Anonymous

The Literature relating to New Zealand

A Bibliography

Anonymous

The Literature relating to New Zealand
A Bibliography

ISBN/EAN: 9783337208806

Printed in Europe, USA, Canada, Australia, Japan

Cover: Foto ©Thomas Meinert / pixelio.de

More available books at **www.hansebooks.com**

THE LITERATURE

RELATING TO

NEW ZEALAND:

A BIBLIOGRAPHY.

WELLINGTON:
BY AUTHORITY: GEORGE DIDSBURY, GOVERNMENT PRINTER.
1889.

BIBLIOGRAPHY OF NEW ZEALAND.

CONTENTS.

	PAGE
PART 1.—CHRONOLOGICAL CATALOGUE	1
Undated publications; and additions	172
PART 2.—CLASSIFIED CATALOGUE :—	
New Zealand generally	176
Provinces	180
Adjacent islands	182
Discovery and exploration	182
Description and physical geography	183
Geology	185
Flora	187
Fauna	188
Maoris generally	190
Morioris	192
Maori ethnology	192
Maori language	192
Maori literature	193
Maori religion	193
Maori history	194
Relations with Europeans	195
Missions	196
Church	197
History	197
Biography	199
Emigration	200
Colonisation and settlement	200
Land	202
Relations with Home Government	203
Government	203
Industry	205
Public works	205
Education	205
Libraries	206
Health resorts	206
Statistics	206
Bibliography	206
Short Classified List	207
PART 3.—ALPHABETICAL CATALOGUE :—	
A.—Authors	208
B.—Titles of anonymous and pseudonymous publications	229
CORRECTIONS.	

NOTE.

An asterisk is prefixed, in the Chronological Catalogue, to publications which the Compiler has had no opportunity of examining. These have been taken from very miscellaneous sources—catalogues (particularly Thomson's and Davis's), references in books, reviews, and advertisements; and the correctness of such titles is not guaranteed. From Dr. Poole's indispensable Index have been derived most of the uninspected articles in periodicals. The Compiler would warmly thank the many gentlemen who have helped him with information or with books, especially his friend Dr. Scheppig, of Kiel, who has had the great kindness to supply the titles of perhaps the majority of the German publications here catalogued.

J. C.

GENERAL ASSEMBLY LIBRARY, WELLINGTON,
June 1, 1889.

THE LITERATURE RELATING TO NEW ZEALAND:

A BIBLIOGRAPHY.

Part 1.—Chronological Catalogue.

1674.

***Tasman**, A. J. Een kort verhael uyt het journael van den Kommander *Abel Jansen Tasman* int' ontdekken van t'onbekende Suit Landt int Jare 1642. Amsterdam: Dirck Rembrantz Van Nierop. 1674.

> All "the published accounts of Tasman's Voyage are derived from his own Journal. The earliest extant, or at present known to have been published, is a very abridged narrative in the Dutch language, entitled" . . . [as above]; "(*i.e.*, *A short relation from the Journal of the Commander* Abel Jansen Tasman, *in the Discovery of the Unknown South Land, in the Year 1642*). . . . . Translations of this abridgment were soon after printed in most of the European languages."— *Burney, Chron. Hist.*, iii. 59.
>
> The complete Journal was reprinted in 1860: see that year. The fullest English translation is in *Burney:* see 1813. The next seven entries relate to Tasman.

1702-5.

Harris, John. Collection of voyages and travels. *See below,* 1744.

1711.

An | Account | of several Late | Voyages and Discoveries: | . . . II. Captain J. *Tasman's* Discoveries | on the Coast of the | South *Terra Incognita*. . . . London, Printed for *D. Brown* without *Temple-* | *Bar*, J. Round in *Exchange-Ally*, *W. Innys* in St. *Paul's* | Church-yard, and *T.* Ward in the *Temple-Lane*. 1711.

> p. 8°. At pp. 129-40 is—
>
> *A Relation of a Voyage made towards the South* Terra Incognita; *extracted from the Journal of Captain* Abel Jansen Tasman, *by which not only a new passage by sea to the Southward of* Nova Hollandia, Vandemens Land, &c., *is discovered, and a vast space of Land and Sea incompassed and sailed round, but many considerable and instructive Observations concerning the Variation of the Magnetical Needle in Parts of the World almost Antipodes to us; and several other curious Remarks, concerning those Places and People, are set forth. Not long since published in the* Low Dutch *by* Dirk Rembrantse, *and now in* English *from Dr.* Hook's *Collections.*

Tasman's Journal—*continued.*
>Tasman's Journal is at pp. 129-40, and the part relating to N.Z. at pp. 139-4.
One of the translations made from the abridged Journal published at Amsterdam.
>"An English translation from Dirk Rembrandt, published in London in 1711 again differs from the French of Thevenot, and the earlier translation (1682) in Dr. Hook's Philosophical Collection."—*Marcus Clarke,* in *Melbourne Review,* i. 453.
>As will be seen, the foregoing volume claims to reproduce the translation in Hook's Collections.

1724-6.

*** Valentijn,** François. Oud en niew Oost-Indien, verwattende een naaukeurige en uitvoerige verhandelinge van Nederlands Mogentheyd in die Gewesten, benevens eene wydluftige Beschryvinge der Moluccos, Amboina . . . en alle de Eylanden onder dezelve Landbestieringen behoorende, *etc.* 5 Deel. Amsterdam, 1724-6.

f°. *From* British Museum Catalogue.
>In 1726, Valentyn published Tasman's Voyage at greater length, accompanied with charts and views, in the IIId volume of his East Indian Descriptions.—*Burney, Chron. Hist.,* iii. 60.
>"Valentyn, the historian, . . . had married into the family of the Secretary of Batavia, and obtained access to the neglected private journal of the navigator. Even this narrative is open to suspicion, for . . . several accounts, each purporting to be the only correct one, had appeared in England and France. The editor of De Hondt's Collection of Voyages asserts that he himself possessed the manuscript journal, though his transcript differs in many important particulars from that of Valentyn."—*Marcus Clarke,* in *Melbourne Review,* i. 452-3.

1744.

Harris, John. Navigantium atque Itinerantium Bibliotheca. | Or, A | Complete Collection | of | Voyages and Travels. . . . Originally published in Two Volumes in Folio, | by John Harris, D.D. and F.R.S. | —— | London: Printed for T. Woodward, &c. &c. | MDCCXLIV.

f°. 2 vols.
>Chapter I, section xxii. contains—The Voyage of Captain Abel Jansen Tasman, for the Discovery of Southern Countries, by Direction of the Dutch East India Company. [Taken from his original journal.] N.Z. i. 326-7.

1756.

*** Brosses,** *President* Charles *de, Count de Tournay, etc.* Histoire des Navigations aux Terres Australes, etc. Paris, 1756.

4°. 2 tom. *See* next entry.

1766-8.

[**Callander,** John.] Terra Australis Cognita : | or, | Voyages | to the | Terra Australis, or Southern Hemi- | sphere, during the Sixteenth, Seven- | teenth, and Eighteenth Centuries. | ——| With | a Preface by the Editor, &c.— | —— | Edinburgh : | Printed for the Author; and sold by Messrs. Hawes, | Clark, and Collins, in Pater-noster-Row, London. | MDCCLXVI.

8°. 3 vols. Maps.
>Tasman's Journal is reprinted, ii. 355-79, from Campbell's edition of *Harris,* with half-a-page of remarks appended. The volume contains the chart drawn, at the instance of the Dutch East India Company, from Tasman's Journal and observations, and "which is yet to be seen in the town-house of Amsterdam" (ii. 379).
>The editor states that he has "drawn many helps" from a French writer whom he does not name. The "French writer" is the President Charles de Brosses, from whose *Histoire des navigations aux terres Australes* it is said to be partly translated.
>"It was in this work that M. de Brosses first laid down the geographical divisions of Australasia and Polynesia, which were afterwards adopted by Pinkerton and succeeding geographers" (*Encyc. Brit.,* ed. 9, iv. 372).
>Callander, who died in 1780, was a Scottish advocate and antiquary. There is a sketch of his life in the *Dict. of nat. biog.,* viii. 255-6.

2

1771.

*Dalrymple, Alexander. An historical collection of the several voyages and discoveries in the South Pacific Ocean. London, 1770–1.
   4°. 2 vols. Maps. Vol. ii : Dutch voyages.
   The account of Tasman's voyage is drawn up from a comparison and examination of Valentyn with the accounts before published, with a selection of the charts and views from Valentyn.—*Burney, Chron. Hist.,* iii. 60.

Dalrymple, Alexander. Scheme of a voyage for the conveyance of domestic animals, corn, iron, &c., to New Zealand; with Dr. Benjamin Franklin's sentiments on the subject. London, 1771.
   It appeared in the *Annual Register,* whence it is reprinted in the *New Zealand Journal,* iv. 42-3. It is summarised in *The New Zealanders,* pp. 408-10, and was reprinted in 1882. The first five and the twelfth and thirteenth paragraphs are apparently Dalrymple's; the rest are Franklin's, whose initials appear at the end of the paper, with the date *April,* 4, 1769. It fills just two columns of the *New Zealand Journal.*

1773.

Hawkesworth, J. An Account | of the | Voyages | undertaken by the | Order of his Present Majesty | for making | Discoveries in the Southern Hemisphere, | and successively performed by | Commodore Byron, | Captain Wallis, || Captain Carteret, | and Captain Cook, || in the Dolphin, the Swallow, and the Endeavour. | Drawn up | From the Journals which were kept by the several Commanders, | And from the papers of Joseph Banks, Esq. | By John Hawkesworth, LL.D. | In three volumes. | Illustrated with Cuts, and a great variety of Charts and Maps relative to | Countries now first discovered, or hitherto but imperfectly known. | —— | London : | Printed for W. Strahan ; and T. Cadell in the Strand. | MDCCLXXIII.

   Vols. ii. and iii. consist of—

An | Account | of a | Voyage round the World, | in the Years | MDCCLXVIII, MDCCLXIX, MDCCLXX, and MDCCLXXI. | By Lieutenant James Cook, | Commander of his Majesty's Bark the Endeavour. |
   4°. Vol. ii. pp. xiv, 410; vol. iii. pp. 395.
   It "was determined that the narrative should be written in the first person, and that I might notwithstanding intersperse such sentiments and observations as my subject should suggest. . . . They will be found most frequent in the account of the voyage of the Endeavour," great part of which "was printed before the others were written."—*Hawkesworth,* Gen. Intro. vol. i. p. v.
   In the Introduction to vol. ii. Hawkesworth describes the circumstances under which Sir J. Banks took part in the expedition ; Banks engaged Dr. Solander, a Swede, and educated under Linnæus, and also two draughtsmen—one for views and figures, the other for natural history subjects. Banks "kept an accurate and circumstantial journal of the voyage, and . . . was so obliging as to put it into my hands, with permission to take out of it whatever I thought would improve or embellish the narrative. . . . The papers of Captain Cook contained a very particular account of all the nautical incidents of the voyage, and a very minute description of the figure and extent of the countries he had visited, with the bearings of the headlands and bays that diversify the coasts, the situation of the harbours in which shipping may obtain refreshments, with the depth of water wherever there were soundings; the latitudes, longitudes, variation of the needle, and such other particulars as lay in his department. . . . But in the papers which were communicated to me by Mr. Banks, I found a great variety of incidents which had not come under the notice of Captain Cook, with descriptions of countries and people, their productions, manners, customs, religion, policy, and language." . . . To Banks also are due the designs of the engravings, except the maps, charts, and views of the coasts as they appear at sea. (Vol. ii. pp. xi.-xiv.)
   The "manuscript account of each voyage was read to the respective Commanders at the Admiralty. . . . The account of the voyage of the Endeavour was also read to Mr. Banks and Dr. Solander, in whose hands, as well as in those of Captain Cook the manuscript was left for a considerable time after the reading. (Vol. i. p. vi.)

Hawkesworth, J.—*continued.*
  Book II, which occupies part of vol. ii. (pp. 281-410) and of vol. iii. (pp. 7-76), relates to N.Z.
    Ch. i. [Passage to N.Z. and incidents in Poverty Bay.] ii. [Poverty Bay and adjacent country; range to Cape Turnagain and back to Tolaga; account of people and country; incidents.] iii. [From Tolaga to Mercury Bay, with incidents; description of views and pahs.] iv. [From Mercury Bay to the Bay of Islands; up the Thames; account of natives, and timber; interviews, and skirmish, with natives.] v. [Round North Cape to Queen Charlotte's Sound.] vi. [Doings in the Sound; through the Straits; cannibalism; mourning; visit to pah.] vii. [Completing circumnavigation.] viii. General account of N.Z.: its first discovery, situation, extent, climate, and productions. ix. Description of the inhabitants, their habitations, apparel, ornaments, food, cookery, and manner of life. x. Of the canoes and navigation of the inhabitants; their tillage, weapons, and music; government, religion, and language: with some reasons against the existence of a southern continent.
    Hawkesworth, born 1715 or 1719, died 1773, was editor of the *Adventurer*. As compiler of the foregoing work he "received from government £6,000 . . . and the work was at first warmly received by the critics. It was soon discovered, however, that in his preface the editor had expressed some ideas apparently at variance with the established religion. . . . Hawkesworth was now suspected of having aimed a secret blow at religion, and his simple and naive descriptions of savage life were represented as dangerous and immoral."—*Encyc. Brit.*, ed. 8, xi. 247.
    The book was translated into French and published at Paris, 1774; and (by Suard) in another edition which was issued twice the same year: see Jackson, *Centenaire*, p. 87. It was translated into German by J. F. Schiller, Berlin, 1774, with an abridgment the same year, and another edition in 1775 (*ibid.* p. 88).
    The eight 4° volumes of which these are a part, were issued by the Admiralty and "are richly ornamented with plates by Bartolozzi, Basire, Pouncey, Lerpinière, and other eminent engravers."—Allibone's *Dict.*, i., 421.

Parkinson, Sydney. A | journal | of a | voyage | to the | South Seas, | in his | Majesty's ship, the Endeavour. | Faithfully transcribed from the papers of the late | Sydney Parkinson, | draughtsman to Joseph Banks, Esq. on his late expedition, | with Dr. Solander, round the world. | Embellished with | views and designs, delineated by the author, and | engraved by capital artists. | London : | Printed for Stanfield Parkinson, the Editor : | and sold by Messrs. Richardson and Urquhart, at the Royal-Exchange ; Evans, in | Pater-noster Row ; Hooper, on Ludgate-Hill ; Murray, in Fleet-street ; | Leacroft, at Charing-Cross ; and Riley, in Curzon-street, May-Fair. | M.DCC.LXXIII.
    roy. 4°. Pp. xxiii, 212 and 2 pp. Errata.
    Preface, nominally by the Editor (Stanfield Parkinson), but said to have been written by Dr. Kenrick, pp. v.-xxiii.
    Part ii. From leaving Yooloo-Etea to departure from New Zealand, pp. 86-131.
    Plate 14. (1) North side of entrance into Poverty Bay, (2) Another side. 15. Warrior in his proper dress and compleatly armed. 16. Head of chief, face curiously tataow'd. 17. Manner in which warriors defy their enemies. 18. War canoe. 19. Warrior and wife. 20. Curious arched rock with river running under it, Tolago Bay. 21. Head of Otegoowgoow, son of chief, the face curiously tataow'd 22. The great peak (Mount Egmont) and the adjacent country. 23. Heads of six men natives, ornamented. 24. Arched rock, with hippa [pah] on top. 25. Map of coast of N.Z. discovered in 1769-70. By I. Cook. 26. Various kinds of instruments and utensils.
    Sydney Parkinson was the son of an Edinburgh brewer, a Quaker, and accompanied Banks as botanical draughtsman on Cook's second voyage to the South Seas, 1768-71. He died on the voyage home in January, 1771.
    Parkinson left behind him a journal of the voyage which was missing after his death. His brother Stanfield, who insinuates that it was secreted by Banks, at length "procured, by purchase, loan, and gift, not indeed the fair copy of my brother's journal, but so many of his manuscripts and drawings, as to enable me to present the following work, in its present form, to the public."
    Friends of Joseph Banks, Dr. Fothergill in particular, offered sums of money to Stanfield to drop the intended publication. Dr. Hawkesworth, the compiler of Cook's voyages, filed a bill in Chancery praying for an injunction to prohibit the publication

Parkinson, Sydney—*continued.*
on the ground that it was an invasion of his property. The injunction was at first granted, but on a re-hearing was dissolved.—From the preface.

The accusations of meanness " against the editor of ' Cook's Voyages' (Dr. Hawkesworth) and Banks . . . have no real foundation." " There was a rigid rule in those days, and long afterwards, which compelled all persons in exploring ships to hand over to the Government all journals kept on voyages."—*Rusden,* i., 76 *note.*

Another edition appeared the same year, with the following words in the title-page after *Endeavour:*—"to which is now added, remarks on the preface (written by Dr. Kenrick at the request of Stanfield Parkinson) by J. Fothergill, and an appendix," &c.—*Jackson, Centenaire,* &c., no. 18.

The work was translated into French by de Nort, roy. 4°, Paris, 1774, and by Henri. 2 vol. 8°, Paris, 1797.—*Ibid.*, nos. 19 and 229.

1777.

* **Cook,** James. A voyage towards the South Pole and round the world. Performed in His Majesties ships the Resolution and Adventure, in the years 1772, 1773, 1774, and 1775. [First edition.] 2 vols. London, 1777.

See for full title second edition in 1779.

* **Forster,** [John] George [Adam]. A Voyage round the World, in His Britannic Majesty's sloop, *Resolution,* commanded by Captain James Cook, during the Years 1772, 3, 4, and 5. London, Printed for B. White, J. Robson, P. Elmsley, G. Robinson, 1777.

4°. 2 vols. Jackson, *Centenaire,* No. 58, and *Lowndes.*

The German translation is entitled :—

J. R. Forster's . . . Reise um die Welt während den Jahren 1772 *bis* 1775, in dem . . . Schiffe, the Resolution, unternommen. Beschrieben und herausgegeben von dessen Sohn und Reisegefährten G. Forster. Vom Verfasser selbst aus dem Englischen übersetzt mit . . . Zusätzen fur den Deutschen Leser vermehrt, und durch Kupfer erläutert. Berlin, 1778, 1779-80 (2nd ed.), 1784 (3rd ed.) —— *Brit. Mus. Cat.,* and *Jackson,* in *Centenaire,* nos. 59, 60, 61.

"2. Mr. Wales, the astronomer of the expedition, published some remarks on the work, which occasioned a *Reply* to Mr. Wales's *Remarks,* 8°, London, 1778 [see Jackson, *Centenaire,* nos. 66, 67], in which the author declares that his father had no concern whatever in the book, but he admits that he had committed some inaccuracies. 3. *A Letter to the Earl of Sandwich,* 4°, London, 1779 [relative to the claims of himself and his father against the government: *Brit. Mus. Cat.*] 4. His *Answer to the Authors of the Literary Journal of Göttingen* . . . candidly admits some errors; it excited further animadversions from Prof. Meiners, who declared himself the author of the criticisms."—*Encyc. Brit.*, ed. 8, ix. 789.

There are biographical sketches of the younger Forster in the *Encyclopædia Britannica,* ed. 8 and (by R. Garnett) ed. 9; and allusions in an article by K. Hillebrand, *Fortnightly,* N.S. xi. 417-21.

1778.

The | Travels | of | Hildebrand Bowman, | Esquire, | into Carnovirria, Taupiniera, Olfacta|ria, and Auditante, in New Zealand ; in | the Island of Bonhommica, and in the power|ful Kingdom of Luxovolupto on the | Great Southern Continent. | Written by Himself ; | who went on shore in the Adventure's large Cutter, at | Queen Charlotte's Sound New Zealand, the fatal 17th | of December, 1773 ; and escaped being cut off and | devoured, with the rest of the Boat's crew, by happen|ing to be a-shooting in the woods ; where he was after|wards unfortunately left behind by the Adventure. | —— | London: Printed for W. Strahan ; and T. Cadell, in | the Strand. 1778.

8°. Pp. xv, Errata, 400. Plates are mentioned in the prefatory "card," but none are in the copy examined.

N.Z., pp. 13-165. Perhaps the first *jeu d'espirit* on N.Z. It bears internal marks of having been written by one who had not visited N.Z., and had not carefully studied the accounts of it.

Forster, J. R.   Observations | made during a | Voyage round the World, | on | Physical Geography, | Natural History, | and | Ethic Philosophy. | Especially on | 1. The Earth and its Strata, | 2. Water and the Ocean, | 3. The Atmosphere, | 4. The Changes of the Globe, | 5. Organic Bodies, and | 6. The Human Species. | By John Reinold Forster, LL.D. F.R.S. and S.A. | And a Member of several Learned Academies in Europe. | —— | London : | Printed for G. Robinson, in Pater-noster-Row | M DCC LXXVIII.

4°. Pp. iv, iv, 649, Errata and list of subscribers.

Geology of N.Z. pp. 15–16, 17–9. Physical geography, pp. 31–2, 41, 50, 51–2, 54. Meteorology, pp. 100–12, 116, 120–31. Climate, p. 133. Flora, pp. 165–6, 169–70, 174–5. Fauna, pp. 185–6, 187, 188, 189–90, 193 and 198 (birds), 197. The following pages have incidental remarks on population, physique, race, progress, food, religion, family, and social institutions generally.

The book was translated into German by the author's son, George, and published, with observations and additions, at Berlin in 1783 and 1785 (Jackson, *Centenaire*, nos. 131, 132, 133).

Johann Reinhold Forster was born in 1729 at Dirschau in Polish Prussia. "In 1772 he was appointed naturalist to the expedition under the command of Captain Cook. . . . For this undertaking F. was abundantly qualified as a man of science and an accurate observer. . . . After the return of the expedition, there were repeated disputes respecting Forster's share in the intended publication of the narrative of the voyage. Two thousand pounds, which had been granted by the government for the plates of the work, were to have been equally divided between Cook and Forster for this purpose; but Forster's performance of his part of the undertaking was disapproved, and he was deprived of the advantage which he expected to have derived from the plates." He was afterwards appointed professor of natural history and inspector of the botanical garden at Halle. He died in 1798.—*Encyc. Brit.*, 4th ed., ix. 788.

"The comparative method . . . became in Reinhold Forster the prevailing tendency. His son Georg adopted the same method and handed it on to his friend Alexander von Humboldt, who in his turn exercised a decisive influence on Karl Ritter."—*Scherer, History of German Literature*, Conybeare, tr., ii. 236–7.

Other works of Forster's relative to the botany of the South Seas are described in Hooker's *Handbook of the New Zealand Flora*, London, 1864, p. 9*.

1779.

Cook, James.   A | Voyage | towards the | South Pole, | and | Round the World. | Performed in | His Majesty's Ships the Resolution and Adventure, | In the Years 1772, 1773, 1774, and 1775. | Written | By James Cook, Commander of the Resolution. | In which is included, | Captain Furneaux's Narrative of his | Proceedings in the Adventure during the Separation of the Ships. | In two volumes. | Illustrated with Maps and Charts, and a Variety of Portraits of | Persons and Views of Places, drawn during the Voyage by | Mr. Hodges, and engraved by the most eminent Masters. | —— | The third edition. | London : | Printed for W. Strahan ; and T. Cadell in the Strand. | MDCCLXXIX.

4°. 2 vols. Pp. xl, 378 ; viii (not numbered), 396. 62 plates.

Vol. I. Book i, ch. iv, pp. 69–91: Transactions in Dusky Bay, with an account of several interviews with the inhabitants. Ch. v, pp. 92–102: Account of the adjacent country, its produce and inhabitants: astronomical and nautical observations. Ch. vi, pp. 103–6: To Queen Charlotte's Sound. Ch. vii (esp. 117–20): Capt. Furneaux's narrative. Ch. viii, pp. 121–30: Transactions in Queen Charlotte's Sound, with some remarks on the inhabitants.

Book ii, ch. iv, pp. 225–34: From Amsterdam to Queen Charlotte's Sound, with an account of interview with the inhabitants. Ch. v, pp. 235–50: Transactions at Queen Charlotte's Sound, with an account of the inhabitants being cannibals.

Vol. II, bk. III, ch. xi, pp. 150–62. Again at Queen Charlotte's Sound.

A table, vol. ii, p. 365, gives specimens of Maori words.

The plates represent—N.Z. spruce, family in Dusky Bay, sketch of the Bay, poi bird, tea-plant, specimens of N.Z. workmanship, man of N.Z., woman of N.Z. Two other original designs by Hodges relating to N.Z. (nos. 8 and 10) are in the Naval Museum, Greenwich : see Jackson, *Centenaire*, p. 91.

Cook, James—*continued.*
Translated into French by A. F. L. de Fréville. Amsterdam, Paris; Pissot, Nyon, 8°, 1777. Also by Suard, 4 vols., 4°, Paris, 1774; with Forster's observations.—*Ibid.*

1782.

Troisième | Voyage | de Cook, | ou | Journal d'une expedition faite dans | la Mer Pacifique du Sud & du Nord, | en 1776, 1777, 1778. 1779 & | 1780. | Traduit de l'Anglois. | —— | A Paris, | Chez Pissot, pere & fils, Libraire, quai des Augustins. Laporte, Libraire, rue des Noyers. | M. DCC. LXXXII. | Avec Approbatim et Privilége du Roi. |
8°. Pp. v, 508. Map and illustration.

Translated from the anonymous English work of an officer(?) of the *Discovery*, "who judges Mr. Cook precipitately and severely, and sometimes gives unfavourable ideas of him." "The author condemns the cruelties practised against the savages." The narrative "contains details that will not be found in Mr. Cook's Journal, and it will form a supplement to the *grande Relation*."—From the avertissement du traducteur.

The visit to N.Z. is described at pp. 105-37. At pp. 119-25, 132-4 is a narrative of an adventure of a sailor with a Maori girl, who instructs him in the manners and customs of the natives.

1783.

Crozet, —. Nouveau Voyage | a la | Mer du Sud, | Commencé sous les ordres de M. Marion, Chevalier | de l'ordre royal & militaire de S. Louis, Capitaine | de brûlot; & achevé, après la mort de cet Officier, | sous ceux de M. le Chevalier Duclesmeur, Garde | de la Marine. | Cette Relation a été rédigée d'après les Plans and Journaux | de M. Crozet. | On a joint a ce Voyage | Un Extrait de celui de M. de Surville | dans les mêmes Parages. | —— | A Paris, | Chez Barrois l'ainé, Libraire, quai des Augustins. | M. DCC. LXXXIII. | Avec Approbation, et Privilège du Roi.
p 8°. Pp. viii, 290+1, 7 planches.

N.Z.: pp. 36-168, 280-7. Description of the country and observations on the inhabitants, pp. 47-54. Description of some northern villages, pp. 54-64. Food, pp. 64-9. Clothing, pp. 69-74. Occupations, pp. 74-85. Religion, pp. 86-8. Events and massacre, pp. 86-126. General remarks, pp. 126-41. Physical observations on N.Z. and some of its products, pp. 147-68. Crozet identifies the Maoris with the American Indians.

The part of De Surville's *Voyage* which relates to N.Z. is at pp. 280-7.

There are sketches of the parts of N.Z. visited by Marion, and four illustrations—of a chief, Tacouri, a Maori girl, warrior, and a woman with her child.

The book appeared under the privilege of the French Academy, and the extract from the Register, May 11, 1782, is signed by Condorcet, Perpetual Secretary.

It was compiled from the papers of Crozet, Marion's first lieutenant, by the Abbé Rochon (*New Zealanders*, p. 43.)

It was translated into German: Reise nach Neuseeland und den freundschaftlichen Inseln. Nürnberg, 1785. 8° (Bibliothek der neuesten Reisebeschreibungen. Bd. vii., 1.)

* **Ledyard,** John. A journal of Capt. Cook's last voyage to the Pacific Ocean and in quest of a North-West passage, performed in the years 1776, 1777, 1778 and 1779, illustrated with a chart shewing the tracks of the ships employed in the expedition. Faithfully narrated from the original MSS. of Mr. John Ledyard. Hartford, Conn., Nathaniel Patten. 1783.
12°. Pp. 208.

Ledyard accompanied Cook on his third voyage and kept a private journal, which was confiscated by the Admiralty. "To satisfy public curiosity till a complete work could be prepared, a very brief sketch of the voyage . . . had been already published by authority in England. This volume L. had procured, and he relied on it for dates, distances, the courses of the vessels, and for other particulars. . . . Extracts are made without alteration in two or three instances, and several of the last pages are literally copied. With no other written materials L. produced his manuscript journal . . . " (*Memoirs*, by Sparks, 1828, p. 49). "The part prepared by himself breaks off, indeed, more than a year before the end of the voyage, and was probably

*Ledyard, John—*continued.*
  filled out by the publisher from the brief account before printed in England" (p. 163).
  "The train of events at the Sandwich Islands, which led to the death of Captain Cook, is narrated by L. in a manner more consistent and natural than appears in any other account of it" (p. 50). See Sparks, *Memoirs*, pp. 137-52, where the account is quoted verbatim.

  Southey reviewed the book in the *Quarterly*, xxxviii. 85-113. The MS. of the Journal is stated to be now in the British Museum.

1784.

Cook, James. A | Voyage | to the | Pacific Ocean. | Undertaken, | by the Command of his Majesty, | for making | Discoveries in the Northern Hemisphere. | To determine | the Position and Extent of the West Side of North America ; its Distance from Asia ; and the Practicability of a | Northern Passage to Europe. | Performed under the direction of | Captains Cook, Clerke, and Gore, | In his Majesty's Ships the Resolution and Discovery. | In the Years 1776, 1777, 1778, 1779, and 1780. | In three volumes. | Vol. I. and II. written by Captain James Cook, F.R.S. | Vol. III. by Captain James King, LL.D. and F.R.S. | Illustrated with Maps and Charts, from the Original Drawings made by Lieut. Henry Roberts, | under the Direction of Captain Cook ; and with a great Variety of Portraits of Persons, Views of Places, and Historical Representations of Remarkable Incidents, drawn by Mr. Webber during the Voyage, and engraved by the most eminent Artists. | Published by Order of the Lords Commissioners of the Admiralty. | —— | London : | Printed by W. and A. Strahan : | For G. Nicol, Bookseller to His Majesty, in the Strand ; and T. Cadell, in the Strand. | MDCCLXXXIV.

  4°. Vol. I. Pp. xcvi. 421.

  Book I, chs. vii and viii relate to N.Z. Ch. vii. Employments in Queen Charlotte's Sound. Transactions with the natives there. Intelligence about the massacre of the Adventure's boat's crew. Account of the chief who headed the party on that occasion ; of the two young men who embark to attend Omai. Various remarks on the inhabitants. Astronomical and nautical observations. Ch. viii. Mr. Anderson's remarks on the country near Queen Charlotte's Sound. Soil. Climate. Weather. Winds. Trees. Plants. Birds. Fish. Other animals. Inhabitants—dress, ornaments, habitations, boats, food and cookery, arts, weapons, cruelty to prisoners, customs, specimen of their language.

  The second edition appeared in 1785, and an undated abridgment was made from the fourth : see Jackson, *Centenaire*, nos. 157, 159. It was translated into French by Demeunier in 1785 ; there were four more French editions and an abridgment the same year, and other French editions in 1816 and 1819 : *ibid.* nos. 160-7. A German translation, with introduction on Cook's services and character, by G. Forster, appeared at Berlin in 1787 : *ibid.* nos. 158, 193. Another German trans., with observations by J. L. Wetzel, was published at Anspach, in 5 vols. 8°, 1787-1812. A Dutch trans., at Rotterdam in 1787.

  Other journals, abridgments and accounts are catalogued in the British Museum Catalogue, *sub nom.* Cook, p. 154. But the fullest bibliography of Cook and his voyages is in Jackson, *Centenaire*.

  "Abridgments of Cook's voyages have been multiplied without number." A prospectus of a new edition to be published by Mr. Smith, Fleet Street, is described in *N.Z. Journal*, ii. 243.

1788.

Kippis, A. The | Life | of | Captain James Cook | *Totque Maris vastæque exhausta Pericula Terræ.* | VIRG. | By | Andrew Kippis, D.D. F.R.S. and S.A. | Dublin : | Printed for Messrs. H. Chamberlaine, W. Colles, | R. Cross, W. Gilbert, W. Wilson, L. White, | P. Byrne, P. Wogan, P. Stewart, | J. Moore, and D. Dorain. | M.DCC.LXXXVIII.

  p. 8°. Pp. xvi, 527.

  N.Z.: First voyage, pp. 54-102 ; second voyage, pp. 205-18, 246-52, 294-6 ; third voyage, pp. 356-64.

Kippis, A.—*continued.*

"In various respects, new information will be found in the present performance; and other things, which were less perfectly known before, are set in a clearer and fuller light." Information was derived from official sources and from his widow. Sir J. Banks read it through before publication.—*Preface.*

"Captain Cook's endeavours to serve the inhabitants of New Zealand, by the vegetables and animals he left among them, are" described in an elegy by Miss Seward (p. 509).

Andrew Kippis (1725–95) a nonconformist divine, edited a new edition of the *Biographia Britannica,* and was author of various works. He was a lecturer at Hoxton Academy and so was tutor to William Godwin: see Paul, *Godwin and his contemporaries,* i. 15.

A life of Cook was written by Bailly, the French astronomer: see Arago's Biographies, p. 108.

Recent statements relating to the circumstances of Cook's death are in *Nature,* viii. 211, xix. 373; Fornander, *Polynesian Race,* iii. 191–4; and in *Centenaire de la mort de Cook,* Paris, 1879.

1800.

Labillardière, [Jacques Julien.] Relation | du Voyage à la Recherche | de La Pérouse, | fait | par Ordre de l'Assemblée Constituante, | Prendant les années 1791, 1792, et pendant la 1ere. et la 2de. année République Françoise. | Par Le. Cen. Labillardière, | Correspondant de la ci-devant académie des sciences de Paris, membre | de la société. d' histoire naturelle, et l'un des naturalistes de l'expédition. | ——— | A Paris, | Chez H. J. Jansen, Imprimeur-Libraire, | Rue des Maçons, No. 406, Place Sorbonne. | An VIII de la République Françoise. |

Ann. 1800. 4° 2 tomes. T. i. pp. xvi, 442; t. ii. pp. 332, 114.

Labillardière stopped near the north coast of the North Island in 1793 and (though he did not land) had an interview with the natives: see ch. xii, vol. ii, pp. 83–8. He advises the importation of the flax-plant to Europe.

See English translation, 1802.

1801.

Vancouver, G. A | Voyage of Discovery | to the | North Pacific Ocean, | and | Round the World ; | In which the Coast of North-West America has been carefully examined | and accurately surveyed. | Undertaken | by His Majesty's Command, | Principally with a view to ascertain the existence of any Navigable | Communication between the | North Pacific and North Atlantic Oceans ; | and performed in the years | 1790, 1791, 1792, 1793, 1794 and 1795, | in the | Discovery Sloop of War, and Armed Tender Chatham, | under the Command of | Captain George Vancouver. | Dedicated, by Permission, to His Majesty. | A New Edition, with Corrections, | illustrated with Nineteen Views and Charts. | In Six Volumes. | ——— | London : | Printed for John Stockdale, Piccadilly. | 1801.

8°. Vol. i. has 410 pp.

The book is edited by John Vancouver, brother to the writer, Captain Vancouver, who "had visited Dusky Bay with Captain Cook in the Resolution," and visited it again in 1790: see vol. i, pp. 185–203. There are charts of the Snares and of Chatham Islands at p. 161.

1802.

Labillardière, [Jacques Julien.] An | Account of a Voyage | in search of | La Perouse | undertaken by order of the | Constituent Assembly of France, | and performed | In the Years 1791, 1792, and 1793, | in the | Recherche and Esperance, Ships of War, | under the command of | Rear-Admiral Bruni D'Entrecasteaux. | Translated from the French of | M. Labillardière, | Correspondent of the *ci-devant* Academy of Sciences, Member of the | Society of Natural History of Paris, and one of the Naturalists | attached to the

Labillardère, [Jacques Julien.] —*continued.*
expedition. | In two volumes. | Illustrated with forty-three engravings, | And a Chart exhibiting the Track of the Ships. | Second edition. | —— | London : | Printed for B. Uphill, No. 30, Brydges-Street, | Covent-Garden. | 1802.
2 vols. 8°. Vol. i. pp. xii, 2, 464 ; vol. ii. pp. viii, 423, 43, 2.

The collection of plates is separate, is in 4°, is dated 1800, and is published by J. Debrett, Piccadilly. The first edition was in 1800.
N.Z. : vol. ii. pp. 89-7.

* **Rochon,** (L'abbé) Alexandre. Voyages aux Indes orientales. Paris, 1802.
8°. 3 tom.

"In 1791 the Abbé Rochon published another volume, containing an account of his own voyages to Madagascar and the East Indies, which was reprinted in 1802, with the addition of two other volumes, in the last of which appears a second narrative of the voyages of De Surville and Marion, in most respects copied from the former, but with a few new remarks interspersed. . . . In his last-mentioned work, Rochon refers to the journals of M. Monneron, supercargo on board the Jean Baptiste, and M. Potier de l'Orme, another of the officers, as his authorities for the account of De Surville's Voyage. The latter, however, he had not seen at the time of his first publication."—*Craik, New Zealanders*, pp. 35-6 note.

1804.

Collins, [David.] An Account | of the | English Colony | in | New South Wales, | from its First Settlement in January, 1788, to | August, 1801 : | with | Remarks on the Disposition, Customs, Manners, &c., of | the Native Inhabitants of that Country. | To which are added, | Some particulars of New Zealand ; | compiled by permission | from the MSS. of Lieut.-Governor King : | and | an Account of a Voyage performed by Captain Flinders and | Mr. Bass ; by which the existence of a strait separating | Van Diemen's Land from the continent of New Holland was | ascertained. | Abstracted from the Journal of Mr. Bass. | By Lieutenant-Colonel Collins, of the Royal Marines ; | several years Judge-Advocate and Secretary of the colony, | and now Lieutenant-Governor of Port Philip. | Illustrated by numerous engravings. | The second edition. | —— | London : Printed by A. Strahan, Printers Street, | For T. Cadell and W. Davies, | in the Strand. | 1804.
4°. Pp. vii, 552. Illus.

At pp. 341-50 is given an "Account of the New Zealanders," derived in 1793 from two Maoris at Norfolk Island, and communicated by Governor King. The two (a warrior and a priest) are described, pp. 341-3 ; their report on N.Z., pp. 343-6 ; King's voyage to N.Z., pp. 346-50.

The second edition is abridged and edited by Maria Collins. The first was published in 1798-1802.

1805.

* **Turnbull,** J. A Voyage round the World, 1800-1804 ; in which the Author visited the Principal Islands of the Pacific Ocean and the English Settlements of Port Jackson and Norfolk Island. By John Turnbull. London, 1805.
12°. 3 vols. Pp. xii, 238 ; xiii-xvi, 237 ; xvii-xx, 204.

Gives an account of the massacre of the crew of the Boyd and of Bruce—the Englishman who lived with the Maoris.

The second edition, re-arranged, appeared in 1813 : see Petherick, *Torch*, no. 4, p. 164.

Traduit de l'anglais par A. J. N. Lallemant, l'un des secrétaires de la marine. Paris, Xhronet, 1807. 8°. Trans. from the first edition : see Ernest de Blosseville, *Histoire des colonies pénales de l'Angleterre dans l'Australie*, Paris, 1831, where there is a reference to N.Z., pp. 285-6.

1807.

Savage, John. Some Account | of | New Zealand ; particularly | the Bay of Islands, and Surrounding Country ; | With a Description of | the Religion and Government, | Language, Arts, Manufactures, Manners, and Customs | of the Natives, &c. &c. | By John Savage, Esq. Surgeon, | and Corresponding Member of the Royal Jennerian Society. | " Remote in Southern Seas an Island lies, | " Of ample space, and bless'd with genial skies ; | " Where shelter'd still by never-fading groves, | " The friendly Native dwells, and fearless roves ; | " Where the tall Forest, and the Plains around, | " And Waters wide, with various Wealth abound." | E. H. | London : | Printed for J. Murray, Fleet-Street ; and A. Constable and Co. Edinburgh ; | *By W. Wilson, at the Union Printing-Office, St. John's Square.* | 1807.

    8°. Pp. viii, 110, Errata, and Directions to the Binder.

    Portrait of Tinorah, a Bay of Islands chief; appearance of North Cape; a N.Z. deity.

    Ch. i.-ii. Bay of Islands in 1805. Ch. iii. Houses. Ch. iv. Natives. Ch. v. Ranks and religion. Ch. vi. Government. Ch. vii. Manners. Ch. viii. Marriage, tattooing, dress. Ch. ix. Cultivation, food, canoes. Ch. x. War, weapons, and tools. Ch. xi. Language, vocabulary of useful words (pp. 74-8) and numerals. Ch. xii. Music, songs, and dancing. Account of a native in London, pp. 94-110.

    Savage visited N.Z. in 1805. He brought to England a native, Moyhanger, who supplied him with much information. The book is probably the first concerned exclusively with N.Z.

    Reviewed in the *Eclectic Review*, vi. 867.

* Savage's account of New Zealand. *Eclectic Review*, vi. 867. 1807.

Burney, J. A | Chronological History | of the | Voyages and Discoveries | in the | South Sea | or Pacific Ocean. | Part III. | From the Year 1620, to the Year 1688. | Illustrated with charts and other plates. | By James Burney, | Captain in the Royal Navy. | London : | Printed by Luke Hansard and Sons, near Lincoln's-Inn Fields ; and sold by | G. and W. Nicol, Booksellers to His Majesty, and T. Payne, Pall-Mall ; | Wilkie and Robinson, Paternoster Row ; Cadell and Davies, in the Strand ; | Nornaville and Fell, Bond-street ; and J. Murray, Albemarle-street. | 1813.

    4°. Ch. iv. pp. 59–112 contains Tasman's Journal. Pp. 59–62 are " introductory " by Burney. Pp. 63–110 are Tasman's Journal, which begins : Journal or Description | By me *Abel Jansz Tasman*, | Of a Voyage from *Batavia* for making Discoveries of the | *Unknown South Land* in the year 1642. | It ends : Your most Humble | and most dutiful Servant, | (Undersigned) Abel Jansz Tasman. | The chapter concludes (pp. 110-2) with remarks by Burney. The parts relating to N.Z. are at pp. 72–80. There is one chart (of part of the east coast) with two engravings—of a boatful of natives and the aspect of Three Kings.

    " Subsequent to the publication of Mr. Dalrymple's *Historical Collection*, a manuscript journal of Captain Tasman's, with charts and views of the lands discovered by him, was brought to this country, and was purchased of the then possessor by Mr. Banks (the present Sir Joseph Banks) shortly after his return from the *South Sea*." Sir Joseph " procured it to be translated into English ; and the Dutch original with the English translation are kept on the same shelf in his Library. From these . . . the account of Abel Jansen Tasman's Voyage is now offered to the public. The English translation was made in 1776, by the Reverend Charles Godfrey Woide, who was then Chaplain to His Majesty's Dutch Chapel at St. James's Palace, and afterwards Under Librarian to the British Museum. . . ."—*Burney*, iii. 59–60.

1816.

The | First Ten Years' Quarterly Papers |:of the | Church Missionary Society: | to which is prefixed | A Brief View of the Society. | [*Sic*, title page, but the papers number 135, and extend to Michaelmas, 1849.] London: | Printed

First Ten Years' Quarterly Papers—*continued.*
by R. Watts, Crown Court, Temple Bar. | Published by Sully & Son, 169, Fleet Street: | Sold also by Hatchard & Son, Piccadilly, | and all Booksellers and Newsmen. | 1826.

8°.

Nos. 3 and 4 (anno 1816) have An account of the New Zealanders, chiefly from Marsden. In No. 10 is a Memoir of Mowhee. In 59 (1830), 70 (1833), 75 (1834), 76, 79 (1835), 81 (1836), 83, 84, 88 (1837), 91 (1838), 99 (1840), 102 (1841), 104, 105 (1842), 109 (1843), 122 (1846), 126 (1847), are extracts from missionaries' letters. All illustrated.

1817.

Nicholas, J. L. Narrative | of a | Voyage | to | New Zealand, | Performed in the years 1814 and 1815, | in company with the Rev. Samuel Marsden, | *Principal Chaplain of New South Wales.* | [including | a Description of the Country, and Incidental Remarks on the | Manners, Customs, and Political Opinions of the Natives ; | together with | Supplementary Observations on the Origin of the People, | and the Soil, Climate, and Productions of the Island.] By | John Liddiard Nicholas, Esq. | —— | In two volumes. | —— | London : | Printed for James Black and Son, | Tavistock-Street, Covent-Garden. | M. DCCC. XVII.

8°. 2 vols. Illus. Pp. xx, 431 ; xii, 397.

Vol. i. and vol. ii. chs. i.-vii. are the journal of a visit to the Bay of Islands and adjacent country with Marsden and Kendall, and to the Thames and Tauranaki; with a description of the coast country from North Cape to Thames. Supplementary observations:—Vol. ii. ch. viii. (physical geography, climate, geology, flora and fauna); ch. ix. (origin of Maoris—Asiatic and congeners of Battas); ch. x. (decline of population, character of natives, expediency of colonising). Vocabulary, and phrase-book and numerals, compiled by Kendall, pp. 327-52. An account of the massacre of the crew of the Boyd, i. 143-50. Appendix 1. Extract from Collins's History of New South Wales, being an account of two New Zealanders left in Doubtless Bay, drawn up by the late Governor King, ii. 353-66. 2. Extract from Turnbull's Voyage round the world between the years 1801 and 1804, ii. 307-80. 3. Memoirs of Duaterra, in a letter from Marsden, ii. 380-97.

Reviewed in the *Christian Observer,* xvi. 803.
The following is a German translation :—
Reise nach und in Neuseeland in den Jahren 1814-15. Mit 1 Kupfer u. 1 Karte.
(Neue Bibliothek der wichtigsten Reise-beschreibungen, bd. xviii.) Weimar, 1819.

* Nicholas's Voyage to New Zealand. *Christian Observer,* xvi. 803. 1817.

* Protestantische Missionen auf Neu-Seeland. Baseler Magazin, II (1817) p. 208 ; III, p. 415; VI, p. 4 ; IX, p. 2 ; XIII, p. 1 ; XV, p. 1.

1820.

Kendall, T. and **Lee**, S. A | Grammar | and | Vocabulary | of the | Language of New Zealand. | Published by the | Church Missionary Society. | London : | Printed by R. Watts, | and sold by L. B. Seeley, Fleet Street ; and | John Hatchard and Son, Piccadilly. | 1820.

fcp. 8°. Pp. viii, 230, with 7 pp. of title-page, advertisement, contents, and preface.

Grammar, pp. 1-60. Praxis, pp. 61-6. Phrases, sentences, &c., pp. 67-94. Familiar dialogues, pp. 95-106. Songs, pp. 107-13. Religious dialogues, pp. 114-24. Prayers, creed, &c., pp. 125-30. Vocabulary, pp. 131-230.

"Mr. Kendall, who had for several years resided as a Settler in N.Z., under the auspices of the Church Missionary Society, having returned early in the summer of the present year [1820], with two Native Chiefs, to England, it was resolved by the Committee, that every advantage should be taken of this opportunity, for the purpose of settling the orthography, and, as far as possible, of reducing the language itself of N.Z. to the rules of Grammar, with a view to the furtherance of the Mission sent out to that country. For this end, Mr. Kendall was, with the Chiefs, sent to Cambridge.
. . . After a residence there of about two months, the MS. of the work now presented

Kendall, T. and **Lee**, S.—*continued.*
to the Public was, with such assistance as I could render, completed, and put to Press. The materials indeed had, for the most part, been previously collected in N.Z., by Mr. Kendall: they received at Cambridge some additions, with the arrangement in which they now appear."—*Preface by Dr. Samuel Lee.*

1823.

* **Sparks**, Jared. New Zealand. *North American Review*, xviii. 828.

1824.

* [**Barrow**, John.†] Australasia. *Encyclopædia Britannica*, Supplement to sixth edition (1824).
  † F.R.S., one of the Secretaries of the Admiralty. Two pages are devoted to N.Z.

There is no mention of N.Z. in the *first* edition (1771) of the Encyclopædia. There is a brief account in the *second* (1783) and the *third* (1797). In the *fourth* (1810), and also in the *fifth* and *sixth*, there is only a short mention of about half a column.

* Colonization of New Zealand. *Blackwood's Magazine*, xlii. 784. 1824.

Cruise, R. A. Journal | of a | Ten Months' Residence | in | New Zealand. | By | Richard A. Cruise, Esq. | Major in the 84th Regt. Foot. | Second edition. | London : | Printed for | Longman, Hurst, Rees, Orme, Brown, and Green, | Paternoster-Row. | 1824.
    8°. Pp. vi, 327. Illus.

"During his residence in N.Z., the Author, being entrusted with the military detachment on board the Dromedary was led from motives of curiosity to maintain a constant intercourse with the inhabitants, and to devote much of his leisure to their society.—The incidents recorded in the following pages were noted down . . . generally on the same day on which they occurred. . . . In the present edition the author has made a few additions."—*Preface.*

The Bay of Islands in 1819 ; the Thames and Taranaki in 1820. Remarks on the natives, pp. 262-303:—tattooing and dress, pp. 263-7 ; religion, pp. 268-70 ; food, pp. 270-1 ; cannibalism, pp. 271-3 ; infanticide, pp. 273-5 ; marriage, pp. 268, 277-8 ; war, pp. 278-82 ; arms and canoes, pp. 282-4 ; dresses, p. 281 ; flora, pp. 285, 288 ; fauna, pp. 285-288 ; characteristics, pp. 292-6, 301-3. Account of massacre of crew of Boyd from *Sydney Gazette*, pp. 309-14. Table of the weather from March to December, 1820, pp. 319-27. First edition was published in 1823.

Reviewed in the *Quarterly Review*, xxxi. 52-65, and *Monthly Review*, cv. 367.

* Cruise's Residence in New Zealand. *Monthly Review*, cv. 367. 1824.

1825.

Cruise —— New Zealand. *Quarterly Review*, xxxi. 52-65.

Hervey, T. K. Australia ; | with other Poems. | By | Thomas K. Hervey, | Trinity College, Cambridge. | Second Edition. | With Additional Poems. | London : | Printed for Hurst, Robinson, and Co. | 90, Cheapside, and 8, Pall Mall ; | and Archibald Constable & Co. Edinburgh. | 1825.
    fcp. 8°. Pp. xxiv, 169.

Six lines descriptive of N.Z. occur at p. 17, and at p. 51 are notes on the storms, mountains, and clouds of N.Z., and the method of reckoning time.

1826.

Blosseville, Jules *de*. Mémoire géographique sur la Nouvelle-Zélande. *Nouvelles Annales des Voyages*, t. xxix. 1826.

Blosseville, afterwards mysteriously lost, with his ship, visited N.Z. in the Coquille in 1824, and acquired from the natives geographical information about the three islands. *Rev. d. D. Mondes*, Sept. 1, 1861, p. 168.

"The researches of M. de B. in a manner sum up the most precise information we possess on this people, and include several useful documents on a number of ports and anchorages in that part of the globe that are still little frequented."—*Rienzi, Océanie*, iii. 186, where an account of the natives of the South Island is reproduced from De Blosseville.

Blosseville, Jules *de*. Voyage du capitaine Edwardson à la côte méridionale de Towaï-Pounamou, du 6 novembre 1822, au 28 mars 1823, rédigé par Jules de Blosseville d'après le journal du capitaine. *Nouvelles Annales*, t. xxix.

> A brief account of the voyage is given in *Revue d. D. Mondes*, Sept. 1, 1861, pp. 168-9.

***Duperrey.** Voyage autour du Monde, exécuté par ordre du Gouvernement sur la corvette la Coquille, en 1822-25. Paris, 1826.

1827.

Adventures | of | British Seamen | in | the Southern Ocean, | displaying | the striking contrasts | which the human character exhibits | in an | uncivilized state. I. (Constable's Miscellany of original and selected publications in the various departments of literature, science, and the arts, vol. IV.) Edinburgh : | Printed for Constable and Co. | 1827.

> Sub-title: Particulars of the destruction of a British vessel on the coast of New Zealand; with anecdotes of some New Zealand chiefs. With a portrait of Tippahee, from an original drawing in the possession of George Brown, Esq. Pp. 323-53.
>
> The "particulars" are contained in a letter from Captain Alex. Berry to Archibald Constable, Esq., dated January, 1819. The vessel was the *Boyd*, the crew of which was massacred at Wangaroa in 1809.

Sparks, Jared. Memoirs | of the | Life and Travels | of | John Ledyard, | from his | Journals and Correspondence. | By Jared Sparks. | London: | Henry Colburn, New Burlington Street. | 1828.

> 8°. Pp. xii. 428. Another edition appeared in 1834; see *Allibone*.
>
> The part relating to Ledyard's voyage to N.Z is at pp. 59-65. Ledyard's *Journal* is described *ante*, 1783.

1829.

Dillon, Peter. Narrative | and | Successful Result | of a | Voyage in the South Seas, | performed by order of the | Government of British India, | to ascertain | the actual fate | of | La Pérouse's Expedition, | interspersed with | Accounts of the Religion, Manners, Customs, | and Cannibal Practices | of the | South Sea Islanders. | By the | Chevalier Capt. P. Dillon, | *Member of the Legion of Honour; of the Asiatic Society of Bengal, and of the Geographical | Society of Paris;* | *Commander of the Hon. East-India Company's Ship Research.* | In two volumes. | —— | London: | Hurst, Chance, and Co., St. Paul's Church-Yard. | 1829.

> 8°. Vol. i., pp. lxxix, 302; vol. ii., pp. 436. 2 illus.
>
> N.Z.: i. 184-256; ii. 320-55.
>
> Dillon was at the Bay of Islands from July 1 to Aug. 2, and from Nov. 5 to Dec. 13, 1827. (He had previously visited it in 1809 and 1826.) He repeats Moyhanger's narrative of his visit to England (i. 200-2), and his account of the massacre of the crew of the Boyd (i. 218-25); mentions circumstances connected with the killing of Marion; is severe on the behaviour of the Church of England Missionaries (ii. 326-31).
>
> Translated into French with the title—Voyage aux iles de la Mer du Sud en 1827 et 1828, et relation de la découverte du sort de La Pérouse, etc. 2 tom. Paris, 1830. 8°. It is referred to in the *Rev. d. D. Mondes*, March 1, 1878, p. 69, where it is said that Dillon gives a novel account of the murder of Marion.

Ellis, W. Polynesian Researches, | during | a Residence of nearly Six Years | in the | South Sea Islands; | including | Descriptions of the Natural History and Scenery of the | Islands, with remarks on the History, Mythology, | Traditions, Government, Arts, Manners, | and Customs of the | Inhabitants. | By | William Ellis, | Missionary to the Society and Sandwich Islands, and author | of the " Tour of Hawaii." | —— | In two volumes. | —— | London: | Fisher, Son, & Jackson, Newgate Street, | M,DCCC,XXIX.

> 8°. Maps and illus.

Ellis, W.—*continued.*
A week's visit to Bay of Islands in 1816, i. 23–39. Description of forest, i. 26–7. Weapons and dress, i. 29. Physiognomy and tattooing, i. 29–31. Sham fight, i. 32–3. War, &c., i. 35, 38. Missions, i. 36–9.

1830.

[**Craik**, G. L.] The Library of Entertaining Knowledge. | The | New Zealanders. | London : | Charles Knight, Pall Mall East ; | Longman, Rees, Orme, Brown, & Green, Paternoster Row ; | Oliver & Boyd, Edinburgh ; Robertson & Atkinson, Glasgow ; | Wakeman, Dublin ; Willmer, Liverpool ; | Baines & Co., Leeds ; and G. & C. Carvill, New York. | MDCCCXXX.
Pp. iv, 424. Map and 46 illustrations.

The book was afterwards reprinted as :—The | New Zealanders, | containing | a Narrative of the First Discovery of the Island and | the Adventures of its Early Visitors ; | with | an Interesting Description of its Present | Inhabitants ; | to which is added | The Personal History of a Sailor who was | detained by them for Several Years. | Illustrated with Cuts. | London : | Nattali and Bond, 23, Bedford Street, | Covent Garden.
Pp. viii, 424. Map of N.Z. as explored by Cook, and 45 illustrations. The map and illus. are reproduced from the previous edition, with the omission of the portrait of Tupai-Cupa, no. 43.

Ch. i. Introduction.—Ch. ii. Progress of discovery—Tasman (two cuts are from Tasman's Journal) and Cook.—Ch. iii. De Surville (pp. 35–40), Marion (pp. 40–53) and Cook.—Ch. iv. Intercourse of New Zealanders with Australia ; with accounts from Collins, Savage, Cruise. Massacre of the "Boyd." Matara. Duaterra. Dillon's visit ; D'Urville's.—Ch. v. John Rutherford's narrative (dictated to a friend on his voyage home). Evidence of cannibalism (pp. 100–107).—Ch. vi. Rutherford's narrative continued. Crying, pp. 114–20. Customs, pp. 120–5, 133–4. Huts, Tools, pp. 125–7, 180. Houses, pp. 125, 128. Carving, pp. 129–31. Tattooing, pp. 135–49. Tapu, pp. 150–4.—Ch. vii. Rutherford's narrative continued. Origin of Maoris, pp. 159–61 (Malay). Physique, p. 161. Dress, pp. 161. Food, pp. 162–3. Scenery, pp. 165–7. Climate, pp. 167–8. Vegetables, pp. 169–70, 183. Wheat, pp. 171–2. Agriculture, pp. 172–4. Timber, pp. 174–8. Flax, pp. 179–83. Minerals, pp. 183–5. Fauna, pp. 185–9 (an illustration of Maoris fishing is from a drawing in the British Museum).—Ch. viii. Rutherford's narrative continued. Funerals, pp. 192–4. Marriage, pp. 195–8. Music, pp. 198–201. Rank, pp. 195–6, 202–5. Notions of theft, pp. 205–11.—Ch. ix. Trophies, pp. 219–23.—Ch. x. Religion, pp. 227–38, 244. Priests, pp. 238–45.—Ch. xi. Rutherford's narrative continued. Mode of procuring fire, pp. 248–51. Fighting, pp. 253–61. Weapons, pp. 262–8. Pahs, pp. 270–2. Canoes, pp. 272–3 (engravings from models in museum of Church Missionary Society, pp. 272–3). Oratory, pp. 259–60.—Ch. xii. Rutherford's narrative continued. Residents in N.Z., pp. 279–82. Omai (painted by Reynolds, apostrophised by Cowper—see quotation), pp. 285–6.—Ch. xiii. Visits of Maoris to England. Shungie, pp. 288–99. George, pp. 308–12.—Ch. xiv. Mowhee, pp. 314–7. Tupai Cupai, pp. 317–35.—Chs. xvi.–xvii. Characteristics of Maoris, pp. 305–93.—Ch. xviii. Franklin's scheme, pp. 408–10. Missions, pp. 410–2.

Dr. Thomson says : "This excellent work was revised and parts written by Lord Brougham," and the statement has been often repeated. The author of it is now known to be George Lillie Craik, afterwards Professor of English Literature at Queen's College, Belfast : see *Dictionary of National Biography*, ed. by L. Stephen, *sub nom*. The book is still one of the best about N.Z., but it owes its chief value now to Rutherford's narrative.

It was trans. into German :—
Die Neuseeländer, nach dem Englischen. Mit 1 Karte und 44 Abbildungen. Leipzig, 1833. klein 8°.

1831.

Beechey, F. W. Narrative | of a | Voyage to the Pacific | and Beering's Strait, | to co-operate with | the Polar Expedition : | performed in | His Majesty's Ship Blossom | under the Command of | Captain F. W. Beechey R.N. | F.R.S. &c. | in the Years 1825, 26, 27, 28. | Published by Authority of the Lords Commissioners of | the Admiralty. | A new edition. | In two

Beechey, F. W.—*continued.*
volumes. | —— | London : | Henry Colburn and Richard Bentley, | New Burlington Street. | 1831.

   8°. Pp. xxii, 472+iv, 452. 3 charts and 23 illus.

   "While we were at anchor [at Otaheite], a whale-ship arrived from New Zealand, with a party of natives of that country on board, whom the master permitted to exhibit their war-dance for our diversion. . . . We learned from the whaler that Shongi, the New Zealand chief who was educated in England, was availing himself of the superiority he had acquired, and was making terrible ravages among his countrymen, whose heads, when dried, furnished him with a lucrative trade."—i. 303–4.

1832.

***Busby**, J. Authentic Information relative to New South Wales and New Zealand. By James Busby, Esq., formerly Member of the Land Board of N.S.W., now British Resident in New Zealand. London, 1832.

   8°. Pp. vii, 72 ; appendix, xxviii.

   Has "A brief memoir relative to N.Z."—Petherick, *Torch*, i. 170. "The work contains some interesting particulars respecting the northern portion of the northern island—the only part of N.Z. of which Mr. Busby had any knowledge."—*N.Z. Journal*, ii. 244.

***Character of the New Zealanders.** *Littell's Museum of Foreign Literature*, xxii. 98.

   Probably a reprint of an article in an English Review.

Earle, A. A | Narrative | of a | Nine Months' Residence | in | New Zealand, | in 1827 ; | together with | a Journal of a Residence | in Tristan d'Acunha, | an Island situated between South America and | the Cape of Good Hope. | By Augustus Earle, | Draughtsman to His Majesty's Surveying-Ship "The Beagle." London : | Printed for | Longman, Rees, Orme, Brown, Green, & Longman, | Paternoster-Row. | 1832.

   8°. Pp. x, 371. Coloured illustrations, full- and double-page.

   A general incidental account of the manners and customs of the natives—at Bay of Islands and north of N.Z., pp. 1–284. Captain Berry's letter describing the massacre of the crew of the Boyd, pp. 43–8.

   Reviewed in *Quarterly Review*, xlviii. 132–65, *Westminster*, xvii. 311, and *Monthly*, cxxviii. 364.

   Part was translated into German in C. F. V. Hoffman's Jahrbuch der Reisen, erster Jahrgang, Stuttgart, 1833, p. 204, under the title : Begegnisse u. Beobachtungen eines Engländischen Malers auf Tristan d'Acunha und Neu-Seeland.

Earle's Residence in New Zealand. *Quarterly Review*, xlviii. 132–65 ; *Westminster Review*, xvii. 311 ; *Monthly Review*, cxxviii. 364. 1832.

   The *Quarterly* reviewer signifies his "belief that, in whatever regards the missionaries, Mr. Earle's statements must be received, for the present, with anything but rash confidence."

Richard, A. Voyage | de Découvertes | de | L'Astrolabe | Executé par ordre du Roi, | Pendant les Années 1826–1827–1828–1829, | sous le commandement | De M. J. Dumont D'Urville. | Botanique | par | MM. A. Lesson et A. Richard. | Paris | J. Taster, Editeur, | N. 4 bis, Rue des Beaux-Arts. | 1832.

   8° 2 tomes. Pp. xvi, 167 ; lvi, 167. Folio atlas of plates—39 representing the flora of N.Z.

   The sub-title of vol. i. is—Essai d'une Flore de La Nouvelle-Zélande, par M. A. Richard. At pp. 135–41 of vol. ii. is—Quelques additions et rectifications sur les Algues de la N.Z.

   "In 1822, Captain Duperrey visited the islands in the French discovery corvette 'Coquille,' when one of his officers, the late Admiral D'Urville, made excellent collections. In 1827, Captain (afterwards Admiral) Dumont D'Urville again visited New Zealand in the same ship, renamed the 'Astrolabe' accompanied by an able naturalist, M. Lesson, when additional botanical collections were made in Cook's Straits, the Thames river, and the Bay of Islands. The materials of this voyage (containing

Dumont d'Urville, J.—*continued.*
upwards of 200 Flowering plants and ferns) were published" in the above work. "Some of Forster's plants, together with extracts from his MSS., preserved in the Paris Museum, were also published in this work.—*J. Hooker, Handbook*, pp. 9*-10.*

1833.

Breton, —. Excursions | in | New South Wales, | Western Australia, | and | Van Dieman's Land, | during the Years 1830, 1831, 1832, and 1833. | By Lieut. Breton, R.N. | —— | London : | Richard Bentley, New Burlington Street. | 1833.
    8°. Pp. xii, 476. Illus.
    A brief account of N.Z. and the Maoris is given at pp. 163–85. See also p. 217.

1834.

Dumont d'Urville, J. Voyage | pittoresque | autour du Monde | Resumé général des Voyages de Découvertes | de Magellan, Tasman, Dampier, Anson, Byron, Wallis, Carteret, Bougainville, Cook, Lapérouse, G. Bligh, | Vancouver, D'Entrecasteaux, Wilson, Baudin, Flinders, Krusenstern, Porter, Kotzebue, | Freycinet, Bellinghausen, Basil Hall, Duperrey, Paulding, Beechey, | Dumont d'Urville, Lutke, Dillon, Laplace, B. Morrell, etc. | Publié sous la direction de M. Dumont d'Urville, | Capitaine de Vaisseau. | Accompagné de Cartes et de nombreuses Gravures en taille-douce sur acier, d'après les dessins | de M. De Sainson, Dessinateur du Voyage de *l'Astrolabe.* | —— | —— | A Paris | chez L. Tenré, Libraire-éditeur, Rue du Paon, 1 ; | et chez Henri Dupuy, Rue de la Monnaie, 11. | M. DCCC. XXXIV.
    4°. 3 vols. Pp. viii ; 576 + 584 ; 70 plates, and a map.
    N.Z. ii. 340–412. Adjacent islands, ii. 412–21.—Description, ii. 340–65. History ii. 365–96. Geography, ii. 396–7. Natural history, ii. 397–8. Indigenes, ii. 343–8. Sojourn among them, ii. 351–61. Rev. Mr. Williams's Journal, 1832, ii. 351–7. Anthropophagy, ii. 378, 386, 406. Wars, ii. 385–95. Manners and customs, ii. 399–403. Houses, ii. 405. Food, ii. 406–7.* Music and dancing, ii. 408–9. Superstitions, ii. 400–10. Funerals, ii. 400. Language, ii. 411. Ch. xliv. describes the Macquarrie, Auckland, Campbell, Chatham, Macaulay, and Norfolk islands.
    D'Urville conceived the general plan of the work, furnished all the materials and wrote the last (second ?) volume: see Notice biographique, D. d'U., *Voyage au pôle sud,* x. 131.

1835.

* **Laplace,** —. Voyage de la Favorite dans les années 1830–33. Paris, 1835.
    Visited the Bay of Islands. Parts of the book are reproduced in Rienzi's *Océanie :* see 1838.

* **Nightingale,** Thomas, Oceanic sketches. With a botanical appendix by Dr. Hooker, of Glasgow. London : Cochrane. 1835.
    8°. Pp. 132.—*Davis.*

* **Martin,** R. Montgomery. History of the British Colonies. In five volumes. Vol. iv : Possessions in Africa and Australasia. London, 1835.
    See 1853.

Yate, W. An Account | of New Zealand ; | and of the | Formation and Progress | of the | Church Missionary Society's Mission | in the Northern Island. | By the Rev. William Yate, | Missionary of the Church Missionary Society. | Second edition. | London : | R. B. Seeley and W. Burnside. | Sold by Hatchard & Son, Piccadilly ; and L. & T. Seeley, | 169, Fleet Street. | MDCCCXXXV.
    p. 8°. Pp. vi, 310, and Index 10 pp. Map, portrait of Samuel Marsden, and 9 full-page illus.
    Ch. i. Description. Ch. ii. Flora, fauna, climate, soil, minerals. Ch. iii. Customs and character. Ch. iv. N.Z. mission; with an account of the mission at Paihia,

Yate, W.—*continued.*
1823–31, from an official report. Ch. v. Effect of missions; observations on language, and (first) translation of liturgy, New Testament, &c., pp. 227-32. At pp. 250-81 are letters to Mr. Yate from converted natives, which seem to have been republished in 1836 with an introduction and notes by G. B.; see *Davis*. Appendix, pp. 307-10, has a catalogue, by J. E Gray, of shells collected on east coast.

The information in this volume "is the result of personal observations by the Rev. W. Yate, during his residence of seven years . . . His materials, collected during that period, and carefully from time to time committed to writing, were collected together by him . . . on the passage" from N.Z.—*Preface.*

1836.

Marshall, W. B. A Personal Narrative | of | Two Visits to New Zealand, | in his Majesty's Ship Alligator, | A.D. 1834. | By | William Barrett Marshall,| Surgeon —— Assistant Surgeon, R.N. | London : | James Nisbet and Co. Berners Street. | MDCCCXXXVI.

12°. Pp. xvi, 351 and Errata, 1 p. One illustration.

Dedicated to Lord Glenelg. Its objects are—(1) To bear testimony to the success of the Church missions; (2) to protest against the punishment of the natives, while these are not protected from the immigrants; (3) to put a stop to military intervention in such cases and substitute a humane policy; (4) to obtain redress from the Imperial Government for wrongs inflicted on the tribes at Cape Egmont.

The first part (pp. 1-145) describes the work of the missionaries at the Bay of Islands; choice of a flag, pp. 107-11. The narrative of the second visit (pp. 149-322) relates the "Alligator's" visit to Cape Egmont and the attack on Waimate Pa, *re* Mrs. Guard; elegy on chief, pp. 227-31; account of extension of missions since first visit, pp. 271-88; mentions an unfinished Maori grammar by Rev. W. Williams, pp. 288-9; achievements of christianity in N.Z., pp. 309-12.

Appendix, pp. 325-51. Letter of Lord Goderich (1832) and address of Mr. Busby (1833) to the chiefs, pp. 330-7. N.Z. hymns, with translations, pp. 338-40. List of ships visiting Bay of Islands in 1833, p. 341. Letter of Governor of N.S.W. to Captain of "Alligator," pp. 342-4. Narrative of Mr. Guard, pp. 344-8. Letter of resident traders to Busby and his reply, pp. 349-51.

Sydney Herald, 1836-7.

A number of excerpts are given in *The British colonisation of New Zealand*, L., 1837: they relate chiefly to the condition of the Bay of Islands, and to the import and export trade of New Zealand.

1837.

Busby, J. Letter from *James Busby*, Esq. British Resident at *New Zealand*, to the Honourable the Colonial Secretary of *New South Wales*.

Enclosure (pp. 6–12) in despatch from Gov. Sir R. Bourke, and dated Bay of Islands, June 16, 1837. (Imperial Parliamentary Papers.)

Describes war between Pomare and Ngapuhi, and rapid depopulation of the country and its causes; suggests establishment of a paramount authority, supported by adequate force, using chiefs as agents, and giving missionaries a share in the government.

Coates, D., **Beecham,** J., and **Ellis,** W. Christianity | the | Means of Civilization: | shown in | the Evidence given before a Committee | of the House of Commons | on Aborigines, by D. Coates, Esq., Rev. John Beecham, and | Rev. William Ellis. | Secretaries of the Church Missionary Society, | The Wesleyan Missionary Society, and | London Missionary Society. | To which is added | Selections from the Evidence of other Witnesses bearing on the same subject. | London : | Published by R. B. Seeley and W. Burnside, L. and G. Seeley, and T. Mason. | MDCCCXXXVII.

p. 8°. Pp. viii, 360.

The evidence "refers chiefly to the following points:

"I. Acts of cruelty and oppression committed by Europeans on the natives, and encroachment on their territories, or diminution of their population.

"II. Measures recommended for the protection of the natives, and their moral and social improvement.

Coates, D., Beecham, J., and Ellis, W.—*continued.*
"III. Whether the experience of the several Societies led to the belief that it would be advisable to begin with civilization in order to introduce Christianity, or with Christianity in order to lead to civilization."
It was given in 1835-6, but is not chronologically arranged. Many of the replies are in the form of papers. Original letters describing outrages by British vessels (pp. 6-20) are incorporated; also letters describing the progress of missions in N.Z. (pp. 111-21). The parts relating to N.Z. are at pp. 6-20, 59-61, 82-6, 111-21, 206-50 (Mr. Yate's evidence on mission work among the natives in 1827-34).

* **Coates, D.** The Principles, Objects, and Plan of the New Zealand Association. In a Letter to the Right Honourable Lord Glenelg. By Dandeson Coates, Esq. London: Hatchards. 1837.
An attack on the N.Z. Association: see *N.Z. Journal*, i. 51. Replied to by E. G. Wakefield, 1837, and Hinds, 1838, below.

* Colonization of New Zealand. *Eclectic Review*, lxvii. 382; *Blackwood's Magazine*, xlii. 784. 1837.
The latter advocates the Association's scheme.

* New Zealand. *Dublin Review*, iv. 67. 1837.

* The present state of New Zealand. [Published by the New Zealand Association in 1837.]
Contains essay by Rev. Montague J. Hawtrey on—Exceptional laws in favour of the Natives of New Zealand, in part reprinted in his *Justice to New Zealand*, pp. 12-15, 22, 28-9, 54-6, 80-3, and printed as an appendix to *The British Colonization of New Zealand*, pp. 399-422. The essay is minutely criticized in Beecham's *Colonization*, 1838, pp. 34-42.

* **Wakefield,** Edward Gibbon. Mr. Dandeson Coates and the New Zealand Association. In a letter to the Right Honourable Lord Glenelg. 1837.
A reply to Coates's pamphlet above. Announced for the first time "that the Missionaries of the Society in N.Z. had made large purchases of land from the natives."—*N.Z. Journal*, i. 51.

[**Wakefield,** E. Jerningham and **Ward,** J.] The | British Colonization | of | New Zealand ; | being an account of the principles, objects, and | plans of the | New Zealand Association; | together with | particulars concerning the position, extent, soil and | climate, natural productions, and native | inhabitants of New Zealand. | With | [5] charts and [5] illustrations. | Published for the New Zealand Association. | London: | John W. Parker, West Strand. | M.DCCC.XXXVII.
fcp 8°. Pp. xvi, 423.
Introduction pp. v-xvi. Ch. i. Principles of colonization. ii. Civilization of the New Zealanders. iii. N.Z. as a field for British colonization. iv. Mode of establishing British dominion in N.Z. v. Mode of colonizing British territory. vi. Government of the settlements. vii. Religious establishment.
Description of N.Z. Section i. General, pp. 75-83. ii. Rivers, harbours and bays —soil and population, pp. 84-138. iii. State of British colonization, pp. 131-65. iv. General character of New Zealanders, pp. 166-251. v. Views of natives as to the settlement of an English colony in N.Z., pp. 252-301. vi. Climate and soil (pp. 302-11), agriculture and implements of husbandry (pp. 311-9), food and fruits (pp. 319-26), fish (pp. 326-9), birds, pp. 330-7. vii. Trade and shipping.
Appendix A. Exceptional laws in favour of the natives of N.Z., by Montague J. Hawtrey, pp. 399-422. B. List of (11) publications relating to N.Z., p. 423.

1838.

* **Bannister,** Saxe. Account of the changes and present condition of the population of New Zealand. *Journal of Statistical Society* (Oct. 1838), i. 366.

Beecham, J. Colonization : | being | Remarks | on Colonization in General, | With an Examination | of the | Proposals of the Association | which has been formed | For Colonizing New Zealand. | By John Beecham. | Second

Beecham, J.,—*continued.*
Edition. | London : | Hatchards, Piccadilly ; Seeleys, Fleet Street ; | and | Hamilton, Adams, & Co., and John Mason, | Paternoster Row. | 1838. | *Price* 1s. 6d.
    8°. Pp. 67.
    <small>Part i inquires why colonization has hitherto proved disastrous to the aborigines. Part ii, pp. 23–67, examines, from this point of view, and condemns the N.Z. Association's plan for the colonization of N.Z. as put forth in *The British Colonization of N.Z.*, and particularly the two chapters on Religious Establishments and Exceptional Laws in favour of the Natives. The pamphlet is replied to by Hinds, *Latest official documents*, 1838.</small>

Beecham, J. Remarks | upon | The Latest Official Documents | relating to | New Zealand : | ordered, by the House of Commons, to be printed, | February 7, 1838 : | In a Letter to a Friend. | By John Beecham.
    <small>The letter is dated Feb. 26, 1838. The first edition was printed for private distribution. The second edition adds :—</small>
With | a Notice of a Pamphlet by Samuel Hinds, D.D. | — | — | — | — | Second Edition. | London : | Hatchards, Piccadilly ; Seeleys, Fleet Street ; | and | Hamilton, Adams, & Co., and John Mason, | Paternoster Row. | 1838. | *Price* 1s. 6d.
    8°. 1st ed. : pp. 58 ; 2nd ed. : pp. 75.
    <small>The documents are—despatch from Sir R. Bourke and letters from Capt. Hobson and J. Busby.</small>
    <small>Again examines Association's plan, Busby's, and that of the Parliamentary Committee. Postscript, pp. 47–63, replies to Hinds. An appendix of letters, despatch, and extracts follows.</small>

* The Bishop of Australia's visit to New Zealand in 1838. (Ppht.) Sydney.

* [**Chapman,** Henry Samuel, *afterwards* Mr. Justice.] The Colonization of New Zealand. *Dublin Review*, no. vii. Jan. 1838.
    <small>A "copious exposition of the principles of Colonization, as explained by Mr. Wakefield in his evidence before the Waste Lands Committee of 1836, which embodied the discoverer's latest development of the system ; and the article concludes with a brief examination of N.Z. as a field for colonization on the principles in question."—*N.Z. Journal*, i. 234.</small>

* The Colonization of New Zealand. *Christian Observer*, xxxviii. 131. 1838.

Cunningham, Allan. Floræ Insularum Novæ Zelandiæ Precursor ; or a Specimen of the Botany of the Islands of New Zealand. *In* Sir W. J. Hooker's Companion to the Botanical Magazine, vol. ii. *and* Annals of Natural History ; or, Magazine of Zoology, Botany, and Geology. Conducted by Sir W. Jardine, P. J. Selby, Dr. Johnston, Sir W. J. Hooker, and R. Taylor. Vol. I. London, 1838.
    8°. *Annals*, i. 210–6, 376–81, 455–62.
    <small>"In 1836, and again in 1838, Allan Cunningham, the eminent Australian botanist and explorer, made extensive botanical explorations . . . chiefly in the Bay of Islands," and the result of his, and his brother Richard's, labours, which "added considerably to the known Flora" are collected in the above work.—J. HOOKER, *Handbook*, p 10*. See his biography in Heaton, *Australian men of the time*.</small>

* First annual report of the Aborigines Protection Society. London : Ball. 1838.
    <small>From *Davis*. There are reports down to 1887 : see Carter's Catalogue.</small>

Hinds, S. The Latest | Official Documents | relating to | New Zealand ; | with | Introductory Observations, | By | Samuel Hinds, D.D., | Vicar of Yardley, Herts ; | and one of the Committee of the New Zealand Association. | London : | John W. Parker, West Strand. | M.DCCC.XXXVIII.
    8°. Pp. 46.

Hinds, S.—*continued.*
Despatches from Sir R. Bourke, Captain Hobson, R.N., J. Busby, Resident; petition from settlers at Bay of Islands *re* Baron De Thierry. Introduced by observations of Dr. Hinds (pp. 5-22) *re* statements of Messrs. Coates and Beecham on probable effect on Natives of a commercial company colonizing New Zealand. Replied to by Beecham, *Latest official documents*, ed. 2, 1838, pp. 47-63.

* **Howitt,** W. Colonization and Christianity: A Popular History of the treatment of the Natives by the Europeans in all their Colonies. By William Howitt. London: Longmans. 1838.
    p. 8°. Pp. 508.
    Ch. 28 relates in part to the colonization of the Pacific islands.—*Davis.*

* **New Zealand.** *Penny Magazine*, vii. 325, 417. 1838.

Polack, Joel Samuel. New Zealand: | being | a Narrative | of | Travels and Adventures | during a Residence in that Country between | the Years 1831 and 1837. | By J. S. Polack, Esq. | Member of the Colonial Society of London. | In two volumes. | —— | London : | Richard Bentley, | New Burlington Street, | Publisher in Ordinary to Her Majesty. | M.DCCC.XXXVIII.
    8°. Pp. xiii, 403; vi, 441 and Errata. Map, and illustrations by the author.
    Vol. I. Chs. i, ii. Progress of discovery. Chs. iii-vii. Journal of journey to Kaipara, with notices of customs, &c. Ch. viii. General description of N.Z. Ch. ix. Climate, soil, botany, zoology. Ch. x. Mineralogy and geology. Ch. xi. Origin and manners of people. Ch. xii. Rank, dress, food.
    Vol. II. Ch. i. Cannibalism, morals, arts. Ch. ii. Warfare. Ch. iii. Ceremonies morals, slavery. Ch. iv. Tolaga Bay. Ch. v. Establishment of Church Mission at Bay of Islands and Wesleyan at Wangaroa. Ch. vi. E'Ongi. Ch. vii. First land-purchases flag. Ch. viii. ix. Religion. Ch. ix. Diseases, language, numerals (comparative) Ch. x. Flax-trade and experiences of a flax collector. Ch. xi. Suggestions on colonization. Appendix, ii. 367-441: note 4, Phormium tenax; note 6, discovery of adjacent islands; note 7, forest trees; note 8, sperm whale fishery; notes 10, 11, proclamation and petition relating to Baron Thierry.
    Polack resided in Hokianga and Bay of Islands, and travelled about. He was a long time among the Maoris, and knew the language. He described himself as a wholesale and retail trader, and admitted that he sold spirits, but denied that he kept a grog-shop. See his evidence in the Report of the House of Lords Committee, 1838, pp. 79, 95. He mentions some autobiographical details in his later work, *Manners and Customs*, &c., ii. 279-80.
    Reviewed in the *Eclectic* and *Monthly* Reviews: see below.

* **Polack on New Zealand in 1831-37.** *Monthly Review*, cxlvii. 161; *Eclectic Review*, lxx. 31; xc. 414.
    The former *Eclectic* article is reprinted in John Foster's *Fosteriana*, London. 1858, pp. 538-57.

Report | from the | Select Committee of the House of Lords, | appointed to inquire into | The Present State | of | The Islands of New Zealand, | and | the expediency of | regulating the settlement of British | subjects therein ; | with | The Minutes of Evidence | taken before the Committee, | and | an index thereto. | *Ordered, by* the House of Commons, *to be Printed*, | 8 *August*, 1838.
    f°. Pp. 376.
    Hon. F. Baring, M.P., Chairman N.Z. Association Committee, pp. 146-56; Beecham, Rev. J., Secretary, Wesleyan Missionary Society, pp. 180-242, 286-315; Brown, O., p. 243; Coates, Dandeson, Lay Secretary to Church Missionary Society, pp. 180-242, 243-75; Elliott, F., Agent-General for Emigrants, pp. 346-52; Enderby, C., pp. 71-9; Evans, G. S., Member N.Z. Association, pp. 317-34; Fitz Roy, Captain, R.N., pp. 161-79. 335-45; Flatt, J., Catechist, Church Missionary Society, pp. 32, 48, 49-55; Garratt, W. A., Member, Committee, Church Missionary Society, pp. 276-66; Hinds, Rev. Dr., pp. 124-46; Montefiore, J. B., pp. 55-71 ; Nayti, a native, pp. 113-7; Nicholas, J. L., pp. 3-12, 117; Petre, Lord, pp. 345-46; Polack, J. S., pp. 75-93, 95; Tawell, J. D., pp. 108-12, 119-24; Watkins, J., pp. 12-32; Wilkinson, Rev. F., pp. 95-108.

Report from Select Committee—*continued*.
> The subjects on which the witnesses gave evidence are—N.Z. in general and Bay of Islands particularly; the natives—their character, customs, wars, religion and traditions, ranks, chiefs and slaves; family and infanticide, cannibalism, &c.; land, its tenure and transfer; the origin and proceedings of the Church Mission and Wesleyan Mission; colonization; N.Z. Association; Mr. Busby as Resident; Baron de Thierry—his scheme to colonize N.Z., proclamation of sovereignty, &c.

Rienzi, G. L. Domeny *de*. Océanie | ou | Cinquième Partie du Monde. | Revue Géographique et Ethnographique | de la Malaisie, de la Micronésie, de la Polynésie | et de la Mélanesie; | offrant les résultats des voyages et des découvertes de l'auteur et de ses devanciers, ainsi que ses nouvelles classifications et divisions de ces contrées, par M. G. L. Domeny de Rienzi, | voyageur en Océanie, en Orient, etc., etc., membre de plusieurs académies de France et d'Italie, de l'Institut Historique, de la Société de Géographie, de la Société de Statistique Universelle, des Sociétés Asiatiques de Paris et de Bombay (Inde), etc., etc. | —— | Tome Troisième. | Paris, | Firmin Didot Frères, Editeurs, | Imprimeurs-Libraires de l'Institut de France, | Rue Jacob, No. 56 | M DCCC XXXVIII.
>
> 8°. Pp. 639. Map and many illustrations.
>
> N.Z., pp. 124–256.
>
> The earlier pages give the geography, aspect, climate, and natural history of N.Z. At pp. 126–31 is an account (from Deterville's *Dictionnaire*) of the seals and sea-lions. The author distinguishes two races, and proposes to call Maoris *Maouiens* (from *Maui*). Chapters follow on the population, political constitution, marriage and the family, tattooing, houses, cultivation, language, poetry and dancing, superstitions, food, salutations, funerals, sacrifices, suicide, anthropophagy, head-preparing, &c. There is a parallel between the New Zealanders and the Battas, pp. 185-6. History, pp. 190–252, from accounts of travellers; that of De Surville and Marion being from French sources. Letters of natives are translated from the Missionary Register of 1830. Pp. 253-6 are on the Chatham and Auckland Isles, &c.
>
> The book is a compilation, sections being taken bodily from D'Urville and Laplace; but part of it is from Rienzi's personal observations.

* **Wheeler**, D. Extracts from the Letters and Journal of Daniel Wheeler, now engaged in a Religious Visit to the Inhabitants of some of the Islands of the Pacific Ocean, Van Diemen's Land, and New South Wales. Accompanied by his Son, Charles Wheeler. Second edition. London, 1838.
> 8°.
>
> Parts 2, 3 and 4 relate to the Society, Friendly, Hawaiian, and Tongan Islands and New Zealand.—*Petherick, Torch*, i. 171. See also Wheeler's *Memoirs, ibid*.

1839.

* **Alison**, Archibald. Speech delivered at the New Zealand colonisation dinner at Glasgow on October 22, 1839. London, 1839.
> The substance of the speech was afterwards reproduced in his *Principles of population*, ch. 15: see 1840. A passage from the speech is given in Jameson's *New Zealand*, &c., pp. 209–11.

* **Bannister**, S. Condition of the population of New Zealand. *Journal of the Statistical Society*, i. 362.

* The Colonization of New Zealand. *Monthly Review*, cl. 38.

Correspondence between Colonial Office and Chairman of Directors, New Zealand Company, 1839. Imperial Parliamentary Papers.
> Has extract from *Morning Chronicle*, Sept. 16, 1839, describing ceremony previous to departure of emigrants. In a speech the Chairman invited the emigrants to sign a social compact agreeing to submit to a voluntary form of government: the document is given at pp. 59–60.

Fitz Roy, *Captain* Robert. Narrative | of the | Surveying Voyages | of His Majesty's Ships | Adventure and Beagle, | between | the years 1826 and

Fitz Roy, *Captain* Robert—*continued.*
1836, | describing their | Examination of the Southern Shores | of | South America, | and | the Beagle's circumnavigation of the Globe. In three volumes. | —— | London : | Henry Colburn, Great Marlborough Street. | 1839.

    8°. Vol. ii : pp. xv, 695. Map and illus. (one N.Z. plate). Appendix to vol. ii : pp. 352 (a separate volume).

        Vol. ii, chs. 24 and 25, pp. 564–618, describe a short visit to the Bay of Islands in 1835, the natives, the missionary station at Pahia and missionary work and influence, Waimate.

        The appendix to vol. ii. contains reprints of early official papers.

        Vol. iii contains C. Darwin's Journal and Remarks (Pp. xiv, 608 and maps), of which pp. 496–514 relate to the same visit to the Bay of Islands. See below, 1845.

Foster, John. Fosteriana. Edited by H. G. Bohn. London, 1858.
        At pp. 538–57 is a review of Polack's first book on N.Z., under the title—"General depravity of the human race."

Mann, W. Six Years' Residence | in the | Australian Provinces, | Ending in 1839 ; | exhibiting their capabilities of colonization, | and containing | The History, Trade, Population, Extent, | Resources, &c. &c. | of New South Wales, Van Diemen's Land, South Australia and Port Philip ; | with | An Account of New Zealand. | By W. Mann, Esq. | —— | London : | Smith, Elder, & Co., Cornhill. | M.DCCC.XXXIX.

    cr 8°. Pp. vi, 360. Map. (at pp. 308–51)

        The account of N.Z. is "extracted from the most recent and authentic works"—chiefly Yate.

* **Important Information** about New Zealand. By a gentleman who was fourteen years at Hokianga. Sydney, 1839.

    Pamphlet.—*Thomson.*

Instructions from the New Zealand Land Company to Colonel Wakefield, Principal Agent of the Company (Enclosed in a despatch dated April 29, 1839.)

    f°. 5 pp. *In* Correspondence with Secretary of State relative to New Zealand, 1840, pp. 59–63.

        The instructions bear upon three points: (1) the purchase of lands for the Company; (2) the acquisition of general information as to the country ; and (3) preparations for the formation of settlements under the auspices of the Company.

Lang, J. D. New Zealand | in | 1839 : | or | Four letters, | to | the Right Hon. Earl Durham, | Governor of the New Zealand Land Company, | &c. &c. &c. | on the colonization of that island, | and | on the present condition and prospects of its | native inhabitants. | By | John Dunmore Lang, D.D. | Principal of the Australian College, and senior minister | of the Church of Scotland in New South Wales. | London : | Smith, Elder, and Co., 65, Cornhill. | 1839.

    8°. Pp. iv, 120.

        Letter i. On the character and influence of the present European population of N.Z., as regards the aborigines. ii. On the character and influence of the missions hitherto established in N.Z., as regards the aborigines. iii. On the prospect which N.Z. affords for the establishment of a British colony. iv. On the principles on which a British colony in N.Z. ought to be established and conducted. Appendix : South Sea Islands, pp. 116–20.

        "Sailing to England he touched at N.Z. in January, 1839. Arriving in England he found the N.Z. Land Company actively at work. . . . Lang addressed four letters to Lord Durham as Chairman of the Company. He urged that the Company ought to make way for a national Colony. He animadverted upon Marsden's plan of civilizing before evangelizing; and upon the 'inefficiency and worthlessness' of the mission. He declared that the church missionaries had actually been 'the principals in the

Lang, J. D.—*continued.*
grand conspiracy of the European inhabitants to rob and plunder the natives of their land,' and that their abuse of their position constituted ' one of the grossest breaches of trust witnessed for a century past.'"—*Rusden, History of N.Z.*, i. 155 note.

H. Williams refers to the Letters as a "wicked production" (*Life*, ii. 24–5).

The book was republished in 1873.

A biographical account of Dr. Lang appeared in the *Melbourne Review*, iii. 352–83

* **Laing's** [sic] Letters on New Zealand. *Tait's Magazine*, n.s. vi. 611. 1839.

Lesson, René Primeverre. Voyage | autour | Du Monde | entrepris par ordre du Gouvernement | sur la Corvette La Coquille ; | par P. Lesson, | Membre correspondant de l'Institut. | —— | Paris. | P. Pourrat Frères, Editeurs, | Rue des Petits Augustins, 5, | Et chez les Libraires et aux Dépôts de Pittoresques de la France | et de l'étranger. | 1839.

roy. 8°. 2 tomes. Pp. 511+519. Portrait, steel and wood engravings, some of them coloured ; 5 are of N.Z. subjects.

The part relating to N.Z. is at vol. ii. pp. 307–411. Ch. xxi describes a sojourn at the Bay of Islands, April 3–17, 1824, and is generally descriptive. Ch. xxii is entitled, Réflexions générales sur les habitants. At pp. 384–403 is a summary of Kendall and Lee's Grammar. At pp. 404–11 is a classified Vocabulary, the majority of the words being taken from the same Grammar, while others were personally collected.

In a note prefixed to ch. xxii the author says: This chapter, the form of which I have carefully retained, saw the light in 1828 in my *Complément aux œuvres de Buffon*. tome ii p. 283 to 352, and the *Voyage pittoresque* which bears the name of M. Durville [sic] appeared only in 1835: the article of M. de Rienzi appeared only in 1837. Lastly, the official narrative of the *Astrolabe* bears the date 1830 (t. ii) and 1831 (t. iii).

* Manners and customs in New Zealand. *Monthly Review*, cli. 575.

Matthew, P. Emigration Fields. | North America, | The Cape, | Australia, | and | New Zealand, | describing these Countries, | and giving a | Comparative View of the Advantages they | present to British Settlers. | By | Patrick Matthew, | Author of "Naval Timber and Arboriculture." | Adam and Charles Black, Edinburgh ; | Longman, Orme, Brown, Green and Longmans, | London. | 1839.

p. 8°. Pp. xi, 237. 2 maps.

Ch. i. Utility of emigration and colonies . . . Ch. viii. Description of New Zealand,—its capabilities for becoming the naval emporium of the southern hemisphere, and of the Pacific, under British colonization. Ch. ix. Especial reasons for colonizing New Zealand. Ch. x. Prefatory observations to a plan for colonizing N.Z., with proposals of a Peace Corps. Ch. xi. Plan of a protective and combinable labour nucleus for the colony. Ch. xii. Location, land-purchase, titles, &c. Ch. xiii. Treatment of natives. Ch. xiv. Bill for colonizing N.Z. Ch. xv. Economy of colonization. Ch. xvi. Remarks on colonial legislation. Appendix, pp. 213–34. Prospectus of a joint-stock company for colonizing New Zealand, pp. 235-7.

Molesworth, Sir William. Lord Glenelg and the Ministry. | Sir William Molesworth's | speech | on the | state of the colonies. | —— | London : | Henry Horper, 13, Pall-Mall East. | 1839.

8°. Pp. 59.

N.Z. pp. 31–3.

With Charles Buller, "as comrades in the cause, were the present Lord Grey and the late Sir William Molesworth, who taken away in the prime of life, but not without having attained high political office, holds his place among the statesmen of his country."—Houghton, *Monographs*, ed. 2, p. 248. See also note on C. Buller's speech.

* **New Zealand.** *Dublin University Magazine*, xiv. 298 ; *Museum of Foreign Literature*, xxxvii. 171.

* **New Zealand and Van Diemen's Land,** 1839. *Monthly Review*, cl. 521.

Owen, Richard. [Sir R. Owen's memoirs on the extinct species of N.Z. begin with a paper in the *Transactions of the Zoological Society of London*

Owen, Richard—*continued.*
for 1839. A list of them to 1861 is given by Hochstetter, *Geologie*, pp. xxv-xxvi, and to 1863 in the Royal Society's *Catalogue of scientific papers*, vol. iv. The memoirs are reprinted in his *Extinct wingless birds of New Zealand*, 1879.]

* Popular Account of New Zealand as a Field for British Colonization. Glasgow: Lumsden. 1839.
Pp. 52.—*Davis.*

Prospectus of New Zealand Land Company. (Enclosure in letter dated May 22, 1839; correspondence with Secretary of State relative to New Zealand, 1840, pp. 64-5.)

***Walton**, J. Twelve Months in New Zealand. 1839.
See *N.Z. Journal*, ii. 245.

Ward, John. Information | relative to | New Zealand, | compiled for | the Use of Colonists, | by John Ward, Esq. | Secretary to the New-Zealand Company. | London : | John W. Parker, West Strand. | 1839.
fcp. 8°. Fourth edition is paged x, 168. Map and outline chart.
The first edition was published in June, 1839, and by Dec. 1840 three large editions had been disposed of. A fourth appeared in 1841.—*N.Z. Journal*, ii. 57-8.
First four chapters are descriptive. Ch. v. Natives. Ch. vi. Colonization. Ch. vii. Emigration; Home meetings. Appendix.

1840.

Alison, [*Sir*] A. The | Principles of Population, | and their Connection with Human Happiness. | By | Archibald Alison, F.R.S.E. | Advocate, Sheriff of Lanarkshire, | and Author of History of Europe during the French Revolution. | In two volumes. | —— | William Blackwood and Sons, Edinburgh : | and Thomas Cadell, | London. | M.DCCC.XL.
8°. Pp. xix, 572 ; viii, 544.
Ch. xv. contains the substance of a speech on emigration to N.Z. delivered in Glasgow in 1839 and reprinted as a pamphlet: see his *Autobiography*, i. 464-5.

***Bell**, [*Sir*] Francis Dillon. New Zealand. *Colonial Magazine*, Nov. 1840.
"An interesting sketch of the proceedings of the N.Z. Company."—*N.Z. Journal*, ii. 245.

* The British Colonization of New Zealand. In *The Colonial Magazine and Commercial Maritime Journal*, Nov. 1840, art. i.
Reviewed in the *N.Z. Journal*, Jan. 2, 1841, (in vol. ii).

Campbell, Edward. The | Present State, | Resources and Prospects | of | New Zealand. | By Edward Campbell. | London : | Smith Elder and Co. Cornhill. | 1840. | *Price One Shilling.*
12°. Pp. 38. Preface is dated—Sydney, April, 1839.
The author was a member of a respectable mercantile firm in Sydney, and his mission was commercial. He visited Hokianga and the Bay of Islands in 1838. An account of his visit to De Thierry is extracted in the *N.Z. Journal*, i. 23.

***Chapman**, H. S. New Zealand. *Dublin Review*, no. xvii, Aug. 1840.
London : Dolman, late Booker, New Bond-street.
A supplement to article in no. vii. History of proceedings of 1839-40 and critical remarks on course of Government in reference to sovereignty. Long extracts are given in *N.Z. Journal*, i. 234-5.

The Colonization | of | New Zealand, | from the Counties of | Devon and Cornwall : | a Brief History of the | New Zealand Company of London ; | a Statement of the Constitution and Plans of the | Plymouth Company of New Zealand ; | and General Instructions for Emigrants. | Seal | Devon-

Colonization of New Zealand—*continued.*
  port: | Published, for the Directors of the Plymouth Company of New
  Zealand, | by H. Granville, (Printer to Her Majesty, and to the Plymouth
  Com | pany of New Zealand,) 99, Fore-street; who will transmit a copy,
  post-free, on receipt of sixpence, secured in a pro-paid letter. | M DCCC XL.
    fcp. 8°. Pp. 43.
    Gives the names of the New Zealand Committee for the West of Scotland, p. 12,
  and of the New Zealand Committee for Ireland, p. 15.

* Description of a View of the Bay of Islands, New Zealand, now exhibiting at
  the Panorama, Leicester Square. Painted by the Proprietor, Robert Burford, from Drawings taken by Augustus Erle, Esq. London: G. Nichols.
  1840.
    Thin pamphlet. No date, but about 1840.—*Davis.*

Dieffenbach, *Dr.* E. Account of the Chatham Islands. *Journal Royal
  Geographical Society,* xi. 195; xii. 142, and *New Zealand Journal,* ii. 125–6.
  1840–1.

Emigration to New Zealand. Report of the speeches delivered by the Rev.
  Dr. Burns and others, at the meeting in the Philosophical Hall, Paisley, on
  Monday, the 27th June, 1840. Paisley, 1840.
    12°. Pp. 12.
    Contains (p. 2) "Appeal on behalf of the Paisley New Zealand Emigration
  Society;" Memorial to Lord John Russell from working men of Paisley (pp. 10-11); and
  (p. 12) "Rules of the Paisley New Zealand Emigration Society."

The | First Report | of the | Directors | of the | New-Zealand Company, | pre-
  sented to | the First General Meeting | of the | Shareholders, | on the 14th
  May, 1840. | London: | Printed by Thompson and Mckewan, 19, Great
  St. Helens. | 1840.
    8°. Pp. 38, with appendices.
    Gives a sketch of the Associations merged in the Company (pp. 6-9) and of the
  formation of the Company, with a statement of its principles.

* Fourteen Years in New Zealand. By an actual Settler. 1840.
    Reviewed in the *N.Z. Journal,* ii. 23. "There is nothing original in this pamphlet.
  The best parts relate to the natives."—*Ibid,* ii. 245.

Gipps, *Sir* G. Speech of Sir George Gipps, Governor of New South Wales, on
  the New Zealand Land Bill. Sydney. 1840.
    The speech is in the Imperial Parliamentary Papers.

* **Hawtrey**, *Rev.* Montague J. G. Earnest address to the New Zealand
  Colonists, in reference to their Intercourse with the Native Inhabitants.
  12°. London, 1840.
    Portions of it are reprinted in his *Justice to N.Z.* pp. 15-16, 18-20, 22-5, 56-7, 58-77.

Holman, James. Travels | in | China, New Zealand, | New South Wales, |
  Van Dieman's Land, Cape Horn, | etc. etc. | By James Holman, R.N.
  F.R.S. | etc. etc. | —— | Second edition. | London: | George Routledge, 11,
  Ryder's Court, | Leicester Square. | 1840.
    8°. Pp. viii, 519.
    Contains a narrative of the massacre on board Captain Stuart's vessel of certain
  Ngatihou Natives, by Te Rauparaha, Hiko, Tungia, and others of the Ngatihoa tribe
  (pp. 480-92). Rough notes (pp. 487-95) on N.Z. and the natives were furnished (in 1832)
  to the author (who does not seem to have visited the country) " by a gentleman who
  commanded a vessel belonging to Sydney, and who collected the substance of the
  following information, while he was trading amongst the natives in different parts of
  the island " (p. 487).

* **H., G.** New Zealand colonisation. By G. H. Martin's *Colonial Magazine*
  ii. 206. 1840.

Johnson, J. Pitts. Plain Truths, | told by a traveller, | regarding our various | Settlements | in | Australia and New Zealand ; | shewing things as they are, | and as they ought to be ; | particularly in | Sydney—Parramatta—Perth—Fremantle—The | Swan River—the Canning—the Murray | — the Darling—King George's Sound | —and in Van Dieman's Land. | The whole drawn up | For the guidance of Emigrants to these Settlements. | By J. Pitts Johnson, Esq. | " Nothing extenuate, nor aught set down [sic] in malice." | London : | Smith, Elder, and Co. Cornhill. | 1840. | *Price Eighteen-pence.*

12°. Pp. 75, with Preface.

A passing visit to Bay of Islands, apparently in 1836, pp. 59-72.

* Journal of a deputation of the London Missionary Society to the South Seas, etc., in 1821-29. 1840.

"At page 182 is a vivid account of the savage treatment the Deputation and others received at the hands of the Maories at Wangaroa Bay."—*Carter.*

* A Letter to the Earl of Chichester, President of the Church Missionary Society, on some matters connected with the New Zealand Mission. By a Clergyman. London : Smith, Elder, and Co. 1840.

* A Second Letter to the Earl of Chichester, on the subject of the Church Missionary Society. By a Clergyman. London : Smith and Elder. 1840.

* A Brief Reply to a Letter, &c. By a Member of the Committee. London : Hamilton and Co. 1840.

The three foregoing pamphlets relate to the land-purchases by missionaries. Long extracts are given in the *N.Z. Journal*, i. 51-3.

* Missions of the Church Missionary Society at Kishnagur and in New Zealand. London : Hatchards. 1840.

12°. Pp. 152.

"N.Z. portion from p. 93 to end. Sub-title runs :—N.Z. mission : Visit of the Bishop of Australia to the C. M. S. Mission in N.Z., and Notices of its State and Progress."—*Davis.*

* New Zealand described ; together with a few words of advice on the subject of Emigration, in a Letter to the Labouring class.—London : G. Mann, 39, Cornhill. 1840. [Price threepence.]

* New Zealand. With illustrations. Martin's *Colonial Magazine*, ii. 5. 1840.

The | New Zealand Journal. | (Published every other Saturday.) | —— | London : | Printed and published by Henry Hobbs Chambers, at the office of the | "New Zealand Journal," 366, Strand. | 1840-9.

f°. Ten annual volumes appeared.

Contains a mass of materials for N.Z. history. N.Z. hemp, i. 7-9. N.Z. colonization societies. Proceedings of N.Z. Company, *passim*. Commercial prospects of N.Z. Catholic mission. Letters from settlers. Reviews of books relating to N.Z. Meeting in Glasgow, i. 118-9. Debates in House of Commons, and evidence before Committees Reports and meetings of Aborigines Society. Speeches at dinners, fêtes. Bennett's Observations on the coniferous trees of N.Z., ii. 81-2. Bibliography, ii. 249-6. Report of expeditions (as to Taranaki, ii. 259-264, and notes of excursions. N.Z. tales (as Koane, iv. 101, 112). Reports of Dieffenbach to Aborigines Protection Society, i. 314, ii. 202-4, 250-1, &c. Letter of M. Hawtrey to Lord J. Russell on native reserves, ii. 76-8.

Polack, J. S. Manners and Customs | of the | New Zealanders ; | with Notes corroborative of their Habits, Usages, etc., | and | Remarks to intending Emigrants, | with numerous cuts drawn on wood. | By J. S. Polack, Esq., | Author of "Travels and Adventures in New Zealand between the Years

Polack, J. S.—*continued.*
    1831 and 1837." [Engraving.] | —— | James Madden & Co., 8, Leadenhall Street, | and | Hatchard and Son, Piccadilly. | MDCCCXXXX.
        p. 8vo. 2 vols. Pp. xxxiv, 288; xviii, 304. Map and 46 illus. in vol. i ; 24 in vol. ii: no. 1 in vol. ii misdescribed in list.
        Vol. I.—Preface, pp. xix-xxii. Introduction (pp. xxiii.-xxxiv) is a personal vindication. Ch. i. Comparative (two races—brown-black and dark-brown, Papuan and Malay). Ch. ii. Traditions. Ch iii, iv, v. Tribes and ranks. Ch. vi. Religion. Ch. vii. Burial, customs. Ch. viii. Feasting, &c. Ch. ix. Assemblies. Ch. x, xi. Burial. Ch. xii-xv. Marriage. Ch. xvi. Flax-trade, arts, fashions. Ch. xvii. Exchange. Ch. xviii. Boils, fishing. Ch. xix. Houses. Ch. xx. Canoes. Ch. xxi, xxii. Religion. Ch. xxiii, xxiv. Priesthood and divination. Ch. xxv. Rites. Ch. xxvi. Witchcraft, and human sacrifices.
        Vol. II.—Ch. i, ii. War. Ch. iii. Fortifications and weapons. Ch. iv. Trophies and tattooing. Ch. v. Slavery. Ch. vi. Internal government. Ch. vii, viii. Land. Ch. ix, x. Causes of decrease of population. Ch. x. Diseases, morals, story-telling. Ch. xi. Occupations. Ch. xii. Eloquence and abilities. Ch. xiii. Titles and names. Ch. xiv. Education. Ch. xv. Terms of relationship, salutations, pastimes. Ch. xvi. Dances. Ch. xvii. Physical geography; Wesleyan and Catholic missions; De Thierry. Ch. xviii. Various climates; forest (pp. 204-10). Ch. xix. Colonization. Ch. xxi. British government of N.Z.; De Thierry. Ch. xxii. Comments on Lords' Committee; qualifications of witnesses examined, pp. 238-40; report, pp. 240-4.
        Appendix, pp. 245-304. Forest timber trees, pp. 249-65. Gums and resins, pp. 265-7. Edible plants, pp. 275-7. Fruits, pp. 278-9. Flax-plant, pp. 291-6.

R., R. Australia, | Van Dieman's Land, | and | New Zealand; | their History and present State, | with their prospects in regard to | Emigration, | impartially examined. | Map | London : Sold by T. M. Cradock, 48, Paternoster Row. | 1840.
        12°. Title-page, preface, contents, and 60 pp.
    N.Z.: pp. 44-60. A compilation from good sources.

Report | from the | Select Committee | on | New Zealand ; | together with the | Minutes of Evidence | taken before them, | and | An Appendix, and Index. | *Ordered*, by the House of Commons, *to be Printed*, | 3 *August* 1840.
        f°. Pp. xii, 207.
    The chairman of the Committee was Lord Eliot, and Mr. Gladstone was a member.
        The witnesses examined were—E. G. Wakefield, pp. 1-57, 97-112; Saxe Banister, p. 58; J. Blackett, pp. 59-70; J. Ward (Secretary of N.Z. Company), pp. 70-5, 90; D. Coates (Secretary to Church Missionary Society), pp. 76-90; J. Beecham (Secretary of Wesleyan Missionary Society), pp. 91-7; Dr. Hinds, pp. 112-21; C. Enderby, pp. 121-4 ; W. Hutt, pp. 124-9; A. Busby, pp. 120-33.
    Rusden (i. 255) describes the Committee as being "among the weapons of the Company." At all events the N.Z. Company was a main subject of the Committee's inquiries. E. G. Wakefield gave an account of the origin and progress of the Association of 1837, the origin of the New Zealand Company and its relations with the Government. The Secretary of the Church Missionary Society described the proceedings of the Society in N.Z., in continuation of his evidence before the House of Lords Committee; as did also the Secretary of the Wesleyan Missionary Society. The purchase of lands by missionaries of both Societies was closely inquired into, and documents connected with are given in the Appendix. Dr. Hinds, afterwards Bishop of Norwich, described the object and progress of the N.Z. Church Society. There is also residential information on the natives.

Reybaud, Louis. Histoire et colonisation de la Nouvelle-Zélande. (Present state of the islands of New Zealand; report brought from the Lords, ordered by the House of Commons to be printed.) *Revue des Deux Mondes*, Jan. 15, 1840, première période, quatrième série, tome xxi. 145-83.
    i. Vues générales sur les îles Polynésiennes. ii. Premiers voyages à la N.Z. iii. Voyages en Europe de quelques Zélandais. iv. Européens naturalisés dans la N.Z. v. N.Z. depuis l'établissement des missions. vi. Colonisation anglaise.

Russell, A. A Tour | through the | Australian Colonies | in | 1839, | with notes and incidents of a voyage | Round the Globe, calling at | New Zealand and South America. | By | A. Russell. | —— | Second edition. | Glasgow : | David Robertson—Duncan Campbell. | Edinburgh : Oliphant & Son. | London : Hugh Cunningham, | Trafalgar Square | MDCCCXL.

    12°. Pp. vii, 332.

    <small>A brief visit to Cloudy Bay is described, pp. 280-9.</small>

* **Rudge,** J. An Address to the New Zealand Emigrants, delivered at the Depot, Deptford, Oct. 11, 1840. By James Rudge, D.D. Published by W. E. Painter, Strand, 1840.

    <small>See *N.Z. Journal*, i. 303.</small>

* **Swainson,** W. Observations on the Climate of New Zealand. By William Swainson. London : Smith, Elder and Co. 1840.

* Third Report of the Aborigines' Protection Society. 1840.

    <small>Cited in *N.Z. Journal*, i. 251.</small>

* **Ward,** J. Supplementary Information relative to New Zealand. 1840.

    12°.

    <small>"This work contains Colonel Wakefield's three first despatches; Dr. Dieffenbach's Report on the Natural History and Physical Condition of Port Nicholson, Queen Charlotte's Sound, &c.; and the first Report of the Directors of the N.Z. Company."—*N.Z. Journal*, ii. 214.</small>

* **Willis,** —. Notes on the acquisition of New Zealand as a Dependency of New South Wales. By Judge Willis. Sydney. 1840.

    <small>Pamphlet.—*Davis.*</small>

* **Young,** W. C. New Zealand described. 1840.

1841.

* **Bright,** John. Handbook for New Zealand emigrants. London : Hooper. 1841.

    12°. *Thomson.*

* ——— State and prospects of New Zealand. 1841.

Bidwill, J. C. Rambles | in | New Zealand. | By John Carse Bidwill, | (Late of Exeter,) | Sidney [*sic*] ; New South Wales. | London : | Published by W. S. Orr & Co., Paternoster Row | and T. Fitze, Exeter. | MDCCCXLI. | (*Price 2s. 6d.*)

    8°. Pp. viii, 104. Map of route.

    <small>The author was in N.Z. from Feb. to April, 1839, and at Port Nicholson in Aug. 1840. His ascent of Tongariro, which was the first, is described at pp. 46-52.—See biographical sketch of Bidwill in *Dictionary of national biog.*, v. 18. Reviewed in *N.Z. Journal*, ii. 176-9, 191; with copious extracts.</small>

Carpenter, W. Emigration and Colonization | considered | with special reference to | The Australasian Colonies | of South Australia | and | New Zealand ; | —— | By William Carpenter. | London : | William Strange, 21, Paternoster-Row. | 1841.

    12°. Pp. 48.

    N.Z., pp. 26-34, 39-40.

Chapman, H. S. Emigration : comparative prospects of our new colonies. With maps. *Westminster Review*, xxxv. 132-87. 1841.

    <small>N.Z., pp. 171-87. Chart of Port Nicholson, by Wilde. Sketch of colonisation and settlement.</small>

* ——— New Zealand. *Encyclopædia Britannica*, seventh edition, vol. xxi. pp. 975-83.

    <small>"A brief view of the principles of Colonization in their application to N.Z."—*N.Z. Journal*, ii. 245.</small>

***Dieffenbach**, Ernst. New Zealand and its native population. (Published for the Aborigines Protection Society). London, 1841.
8°.
Probably a reprint of the Reports in *N.Z. Journal*, I. 314, II. 202-4, 250-1, &c.

Du Petit-Thouars, A. Voyage | autour du Monde | sur la Frégate | La Venus, | pendant les Années 1836–1839, | publié par ordre du Roi, | sous les Auspices du Ministre de la Marine, | par Abel du Petit-Thouars, | Capitaine de vaisseau, Commandeur de la Légion-d'Honneur. | —— | Paris, | Gide, Éditeur, | Rue de Seine-Saint-Germain, 6 bis. | 1840–1.
roy. 8°. 2 tomes, xliv; 402+404.
Tome iii. appears to relate to N.Z.

***Hodgskin**, Richard, *jun.* Narrative of eight months' sojourn in New Zealand; with a description of the habits, customs, &c. of the islanders, the climate, soil, birds, fishes, &c. Coleraine, 1841.
Pamphlet.

***Information** relative to New Plymouth Settlement. London. 1841.
Thomson.

***Letters** from Emigrants, two sets. London. Published by N.Z. Company.
Ibid.

***New Zealand** in 1841. *Monthly Review*, clvi. 543.

The **New Zealand Journal**. Vol. ii. London. 1841.
Mr. Hanson at Chatham Islands, pp. 100-1, and description of the Islands by Dieffenbach, pp. 125-6. Stokes's report of an expedition to Taranaki by land, pp. 121-4, 133-6, 253-7, 265-8. Major Bunbury's report on the Middle Island, &c., pp. 233-6.

***Petition** for the recall of Governor Hobson. Martin's *Colonial Magazine*, vi. 110.

***Petre's** Account of New Zealand. *Littell's Museum of Foreign Literature*, xliv. 377.

The | Third Report | of the Directors of the New Zealand Company, presented to | the Annual General Meeting | of the | Shareholders, on the 1st May, 1841. | London : | Printed by L. Thompson, 19, Great St. Helens. | 1841.
8°. Pp. 61.
Relates in part to the foundation of the proposed second colony—Nelson.

***Tristan d'Acunha's** New Zealand [*sic*]. *American Quarterly Register*, Andover, xiii. 167.

1842.

***Beaven**, ——. Narrative of a voyage to New Zealand. London. 1842.
Thomson.

***Bell**, F. Dillon, *and* **Young**, F. Reasons for Promoting the Cultivation of New Zealand Flax. London : Smith, Elder, and Co., Cornhill. 1842.
Reviewed in *N.Z. Journal*, iii. 274.

***Birt**, J. N. Emigration and Colonisation of Chatham Islands. London : 1842.
Thomson.

Index Reference | to accompany the plan | of the | Town of New Plymouth, | at | Taranaki | in | New Zealand, | from the original survey, | by | Frederick A. Carrington, | Principal Surveyor at the Settlement. | London : | Smith, Elder and Co., | 65, Cornhill. | 1842.
8°. Pp. 62.

***Colenso**, William. Description of some new ferns lately discovered in New Zealand. *Tasmanian Journ. Nat. Sci.*, 1842, i. 375–80.

* Dieffenbach's Travels in New Zealand, 1839–41. *Monthly Review*, clx. 369. 1842.

* **Etonian.** New Zealand: a Poem. By an Etonian. London: L. and G. Seeley. 1842.
    Reviewed in the *N.Z. Journal*, iii. 105-6. Designed as a tribute to Bishop Selwyn.

The | Fifth Report | of the | Directors | of the | New Zealand Company, | presented to | the Annual Court of Proprietors, | held | on the 31st May, 1842. | London : | Printed by Johnston and Barrett, 13, Mark Lane. | 1842.
    Foundation of Nelson. Progress at Wellington.

* **Fox,** W. Colonization and New Zealand. By William Fox, of the Inner Temple. London: Smith, Elder and Co., Cornhill. 1842.
    Pp. 24.
    Reviewed in the *N.Z. Journal*, iii. 57-8.

* **Hamlin,** James. The Mythology of the New Zealanders. *Tasmanian Journal*, vol. i. Hobart Town. 1842.
    Thomson.

* **Heale,** Theophilus. New Zealand and the New Zealand Company, and a consideration of how far their interests are similar. London, 1842.
    Extract in Martin, *Brit. Colonies*, iii. 162, 173.

* ——— New Zealand and the New Zealand Company, or considerations how far the interests of the Colony and the Company are similar. In answer to a pamphlet [by Ross D. Mangles, M.P.] entitled "How to Colonise: The interest of the country, and the duty of the Government." By Theophilus Heale, Esq. London: Sherwood, Gilbert, and Piper, Paternoster-row. 1842.
    Reviewed in *N.Z. Journal*, iii. 8-9, 31-2.

Jameson, R. G. New Zealand, | South Australia, | and | New South Wales: | a Record of | Recent Travels in these Colonies, | with Especial Reference to Emigration | and | the Advantageous Employment of Labour | and Capital. | By | R. G. Jameson, Esq. | Late Surgeon Superintendent of Emigrants to South Australia. | "Ubi bene ibi Patria." | London : | Smith, Elder, and Co. | 65, Cornhill. | 1842.
    p. 8°. Pp. xii, 372. Map of N.Z. from official documents. Illus.
    Chapters xiv to xxiv and Appendices v, vi, and vii relate to N.Z., which it is his chief object to describe (p. v). The author's two visits (from N.S.W.) were in 1839 and 1840, and extended from Bay of Islands to Hot Lakes and Tongariro. The country, native characteristics and usages, and the effect on them of colonisation are incidentally described. The missionaries are vindicated from "Dr. Lang's misrepresentations" (ch. xix). Intercourse with Bishop Pompallier, pp. 192-3. Cultivable productions, ch. xxiv. The South Island is described from Major Bunbury's Report, pp. 321-2. The three appendices consist of official documents.

Heaphy, C. Narrative of a Residence | in various parts of | New Zealand. | Together with | a Description of the Present State | of the | Company's Settlements. | By Charles Heaphy, | Draftsman to the New Zealand Company. | London : | Smith, Elder and Co., 65, Cornhill. | 1842.
    p. 8°. Pp. viii, 142.
    Ch. i. Arrival of the preliminary expedition. Ch. ii. Early progress of the settlement. Chs. iii, iv. Climate, soil, and natural productions. Ch. v. Natives. Ch. vi. Wellington. Ch. vii. Wanganui river and district, and New Plymouth settlement. Ch. viii. Nelson country. Ch. ix. Parts best adapted for colonization. Ch. x. Conclusion. Appendix A. Chatham Islands as a field for colonization, pp. 117-32. B. Progress at the Settlements, pp. 133-41. C. Tariff, p. 142.

* ——— Views of the Settlements in New Zealand. Drawn by Charles Heaphy,

Heaphy, C.—*continued.*
Draughtsman to the New Zealand Company. London: Smith, Elder & Co. 1842.
Davis.

Kappa: see **Ward.**

** Latest Information from the Settlement of New Plymouth, on the Coast of Taranake, New Zealand. Comprising Letters from Settlers there, &c. Published under the Direction of the West of England Board of the New Zealand Company. London: Smith, Elder and Co. 1842.
Reviewed in the *N.Z. Journal,* iii. 107, 118-9; with long extracts.

* Letter to J. Somes, Esq., about the Capital of New Zealand. London. 1842.
Thomson.

***Mangles,** Ross D. How to Colonize: the Interest of the Country, and the Duty of the Government. By Ross D. Mangles, Esq., M.P. London: Smith, Elder and Co. 1842.
Reviewed in *N.Z. Journal,* iii. 31-2. Advocates the Wakefield theory of colonization, and infers—(1) that the interests of such a Company as the N.Z. Company are identical with those of the settler and the public; and (2) that such a Company is the best agent which the Government could employ for the colonization of their waste lands.

Maunsell, R. A | Grammar | of the | New Zealand Language, | by the | Rev. R. Maunsell, A.B., T.C.D. | of the Church Missionary Society. | —— | Auckland : | Printed and published by J. Moore, High-street, | 1842.
8°. Pp. xv. 186. Preface is dated Waikato Heads, February, 1842. It was issued in monthly parts.
Introduction, pp. v-xv. Ch. i. Pronunciation of Maori (p. 10, Table of principal dialects). Ch. ii-xii. Parts of speech. Ch. xiii-xx. Syntax. Index, pp. 179-182. Errata, pp. 183-4. Favourable notices, p. 185. Donations and subscriptions, p. 186.
The orthography is on the established basis of the Ngapuhi dialect; the grammar is founded on the Waikato dialect. Lee's theory of the Hebrew tenses is applied to the Maori.
"To accommodate the English reader, the following grammar has been constructed as much as possible on the model of that of the English by Lindley Murray. . . ."—*Intro.* p. xiii.

* The Natives of New Zealand. *Penny Magazine,* xi. 132. 1842.

***Norris,** Edwin. Grammar of the New Zealand Language, &c., By E. Norris, Esq., A. Secretary of the Royal Asiatic Society.
Small 8°. Pp. 14, and 12 pages of a translation of St. Luke's Gospel in Maori, with an interlinear version.
"Printed in one copy only, which was presented by the author to Professor A. Hoefer, London, 30th Sept., 1842."—*Bleek.*
The copy is now in the Auckland Free Public Library. Sir G. Grey, who says that "by some mistake the type was lifted" after only one copy had been printed, tells how he acquired the unicum: *Address,* Auckland, June 5, 1883, p. 24.
See German translation, *ann.* 1846.

Petre, *Hon.* H. W. (*afterwards Lord*). An Account of | the Settlements | of the | New Zealand Company, | from Personal Observation during a Residence there. | By | The Honble. Henry William Petre. | Fourth edition. | London : | Smith, Elder and Co. 65, Cornhill. | 1842.
8°. Pp. 94 and map (same as in Jameson's book).
Introduction, pp. 7-8 (formed one of the "First Colony" in 1839, and writes of what came under his own observation or could gather from authentic sources). Ch. i. Expedition and settlement of First Colony. Ch. ii. Recent progress of the Company's settlements. Ch. iii. Difficulties overcome by the colonists. Ch. iv. Soil, climate, and productions (flax—efforts to discover machinery for making it available as export, pp. 61-74).

Petre, *Hon.* H. W.—*continued.*
Chiefly relative to the early settlement of Port Nicholson; town of Britannia at Pitone, 1839-40.
The book had a large circulation: a fifth edition is reviewed in the *N.Z. Journal*, iii. 107. The first edition appeared in 1841.

* The Present State of New Zealand. Martin's *Colonial Magazine*, vii. 81. 1842.

* **Ritter,** Carl. Die Colonization von Neu-Seeland: ein Vortrag im wissenschaftlichen Vereine zu Berlin am 22 Januar 1842. Mit 1 Kartenskizze. Berlin, Besser. 1842.
  gr. 8°.
  Written after a visit to England in 1841.

* ——— The Colonization of New Zealand. By Professor Charles Ritter of Berlin. London: Smith, Elder and Co. 1842.
  Translation of the foregoing.
  Reviewed in the *N.Z. Journal*, iii. 106-7, where two long extracts are given.

* Ritter on the colonization of New Zealand. *Monthly Review*, clviii. 264.

* **Russell,** *Bishop* M. Polynesia: | or, an Historical Account | of the | Principal Islands in the South Sea, | including | New Zealand; | the Introduction of Christianity; and the Actual Condition | of the Inhabitants in Regard to Civilisation, | Commerce, and the Arts of Social Life. | By the Right Rev. M. Russell, LL.D. and D.C.L., | (of St. John's College, Oxford); | Author of "View of Ancient and Modern Egypt," "Palestine or the Holy | Land," "Nubia and Abyssinia," "History and Present Condition | of the Barbary States," &c. | With a map and vignette. | [Edinburgh Cabinet Library.] Edinburgh: Oliver and Boyd, Tweeddale Court; and Simpkin, Marshall, & Co., London. | MDCCCXLII.
  fcp 8°. Pp. 440.
  Ch. x. relates to N.Z., pp. 335-76; it is general and a compilation.

Terry, C. New Zealand, | its Advantages and Prospects, | as a | British Colony; | with a full account of | the Land Claims, Sales of Crown Lands, | Aborigines, etc. etc. | By | Charles Terry, F.R.S. F.S.A. | London: | T. & W. Boone, 29, New Bond Street. | MDCCCXLII.
  8°. Pp. xii, 367. Map of Auckland and adjacent districts, and 12 illus.
  Part i. History of the colony, pp. 3-68. (List of officials in 1841 and Governor's speech in first session of Legislative Council, pp. 48-51; prices, rents and wages in 1841, pp. 60-1; meteorological tables, pp. 65-7; European population, p. 68.)—Part ii. Land claims, pp. 71-125. (History; abstract of claims, pp. 121-5.)—Part iii. Sale of Crown lands, pp. 129-71.—Part iv. Aborigines, pp. 175-224.—Part v. Prospects. Ch. i. Resources and exports. Ch. ii. Labour and agriculture. Ch. iii. Revenue and expenditure. Ch. iv. Proposed measures.
  Appendix, pp. 303-66, consists of official documents.

Wade, W. R. A Journey | in the Northern Island | of | New Zealand: | interspersed with Various Information relative | to the Country and People. | By | William Richard Wade, | Minister of Harrington-Street Chapel, Hobart Town; | formerly a Resident Missionary in New Zealand. | Hobart Town: | Printed by W. Pratt, Elizabeth Street: | Published by George Rolwegan, Collins-Street. | 1842.
  p. 8°. Pp. 206.
  Dedicated to Lady Franklin, "who has taken a deep interest in the country and people of N.Z." Lady Franklin's visit to the islands is referred to, p. 24.
  From Waimate via Tauranga and Coromandel to the Hot Lakes in 1838. A pa is described in a quotation from the *Protestant Guardian* for 1841, published at Madras, pp. 29-31, from which is also taken the journal of a trip to the Waitangi, pp. 32-4. Forest trees, pp. 38-43. Visit to De Thierry, pp. 47-9. Infanticide and other destruc-

Wade, W. R.—*continued*.

tives, pp. 60-74. Ranks, pp. 83-6. Maui-myth (personally collected from a chief), pp. 87-98. Language, pp. 102-8. Hot Lakes, pp. 140-62. Native letter, pp. 185-7.

Appendix (pp. 193-206) contains a list of the plants of N.Z. "furnished by the late Allan Cunningham, Esq., when on his last visit to the Island; and it has been revised and arranged according to the Lindleyan classification through the kindness of Dr. Milligan. The native names, where known, are given in notes at the foot of the page."

*[**Ward**, —.] Nelson, the latest Settlement of the New Zealand Company. By Kappa. Price 1s. Smith, Elder and Co. 1842.

Reviewed in *N.Z. Journal*, iv. 261. A naval surgeon who resided in Canada. Favours social settlement—settlement in community; apparently a plan of settlement on the Seignorial tenure in the villages on each shore of the St. Lawrence. He writes a letter, *ibid.* iv. 280-1.

1843.

***Butler**, S. The Emigrant's Hand-book of Facts, concerning Canada, New Zealand, Australia, Cape of Good Hope, &c., with the relative advantages each of the Colonies offers for Emigration, and practical advice to intending Emigrants. By Samuel Butler, Esq., Author of the "Hand-Book for Australian Emigrants." Glasgow: W. R. McPhun, 84 Argyll Street, and H. N. Cotes, Cheapside, London, 1843.

Reviewed in the *N.Z. Journal*, iv. 70. Suggests a plan for carrying out a system of emigration from Scotland by means of a Joint Stock Company.—*Ibid.* iv. 75.

Chapman, H. S. and others. The | New Zealand Portfolio; | embracing | a Series of Papers on Subjects of Importance | to the Colonists. Conducted by H. S. Chapman, | of the Middle Temple, Barrister at Law. | London : | Smith, Elder & Co., 65 Cornhill. | 1843.

8°. Pp. viii, 136.

1. Administration of justice in New Zealand. Chapman, H. S. 2. Advantages of a loan company for N.Z. Chapman, H. S. 3. Address to New Zealand land proprietors resident in England. Chapman, H. S. 4. Financial condition of N.Z. Terry, Charles. 5. Voluntary emigration and charges for passages to N.Z. Chapman, H. S. 6. Banks for N.Z. Holroyd, A. T. 7. Advantages of a Representative Assembly for N.Z. Chapman, H. S.

Published as monthly papers—the first no. on Aug. 1, 1842: see *N.Z. Journal*, 1842.

***Colenso**, William. An account of some enormous fossil bones of an unknown species of the class Aves, lately discovered in New Zealand. *Tasm. Journ. Nat. Sci.*, 1843, ii. 81-96; *Ann. Nat. Hist.*, 1844, xiv. 81-96.

*Description of New Zealand. *Christian Remembrancer*, vii. 393.

Dieffenbach, Ernest. Travels | in | New Zealand ; | with Contributions to the | Geography, Geology, Botany, and Natural | History of that Country. | By Ernest Dieffenbach, M.D., | *Late Naturalist to the New Zealand Company.* | In two volumes.— | —— | London : | John Murray, Albemarle Street. | 1843.

8°. 2 vols. Pp. viii, 431 ; iv, 396. 6 illustrations (including perhaps the first published of Taupo, White Terrace, Ruapehu and Tongariro).

Vol. I.—Part i. Cook's Straits region, pp. 21-195. (Ch. ix. Climate of Straits and N.Z. generally. Ch. xi. Straits natives.) Vol. I.—Part ii. North Island—northern districts, pp. 197-418. (Ch. xxix. Some remarks on the botany of N.Z.: historical sketch, pp. 419-20; description, pp. 420-31. Chs. xxiv-vi describe Taupo, Tongariro, Tarawera, Rotomahana, Rotorua, and hot springs.) Vol. II.—Part i. Ch. i. Natives (two races—dark and fair, due to difference of castes, pp. 7-11). Ch. ii. Native diseases. Ch. iii. Children, names, incantations, tattooing, marriage. Ch. iv. Food, clothing, dances, burial, religious ideas. Ch. v. Villages and houses; tribal divisions and strength (pp. 72-83). Ch. vi. Traditions of origin; tapu. Ch. vii. Characteristics, ranks, property, religion. Ch. viii. Reckoning. tillage, war. Ch. ix. How to legislate for the natives—summed up at pp. 171-2.

Dieffenbach, Ernest—*continued.*

Vol. II.—Materials towards a fauna of N.Z., Auckland Islands, and Chatham Islands, [edited by John Edward Gray, F.R.S., Keeper of the Zoological Collections in the British Museum,] vol. ii. pp. 177-296: Historical sketch, pp. 178-81. 1. Mammalia, by J. E. Gray, pp. 181-5. 2. Birds, by G. R. Gray, pp. 186-201. 3. Reptiles and Amphibia, pp. 202-6. 4. Fishes, by J. Richardson and J. E. Gray, pp. 206-28. 4 (sic). Mollusca, by J. E. Gray, pp. 228-65. Annulose animals, pp. 265-95, by A. White and E. Doubleday. Fossil shells, by J. E. Gray, p. 296.

Vol. II.—Part ii. N.Z. language. Ch. i. Introductory. Ch. ii. Specimens (8 proverbs, pp. 307-10; 3 songs, pp. 310-4; letter, p. 314; Maori translations, pp. 314-6; 260 sentences, pp. 316-25.)

Vol. II.—Part iii. N.Z. Grammar, in 8 chapters, pp. 326-54. Ch. ix. N.Z. Dictionary, pp. 355-96.

Incantations are given in vol. ii, pp. 29, 30-32, 51, 61; funeral ode, pp. 64-5; native names, pp. 27-8, *note.*

These volumes contain accounts of several journeys into various parts of N.Z. in 1839, 1840, and 1841, when the Chatham Islands were also visited. " I have been over much untrodden ground. I was the first to visit or describe Mount Egmont, many places in the northern parts of the island, and some of the picturesque and interesting lakes and thermal springs in the interior."—*Preface.*

Hochstetter (*Geologie*, p. xxiv) says that the work "comprises numerous geological observations, relative to the North Island particularly, and asserts (*Neu-Seeland*, p. 549) that it is still one of the best books on N.Z. Gray's *Fauna* is still the completest (*ibid.* p. 553).

Reviewed in the *Journal of Agriculture*, Edin., 1843-5. Portions of the work had been published in the *N.Z. Journal* and as reports to the Aborigines Protection Society.

* **Information** for the Use of the Missionary Deputation to Lord Stanley. London : 1843.
    Davis.

* **Jennings, J.** New Zealand Colonization ; Details of the New Zealand Company, and of the proceedings of the Local Government ; with Objections stated and Remedies proposed, in a Plan for the Next Settlement ; suggested with a view of preserving all the advantages of colonization to the Colonists themselves. By John Jennings, New Zealand Agent. London : Pelham Richardson, Cornhill, 1843.

    "The object of the pamphlet is to prove that Absentee Land-owners, the N.Z. Company included, are useless if not pernicious to a colony; that colonization is nevertheless a commercial undertaking, and ought not to be managed in its commercial details by Government. . . . The proper instrument of colonization . . . is the body of colonists themselves."—*N.Z. Journal*, iv. 35.

* **Joplin, R. C.** New Zealand : A Poem, in three cantos. Auckland : "Chronicle" office. 1843.

* **Letters** from Settlers and Labouring Emigrants in the New Zealand Company's Settlements of Wellington, Nelson, New Plymouth. From February, 1842, to January, 1843. London : Smith, Elder and Co.
    Pp. 211.—*Davis.*
    Probably reprinted from *N.Z. Journal.*

* **Mantell, G. A.,** *and* **Deane,** James. Correspondence on the Ornithichnites of the Connecticut River Sandstones and the Dinornis of New Zealand. *Silliman's Journ.*, 1843, xlv. 177-83.

* **Randall,** —. Address on New Zealand Emigration. London. 1843.
    Thomson.

* **Suttor, G.** The Culture of the Grape Vine and the Orange in Australia and New Zealand. By Geo. Suttor, F.L.S. London : Smith, Elder and Co. 1843.
    p. 8°. See Thomson's note.

***Wood,** *Lieut.* John. Twelve Months in Wellington, Port Nicholson. London: Richardson, Cornhill. 1843.
: Reviewed in *N.Z. Journal,* iv. 289-90.

1844.

***Bridges,** W. New Zealand and Ireland: a new mode of combining land, labour and capital in the development of our colonial resources. London, 1844.

Burns, Barnet. A | Brief Narrative | of a | New Zealand Chief | being the | Remarkable History | of | Barnet Burns, | an English Sailor, | with a faithful account of the way in which he became | A Chief | of one of the | Tribes of New Zealand, | together with | a few remarks on the manners and customs of the people, | and other interesting matter. | Written by Himself. | ——— | Belfast: | Printed by R. & D. Read, Crown-entry. | 1844.
: 8°. Pp. 26. Two portraits of Burns tattooed, engravings of weapons, tattooing instruments, idols, canoe, flax-plant.
: An account of his adventures; translation of a song; vocabulary, pp. 21-6.

***Coates,** Dandeson. The New Zealanders and their Lands. London: Hatchard. 1844.
: 8°. Pamphlet.—*Thomson.*

***Coates** on the New Zealanders. *Christian Observer,* xliv. 693. 1844.
: See previous pamphlet by Coates, 1837, and note to one by Beecham, same year.

Colenso, W. Excursion | in the | Northern Island | of | New Zealand; | in the Summer of 1841-2. | By William Colenso, Esq. | Launceston, V.D. Land: | Printed at the Office of the Launceston Examiner. | 1844.
: A sub-title is—Memoranda of an Excursion, made in the Northern Island of New Zealand, in the summer of 1841-2; intended as a contribution towards the ascertaining of the Natural Productions of the New Zealand Groupe: with particular reference to their Botany.
: 8°. Pp. 95. Dated—Bay of Islands, Jan. 1843.
: A missionary expedition on the East Coast, North Island, and in Urewera Country; with notes on the natural history of the locality.

* ——— Journal of a naturalist in some little known parts of New Zealand. *Hooker's Lond. Journ. Bot.,* 1844, iii. 1-62.

Domett, A. Narrative | of the | Wairau massacre, | 17th June, 1843. | By | Alfred Domett. | Published by the New Zealand Company. | 1844.
: 8°. Pp. 131-97. Domett's narrative is an enclosure sent by Mr. Fox for the Directors of the N.Z. Company.
: § i. Rauperaha and Rangihaiata, pp. 132-6. § 2. The Wairoa: proceedings between the natives and the surveyors, pp. 136-9. § iii. Fight and massacre, pp. 139-51. § v. Notices of sufferers, pp. 151-64. § xiii. Causes and consequences of the massacre, pp. 165-97. (Characteristics of Maoris, pp. 175-81, 183. Opposition of missionaries—their influence generally, pp. 183-9.)
: A biographical sketch of Domett is in Cox, *Men of mark of New Zealand,* a political in Gisborne, *New Zealand rulers and statesmen,* p. 199 ff.

***Donlan,** ——. Letter to absentee landlords. London: Aird. 1844.

New Zealand. *Colonial Quarterly Review,* 1844. Reprinted in *N.Z. Journal,* v. 638, 656; vi. 9.

Report | from the | Select Committee | on | New Zealand; | together with the | Minutes of Evidence, | Appendix, and Index. | *Ordered, by* The House of Commons, *to be Printed,* | 29 *July* 1844.

Report from Select Committee on New Zealand—*continued.*
 f°. Pp. xxxi (proceedings), 256 (evidence), 826+4 (appendix), and map.
 The Committee was appointed to inquire into the state of the Colony and the proceedings of the N.Z. Company. Lord Howick was chairman, and drafted the Resolutions and the Report.
 The evidence given bore upon the natives—their character, chiefs, slavery, customs, land usages, language, &c.; description and capabilities of the various parts; climate; minerals; soil and vegetation; flax; ornithology; fisheries; land-purchases; the N.Z. Company; the treaty of Waitangi; the Wairau massacre; the Church in N.Z.
 The bulk of the voluminous appendix relates to the N.Z. Company—Its land claims, relations with the aborigines, state of its affairs, accounts, despatches from its agents. The famous Twelfth Report is reprinted (pp. 501-746) and there is a Memorandum on it at pp. 1-3.
 Rusden's account of the Committee is in vol. i, pp. 373-6 of his *History*.

Richardson, Sir John. See *infra, Voyage of the Erebus and Terror.*

***S.,** W. H. A brief survey of the northern districts of New Zealand. Simmonds' *Colonial Magazine*, May, 1844.
 See Martin's *Brit. Colonies*, iii. 278, 280.

Selwyn, G. A. Letters from the Bishop, &c. See 1847.

***Stokes,** —. Letter on the Wairau Massacre. London: Longmans. 1844.
 Thomson.

Voyage of H.M.S. Erebus and Terror. London, 1844-1848. One volume has no title-page. The other is titled: Ichthyology | of the | Voyage of H.M.S. Erebus & Terror, | under the command of Captain Sir James Clark Ross, R.N., F.R.S. | By | Sir John Richardson, Knt., M.D., F.R.S., &c., | Inspector of Naval Hospitals, etc., etc. | London: | M.DCC.XLIV.—M.DCCC.XLVIII. | but it contains as well—The Insects of New Zealand; the title is evidently that of one part.
 4°. 2 vols. With plates, some coloured.
 Birds of N.Z., 20 pp., with coloured plates, in vol. i. Insects of N.Z., 24 pp., with plates, in vol. ii. A note prefixed to the Birds of N.Z. describes the history of the successive accretions to the species.

***Williams,** W. A Dictionary of the New-Zealand Language, and a concise Grammar; to which are added a Selection of colloquial sentences. By William Williams, B.A., Archdeacon of Waiapu. Paihia: printed at the Press of the Church Missionary Society. M.DCCC.XLIV.
 Sm. 8°. Pp. xli, 195. The dictionary contains 5380 words. See also 1852 and 1871.

1845.

Brodie, W. Remarks | on | the Past and the Present State | of | New Zealand, | its Government, Capabilities, and Prospects; | with | a Statement of the Question of the Land-claims, | and Remarks on | the New Zealand Company; | also, | a Description (never before published) of its | Indigenous Exports, | and | Hints on Emigration, | the Result of Five Years' Residence in the Colony. | By | Walter Brodie. | London: | Whittaker and Co. Ave Maria Lane. | 1845.
 8°. Pp. viii, 171.
 The book is dedicated to Lord Stanley, Secretary for the Colonies, and in the preface (dated Eastbourne, Jan. 1, 1845) the author says he "travelled over the greatest part of N.Z. with the view of ascertaining, among other resources available for colonization, the natural products of the islands."
 Appointment of Mr. Shortland, pp. 4-14. Russell, pp. 15-21. Bad policy of Local Govt. towards Aborigines, pp. 21-44. Non-settlement of land-claims, pp. 44-77. N.Z. Company, pp. 78-86. Capt. Fitzroy, pp. 86-90. Exports—flax, pp. 90-8; 24 others, pp. 98-105. Emigration, pp. 106-31. Rotorua lakes and district, pp. 131-46. Postscript (origin of Heke's war), pp. 146-54. Traditions of origin, from oral narration, pp. 157-65. Puckey's visit to Reinga in 1834, pp. 166-71.

Brown, W. New Zealand | and | its Aborigines : | being an Account of | the Aborigines, Trade, and Resources | of the Colony ; | and the Advantages it now presents as a Field for Emigration and the Investment of Capital. | By | William Brown, | lately a Member of the Legislative Council of New Zealand. | London : Smith, Elder, and Co., 65, Cornhill. | 1845.
    p. 8°. Pp. viii, 320.

<small>Introduction, pp. 1-8. Part I. Description of aborigines (chs. i, ii, iii) and the means of advancing them in civilization (ch. iv), pp. 9-186. Part II. Changes in the administration of the government, and the colony considered as a field for emigration, pp. 187-252.
Appendix i. Rev. Mr. Turton's letters to Dr. Selwyn, pp. 253-74 (conflicts between Wesleyan and Episcopalian missions).—ii. Protest against the Native Trust Bill, pp. 275-6, June 27, 1844, signed by W. Brown, S. M. D. Martin, and C. Clifford.
Postscript, pp. 293-320 (free-trade in land and commerce necessary ; native rights to land absolute ; representative government needed).</small>

*Buch, L. von. Ueber die vulkanischen Erscheinungen auf Neu-Seeland. Monatsberichte über die Verhandlungen der Ges. f. Erdkunde zu Berlin. N.F., ii. pp. 273-5.

Buller, Charles. Speech in House of Commons : see below—A corrected report, &c.

*Churton, —. Letters from Wanganui. London : 1845.
    8°. Pamphlet.—*Davis.*

Colenso, W. A | Classification and Description | of some | Newly-Discovered Ferns, | collected in | the Northern Island | of | New Zealand, | in the Summer of 1841-2. | By William Colenso, Esq. | Launceston, V.D. Land : | Printed at the office of the Launceston Examiner. | 1845.
    8°. Pp. 29. Dated Paihia, Jan. 3, 1843.
<small>The total number of N.Z. ferns now known is about 140 species.</small>

A Corrected | Report of the Debate | in the | House of Commons, | on the 17th, 18th, and 19th of June, | on the | State of New Zealand | and the | Case of the New Zealand Company. | London : | John Murray, Albemarle Street. | 1845.
    8°. Pp. 287.

<small>Speeches by—C. Buller, Monckton Milnes, G. W. Hope, Capt. Rous, Aglionby, Barkly, Sir R. Inglis, Hawes, Sir Howard Douglas, Lord Howick, E. Ellice, Cardwell, Mangles, Colquhoun, R. L. Sheil, Sir J. Graham, Lord J. Russell, Sir R. Peel.
Appendix :—1. Petition of N.Z. Company. 2. Petition of N.Z. colonists. 3. Resolutions annexed to report of Select Committee of H. of Commons, July 29, 1844. 4. Division list.
E. G. Wakefield, in *Founders of Canterbury*, pp. 94-95, gives the main points then established by Buller, Hawes, E. Ellice, Howick, Sheil, J. Russell, &c. (who corrected their speeches for the Book).
C. Buller's speech is at pp. 1-54. Lord Houghton has reminiscences of Buller in *Monographs*, ed. 2, pp. 248-57.</small>

Correspondence between Her Majesty's Secretary of State for the Colonies and the New Zealand Company, relative to the establishment of a Proprietary Government in the Islands of New Zealand. *Ordered, by* The House of Commons, *to be Printed,* 6 *June,* 1845.
    f°. Pp. 10.

<small>The scheme is the suggestion of the N.Z. Company, and is described at pp. 3-8. It was on the basis of constituting a new Company for the government of the whole of the Middle Island, and of so much of the Northern Island as it might be advisable to include. The new government was to be on the model of the old proprietary governments in the N. American Continent : Lord Stanley found that the difficulties were insuperable.</small>

Correspondence between Secretary of State and N. Z. Company—*continued.*
  The N.Z. Company's letters are probably written by E. G. Wakefield, though signed by the Chairman, and Lord Stanley's by Sir J. Stephen.
  The character of Mr., afterwards the Right Hon. Sir James, Stephen, and his connection with the Colonies, are described from opposite points of view in articles quoted in the *N.Z. Journal*, vii. 306-8. Sir H. Taylor's *Autobiography* and *Correspondence* abound in allusions to him, and there is a brief sketch in the *Encyclopædia Britannica*, ed. 9.

Darwin, C. Journal of Researches | into the | Natural History and Geology | of the | Countries visited during the voyage of | H.M.S. Beagle round the World, | under the | Command of Capt. Fitz Roy, R.N. | By Charles Darwin, M.A., F.R.S. | Second edition, corrected, with additions. | London : | John Murray, Albemarle Street. | 1845.
  cr 8°. Pp. viii, 519.
  Pp. 416-30 describe a brief visit to the Bay of Islands in 1835. Darwin found the country and the people equally unattractive. "I look back but to one bright spot, and that is Waimate, with its Christian inhabitants."
  The first edition appeared as part of Fitz Roy's *Narrative*: see 1839; The third in 1860. It was translated into German :—
    Ch. Darwin's Naturwissenschaftliche Reisen. Deutsch von E. Dieffenbach. 2 Theile. Braunschweig, 1844. The part relative to N.Z. is in Theil 2, S. 190-207. The trans. is evidently from the first edition.

Dieffenbach, E. On the geology of New Zealand. Proceedings Brit. Ass., 1845, Abstract in *Report*, ii. 50.

* A few plain facts concerning the settlement of Nelson. London, 1848. Extract in Martin, *Brit. Col.* iii. 242.

* **Majoribanks**, A. Travels in New Zealand, with a map of the country. By Alexander Majoribanks, of Majoribanks. Smith, Elder, and Co., London; Oliver and Boyd, Edinburgh. 1845.
  Reviewed in *N.Z. Journal*, vi. 129-31.

Martin, S. M. D. New Zealand; | In a series of Letters : | containing | an Account of the Country | both before and since its occupation by the British Government; | with Historical Remarks | on the Conduct of the Government, the New Zealand | and the Manakau Companies ; | also | a Description of the Various Settlements, | the Character of the Aborigines, and the Natural | Productions of the Country. | By | S. M. D. Martin, M.D. | lately a Member of the Legislative Council of New Zealand. | London : | Simmonds & Ward, 18, Cornhill. | 1845.
  8°. Pp. xii, 379.
  The Letters extend from 1839 to 1844. Introduction, pp. 9-25. Letter i. [Bay of Islands in 1839.] ii. [Bay of Islands natives.] iii. [Thames district, settlers and natives.] iv. [N.S. Wales and N.Z.] v. [N.Z. Company and its immigrants. Governor Hobson.] vi. Unsettled state of N.Z. affairs. vii. [Removal of seat of Government to Auckland; Auckland.] viii. [Land claims; Governor Hobson; Acting-Governor Shortland.] ix. Wairau massacre. x. [Governor Shortland.] xi. [Governor Fitzroy; legislation.] xii. [New direct taxes.] xiii. Capabilities and resources of N.Z. xiv. New Zealand Company; [Manakau Company.] xv. Aborigines. xvi. Colonial society. Concluding remarks, pp. 333-59. Appendix 1. Government official translation of Treaty of Waitangi; literal and true translation. 2. Protest of land-purchasers against recent Act. 3. Property-rate ordinance, 1844. Appendix 3*. Address to Gov. Fitzroy. 4. Proclamation of Gov. Fitzroy [respecting waiver of pre-emptive right.] 5. [Meteorological tables, Auckland, 1840-4.]
  Dr. Martin, at one time editor of the *Auckland Gazette*, was one of the signers of a letter to Lord Stanley, intimating the intention of settlers at the Bay of Islands to emigrate to an island in the Pacific for the purpose of forming a permanent (republican) settlement. See *N.Z. Journal*, Feb. 4, 1843.

* Manners and customs in New Zealand. U.S. *Catholic Magazine*, Baltimore, iv. 375, 457.

*Montagne, —. Voyage au Pôle sud, Bot. crypt. Paris 1845.
 8°. With folio atlas of 20 plates.
 Describes cryptogamia of Auckland Islands; "figures of some of the Flowering plants and Ferns have likewise been published in the same form, but without descriptions."—*Hooker, Handbook*, p. 13°.

*New Zealand. *Chambers's Journal*, iv. 53, 85, 268; *Dublin University Magazine*, xxvi. 405; *Westminster Review*, xlv. 133.

New Zealand. A review of Dieffenbach's *Travels*. *Journal of Agriculture*, 1843–5. Edinburgh, 1845.

*New Zealand and its claims. London: Richardson. 1845.
 Davis.

*The New Zealand Company; its claims to compensation considered. 1845.
 Extracts are given in Martin, *Brit. Colonies*, iii. 155-7, where the author is described as "an able and well-informed writer."

The | Petition | of the | New Zealand Company, | presented to | the House of Commons, | by | Joseph Somes, Esq., M.P., | the Governor of the Company, | 16th April, 1845. | [Seal] | London : | Printed by Stewart and Murray, Old Bailey. | 1845.
 8°. Pp. vi, 40.
 Describes the origin of the Company and its proceedings, conflicts with Governors, erroneous theory of missionaries, hostility of Colonial Department, Government and Company's systems of colonisation, disastrous effects of policy of Government. Crown should administer waste lands and prohibit private purchases. By "accustoming the Savage to the habits and occupations of civilised Men, we may ultimately effect his amalgamation with the Race which must eventually be master in N.Z." (p. 34). The Directors describe themselves (p. 34) as "persons who have united together for no selfish end; who have devoted themselves to what they believed to be an honourable and beneficial purpose; who have been baffled by measures which they could not control, which they had no right to anticipate, and which appeared to them to be directed not less against the public good than against their personal success; and who, whatever their mistakes or their failures, have at least succeeded in securing for their country an extensive and valuable territory, when it was all but sacrificed by the servants of the Crown."
 The Petition of the Merchants, Bankers, and Traders of the City of London is at pp. 37–40.

Results of the New Zealand Inquiry. Second sheet of the *Spectator*, Jan. 4, 1845. [London.]
 f°. Pp. 24.
 Some passages in the history of N.Z. (early history of N.Z. Association and Company), pp. 1–3. Natural advantages of the country, pp. 3–4. Aborigines, p. 5. Missionaries, p. 5 (an unfavourable account). Treaty of Waitangi (adverse criticism), pp. 6–8. Hobson-Shortland administration, pp. 8–11. The Company's settlements, pp. 11–12. Auckland and northern settlements, pp. 12–3. Wairau massacre, pp. 13–14. Case of N.Z. Company, pp. 14–7. House of Commons Committee, pp. 17–22. Mr. Stephen, pp. 22–3. Lord Stanley, pp. 23–4. Governor Fitz Roy, p. 24.
 Written in the interests of the N.Z. Company and from its point of view throughout.
 Issued also with *N.Z. Journal*, 1845.

*Scenes in New Zealand.
 "A little book on missionary work, with the first diocesan map of N.Z., dated 1841."—*Carter*.

Selwyn, G. A. Church in the Colonies. | No. VII. | New Zealand. | Part II. | Journal | of the | Bishop's Visitation Tour, | from August to December, 1843. | To which is prefixed | An Extract of a Letter | from the Bishop to a Friend in England. | 1845.
 See other Parts under years 1846, 1847, 1851.

Wakefield, E. J. Adventure | in | New Zealand, | from 1839 to 1844 ; | with some Account of the Beginning of the British | Colonization of the Islands. | By | Edward Jerningham Wakefield, Esq. | In two volumes. |——| London : | John Murray, Albemarle Street. | 1845.

8°. Pp. x, 482 ; x, 546.

Describes the expedition of the "Tory;" foundation of Wellington and Wanganui; trips about Cook Strait (chs. iii and xi); political incidents of early history of Wellington. Rauparaha is described in vol. i, ch. 5. A table of manufactured Maori words is given, i. 174-8. Social compact of N.Z. Company's settlers, i. 208-10. Whalers' code of laws, i. 316-7. Visit of Lady Franklin, i. 414-5. Wanganui, vol. ii. chs. 4, 5. Nelson, ii. chs. 6, 7. Wairau massacre, ii. chs. 15, 16.

A biographical sketch of E. J. Wakefield is in Cox, *Men of mark of N.Z.*

* Illustrations to ' Adventure in New Zealand.' Lithographed from original drawings by Mrs. Wicksteed, Miss King, Mrs. Fox, Messrs. John Saxton, Charles Heaphy, S. C. Brees, and Capt. W. Mein Smith. London, 1845.

Fifteen plates, coloured. Oblong folio. From the Catalogue of the Library of the Royal Colonial Institute.

1. Vignette: Mount Egmont. 2. Two head chiefs of Port Nicholson, Warepori and Epuni. 3. Sawyers clearing a Kauri forest. 4. Panorama of Wellington and Harbour. 5. Papitea pah, Wellington ; Hiko, Native chief. 6. Town of Petre ; Wanganui river. 7. Town and harbour of Nelson. 8. View of country near Nelson. 9. Plain of Ruamahauga. 10. Town of New Plymouth. 11. Wahi tapu, or burial place; wata, or storehouse. 12. Porirua harbour ; whaling station. 13. Titoki tree ; tana tree. 14. Tutu shrub ; rata forest tree. 15. Phormium tenax. [Names as in Catalogue.]

Wilkes, C. Narrative | of the | United States | Exploring Expedition. | During the Years | 1838, 1839, 1840, 1841, 1842. | By | Charles Wilkes, U.S.N., | Commander of the Expedition, | Member of the American Philosophical Society, etc. | In five volumes, and an atlas. | Vol. II. | Philadelphia : | Lea & Blanchard. | 1845.

4°. Pp. xvi, 505.

A visit to the Bay of Islands in 1840 is described at pp. 391-436. Some of the officers witnessed the signing of the Treaty of Waitangi, pp. 397-9. Pomare's pa, pp. 407-10. Dress, pp. 410-1. Houses, pp. 411-2. Pomare, Mauparawa, pp. 413-6. Tribes, pp. 416-7. Maori characteristics, traditions, cannibalism, &c., pp. 420-5. War-dance, pp. 426-7. Report of visit to southern parts, pp. 428 ff. Southern natives, pp. 432-3. Captain Wilkes mentions having previously to his arrival at the Bay seen Burford's "splendid panorama" (p. 395).

Pickering's *Races of Man* (see 1863) is said to be a reprint of vol. vii. H. Hale's Ethnography and Philology of the Expedition appeared in 1846.

1846.

*The Affairs of New Zealand. *Westminster Review*, March, 1846.

Angas, George French. The | New Zealanders | Illustrated. [Frontispiece has :] London : Published for the Proprietor by Thomas Maclean, 26 Haymarket. | 1846. [Title-page —] London : | Thomas McLean, No. 26 Haymarket, | 1847.

imp. f°. 60 coloured plates and frontispiece, with descriptions.

General remarks, 5 pp. Plate 1. Heki and Patuone. 2. Mount Egmont ; war canoe. 3. Ngeungeu, and her son James Maxwell. 4. Rangihaeata's house on the island of Mana. 5. Te Awaitaia and Te Moanaroa : Waingaroa. 6. Scene in a New Zealand forest near Porirua. 7. Daughter of the Barrier Island chief. 8. Tongariro from Roto-aire lake. Motupoi pah in the distance. 9. Nieces of Rauparaha. 10. Monument to Te Whero Whero's daughter, at Raroera pah. 11. Hongi Hongi. 12. Roperta, and a half-caste nephew of Rauparaha. 13. Women of the Ngatitoa tribe. 14. A woman of the Ngatitoa tribe and her children. 15. The pah of Te Whero Whero on the Waikato, Taupiri mountain in the distance. 16. Te Mutu, with his sons Patuone and Te Kuri. 17. Nene, or Tamiti Waka. 18. Waitahanui pah. 19. Na Horua, or Tom Street, with his wife and son. 20. E Pori and her daughter. 21. The house of Hiwikau and the falls Kowaihi, at Te Rapa, Taupo lake. 22. Children on the banks of the Waipa. Children at the boiling springs, near Taupo lake. 23. Tomb of Huri-

Angas, George French—*continued.*
wenua, a late chief of the Ngatitoa tribe, Queen Charlotte's Sound. 24. Raugitakina, a chief of the Bay of Plenty. 25. Maketu house at Otawhao, built by Puatia to commemorate the taking of Maketu. 26. A young woman of Barrier Island. 27. Mungakahu, chief of Motupoi, and his wife. 28. The volcanic region of pumice hills, looking towards Tongariro and the Ruapahu. 29. Blind Solomon. 30. Storehouses for food. 31. Native girls and boy at Port Nicholson. 32. Motupoi pah, with Roto-airo lake. Tongariro in the distance. 33. Two lads of Poverty Bay; children of Te Pakarau. 34. Tara. 35. Paratene Maioha. 36. Native feast at Mata-ta; throwing the spear. 37. Nga Porutu and his wife Rihe; Nga Whea and Nga Miho. 38. Entrance to a dwelling house at Raroera pah, Waipa. 39. Ornaments and decorations. 40. Group at Te Aro pah. 41. An old tohunga; Ko Tauwaki and Ko Teonionga, Taupo. 42. Canoe heads, paddles, &c. 43. Bay of Waikato; young chief of Nga-ti-pou tribe; a chief of Taupo, with his wife. 44. Te Whero-Whero or Patatau; Te Waru and Te Pakaru. 45. Weeping over a deceased chief. 46. Ornamental carvings in wood. 47. Christian chief of Waikato, with his attendant boy. 48. Taupo pah, Cook's Straits. 49. Aboriginal inhabitants: typical portraits. 50. Tombs. 51. Chiefs. 52. Ceremony of *ongi*, or pressing noses. 53. Maori swing; war-dance. 54. Toca and slave boy. 55. Implements and domestic economy. 56. Te Kawaw and his nephew, Te Heuheu, and Hiwikaw. 57. Rangihaeata's pah, with the island of Mana and the opposite shores of Cook's Straits. 58. Weapons and implements of war; warriors preparing for a fight. 59. Domestic economy; women making mats, &c. 60. Colossal tiki at Raroera pah.

Some of the illustrations are copied, on a reduced scale, in *Annals of the diocese of New Zealand*, London, 1847; and in White, *Ancient history of the Maori.*

***Despard,** Col. Narrative of the North Campaign. *United Service Magazine*, 1846–7.

Domett, A. Petition to Parliament | for the | recall of Governor Fitzroy ; | together with a narrative | of the Wairau Massacre. | By | Alfred Domett. | Published by the New Zealand Company. | London, [1846.]

The inner title is—Petition to Parliament | for the | recall of Governor Fitzroy ; | from the | inhabitants of the southern settlements of New | Zealand.

p. 8°. Pp. 190. Also f°. Pp. 34.

Injustice of Governor Fitzroy's administration towards southern settlers, his temporising with the Natives in their aggressions on settlers' land, &c., erroneous financial policy, harsh treatment of settlers—review of Fitzroy's whole proceedings necessitates declaration of want of confidence.

Dumont-d'Urville, Jules-Sébastien-César. Voyage | au Pôle Sud | et dans L'Océanie | sur les corvettes | L'Astrolabe et La Zélée, | exécutée par ordre du Roi | pendant les années 1837–1838–1839–1840, | sous le commandement | de M. J. Dumont D'Urville, | Capitaine de vaisseau. | Publié par Ordonnance de sa Majesté. | Histoire du Voyage, | par M. Dumont D'Urville. | —— | Paris, Gide, Editeur, | Rue des Petits-Augustins, 5 près le Quai Malaquais. | [1841–6.]

10 vols. 8°. Maps.

The parts relating to N.Z. and the neighbouring islands are chs. 64, 65, 66 and 67, t. ix. pp. 93–204, and notes 5 to 24, pp. 264–323. The Auckland Isles are described ix. 94–116 ; Otago harbour (Port Chalmers), with details about the natives, pp. 122–42 ; Akaroa, pp. 145–57 ; Bay of Islands, pp. 164–204. At pp. 172–4 is an adverse account, on the report of a M. Bonnefin, of the signing of the Waitangi Treaty. The remaining pages describe the natives, the Catholic mission, and a visit from Baron de Thierry. Notes 5, 6, 7 and 8 by MM. Jacquinot, Dubouzet, Roquemaurel, and Desgraz, are on the Auckland Isles. Notes 9, 10, 11, 12 and 13 are on Otago Bay, the natives and their houses, and are also by the officers. Notes 14–18, Akaroa and its natives. Note 19 is on Poverty Bay. Notes 20 to 24 are on the Bay of Islands. An official report relates partly (x. 196-9) to the anchorages of N.Z. In t. iii are given, as *pièces justificatives*, translations of missionaries' reports and of other documents down to 1822.

There is a biographical notice of Dumont-D'Urville (whose name, on the title-page of tome i without a hyphen, becomes a compound in tomes ix and x) in t. x. 55–148.

The first three volumes and the first three chapters of the fourth were alone edited by Dumont.

Fitz Roy, Robert. Remarks on New Zealand in February 1846. London, 1846.
 8°. Pp. 67.
  Ch. i. (events previous to 1844). ii. 1840-44. iii. 1844. iv. 1844. v. 1844-5. vi. 1845. vii. General reflections; 1846. Commercial resources; 1846.
  Fitz Roy was Governor, 1843-5: see Cox, *Men of mark*, pp. 70-1; Gisborne, *N.Z. rulers*, pp. 36-9; Rusden, *History of N.Z.*, vol. i. Darwin's account of him is in *Life and letters*, vol. i.
  Copious extracts are in Martin, *British Colonies*, vol. iii, where his policy is described, pp. 193-225.

***Kean,** C. Adventures in New Zealand. *Bentley's Miscellany*, xx. 314. 1846.
  Probably a review of E. J. Wakefield's *Adventure in N.Z.*

* A letter to the Directors of the New Zealand Company from the resident purchasers of land. Wellington, New Zealand. Printed by R. Stokes, 'Spectator' Office: To Aro. [1846?]

* Marsden's missionary visits to New Zealand. *Christian Observer*, xlvi. 10, 75, 145. 1846.

***Norris,** Edwin. Abriss der Neuseelandischen Grammatik nebst Sprachproben und einem Anhange Nach dem englischen Original von Mr. Norris übersetzt vom Herausgeber. *Zeitschrift für die Wissenschaft der Sprache*. Herausgegeben von Dr. Hoefer, Professor a. d. Universität zu Greifswald.— Erster Band, Berlin, Druck und Verlag von G. Reimer. 1846.
 8°. *In* zweites heft, pp. 187-209.
  "Contains Notice of the editor, p. 187; i. Grammatik, p. 188; ii. Sprachprobe, Evangel. St. Luc. Cap. i. (v. 1-25, with an English interlinear version) p. 202; iii. Die Behandlung der Fremdnamen im Neuseeländischen. Zusatz des Herausgebers, p. 206."—*Bleek*.

* On the British colonization of New Zealand. By the Committee of the Aborigines Protection Society. London: Smith, Elder and Co. 1846.
 8°. Pp. 67.
 Noticed in *Martin, British colonies*, iii.

***Raoul,** E., *and* **Decaisne,** —. Choix de plantes de la Nouvelle-Zélande. Paris, 1846.
  "During the visits of the French frigates 'L'Aube' in 1840-1 and the 'Allier' in 1842-3 M. Raoul explored Bank's Peninsula and the Bay of Islands; "most of the new species discovered were published first in the 'Annales des Sciences Naturelles' . . . and more recently were described and figured in" the above work, "which further contains thirty plates, and an enumeration of all then known New Zealand plants."—*Hooker, Handbook*, p. 10*.

Selwyn, G. A. Church in the Colonies. | No. VIII. | New Zealand. | Part III. | Journal | of the | Bishop's Visitation Tour, | from December 1843, to March 1844. | Including | An Account | of his | Visit to the Southern Island. | Second edition. | London | —— | 1846. |
 fcp. 8°. Pp. 48. [Third edition, 1851.]
  Journal of a visit to Wellington province, Otago, and Stewart's Island. Parts I, II and IV appear under 1847, and part V under 1849.

***United States Exploring Expedition** (see *ann.* 1845). Ethnography and Philology. By Horatio Hale, Philologist of the Expedition. 1846.
  A general account of the Polynesian nation is given at pp. 4-13. Migrations of the Oceanic tribes, pp. 117-196; with chart. N.Z. is discussed at p. 146 and Chatham Islands p. 148. At pp. 229-289 is a comparative grammar of the Polynesian dialects; at pp. 291-339, essay at a lexicon of the Polynesian language; and at pp. 341-356, an English and Polynesian vocabulary.—*Bleek, Library of Sir G. Grey*, vol. ii. pt. iv, pp. i-li.

Wohlers, J. F. H. Ostküste der neuseeländischen Insel Poenamu. *Monatsber. über die Verh. des Ges. f. Erdk. zu Berlin*, N.F., iii, p. 191 (1846).

1847.

Angas, G. F. Savage Life and Scenes | in | Australia and New Zealand; | being an Artist's Impressions of Countries and | People at the Antipodes. | With numerous Illustrations. | By George French Angas, | Author of " The New Zealanders Illustrated ;" " South Australia | Illustrated ;" " A Ramble in Malta and Sicily," &c. | In two volumes. | —— | Engraving | London : | Smith, Elder, and Co., 65 Cornhill. | 1847.

p.8°. Vol. i : pp. xi, 330 ; vol. ii.

Vol. i.—Ch. vii describes visits to the natives in the neighbourhood of Wellington. Massacre of Wairau, pp. 250-61. Carvings, pp. 264-7. Ch. viii. Cloudy Bay, Queen Charlotte's Sound, Auckland. Tombs, p. 275. Mausoleum, pp. 278-80. Vestiges of extinct tribes, pp. 296-7. Ch. ix. General remarks on natives. (Descendants of ancient Mexicans, pp. 307-8.) Physical characters, pp. 308-11; clothing, pp. 321-8.) There are many artistic descriptions: as of landscape, i. 277, 289; fleet of canoes, i. 295-6; atmospheric effects, i. 294.

Vol. ii not examined.

Brees, S. C. Pictorial Illustrations | of | New Zealand. | By | S. C. Brees, C.E. | Late Principal Engineer and Surveyor of the New Zealand Company, from the years 1841 to 1845 ; | Author of | " Railway Practice," " Glossary of Terms used in Civil Engineering," | " Present Practice of Surveying and Levelling," etc. | London : | John Williams and Co., Library of Arts, 141, Strand. | MDCCCXLVII.

roy.4°. Pp. 36, 64 engravings, and map of New Zealand, New Ulster and the several harbours.

With a sketch of the country and descriptions of the views, which are chiefly of Wellington district.

Church Missionary Society. | New Zealand land question. | Minute and resolutions | of the | Special Committee of Feb. 22, 1847, | in reply to the | statements made by Governor Grey | respecting the | large landed missionaries. | Communicated to the Committee by the | Right Hon. Earl Grey. | Extracted from the New Zealand parliamentary papers | printed by order of the House of Commons, | June, 1847. (Pp. 70-73.) | (*This Reprint is intended to accompany Mr. Kempthorne's Exami-|nation of the Minute, &c., as addressed to Earl Grey.*) | London : | G. J. Palmer, Printer, Surrey Street, Strand.

8°. Pp. 11.

The Committee resolved that " no Missionary or Catechist of the Society can be allowed to continue in connexion with the Society, who shall retain for his own use and benefit large tracts of unoccupied land " (p. 7).

Enderby, Charles. Proposal | for re-establishing | the British Southern Whale | Fishery, | through the medium of | a Chartered Company, | and in combination with | the Colonisation of the Auckland | Islands, | as the site of the company's whaling station. | By | Charles Enderby, Esq., F.R.S. | [Being in reply to a letter addressed to him on behalf of certain | parties connected with the British shipping interest, | inviting the expression of his sentiments | on the first-named subject.] | Third Edition. | London : | Effingham Wilson, 11, Royal Exchange. | 1847.

8°. Pp. 67. Map prefixed.

1. Letter from Mr. Preston to Mr. Enderby. 2. Reply by Mr. Enderby. Appendix. Narrative of the United States' Exploring Expedition. Prospectus of Southern Whale Fishery Company is appended.

Grimstone, S. E. The | Southern Settlements | of | New Zealand: | comprising statistical information from the earliest period | to the close of the year 1846; together with | a summary of the local ordinances, proclamations, | &c. &c. &c. | From the most authentic sources. | By | S. E. Grimstone, Esq. | Wellington : New Zealand. | Printed by R. Stokes, Spectator Office, Manners Street. | 1847.
    8°. Pp. 104.
    Wellington, Nelson, Petre, Akaroa, New Plymouth.

Hooker, J. D. The Botany | of | The Antarctic Voyage | of | H. M. Discovery Ships *Erebus* and *Terror*, | in the Years 1839–1843. | Under the Command of | Captain Sir James Clark Ross, Kt., R.N., | F.R.S., &c. | By | Joseph Dalton Hooker, M.D., R.N., F.L.S., | Assistant Surgeon of the " Erebus " and Botanist to the Expedition. | —— | Published under the Authority of the Lords Commissioners of the Admiralty. | London : | Reeve, Brothers, King William Street, Strand. | 1847.
    Part i. Botany of Lord Auckland's Group and Campbell's Island.
    roy. 4°. Vol. i : pp. xii, 208. Map and 80 coloured plates.
    " In the beginning of the year 1839, the British Government having determined on fitting out an Expedition, for the purpose of investigating the phenomena of Terrestrial Magnetism in various remote countries, and for prosecuting Maritime Geographical Discovery in the high southern latitudes, H.M. Ships Erebus and Terror . . . sailed from Chatham on the 29th of September 1839. In addition to carrying out the above-mentioned leading views, it was enjoined to the officers, that they should use every exertion to collect the various objects of Natural History which the many heretofore unexplored countries about to be visited would afford." P. v.

Hoole, E. The | Year-Book of Missions : | containing | a Comprehensive Account | of | Missionary Societies, | British, Continental, and American. | With | a Particular Survey of the Stations, | arranged in geographical order. | By Elijah Hoole, | one of the General Secretaries of the Wesleyan Missionary Society. | London : | Longman, Brown, Green, and Longmans, | Paternoster-Row. | MDCCCXLVII.
    8°. Pp. viii, 423.
    A brief account of both Church and Wesleyan missions in both islands is given at pp. 211–28. See also Alder's *Wesleyan missions* (1842), pp. 53–6; and (for Church of England mission) *Quarterly Review*, Dec. 1844, pp. 216–8.

* Letters from New Zealand. *Sharp's London Magazine*, v. 180, vii. 91. 1847–48.

* **Martin,** *Sir* W. England and the New Zealanders. Remarks upon a dispatch from the Right Honourable Earl Grey to Governor Grey, dated 23rd December, 1846. Bishop's Auckland, 1847.
    " The Chief Justice drew up a clear and cogent statement, which was printed at the Bishop's College Press, but was not published." *Rusden, History of N.Z.*, i. 459. See also i. 463–5.
    A protest against Earl Grey's Royal Instructions of 1846.

* Otago. *Chambers's Journal*, viii. 185. 1847.

* Plain Facts Relative to the War in the North of New Zealand. Auckland. 1847.
    Pamphlet.—*Davis.*

Ross, *Sir* J. C. A | Voyage | of | Discovery and Research | in the | Southern and Antarctic Regions, | during the years 1839–43. | By | Captain Sir James Clark Ross, R.N. | Knt., D.C.L. Oxon., F.R.S., etc. | With plates, maps, and woodcuts. | In two volumes. | —— | London : | John Murray, Albemarle Street. | 1847.
    8°. Vol. i : pp. liii, 366. Vol. ii.

Ross, Sir J. C.—*continued.*

Auckland Islands, i. 131-54 (discovery, pp. 137-8; geological formation, pp. 143-4; flora, pp. 144-8; fauna, pp. 148-50.) Campbell Island, pp. 154-63 (discovery, p. 157 flora, pp. 156-63; geology, p. 163.)
Bay of Islands in 1841, ii. 59-128. Climate, with tables, pp. 74-80. Aspect of the country, pp. 91-100. *Jean Bart* and *Héroine* at Chatham Islands, pp. 110-6.
Geology of N.Z. (Bay of Islands and vicinity) ii. 404-11. Geology and zoology of southern islands, ii. 412-5. Captain Cecille's observations at and description of Chatham Islands, ii. 423-5.

[Selwyn, C. J. *and* L. F.] Annals | of the | Diocese of New Zealand. | Published under the direction of | the Committee of General Literature and Education, | appointed by the Society for promoting | Christian Knowledge. | London : | printed for the | Society for promoting Christian Knowledge ; | sold at the Depository, | Great Queen Street, Lincoln's Inn Fields, | and 4, Royal Exchange. | 1847.

fcp. 8°. Pp. x (besides Title-page and Preface), 247. Map. Illus.
Introduction, pp. i-x. Ch. i. From 1814 to 1830. ii. 1831-1842. iii. 1842-3. iv. 1843. v. 1844. vi. 1844-5. vii. 1845-6. viii. State of the mission, 1845-6. ix. Recent accounts from the Mission. Description of St. John's College, Auckland. Appendix, pp. 224-47. N.Z. itinerary, pp. 234-8. Names, uses and properties of N.Z. trees, pp. 239-44.
"The first part of the Work is principally compiled from the letters of the Missionaries, which have been published. . . ." The letters of Bishop Selwyn (see below) have been abridged. The general details are from despatches. The account of plants and trees is from MS. by Cunningham, revised by Sir W. Hooker. The illustrations are reduced from Angas.—*Preface.*

Selwyn, G. A. New Zealand. | Part I. | Letters from the Bishop | to | the Society for the Propagation of the Gospel, | together | with Extracts | from his | Visitation Journal, | from July 1842, to January 1843. | Third edition. | London : | Printed for | the Society for the Propagation of the Gospel ; | sold by | Rivington's, St. Paul's Churchyard and Waterloo Place ; | Burns, Portman Street ; Hatchards, Piccadilly ; T. B. Sharpe, Skinner Street, Snow Hill ; | and by all Booksellers. | 1847. [First ed. 1844.]

fcp. 8°. Pp. x, 111. Map.
The preface, signed C.B.D. (Rev. C. B. Dalton) is dated Aug. 1844. The Journal is —the Waimate to Auckland (Letter i); Nelson (ii); Nelson to Wollington (iii); to Otaki (iv); to Kapiti (v); by Lake Rotorua to Waimate (vi); special contributions to the Diocese of N.Z., pp. 105-11.

Selwyn, G. A. Church in the Colonies. | No. XII. | New Zealand, | Part IV. | A Letter | from | the Bishop of New Zealand, | to the | Society for the Propagation of the Gospel ; | containing | An Account of the Affray between the Settlers and the Natives at Kororareka. | Second edition. | 1847.

fcp. 8°. Pp. 40.

Selwyn, G. A. Charge to the clergy of the diocese of New Zealand : see 1850.

1848.

Arrangements | for the | Adjustment of Questions | Relating to | Land in the Settlements | of the | New Zealand Company. | —— | London : | Printed by Stewart and Murray Old Bailey. | 1848.

8°. Pp. ii, 75.
Correspondence between Governor Grey, Earl Grey, Mr. Fox, the Secretary of the Company, Mr. Hawes, &c.
Nelson, pp. 1-58. Cook's Strait settlements, pp. 58-74.

Byrne, J. C. Twelve Years' | Wanderings | in the British Colonies. From 1835 to 1847. | By J. C. Byrne. | In two volumes. | —— | London : | Richard Bentley, | New Burlington Street. | Publisher in Ordinary to Her Majesty. | 1848.

Byrne, J. C.—*continued.*
  8°. Pp. vii, 431; vii, 411. Two maps.
  Vol. i, pp. 47-94, relate to N.Z. Aims at "affording general information with regard to the manners, habits, customs, and prospects . . . together with particulars of the climate, rates of wages, and value of property. . . ."
  "The soil does not produce grass, or any substitute, to such an extent, as to render it advisable to rear cattle and sheep as articles of export, either in their live state, or as wool, tallow, hides, &c. The dense forests also render the space over which they can roam very confined; so that, at least for ages to come, the colonists can never expect to realise wealth or competence from grazing and breeding live stock. . . ." (i. 62.)

Chamerovzow, L. A. The | New Zealand Question | and the | Rights of Aborigines. | By | Louis Alexis Chamerovzow. | London: | T. C. Newby, 72, Mortimer Street, | Cavendish Square. | 1848.
  p. 8°. Pp. vi, 418. Appendix, pp. iv, 53.
  Ch. i. History. Chs. ii, iii. "Right by discovery." Chs. iv, v, vi. Treaty of Waitangi. Ch. vii. Abstract principles of land-tenure and rights of Aborigines. Ch. viii. N.Z. under Hobson, Shortland and Fitzroy. Ch. ix. Charter of 1846. Ch. x. Summary. Postscript, pp. 417-8.
  Asserts "that the principle 'in regard to property in land,' as laid down by Earl Grey, in the Letter of Instructions which accompanied the Charter of 1846, is not only radically unsound and unjust, but specially inapplicable to New Zealand" (p. 408). The native rights extend over the whole of the Northern Island and the Middle Island offers no exception (p. 409).

  The following is bound up with the work:—Appendix | to the | New Zealand Question, | being the | opinions thereupon | of | Joseph Phillimore, Esq., D.C.L. | and | Shirley F. Woolmer, Esq., | of the Middle Temple, | Barrister-at-law. | London: | Thomas Cautley Newby, Publisher | 72, Mortimer St., Cavendish Sq. | 1848.
  Pp. iv, 53.
  "The opinions which follow were in reply to certain Queries propounded by the Aborigines' Protection Society, on behalf of the natives of N.Z.," relating (1) to the Native land-rights under the Treaty of Waitangi, (2) to the Crown rights, and (3) to the principle of International Law which regulate intercourse with barbarous races.
  Chamerovzow was Assistant Secretary to the Aborigines' Protection Society.

* **Chapman**, H. S. Earthquakes in New Zealand. *Westminster Review*, li. 390.

* A Cookery book from New Zealand. *Colburn's Monthly Magazine*, lxxxv. 441.

New Zealand: | Correspondence | between the | Wesleyan Missionary Committee | and the | Right Hon. Earl Grey, *Her Majesty's Principal Secretary of State for the Colonial Department*, | on the | Apprehended Infringement | of the | Treaty of Waitangi: as published in the Report of the Wesleyan Missionary Society, | for 1848. | London.
  8°. Pp. 36. Correspondence is dated, Feb.–April, 1848.
  Gives statistics of Wesleyan mission in N.Z., pp. 4-5. Committee alarmed by Lord Grey's despatch, Dec. 23, 1846, respecting native claims to unoccupied land.
  It is continued by—
  Correspondence | between the Wesleyan Missionary Committee and the Right Honourable Sir John Pakington, Bart., M.P., Her Majesty's Principal Secretary of State for the Colonial Department, on the importance of framing the Bill for giving a Representative Constitution to New Zealand with due regard to the Treaty of Waitangi.
  Pp. 8. Dated, May 1852.

* **Mantell**, Gideon Algernon. On the fossil remains of birds collected in various parts of New Zealand by Mr. Walter Mantell of Wellington, with additional remarks on the geological position of the deposits in New Zealand

Mantell, Gideon Algernon—*continued.*
which contain bones of birds. *Quarterly Journal of the Geological Society*, iv. 225–41. *Silliman, Journal*, 1849, vii. 28–44. 1848.

    Compares N.Z. with European countries during coal- and trias-period.—*Hochstetter.*

* Neu Volkszählungen in Neu-Seeland. *Ausland*, 1848, no. 43.

* **New Zealand.** *People's Journal*, vii. 259. 1848.

* **New Zealand** under Governor Grey. *Fraser's Magazine*, xxxix. 70. 1848.

* **Otago.** *Chambers's Journal*, x. 209, 353. 1848.

The **Otago Journal.** No. 1 appeared in Jan. 1848; no. 2 is dated June, 1848; no. 3, Nov. 1848; no. 4, June, 1849; no. 5, Nov. 1849; no. 6, Nov. 1850; no. 8, Aug. 1852. All printed by Wm. Forrester, S.E. Thistle St. Lane, Edinburgh. Certain of the nos. bear—Sold at the Otago offices, 27 Hanover Street, Edinburgh, and 3 West Nile Street, Glasgow. Others—Published by James Nichol, Edinburgh, 40 George Street; James Nisbet & Co., London.

    imp. 8°. Pp. 128.

    Reports of Association, and of Colonial Committee of Free Church of Scotland; letters from settlers; accounts of departure of emigrants; Otago scheme; despatches from Captain Cargill; letters from Rev. T. Burns and Capt. Cargill; terms of purchase of land; progress of settlement; journey from Dunedin to the Clutha (pp. 124–7).

    Accounts of the inception and execution of the Otago emigration scheme are also in *N.Z. Journal*, 1845–49. Tuckett's report of exploration is in *idem*, vi. 54–9, 95, 119, 131.

Plan | of the | Association for founding the Settlement of Canterbury, New Zealand. London : John W. Parker, West Strand. | 1848.

    8°. Pp. 23.

    Included in Canterbury Papers, 1851 (no longer in double columns, and with verbal alterations).

* The **Question** and rights of the aborigines. *Eclectic Review*, lxxxviii. 579; *Colburn's Monthly Magazine*, lxxxiv. 250.

* **Taylor**, Rev. R. A Leaf from the Natural History of New Zealand; or, A Vocabulary of its Different Productions, &c., with their Native Names. Wellington, 1848.

    Appeared in an enlarged edition, as a Maori and English Dictionary, in 1870, q. v.

[**Wakefield**, E. Jerningham.] The Handbook | for | New Zealand : | consisting of the | Most Recent Information. | Compiled | for the use of intending Colonists. | By | a late Magistrate of the Colony, | who resided there during four years. | London : | John W. Parker, West Strand. | M DCCC XLVIII.

    12°. Pp. viii, 493.

    Ch. ii. Canterbury Association—plan. Ch. iii. Resources and character of N.Z. Ch. iv. Historical summary. Chs. v, vi. Wellington district. Ch. vii. Nelson. Ch. viii. Taranaki. Ch. ix. Otago and Scotch colony. Ch. x. Canterbury. Ch. xi. Auckland. Ch. xii. North of Auckland. Ch. xiii. Officers of N.Z. Co. Chs. xiv, xv are miscellaneous. Statistical appendix. Bibliography, pp. 480–7.

1849.

Australia, | Van Dieman's Land, | and | New Zealand ; | their history and present state, | with their prospects in regard to | Emigration | impartially examined. | —— | New edition. | London : Cradock and Co., 48 Paternoster Row.

    fcp. 8°. Pp. 60. In or after 1848.

    N.Z.: pp. 44–58. A general compilation.

*Dana, James. [United States Exploring Expedition, Vol. X. Geology, ch. viii. p. 437.] 1849.
Relates to the Bay of Islands.—*Hochstetter*.

*Enderby, Charles. The Auckland Islands: a short account of their climate, soil and productions, and the advantages of establishing a settlement at Port Ross for carrying on the southern whale fisheries. Map and panoramic view of Port Ross. London, 1849.
8°.

Fox, W. Report | on the | Settlement of Nelson | in | New Zealand. | By William Fox, Esq., | late Resident Agent of the New Zealand Company. | With Statistical Returns | From 1843 to 1847. | —— | London: Smith, Elder and Co., 65, Cornhill. | 1849.
8°. Pp. 45.
Blind Bay, harbour, &c. pp. 3-6. Location, pp. 6-11. Soil, produce and weather, pp. 11-12. Population, pp. 13-20. Natives, pp. 20-3. Education, pp. 23-5.

Guide and description | of the | panorama of New Zealand: | illustrating | the country, habits of the colonists, | public buildings, houses, farms, and clearings, | customs of the natives, | pa's, habitations, canoes, &c. | and | life in the colony and in the bush | Painted | under the immediate superintendence of | S. C. Brees, Esq. | formerly principal engineer and surveyor to the | New Zealand Company, | from drawings made by him on the spot, | by Messrs W. A. Brunning, M.S.B.A.; J. Zeitter, M.S.B.A.; | H. S. Melville ; W. Wilson; E. Hassel, M.S.B.A. | and assistants. | London: | Printed by Savill and Edwards, Chandos Street, Covent Garden.
8°. Pp. 32. Small skeleton map, 1849. Advertisement of the N.Z. Company.
The scenes illustrated in the Panorama were different from those of the Pictorial Illustrations of New Zealand, published in 1847.

The | Hand-Book | to the | Suburban and Rural Districts | of the Otago Settlement. | Re-printed from the "Otago News." | Dunedin : | Published at the "News" Office, Princes Street. | 1849.
16°. Pp. 18, not numbered.
Descriptive.

Hursthouse, Charles. An Account | of the | Settlement of New Plymouth, | in | New Zealand, | from Personal Observation, during a Residence there of Five Years. | By | Charles Hursthouse, Jun. | With a plan and views. | London: Smith, Elder and Co., 65, Cornhill. | 1849.
p. 8°. Pp. xvi, 160.
Introductory. Ch. i. Physical geography. Ch. ii. Timber, minerals, birds, fish, insects. Ch. iii. Natives. Ch. iv. Land-question. Ch. v. Statistics. Ch. vi. Roadstead. Ch. vii. Capabilities and resources. Ch. viii. Requirements. Postscript, pp. 157-60.

McKillop, H. F. Reminiscences | of | Twelve Months' Service | in | New Zealand | as a Midshipman, during the late Disturbances | in that Colony. | By Lieut. H. F. McKillop, R.N. | London : Richard Bentley, New Burlington Street. | 1849.
fcp. 8°. Pp. viii, 275.
Personal narrative of the war at the Hutt, Porirua, and Wanganui; capture of Te Rauparaha; sketch history of war at Bay of Islands; the Wairau Massacre; with accounts of the natives.

* New Zealand and the Polynesians. *Littell's Living Age*, xxv. 407.

* New Zealand, its history, geographical importance, population and present state. By a young missionary. London, 1849.

* **Pompallier,** Jean Baptiste François. Notes Grammaticales sur la Langue Maorie ou Néo-Zélandaise. Par Mgr. Pompallier. — Lyon. Imprimerie d'Antoine Perisse, Imp. de N.S. P. le Pape et de S. Em. Mgr. le Cardinal-Archevêque. 1849.
    8°. Pp. 40.
    Notes grammaticales, pp. 3-22. Petite collection de mots Maoris (a French-Maori vocabulary of about 440 words), pp. 23-40.
    There is a brief sketch of the Bishop of Oceania in *Cox, Men of mark*, &c. And see Pompallier's journal, 1888.

Power, W. Tyrone. Sketches in New Zealand, with pen and pencil. By W. Tyrone Power, D.A.C.G. | From a Journal kept in that Country from July 1846, to June 1848. | Frontispiece. | London : | Longman, Brown, Green, and Longmans, | Paternoster-row. | 1849.
    cr. 8°. Pp. viii, 200. 10 illustrations (by Hon. W. Yelverton, afterwards Lord Avonmore, Sir F. Dillon Bell, &c.).
    The introduction and the first 21 chapters relate to N.Z.: they describe the incidents of a two years' residence in Wellington province.

Selwyn, G. A. Church in the Colonies. | No. XX. | New Zealand, | Part V. | A Journal | of the | Bishop's Visitation Tour | through his Diocese, | including a | Visit to the Chatham Islands, | in the Year 1848. | London | ——— | Society for promoting Christian Knowledge. | ——— | 1849.
    fcp. 8°. Pp. 134.

* **Sidney's Emigrant Journal for 1849.**
    Has "coloured map admirably illustrating the physical features of the country surveyed to form the settlement of Nelson."—*Martin, Brit. Col.* iii. 305.

* **Stokes,** *Capt.* J. L. Surveys in the Middle Island of New Zealand. *Journal, R.G. Society,* xxi. 25. 1849 ?
    See Stokes, 1851.

Wakefield, Edward Gibbon. A View | of the | Art of Colonization, | with present Reference to the | British Empire ; | in Letters between a Statesman and a Colonist. | Edited by | (one of the writers) | Edward Gibbon Wakefield. | London : | John W. Parker, West Strand. | M DCCC XLIX.
    8°. Pp. xxiv, 513.
    Besides an exposition of the principles on which the N.Z. Company's and Canterbury Association's settlements were founded, there are references throughout the volume to controversies between the Colonial Office and the N.Z. Company, and to features of the early social state of New Zealand.
    Appendix ii. (pp. 501-13) is—A letter from certain New Zealand colonists to Mr. Hawes, Under-Secretary of State for the Colonies, relating to the conditons under which self-government should be granted.
    C. Buller's speech on Systematic Colonization in 1843 is reprinted, pp. 457-500; with personal reminiscences, pp. 453-7. To that speech rather than to the speech of 1845 apply Lord Houghton's remarks (*Monographs*, ed. 2, p. 248).
    There are frequent references to the composition of the book in the *Founders of Canterbury*, pp. 31-47, where Wakefield writes of it as wholly his own.
    Wakefield's views on colonization were first expounded in his *Letter from Sydney*, London, 1829, professedly by Robert Gouger, with its appendix.—"Outline of a system of colonization ;" and afterwards in his *England and America* (1833), which has an appendix entitled "The art of colonization." The theory is discussed by Merivale, *Lectures on colonization and colonies*, esp. lecs. xiii, xiv, and its application to N.Z., pp. 475-7 : also by Leroy-Beaulieu, *De la colonisation chez les peuples modernes*, ed. 3, pp. 567-75. As applied to N.Z. it was expounded by Mr. Justice Chapman, *Encyc. Brit.*, ed. 7, xxi. 975-83; and criticized by J. Hill Burton in ed. 8, vii. 150.
    There is a good biographical sketch of W. in the *Encyc. Brit.*, ed. 9, by R. Garnett, who concludes :—" After every deduction it remains true that no contemporary showed equal genius as a colonial statesman, or in this department rendered equal service to his country " (xxiv. 319).

Wakefield, Felix. Colonial surveying | with a view to the | disposal of waste land : | in a report to the New-Zealand Company. | By | Felix Wakefield. | London : | John W. Parker, West Strand. | MDCCCXLIX.

8°. Pp. v, 89. Dated, Nayland, *10th September*, 1849.

Introduction, pp. 1-17. i.—Mode of sale, pp. 17-46. ii.—Mode of surveying, describing, and mapping, pp. 46-67. iii.—Mode of selection, giving possession, and completing the title, pp. 67-9. Cost, make-shift, scale, conclusion, pp. 69-89.

Apparently referring to this publication, E. G. Wakefield says (*Founders of Canterbury*, p. 109):—" Of course, I had a good deal to do with the literary composition of Felix's Report; but though the exposition of the ideas may be regarded as in a good measure mine, the ideas were not mine last year, and I still dissent from some of them."

There is a brief sketch of F. W. in *Cox*.

Captain R. K. Dawson made in 1840 a "Report on Surveying; Considered with reference to *New Zealand*, and applicable to the Colonies generally," which is appended to the Imperial Report from the Select Committee on South Australia, 1837.

1850.

* **Busby**, J. A Letter to the Right Hon. the Earl of Chichester, President of the Church Missionary Society. Auckland : Williamson & Wilson.

  Pp. 75, with postscript.—*Davis*.

* Canterbury Association for emigration to New Zealand. *Christian Remembrancer*, xix. 445.

* Canterbury Settlement in New Zealand. *Fraser's Magazine*, xlii. 463.

A Letter to the Right Rev. the Lord Bishop of the Church of England, New Zealand. Auckland. 1850.

* **Mantell**, G. A. Notice of the remains of the Dinornis and other birds, and of fossils and rock specimens, recently collected in the Middle Island of New Zealand ; with additional notes on the Northern Island. With note on Fossiliferous deposits in the Middle Island by Edw. Forbes. *Quarterly Journal of the Geological Society*, vi. 319-43. 1850.

  Geological sketch of east coast of South Island. Fossils first described and strata distinguished accordingly.—*Hochstetter*.

* **Mantell**, G. A. Notice of the discovery by Mr. Walter Mantell in the Middle Island of New Zealand of a living specimen of the Notornis, a bird of the Rail family, allied to the Brachypteryx, and hitherto unknown to naturalists except in a fossil state. Zool. Soc. Proc. 1850, xviii. 209-12 ; *Silliman, Journ.* 1851, xi. 102-5 ; Zool. Soc. Trans. 1862, iv. 69-72.

* **Mantell**, Reg. Neville. On the probable age of the deposits containing the remains of extinct colossal birds in New Zealand. Amer. Assoc. Proc. 1850, pp. 252-4.

Melville, Henry. The | Present State | of | Australia, | including | New South Wales, Western Australia, South Australia, | Victoria, and New Zealand, | By Henry Melville | —— | London : | G. Willis, Great Piazza, Covent Garden.

p. 8°. Pp. xiv, 392. Illus.

Cursory sketch of New Zealand as a colony, pp. 79-80, 344.

* New Zealand Zauberflöte. *Household Words*, ii. 75, 128. 1850.

The Polynesians : and New Zealand. *Edinburgh Review* (April, 1850), vol. xci. 443-71.

Discusses the decrease of the native population.

Selwyn, G. A. A | Charge | delivered to | the Clergy | of the | Diocese of New Zealand, | at | the Diocesan Synod, | in the Chapel of St. John's College, |

Selwyn, G. A.—*continued.*
>On Thursday, September 23, 1847. | By George Augustus | Bishop of New Zealand. | Fourth edition. | London : | Francis & John Rivington, | St. Paul's Church Yard, and Waterloo Place. | 1850.
>>fcp. 8°. Title-page, advertisement, dedication, and 106+1 pp.
>>
>>In Sept. the Bishop "held his second Synod, and delivered his primary Charge. This was a remarkable document. . . ."—*Tucker, Memoir,* &c., i. 234, where (pp. 235–48) large portions of the Charge are reprinted.

Steam to Australia | and New Zealand. | A collection of letters, etc., which have recently | appeared in the public journals relative | to the various routes proposed for | steam communication with | Australia and New | Zealand. | With an appendix. | London : | Effingham Wilson, 11, Royal Exchange. | 1850.

* **War** with the Maoris. *Dublin University Magazine*, lvii. 175.

1851.

***Brunner**, T. Explorations in the Middle Island of New Zealand. *Journal, Royal Geographical Society,* xx. 344. [Date unknown.]
>"In 1851 the Council awarded £25 to Mr. Thomas Brunner, for a very enterprising journey among the Alps and along the western shore of the Middle Island of N.Z., which, in those early days of colonisation, was an undertaking of some risk and difficulty."—*C. R. Markham, Jour. R.G. Soc.,* i. 63.
>
>The paper seems also to have appeared as—Journal of an expedition along the west coast of the Middle Island, in a no. of the *New Zealand Gazette.*

Buddle, T. The | Aborigines of New Zealand : | Two Lectures | delivered by | The Rev. Thos. Buddle, | Wesleyan Minister, | at the Auckland Mechanics' Institute, on the | Evenings of the 25th March, and 12th May, 1851. | Published by request. | Auckland :—Williamson and Wilson, | M DCCC LI.
>8°. Pp. 51.
>
>Origin of New Zealanders (pp. 7–13 ; Asiatic *via* Malaysia). Religion, pp. 13–21. Priesthood, pp. 21–5. Tapu, pp. 25–8. Witchcraft, pp. 28–9. Fairies, pp. 29–31. War customs, pp. 32–41. Cannibalism, pp. 41–43. Tatooing, pp. 44–5. Social and domestic condition, pp. 45–8. Mourning, pp. 48–51.
>
>Translations are given of canoe-songs, war-songs, laments, spirit-songs, birth-songs, ballads, songs sung during tattooing, and love-songs.

Canterbury Papers. | Information | concerning the | Principles, Objects, Plans & Proceedings | of the Founders | of the | Settlement of Canterbury, | in | New Zealand. | —— | London : John W. Parker and Son, West Strand. | 1851.
>8°. Pp. 318. Sketch map of the site of Canterbury Settlement and four illustrative views.
>
>Eleven numbers ; there were twelve in all. Plan for settlement, pp. 5–8. Capabilities of N.Z. for colonization, pp. 9–14. Preliminary arrangements and economy, pp. 14–22. Information respecting district, pp. 22–31. Letter from Bishop Selwyn (pp. 32–6) with *Times* leader, pp. 36–8. Correspondence between Lord Lyttelton and Earl Grey, pp. 38–41. Terms of purchase, pp. 41–4, 62–4, and 135–7. Instructions to Godley, pp. 44–7. Charter, pp. 57–60. Reports of public meetings. Scheme for college, pp. 101–2, 234–8. Proposed relation between Association and Colonists, pp. 103–7. Geological formation of Middle Island, by Walter Mantell, pp. 150–4. Reports of progress. Despatches to and from Godley. Sermons by Archbishop of Canterbury, pp. 217–23, and Bishop of Oxford, pp. 252–8.
>
>The preface is dated Feb. 1850 ; the first no. is stated to have been issued in 1848.
>
>E. G. Wakefield refers to the projected Canterbury Papers in his correspondence (*Founders of Canterbury,* pp. 200, 203, 206–7).
>
>Two nos. of a second series appeared in 1859, q.v.

Cooper, George Skidmore. Journal | of an | Expedition overland | from | Auckland to Taranaki, | by way of | Rotorua, Taupo, and the West Coast. | *Undertaken in the Summer of* 1849-50, | By His Excellency the | Governor-in-chief of New Zealand. | Auckland: | Printed by Williamson and Wilson, | 1851.

    16°. Pp. 310 and title-page. The *even* pages, pp. 2-310, give the English text; the *odd*, pp. 3-309, the Maori translation.

    This Journal was at first published in the *Maori Messenger* (No. 112), Nos. 43-48, 50-53, 55-67, 69 (Aug. 15, 1850 to Aug. 14, 1851).

    The English Journal was written by Mr. Cooper, Assistant Private Secretary, and translated into Maori by Mr. Charles Oliver B. Davis, Interpreter.

    The pieces of native literature contained in this publication were collected by Sir George Grey. They are—the fishing imprecation, p. 33 (trans., pp. 32, 34); another karakia, p. 41 and p. 40; legend of the Taniwhas, pp. 129-63 and pp. 128-62; welcome to strangers, p. 171 and p. 170; and the legend of Hine Moa, taken down from dictation (pp. 191-209) and translated by Sir G. Grey, pp. 190-208.—See *Catalogue of Sir G. Grey's Library*, vol. ii. pt. iv., pp. 47-8.

Fox, W. The | Six Colonies | of | New Zealand. | By | William Fox. | London: | John W. Parker and Son, | West Strand. | MDCCCLI.

    fcp. 8°. Pp. viii, 168.

    Ch. i. Descriptive and statistical. Ch. ii. Natives (Missionary influence, pp. 76-89.) Ch. iii. Government (describing the existing form); and two chapters are historical: Self-government, pp. 144-53; Constitutions—existing and proposed, pp. 153-62. Appendix: transfer of land, pp. 163-8.

***Gouland,** H. G. Plan of a Proposed New Colony, to be called Britannia. Lyttelton. 1851.

    "A pamphlet, in the form of a letter to Mr. Gladstone."—*Davis.*

Grey, Sir G. Address | of | Sir George Grey, K.C.B., | to the | Members of the | New Zealand Society, | as their first president, | September 26, 1851. | New Zealand: | Printed by R. Stokes, at the "Spectator Office," Wellington. | 1851.

    8°. Pp. 15.

    Describes the duties that lie before the scientific men of N.Z. to discover and describe the flora, the fauna, and the geology of the islands, the mythology and social state of the aborigines, their past and present history, "as tending to illustrate and clear up the history of the entire human race, and of all time, considered as one harmonious whole." Paragraphs of the address are quoted by Cholmondeley, *Ultima Thule*, pp. 338-9.

Grey, *Sir* G. Speech | of | Sir George Grey, K.C.B., | in answer to | Mr. Cautley's enquiry | for information as to the proposed extension | of the Canterbury block, | in the Legislative Council, | on the 18th June, 1851. | New Zealand: | printed by R. Stokes, at the "Spectator Office," Wellington. | 1851.

    Replied to by E. J. Wakefield: see below, 1851.

***Hursthouse,** C., *jun.* New Zealand: the Emigration Field of 1851. An Account of New Plymouth; or Guide to the Garden of New Zealand. 1851.

    8°. Pp. 195.

***New Zealand.** *North British Review*, xvi. 336. 1851.

***New Zealand Emigrants' Manual.** London: Orr & Co. 1853.

    Pamphlet.—*Davis.*

New Zealanders. *Blackwood's Magazine*, lxx. 414-30. Oct. 1851.

    Founded on Earle, Augas, and official papers.

***Richardson,** *Sir* John Larkins Cheese. The First Christian Martyr in New Zealand. A Poem in blank verse. 1851.

    Davis.

Shortland, E. The Southern Districts | of | New Zealand ; | a Journal, | with | Passing Notices of the Customs | of | the Aborigines. | By | Edward Shortland, M.A. Cantab. | Extra-licentiate of the Royal College | of Physicians. | London : | Longman, Brown, Green, and Longmans, | Paternoster Row. | MDCCCLI.

    8°. Pp. xiv, 315. Map of southern districts and map of lakes in interior of Middle Island. Three illustrations. Genealogical tables. Preface, pp. v–x. Contents, pp. xi–xiv. Illustrations, p. xv.

    Ch. i. Banks' peninsula and Otago. ii. Otago Maoris. iii. Native population. iv. Land claims. v. Native pedigrees. vi. Waikouaiti. vii. Whaling station and native village. viii. Southland and Stewart's Island. ix. Otago and Dunedin. x–xiii. From Otago to Akaroa. xiv–xv. Akaroa and Canterbury.

    Appendix: various; natural religion of New Zealander, pp. 292-7. Vocabulary of Kaltahu dialect, pp. 305-15.

    " . . . Compiled from the notes of a journal written during part of the years 1843-4, while the author was employed in the service of the Colonial Government of N.Z., as a Protector of the Aborigines " (p. v).

Stokes, J. L. Survey of the southern part of the Middle Island. Proc. Brit. Ass. 1851, *Report*, ii. 97-8.

    Captain Stokes was employed in 1844 by the N.Z. Company to explore the eastern and southern coast in order to select a site for the settlement of New Edinburgh. No eligible site south of Mataura river. Otakau (Otago) was recommended; Banks' peninsula rejected. A small community of Europeans at Bluff and Aparima, who have intermarried with natives and pursue whaling, sealing and husbandry. See 17th Report, N.Z. Co. and Martin, *Brit. Colonies*, N.Z., Topography.

Thomson, Arthur S., *M.D., Surgeon of the 58th Regiment.* A statistical account of Auckland, New Zealand, as it was observed during the year 1848. *Journal of the Statistical Society*, xiv. 227–49. London : J. W. Parker, Sept. 1851.

    8°.

    Auckland and its population are treated of in every aspect.

Thomson, A. S. [?] Statistics of New Munster, New Zealand, down to 1848, compiled from official records in the Colonial Secretary's Office. [Read before the Statistical Society of London, in continuation of the preceding paper, 17th February, 1851.] *Ibid.* xiv. 250–61.

***Wakefield,** E. Jerningham. Letter to Sir George Grey, in Reply to his Attack on the Canterbury Association. Lyttelton.

    Thomson.—A reply to the speech in Council, above.

Weld, F. A. Hints to intending Sheep-farmers in N.Z.

    See 1864.

***Wilson,** *Mrs.* R. New Zealand ; and other poems. London : Masters. 1851. 12°.—*Davis.*

1852.

***Brandes,** *Dr.* C. H. Neu-Seeland in geschichtlichen Umrissen von seiner Entdeckung bis zur Gegenwart. *In* von Raumer's historischem Taschenbuch, dritte Folge, dritter Jahrgang, 1852. Referred to in Hochstetter, *Neu-Seeland*, pp. 62-3 *note.*

    Gives passages from German school-books and geographies of the eighteenth century to show the ignorance then prevailing about New Zealand.

Correspondence showing the reason why Mr. Thomas quitted the service of the Canterbury Association.

    Without other title-page. But p. 16 has : London : printed by Stewart and Murray, Old Bailey. The correspondence ranges over 1851 and runs into 1852. It was probably published at London in 1852.

Golder, W. New Zealand Minstrelsy | containing | Songs and Poems | on Colonial Subjects, | With an Appendix, | By William Golder, | Author of "Recreations for Solitary Hours." | —— | Wellington : | R. Stokes and W. Lyon, Lambton-Quay ; | and sold by the Author, River Hutt. | 1852.

12°. viii+46 (continuous)+xxii+3.

Of the few of the poems which are distinctively Colonial one is "Wairau:—or Col. W——'s dirge to the memory of his brother," written to the tune of "Wallace's Lament." The appendix (xxii pp.) consists of earlier poems. The last three pages have subscribers' names.

***Hursthouse,** C. Emigration: Where to go, and who should go. London : Saunders. 1852.

12°. Pamphlet.—*Davis.*

Mundy, G. C. Our Antipodes: | or, Residence and Rambles | in | The Australasian Colonies. | With | A Glimpse of the Gold Fields. | By Lt. Colonel | Godfrey Charles Mundy, | Author of "Pen and Pencil Sketches in India." | —— | —— | London : | Richard Bentley, New Burlington Street, | Publisher in Ordinary to Her Majesty. | MDCCCLII.

3 vols. Vol. ii (relating mainly to N.Z.) : pp. viii, 405.

Chs. 3 to 14 describe a visit to Auckland, Bay of Islands, Wellington, and Wanganui in 1847-8, with accounts, apparently from oral narratives, of Heke's war, the war in the Hutt Valley, the Wairau massacre, and the capture of Rauparaha. Descriptions of the natives are interspersed.

Oliver, R. A. A Series | of | Lithographic Drawings | from | Sketches in New Zealand, | etc. | By R. A. Oliver, | Commander, R.N. | Dedicated by Permission to | His Royal Highness Prince Albert. | Lithographed and Published by | Dickinson Bros., Publishers to the Queen, 114, New Bond Street.

roy. f°. 8 sheets—9 engravings ; not coloured.

Rangihaeata; a kororo; a tangi; falls of the Kirikiri; stranger's house; half-castes of Pomare's pah ; Puebo, New Caledonia; Harry Bluff; and Johnny.

***Peppercorne,** Fr. S. Geological and topographical sketches of the province of New Ulster. Auckland, 1852.

Progress of Comparative Anatomy. *Quarterly Review,* March 1852, xc. 362-413.

Gives an account of arrival of first moa bone and subsequent consignment, pp. 401-3. See also note on Owen's Discovery, under *Owen*, 1879.

***Rough,** D. The North of New Zealand. London: S.P.C.K. 1852.

18°. *Davis.*

Shaw, J. A | Tramp to the Diggings; | being | Notes of a Ramble in | Australia and New Zealand | in 1852. By John Shaw, M.D. | F.G.S., F.L.S. | London: | Richard Bentley, 8, New Burlington Street. | Publisher in Ordinary to Her Majesty. | 1852.

cr. 8°. Pp. 317.

Only 10 pp. are given to N.Z.; of which 7 are descriptive of the country and 3 of the aborigines.

Williams, W. A | Dictionary | of the | New Zealand Language, | and | a Concise Grammar; | to which is added | a Selection of Colloquial Sentences. | By | William Williams, D.C.L., | Archdeacon of Waiapu. | Second edition. | London: | Williams and Norgate | —— | MDCCCLII.

p. 8°. Pp. xxxix, 323.

In the preface to the first edition, dated Tauranga, 1844, it is stated that "the following Compilation was prepared for the press six years ago. . . ." See also 1844 and 1871.

1853.

Adams, C. Warren. A | Spring | in the | Canterbury Settlement. | By | C. Warren Adams, Esq. | With engravings. | London: | Longman, Brown, Green, and Longmans. | 1853.
 p. 8°. Pp. ix, 92, xi. Illus.
  Ch. i. Voyage. ii. First impressions. iii. Lyttelton and Christchurch. iv. The bush. v. Banks's Peninsula. vi. Excursion through the Plains. vii. Sheep farms. viii. Maories. ix. General observations. 4 Plates. Addendum on finances of Canterbury Association.

* Auckland (New Zealand) and its neighbourhood. London, 1853.
 Pamphlet. Quotation in Fitton, *New Zealand*, pp. 34-5.

* **Busby,** James. A Picture of Misgovernment and Oppression in the British Colony of New Zealand. 1853.

* Canterbury Settlement in New Zealand. *Christian Remembrancer,* xxvi. 300.

Collinson, [T. B.] Remarks | on the | Military Operations in New Zealand. | By Captain Collinson, Royal Engineers.
 Described as "Paper II.," apparently of some Transactions, but without title-page. The date of the preface is Jan. 1, 1853.
 roy. 8°. Pp. 73. Map of N.Z. by Arrowsmith, 1853; of Bay of Islands. Sketch of pah at Ruapekapeka, and of Ruapekapeka.
  Part i. General Description.—Introduction. § 1. General physical description. 2. Native population. 3. British population and description of the six settlements. 4. Government and land. 5. Climate and productions. 6. Communication and harbours. 7. Defences. 8. Geographical advantages. 9. Recapitulation and statistics.
  Part ii. Northern campaigns. § 1. General history to 1844. 2. Tauranga. 3. Wairau. 4. Kororarika. 5. Okaihu. 6. Ohaiawai. 7. Ruapekapeka.
  "This paper is intended to be a short connected account of all the military operations that have occurred in N.Z. since the commencement of the colony. . . . It is a compilation from some of the many books that have been printed about N.Z., and from some private sources, and from three years' personal experience, from 1846 to 1850."—*Introduction.*

Earp, G. B. New Zealand: | its | Emigration and Gold Fields. | By | George Butler Earp, | Author of "Gold Colonies of Australia;" formerly Member of the | Legislative Council of New Zealand. | With a Map. | London : | George Routledge and Co., | Farringdon Street. | 1853.
 12°. Pp. xii, 192.
  Ch. iii. Climate. iv. Outline sketch of N.Z. v. Auckland. vi. Geological sketches of New Ulster. vii. Wollington. viii. Valley of the Wairarapa. ix. Nelson and the Wairau. x. New Plymouth. xi. Otago. xii. Canterbury. xv. First steps in the Colony. xvi. Agriculture and land-clearing. xvii. Auckland gold-fields.
  The book is dated from the Australian Gazette Office, and the author describes his qualifications as being "a pretty long experience in the colonies of the South Pacific, and . . . a still longer experience in despatching emigrants from the mother country."—*Preface.*

* **Gray,** Asa. Hooker's Flora of New Zealand. *American Journal of Science,* New Haven, lxvii. 241, 334. 1853.

Grey, Henry George Grey, *Earl.* The | Colonial Policy | of | Lord John Russell's Administration. | By Earl Grey. | In two volumes. | —— | London: Richard Bentley, New Burlington Street, | Publisher in Ordinary to Her Majesty. | 1853.
 8°. Vol. i: pp. xii, 414. ii: pp. 473.
  Letters addressed to Lord J. Russell. Letter x. (vol. ii. pp. 112-60) relates to N.Z. It has a long extract (pp. 116-34) from a despatch of Governor Grey, July 9, 1849, whose policy is eulogized. " . . . we adopted the only course likely to lead to a happy result, in resolving to embarrass him by few positive and no minute instructions, but to leave it almost entirely to his own judgment to determine upon the measures to be

Grey, Henry George Grey, *Earl—continued*.
taken by him, and to be guided mainly by his advice in what we were ourselves called upon to do" (ii. 140). Appendix 13 (ii. 334-46) is an extract from a speech of Lord Grey in the House of Lords, June 1852, on the second reading of the New Zealand Bill.

Lord G. was Secretary of State for the Colonies, 1846-52. A second edition of the book appeared the same year.

Reviewed by Sir C. Adderley: see 1869.

***Hogg**, *Rev.* Lewis M. A letter to His Grace the Duke of Newcastle on behalf of the Melanesian mission of the Bishop of New Zealand. London, 1853.

The title is in *Quarterly Review*, xc. 165.

Hooker, J. D. The Botany | of | The Antarctic Voyage | of | H.M. Discovery Ships *Erebus* and *Terror*, | In the Years 1839-1843, | under the command of | Captain Sir James Clark Ross, Kt., R.N., F.R.S. & L.S., etc. | By | Joseph Dalton Hooker, M.D., R.N., F.R.S. & L.S., etc. | Assistant Surgeon of the "Erebus" and Botanist to the Expedition. | II. | Flora Novæ-Zelandiæ. | Part I. Flowering Plants. | Published under the Authority of the Lords Commissioners of the Admiralty. | London : | Lovell Reeve, Henrietta Street, Covent Garden. | 1853.

imp. 4°. Pp. xxxix, 312 ; 95 coloured plates.

Part II. Flowerless Plants.

imp. 4°. Pp. 378 ; 35 coloured plates. The plates are numbered I to CXXX.

Introductory essay, pp. i.-xxxix. Ch. i. Summary of the history of the botany of N.Z., pp. ii-vii. Ch. ii. On the limits of species; their dispersion and variation, p. vii (application of Forbes's views to N.Z. flora). Ch. iii. §1. Physiognomy and affinities of N.Z. flora ; §2. Variation of N.Z. species.

The expedition "cast anchor in the Bay of Islands, August 16th, 1841, where we remained three months. This time was spent in collecting materials for a Flora of N.Z., in which object we received great assistance from Mr. Colenso and many other gentlemen. . . ." Part I, p. vii.

Reviewed by Asa Gray: see above, 1853.

Hursthouse, C. Emigration. | Emigration Fields Contrasted. | The Diggings. | Practical Hints on Emigration. | Mechanics. | Farmers. | Small-Capital Families. | Younger Sons. || Clerks and Shopmen. | Female Emigrants. | Outfit. | Voyage. | New Zealand. | By | Charles Hursthouse, Jun., | Author of "Emigration: Where to Go, and Who Should Go" (Dedicated to | Caroline Chisholm) ; and other Works. | London : | Robert Hardwicke, 38 Carey Street, | Lincoln's Inn. | MDCCCLIII.

cr. 8°. Pp. 57+2 pp. of notices of the Press of past works, and 3 pp. advertisements.

Two lectures, one on Emigration, the other on N.Z. generally. Mr. H. advertises as an emigration-agent. "Private interviews, by appointment, every morning from 11 to 3 o'clock, and Country Correspondents duly attended to by letter.—Terms—Half-a-guinea."

Martin, R. Montgomery. | The | British Colonies; | their | History, Extent, Condition, and Resources: | By R. Montgomery Martin, Esq., | late Treasurer to the Queen at Hong Kong; and Member of Her Majesty's | Legislative Council in China. | Vol. III. | New Zealand, Tasmania, Etc. | Printed and published by | The London Printing and Publishing Company, | London and New York.

imp. 8°. Pp. 381+175. Portraits (one of Banks) and maps (one of N.Z.). [1853?]

Bk. iii, pp. 108-356, relates to N.Z.

Ch. i. Discovery and history. ii. Position and physical geography ; governmenta divisions; settlements ; chief towns, and general topography. iii. Geology, palæontology, soil, mineralogy, climate, and diseases. iv. Population ; Maoris and their pro-

Martin, R. Montgomery—*continued.*
gross; religion; education; government. v. Revenue, customs and taxation; expenditure; commerce; staples; shipping; wages and prices. vi. Natural productions—flora and fauna.

Native population in 1835, p. 131. A full, but not impartial, history of the New Zealand Company is at pp. 145-93, 197, 205-15, 236-42, 250-4. Tuckett's report on Nelson, pp. 178-86. Tuckett's account of Wairau massacre, pp. 198-205. Quotations from Fitz-Roy's pamphlet, pp. 210-1, 216, 221-2, with a sympathetic account of his administration. Brunner's explorations in 1847-8, pp. 303-4 (extract, &c.).

The book has long extracts from now rare pamphlets and reports.

The | Mutual Relations | between the | Canterbury Association | and the | Purchasers of Land | in | the Canterbury Settlement | Briefly considered. | With | a copious Appendix of authentic Documents. | By authority of a committee of land-purchasers resident | in England. | London : | 1853.

    8°. Pp. 147 (ix pp. in Roman numerals) + 2 at beginning not numbered. Four pamphlets (apparently connected with the foregoing) of 16, 24, 8 and 4 pages respectively are appended.

Preface, pp. iii-ix (describes a meeting of Canterbury land-purchasers held on Feb. 1, 1853, attended by Mr. Felix Wakefield, which complained that the Association had signally failed in its engagements, charged it with misappropriation of money paid by land-purchasers, and resolved to seek an interview with Lord Lyttelton). Summary of a report made by the member of the committee deputed to communicate with Lord L., pp. 11-38. Principal events from the origin of the scheme to the return of the Land Agent, with his report of the actual state of the colony, pp. 41-49. Appendix A. Extracts from Canterbury papers, pp. 50-71. B. Land Agent's report on Canterbury Settlement, pp. 72-85. C. and D. Correspondence. E. Newspaper extracts and letters. F. and G. Canterbury Association Audit and balance-sheet.

The | New Zealand | Emigration Circular | for 1853. | Contents. | Introduction. | Gold or Corn. | Labour. | Remedy for Poor Rates. | New Zealand, its Products, &c. | Natives. | Climate. | Settlements. | Auckland. | New Plymouth. | Wellington. | Nelson. | Canterbury. | Otago. | Maps. | Land, Cost of Clearing, Produce. Wages, &c. | Books, Voyage, Outfit, &c. | Statistics. | Third Edition. | London : | Saunders and Stanford, 6, Charing Cross. | 1853. | *Price Twopence.*

    cr. 8°. Pp. 34.

The 1853 edition of the Circular occupies only pp. 1-2; the rest being a republication of the Circular for 1852.

* Reise- und Lebensbilder aus Neu-Holland, Neu-Seeland und Californien. Aus dem Tagebuche eines Verwandten herausgegeben von W. Schulze. 2. verbesserte Auflage. Magdeburg: Baensch, 1853.
    gr. 8°.

* **Rochfort,** John. Adventures of a surveyor in New Zealand and Australia. 1853.

Strachan, Rev. Alexander. Remarkable incidents in the life of the Rev. Samuel Leigh, missionary to the settlers and savages of Australia and New Zealand. London, 1853.
    See 1855.

[**Swainson,** William.] Auckland, | The Capital of New Zealand, | and the | Country Adjacent : | including some account of | The Gold Discovery in New Zealand. | —— | With a Map of the Auckland District from recent surveys. | London : | Smith, Elder & Co., 65, Cornhill. | Auckland : J. Williamson. | 1853.

    8°. Pp. xii, 163. Map.

Ch. 1. Captain Hobson. 2, 3. Auckland. 4. Climate—careful observations. 5. Auckland—social and domestic. 6. Gold discovery—Coromandel. 7. Bush travelling. 8. Past and present of N.Z.—Appendix of documents.

***Thomson,** *Dr.* A. S. Physique of the inhabitants of New Zealand. *Jour. R. G. Society* [?], xxiii. 87.

"The loose statements of casual observers respecting the physical condition of the Maori race have been brought to something approaching a test of exact comparison by Dr. Thomson, surgeon to the 58th Regiment, whose remarks on the subject have been included in a late number of the Journal of the Statistical Society of London, and in the British and Foreign Medico-Chirurgical Review for April of the present year."—*Quarterly Review,* xcv. 189-90, where a summary of the results is given. See article by Thomson, 1854.

1854.

[**Carleton,** Hugh.] A Page | from the | History of New Zealand. | By Metoikos. | "Grudge not one against another, brethren, lest ye be condemned: behold, the Judge standeth before the door." | Auckland : | Printed, for the Author, by Williamson and Wilson. | 1854.

4°. Pp. ii, 69—double columns.

In the preface, which is dated Auckland, 15th October, 1853, and is signed Hugh Carleton, it is stated: "The following analysis of the CHURCH MISSIONARY LAND QUESTION was published about eighteen months ago, as a series of letters to the *Southern Cross;*" and that " many additions are made, but no material alterations."

"The three most interesting episodes in the annals of the Colony are the native war, the struggle for self-government, and the contention raised with the Church Missionary Grantees by Bishop SELWYN and Governor GREY. Of those, I shall undertake the latter for my share." (P. 1.)

An *ex parte* history of the proceedings arising out of the purchase of land by the missionaries, the controversies of the missionaries with the Church Missionary Society, Governor Grey and Bishop Selwyn.

It includes correspondence with Bishop Selwyn, Archdeacon Williams, Mr. Venn, Dr. Maunsell, &c.

[**Carleton,** Hugh.] Postscript to " A page from the history of New Zealand " by Metoikos. Being a short exposition of the pusillanimous compliance of the Secretaries of the Church Missionary Society, with the political intrigue of Sir George Grey, Governor of New Zealand, set forth in his calumniatory despatches, to the Secretary of State for the Colonies.

8°. Pp. 19. No place and no date.

Cholmondeley, T. Ultima Thule; | or, | Thoughts | suggested by | A Residence· in New Zealand. | By | Thomas Cholmondeley. | London : | John Chapman, 142, Strand. | M.DCCC.LIV.

p. 8°. Pp. iv, 344.

A book of reflection mainly, garnished with observations, suggestions and advice. A chapter on the English peopling of N.Z. describes (pp. 9-11) the dispersion of one of the old whaling villages. The book treats of immigration, the various classes, the conditions of success, agriculture and pasture lands, the Maories (ch. xvi), the Constitution of N.Z. (ch. xvii), the church (ch. xviii; the general principles recommended by Bishop Selwyn for the basis of a constitution, pp. 249-50; constructive free-thinking, pp. 276-80), society and its institutions (ch. xix), thoughts on the history of N.Z. (ch. xx). At pp. 338-44 the author gives his "conception of the arrangement of our materials for a history of N.Z."

Christianity in Melanesia and New Zealand. *Quarterly Review,* xcv. 165-206.

N.Z. pp. 180-206.

Grey, *Sir* G. Memorandum | upon | A Letter | addressed by Lord Lyttelton | to | Sir George Grey. | London : | Printed by G. Norman, Maiden Lane, Covent Garden. | 1854.

8°. 50 pp. Dated July 6th, 1854.

A self-vindication against the charges, made by Mr. Adderley (now Lord Norton) and Sir J. Pakington, that the Governor had called together the Provincial Councils, had delayed the meeting of the General Assembly, had delayed proclaiming the Constitution Act and issuing the writs, had failed to make nominations to the Council, had dealt illegally with the revenue and with Crown lands, and had prematurely left New Zealand,

*Heaphy, Charles. On the Coromandel gold-diggings in New Zealand. *Quarterly Journal of the Geological Society*, x. 322-4. 1854.

Malone, It. E. Three Years' Cruise | in the | Australasian Colonies. By | R. Edmund Malone. London: | Richard Bentley, New Burlington Street. | —— | 1854.
    p. 8°. Pp. viii, 304.
    Ch. vii. Auckland islands, pp. 59-82 (three months' wind and weather journal, pp 79-82). Ch. ix. Brief account of a visit to Mana, Porirua, Wellington, Taranaki, Nelson, and Auckland, pp. 98-121.
    The author was an officer in H.M.S. Fantôme, which was on the Australian station from 1850 to 1853.

*Paul, *Rev.* R. B. Account of Canterbury Settlement, N.Z. London: Rivington. 1854.
    18°. Pamphlet.—*Thomson.*

Peel, *Sir* Robert. The | Speeches | of | the late Right Honourable | Sir Robert Peel, Bart. | delivered in | the House of Commons. | With a General Explanatory Index, | and a | brief chronological summary of the various subjects on which | the speeches were delivered. | In four volumes. | Volume IV. | From 1842 to 1850. London: | George Routledge and Co., | 1853. 8°.
    New Zealand, July 23, 1845, pp. 555-64. See also *Hansard*, Third series, vol. 82, pp. 991-1009.

*Pemberton, Robert. The Happy Colony. London: Saunders & Otley. 1854.
    See Thomson's note, ii. 359.

*Richardson, *Sir* J. L. C. A summer's excursion in New Zealand; with gleanings from other writers. By an Old Bengalee. Exeter, 1854.
    12°. Thomson gives it as—London, 1855.

*Thomson, Arthur S. Description of two caves in the North Island of New Zealand containing bones of the Moa. *Edinburgh New Philosophical Journal*, lvi. 268-95. 1854.

*Thomson, A. S. Native race of New Zealand. *Journal of the Statistical Society*, xvii. 27.
    See note to article by Thomson in previous year.

1855.

*Abraham, Charles John, *Archdeacon*. Journal of a walk with the Bishop of New Zealand from Auckland to Taranaki, August, 1855.
    Davis.—A biographical notice of Bishop Abraham is in *Cox.*

*Catechism of the Constitution. By a Member of the Provincial Council. Lyttelton. 1855.
    Pamphlet.—*Davis.*

*Crawford, James Coutts. On the geology of the Port Nicholson district. *Quarterly Journal of Geol. Soc.*, xi. 530.

Davis, C. O. B. Maori Mementos; | being | A Series of Addresses, presented by | the Native People | to | His Excellency Sir George Grey, K.C.B., F.R.S. | Governor and High Commissioner of the Cape of Good Hope, | and late Governor of New Zealand; | with Introductory Remarks and Explanatory Notes, | to which is added | a Small Collection of Laments, &c. | by | Charles Oliver B. Davis, | Translator and Interpreter to the General Government. | Auckland: | Printed by Williamson and Wilson. | 1855.
    8°. Pp. iii+227.

Davis, C. O. B.—*continued.*
Farewell Addresses of natives, clergy, &c, with 29 songs; most in both English and Maori. The Governor's farewell—in English, pp. 120-2; in Maori, pp. 121-5. Two native feasts at Auckland, in 1850-1, pp. 126-31, 158-61; with 6 songs. Account of meeting at Coromandel on the gold question, with speeches by natives and one song, pp. 132-57. Nineteen Maori songs and laments, with translations, pp. 162-78, 191-209. Ancient Maori stories, with song, pp. 179-87. Two Maori fables, pp. 188-90. Eight hymns and songs, pp. 210-26. Maori legend (in English only), p. 227. Most of the Maori originals have English translations.

***Davis,** C. O. B. The renowned Chief Kawiti, and other New Zealand Warriors. Auckland. 1855.

***Forbes,** Ch. On the geology of New Zealand. With notes on its carboniferous deposits. *Quarterly Journal of the Geolog. Soc.*, xi. 521. 1855.
Geological features along coast of both Islands.—*Hochstetter.*

Grey, *Sir* G. Polynesian Mythology, | and | Ancient Traditional History | of the | New Zealand Race, | as furnished by their priests and chiefs. | By Sir George Grey, | late Governor-in-Chief of New Zealand. | —— | London : | John Murray, Albemarle Street. | 1855.
p. 8°. xiii pp., Contents, List of illustrations, and 333 pp. 15 illus.

There are 23 myths and legends illustrative of Maori cosmogony, early history and emigration to N.Z., and life there. An appendix (pp. 313-33) on the native songs is by James A. Davies: it has (pp. 329-33) the music of 4 N.Z. airs, and seems to have been previously published: see the Catalogue of the Grey Library at Capetown, vol ii, pt. iv, no. 128.

The legends are translations of *Ko nga Mahinga a nga Tupuna Maori he mea kohikohi mai,* London, 1854, translations of parts of which exist only in MS.: see Grey, *Catalogue,* vol. ii, pt. iv, no. 126. A second edition appeared in 1886, with the date 1885.

In an interesting preface the author describes how he came to collect the legends. The work has been the chief storehouse of information on Polynesian mythology, and has furnished materials for many chapters and articles. It was translated into French, with very long notes, by Lesson, and addressed in December 1865 to the Anthropological Society of Paris, which reported on it through M. Gaussin in July 1867: see Lesson's *Polynésiens,* iii. 344. The translation seems not to have been published.

***Heaphy,** Ch. On the gold-bearing district of Coromandel harbour, New Zealand. *Quarterly Journal of the Geological Society,* xi. 31-6. 1855.

*The Maoris of New Zealand. *Littell's Living Age,* l. 229.

Polynesian mythology. *New Quarterly Review,* iv. 211.
Extracts from *Grey* mainly.

Strachan, A. Remarkable Incidents | in the Life | of | the Rev. Samuel Leigh, | missionary to the settlers and savages of | Australia and New Zealand : | with | a Succinct History | of | the Origin and Progress of the Missions | in Those Colonies. | By the Rev. Alexander Strachan, | author of the Life and Times of the Rev. George Lowe, | etc. | Second edition. | London : | Printed for James Nichols, 46, Hoxton-Square ; | and may be had of all booksellers. | MDCCCLV.
p. 8°. Pp. iv, 418. Portrait.

Chs. iv to ix (pp. 83-216) and chs. xiv, xv, xvi (pp. 303-77) relate to N.Z.
Mr. Leigh, the first Wesleyan missionary in N.Z., visited the country in 1818. He returned in 1822 and remained till 1827. The six earlier chapters describe his work at the Bay of Islands; the three later, the subsequent history of the mission. An account of Hongi and Waikato in London is given in ch. iv, and many incidents of Native history are related.

The Index is exceptionally full.

Taylor, R. Te Ika a Maui, | or | New Zealand and its Inhabitants, | illustrating the | Origin, Manners, Customs, Mythology, Religion, Rites, | Songs,

61

Taylor, R.—*continued.*
Proverbs, Fables, and Language of | the Natives. | Together with the | Geology, Natural History, Productions, and Climate | of the Country ; | its State as regards Christianity ; | Sketches of the Principal Chiefs, and their Present Position ; | with a Map and numerous Illustrations. | By the | Rev. Richard Taylor, M.A., F.G.S., | Many years a missionary in New Zealand. | London : | Wertheim and Macintosh, 24, Paternoster-Row. | MDCCCLV.
 8°. Pp. xiv, 490. 8 coloured plates.
  The contents are similar to, but not coextensive with, those of the second edition, published in 1870, q.v.
  The chapters on zoology and botany, mythology and traditions are translated by Lesson, *Polynésiens,* iv. 200-378, who refers (iii. 2) to a complete translation by him which is still unpublished.

* Traditions and superstitions of the New Zealanders. *Dublin University Magazine,* xlvii, 221. 1855.

Tucker, *Miss.* The Southern Cross and Southern Crown.
 See 1858.

1856.

Busby, James. The first settlers in New Zealand, and their treatment by the Government ; being a speech delivered at the table of the House of Representatives, August 1st, 1856. Revised and enlarged. Auckland, 1856.
 8°. Pp. vi, 54.
  Preface, pp. iii-vi. Address, pp. 1-49. Appendix A, pp. 50-3. Appendix B, pp. 53-4.

The | Church Missionary | Intelligencer, | A Monthly Journal | of | Missionary Information. | —— | —— | London : | Seeley, Jackson, and Halliday, Fleet Street, | and Hanover Street, Hanover Square ; | T. Hatchard, Piccadilly ; | and J. Nisbet and Co., Berners Street.
 imp. 8°. Vols. vii (1856), viii (1857), ix (1858), x (1860), xi (1861). Illus.
  Missions in New Zealand: Vol. vii. 145-62 (Native church of N.Z.). viii. 29-31. ix. 149-58, 177-61, 277-88 (sketch of history of mission). xi. 1-21 (Episcopate, Church Missionary Society, and native race), 217-29 (Christianity in its influence on colonization), 239-40 (war), 241-57 (colonial N.Z.). xii. 10-14 (Maori N.Z.), 210-22.

Curr, E. M. The | Waste Lands | of | the Province of Wellington, | New Zealand. | In a Series of Letters. | By Edward M. Curr. | Wellington, New Zealand : | Printed at the office of the " New Zealand Spectator and | Cook's Strait Guardian." | 1856.
 8°. Pp. 37.
  A denunciation of the land-purchase regulations of the Province.

Fitton, E. B. New Zealand : | its | Present Condition, Prospects | and Resources ; | being a | Description of the Country | and General Mode of Life among New | Zealand Colonists, | for the | Information of Intending Emigrants. | By | Edward Brown Fitton, a Landowner and late Resident in the Colony. | London : | Edward Stanford, 6, Charing Cross. | 1856.
 12°. Pp. vi, 358. Map.
  Ch. i. Early history of N.Z. ii. General description. iii. Auckland. iv. Wellington. v. Nelson. vi. New Plymouth. vii. Otago. viii. Canterbury. ix. Pastoral occupations. x. Agricultural. xi. Domestic life. xii. Colonial life, etc. xii, xiii. Emigration. xiv. Price of waste lands. xv. Conclusion : mainly a speech of Godley's.
  Expanded from a lecture ; filled out with extracts from newspapers and official documents.

A Hand Book | for | Emigrants to New Zealand ; | being | a Digest | of the most | .Recent and Authentic Intelligence | respecting | Auckland, | the

Hand Book for Emigrants to New Zealand—*continued.*
Capital of the Colony. | London : | Printed and sold by J. S. Forsaith, Bethnal Green Road. | 1856. | [*Price Threepence.*]
12°. Pp. 85.

* Ika-na-Mawi. Sagen und Gewohnheiten der Neuseeländer. *Ausland*, 1856, no. 30.

List | of | Original Land Purchasers | and Holders | of | Pasturage Runs ; | to Accompany Map | of the | Canterbury Province, | New Zealand. | London : | Edward Stanford, 6, Charing Cross. | 1856.
8°. Pp. x. Map.
On the wrapper is a list of maps, plans and views of N.Z., published by Stanford.

Mills, Arthur. Colonial Constitutions : | an Outline | of the | Constitutional History and Existing Government | of the | British Dependencies : | with Schedules of the | Orders in Council, Statutes and Parliamentary Documents | relating to each Dependency. | By Arthur Mills, Esq. | of the Inner Temple, Barrister-at-Law. | ——— | London : | John Murray, Albemarle Street. | 1856.
8°. Pp. lxxi, 399.
Brief history of the N.Z. Constitution, pp. 331-6 ; Orders in Council, 1840-55, pp. 338-9 ; Imperial Acts, pp. 339-40 ; Parliamentary reports, &c., pp. 340-2.

Schirren, C. Die | Wandersagen der Neuseeländer | und | der Mauimythos. | Von | C. Schirren. | Riga, | Verlag von N. Kymmel. | 1856.
roy. 8°. Pp. iv, 209.
i. Sources and contents of the myths, pp. 1-42. ii. Ethnological interest of an examination of the myths ; method of inquiry, pp. 43-53. iii. Character of the migration-sagas ; Maui as first man, pp. 53-67. iv. The Maui-myth and the migration-legends, pp. 67-115. v. Kindred gods and myths in the North-west, pp. 115-33. vi. Interpretation of the Maui-myth and the migration-sagas, pp. 133-68. vii. Results of the inquiry ; characteristics of sun-worship, pp. 168-94. Appendix on proportional numbers in myths, pp. 195-208.

Hawaiki has "a mythical signification. It denotes the lower regions, the realms of the dead." The migration-legends are also fables. "Just as Maui, the god of the lower regions, and at the same time the first man, lord of water, air and sky, raised the earth out of Hawaiki, so also all the first immigrants hailed from Hawaiki. Maui . . . is the prototype of the migrating heroes, whom we may regard as humanized gods or deified men. Notwithstanding the change of scenes and names, there is a certain uniformity, a repetition of stereotyped personal transactions, such as abductions, pursuits, open feuds and treacherous stratagems, in all the stories of migration. The adventures and experiences of the heroes are traceable to natural phenomena, and their great number to the dispersion of the N.Z. tribes. Each tribe endeavours by means of an artfully arranged line of ancestors to derive its descent from one of those mythical heroes. . . . The traditions of the New Zealanders are nothing but versions of the Maui mythos. Thus every single link is removed that might aid in tracing the descent of the New Zealanders to the immigration from this or that South Sea Island. . . . Schirren proves that the Maui-myths, varying in individual features, but identical in the main, exist throughout Polynesia. . . . Maui is the national deity of all the Polynesian tribes. Hence the Maui-mythos proves . . . the original unity of the Polynesian race." But the mythology supplies no evidence of the origin of the race ; it is a system of nature-myths, peculiar to the Polynesians.—*Hochstetter, New Zealand,* English trans., pp. 207-10 ; *Neu-Seeland*, pp. 54-7.

"Schirren . . . and Hochstetter place Hawaiki in the lower world, and allow it only a legendary signification. Gerland, however, has skilfully vindicated the older opinion of H. Hale."—*Peschel, Races of man,* p. 352, *note.*

Shortland, E. Traditions and Superstitions | of the | New Zealanders : | with | illustrations of their manners and | customs. | By | Edward Shortland, M.A. | of the University of Cambridge ; | extra-licentiate of the Royal College of Physicians ; author of | "The southern districts of New Zea-

Shortland, E.—*continued.*
land." | Second edition. | London : | Longman, Brown, Green, Longmans and Roberts, | Paternoster Row. | 1856.

 cr. 8°. Pp. xi, 316. Map and two genealogical tables.

Ch. I. Traditions of origin and colonisation. ii. Colonisation and race. iii. Prior traditions. iv, vi, vii. Religious Ideas. v. Rites. viii. Institutions. Songs. ix. Songs. x. Oratory. Proverbs. xi. Arts. Knowledge. xii. Political divisions and institutions. xiii. Military. xiv. Landed property—gives a good description of land-title by descent, gift, and conquest, individually and tribally.

Appendix (various), pp. 230-310. Vocabulary of words occurring in the foregoing pages not to be found in Williams's dictionary, pp. 313-6.

"Several years' residence in N.Z., passed for the most part in constant intercourse with its native inhabitants, either while travelling or while stationed at Maketu—a large village on the shore of the Bay of Plenty, where the influence of the Missionaries had made little or no impression—gave the writer of the following pages opportunities of studying the manners of the Aborigines, such as they were before they were modified by intercourse with Europeans."—*Pref. to first edition*, 1854.

"In this edition a more complete account of the tribal divisions of the New Zealanders is given. The first and third chapters have been partly re-written; and some additional matter introduced, which has been obtained in reply to inquiries made through friends who have been resident in New Zealand, and who, from their knowledge of the *Maori* language, are competent to extract information from the most trustworthy sources."—*Preface to second edition.*

Swainson, W. New Zealand. | The Substance of | Lectures | on the | Colonization of New Zealand, | delivered at | Lancaster, Plymouth, Bristol, Hereford, | Kirkby Lonsdale, Richmond, and | The Charter House, London. | By | William Swainson, | H.M. Attorney General for New Zealand, and Speaker of the | Legislative Council of the General Assembly. | With Notes. | London : | Smith, Elder & Co., 65 Cornhill. | 1856.

 cr. 8°. Pp. vi (not numbered), 64.

Historical summary—Constitution—Natives—Progress of the Colony—Climate, scenery, &c.—Past and present.

The book was written after 14 years' residence.

Tancred, *Sir* T. Notes | on the | Natural History | of the | Province of Canterbury, | in the | Middle Island of New Zealand. | By | Sir Thomas Tancred, Bart. | *From the Edinburgh New Philosophical Journal, New Series, for January* 1856. | Edinburgh: | Printed by Neill and Company. | MDCCCLVI.

 8°. Pp. 36.

Physical geography, pp. 3-11. Fauna, pp. 11-16. Flora, pp. 16-24. Climate, pp. 24-9. Natives, pp. 29-36.

Waitt, Robert. The Progress of Canterbury, New Zealand. | A Letter | addressed to | Joseph Thomas, Esq., | late Principal Surveyor and acting Agent of the | Canterbury Association. | London : | Sumfield & Jones, Printers, West Harding Street, Fetter Lane. | 1856.

 cr. 8°. Pp. 16.

White, John. Maori superstitions. By John White, Interpreter to the Land Purchase Department. Auckland. 1856.

 See 1861 and 1885.

1857.

*****Baker**, A. New Zealand compared with Great Britain in its Physical and Social Aspects. A Lecture. By the Rev. A. Baker, M.A. Wellington, 1857.

 Thomson.

Buller, J. New Zealand; | the future | England of the Southern Hemisphere; | or the | Natural Advantages of New Zealand | compared with those of the |

Buller, J.—*continued.*
Australian Colonies. | A Lecture, | by the | Rev. James Buller, | *Wesleyan Minister.* | Wellington: | Published by William Lyon. | *Price* 6d. |
fcp. 8°. Pp. 21.
Delivered in the Mechanics' Institute, April 14, 1857, in connexion with the Wellington Sunday School Union; reprinted from the *Wellington Independent*. It is reprinted in the author's *Forty Years in N.Z.*, pp. 457-72.

*****Busby,** James. Colonies and Colonization: A lecture with especial reference to New Zealand. Auckland: Philip Kunst, "Southern Cross." Office. 1857.
Pp. 27.

*****Busby,** J. Responsible Government and the Governmental Institutions of New Zealand: a letter to Governor Gore Browne. Auckland. 1857.

*****Cooper,** *Capt.* I. Rhodes. The New Zealand settlers' guide. London, 1857.
8°.—*Thomson.*

D'Ewes, J. China, Australia | and | the Pacific Islands, | in the Years 1853–56. | By J. D'Ewes Esq. | —— | London: | Richard Bentley, New Burlington Street. | 1857.
p. 8°. Pp. 340. Illus.
Auckland in 1855-6, pp. 212-34.

* Edw. Shortland über Neu-Seeland. *Ausland*, 1857, no. 31.

Grey, *Sir* G. Ko nga Whakapepeha | me | nga Whakaahuareka a nga Tipuna | o | Aotea-Roa. | Proverbial and Popular Sayings | of the | Ancestors of the New Zealand Race. | By | Sir George Grey, K.C.B., Governor and Commander-in-chief of the Cape of Good Hope | and Her Majesty's High Commissioner. | Cape Town: | Saul Solomon and Co., Steam Printing Office, | 63, Longmarket-Street. | Sold by Trübner and Co., No. 12, Paternoster-Row, London. | 1857.
8°. Pp. v, 120.
Pp. 1-96 are the proverbs in Maori and English. An Appendix, pp. 97-102, contains "the narratives from which some of them are derived" (p. v.). Follows (pp. 103-8) "The Proverbs of Te Paki," with the prefatory paragraph:—"The following treatise on N.Z. Proverbs, in the native language, was drawn up in January and February, 1849, by a native, from the dictation of Te Paki, the chief of the Ngaungau tribe, and formerly the High Priest of the Waikato tribes." A translation is at pp. 109-18. An explanation of the proverb, Ngati-Awa a Awa-nui-a-rangi, is given in Maori, p. 119, with note, pp. 119-20.

Hursthouse, C. New Zealand, | or | Zealandia, | The Britain of the South. | With Two Maps and Seven Coloured Views. | By | Charles Hursthouse, | a New Zealand Colonist, and Former Visitor in the | United States, the Canadas, the Cape Colony, | and Australia. | In two volumes. | —— | London: | Edward Stanford, 6, Charing Cross. | 1857.
p. 8°. Vol. i: pp. xv, Errata, 328; vol. ii: pp. vii, Errata, 329 to 664.
Ch. i. Introductory. ii. Historical sketch. iii. Physical features. iv. Climate. v. Animal kingdom. vi. Vegetable kingdom. vii. Minerals. viii. Natives. ix. Provinces. x. Government. xi. Exports and markets. xii. Agriculture and horticulture. xiii. Pastoral. xiv. Investments and pursuits. xvii. Land regulations. xviii. Statistics and prices. Chs. xv, xvi, xix, xx relate to emigration. Appendix.
A second edition was published in 1861.

* New Zealand in 1857. *Littell's Living Age*, Boston, lv. 599.

Paul, R. B. Letters | from | Canterbury, New Zealand. | By | Robert Bateman Paul, M.A. | Archdeacon of Waimea, | formerly Fellow of Exeter College, Oxford, | author of " Grecian Antiquities," | " Markham's History

Paul, R. B.—*continued.*
of Germany," | &c. &c. &c. | With a Map of the Province, | and a considerable part of the Province of Nelson, | showing the purchased land, reserves, sheep and cattle runs, | Mr. Weld's overland route | from Nelson to Canterbury, &c. &c. | By Edward Jollie, C.E. | London : | Rivingtons, Waterloo Place. | 1857.
12°. Pp. viii, 160. Map.

The substance of information collected during a residence of four years, for the use of emigrants. "I am indebted for the excellent article on the establishment of a sheep-station to Mr. Charles Hunter Brown of Double Corner; for information on agricultural matters, to Mr. W. G. Brittan and other experienced N.Z. farmers; for church and educational statistics, to the Rev. Henry Jacobs. . . ."—*Preface.*

The letters give a general account of the Province in 1857. In the Appendix are —Narrative of overland journeys from Nelson to Christchurch by E. J. Lee and F. A. Weld, pp. 105–29; Census of 1854; table of exports; list of runholders.

[**Puseley**, D.] The Rise and Progress | of | Australia, Tasmania, | and | New Zealand. | In which will be found | a Colonial Directory ; | Increase and Habits of Population ; | Tables of Revenue and Expenditure ; Economical Growth and Present Position of Each | Dependency ; | Intellectual, Social and Moral Condition of the People, &c., | gathered from | Authentic Sources, Official Documents, | and Personal Observation | in Each of | the Colonies, Cities, and Provinces | enumerated. | By an Englishman. | Author of "Commercial before Military Glory," "Sketches of English | and Scottish Scenery," and "A Traveller's Diary," | "Five Dramas," etc., etc. | London : | Saunders and Otley, Conduit Street. | 1857.
p. 8°. Pp. xvi, 496. The preface is signed D.P. = D. Puseley. Fifth thousand.
N.Z.: pp. 223–420, 449–71.

Introduction, pp. 225–30. Introductory description of the colony, pp. 231–56. Auckland, pp. 257–78. Taranaki, pp. 279–90. Nelson, pp. 291–309. Black Ball Line, pp. 310–2. Wellington, pp. 313–28. Canterbury, pp. 329–50. Otago, pp. 351–64. Bishop of N.Z. (Selwyn), pp. 364–6. Governor (Gore Browne), p. 367. N.Z. Directory, by Provinces, pp. 449–71. A fourth edition was published in 1858, with the author's name, by Warren Hall and Co., Camden Town, London. There are only 416 pp.; the Colonial Directory being omitted.

Social progress at the Antipodes. Concluding article. *Chambers's Journal,* xxviii. 152 ; Sept. 12, 1857, pp. 173–5.

Experiences in the neighbourhood of Cape Kidnapper. "The settlements of the Middle Island appear to have fallen into a state of permanent commercial paralysis. A few years ago some wealthy Port Phillip squatters endeavoured to grow wool on the Canterbury plains, . . . but were obliged to abandon the attempt on account of the cold wintry winds and the scarcity of pasturage" (p. 173).

* **Stratford**, S. P. Natural history of New Zealand. *Canadian Journal of Industry,* Montreal, N.S., ii. 357.

1858.

***Adam**, G. J. Description of the Province of Otago. Edinburgh : Bell and Bradfute. 1858.
Thomson.

Boyce, *Rev.* W. B. New Zealand. *Encyclopædia Britannica,* ed. 8, v. 16, pp. 232–9. Edinburgh : Adam and Charles Black. 1858.
See also v. 4, pp. 265–8.

* **Busby**, James. The Federation of Colonies and the system called ' Responsible Government.' Auckland : Richardson & Sansom. 1858.
Pp. 17.
Shows the necessity of a paramount local authority for each of the provinces of N.Z.

* Description of the Province of Nelson; and of Wellington. Kent & Co. 1858.
  Thomson.
* Description of the Province of Wellington. Also, of Nelson. Tweedie. 1858.
  Both written by the Editor of the *Australian and N.Z. Gazette.*—Thomson.
* Emigrants' Manual to New Zealand. Edinburgh: Chambers. 1858.
  12°. Pamphlet.—Davis.
* **Hodgkinson,** S. Description of the Province of Canterbury, N.Z. Ed. 2. Tweedie. 1858.
  Sic Davis. Thomson has—Description of the Province of Canterbury. By G. S. Hodgkinson, M.R.C.S. Kent and Co.

Grey, Sir George, *and* **Bleek,** W. H. I. The Library | of His Excellency | Sir George Grey, K.C.B. | Philology. | Vol. II. Part IV | New Zealand, | the Chatham Islands and the Auckland Islands. | Sir G. Grey and W. H. I. Bleek. | Sold by Trübner and Co., 60 Paternoster Row, London, | and by F. A. Brockhaus, Leipzig. | 1858.
  8°. Pp. 76. Printed at Capetown.
  Bibliography of 198 publications and manuscripts (the bulk of them Maori) in the Grey Library at Capetown.
  Grammars, pp. 1-4. Dictionaries, p. 5. Vocabularies, pp. 5-6. Phraseologies, pp. 6-8. Elementary books (for teaching the natives English), pp. 8-10. Maori spelling book, p. 10. Catechisms: Church of England missions, pp. 10-12; Roman Catholic missions, pp. 12-16; Wesleyan missions, p. 16. Hymn books: Church of England missions, p. 16; Wesleyan missions, p. 16; Roman Catholic missions, p. 16. Prayer books: Church of England missions, pp. 17-20; Wesleyan missions, pp. 20-1; Roman Catholic missions, p. 21. Scripture history, pp. 21-2. Scripture extracts: Old Testament, pp. 22-4; New Testament, pp. 25-8. Old Testament, pp. 28-36. Tracts, pp. 37-42. Sermons, pp. 42-3. Songs, fables and tales, pp. 43-5. Books of history and travels, pp. 45-8. Geography, p. 49. Books of instruction, pp. 49-51. Periodicals, pp. 51-2. Proclamations and addresses, pp. 53-7. Native literature: publications, pp. 57-64; manuscripts, pp. 64-76.—See also a letter from Bishop Patteson (part iii, p. 18) partly relating to the diffusion of the N.Z. language.
  "I have, from the earliest time to the present, done my utmost to preserve and record the languages and dialects of each of the nations amongst whom I have lived." *Grey, Address at Auckland*, 1883, p. 21.
  "Sir George Grey's services to the science of language have hardly been sufficiently appreciated as yet, and the Linguistic Library which he founded at the Cape places him of right by the side of Sir Thomas Bodley."—*Müller, Chips from a German workshop,* iv. 360.
  A biographical sketch of Dr. Bleek is given in the *Dict. of national biography,* vol. v, where the Catalogue is described as "virtually a handbook of African, Australian and Polynesian philology."

* Die Maori und Neu-Seeland. *Ausland,* nos. 50, 51.

Marsden, J. B. Memoirs | of | the Life and Labours | of the | Rev. Samuel Marsden, | of Paramatta, | Senior Chaplain of New South Wales; | and of his Early Connexion with the Missions | to New Zealand and Tahiti. | Edited by the | Rev. J. B. Marsden, M.A., | Author of "The History of the Early and Later Puritans," etc. etc. | London: | The Religious Tract Society; | 56, Paternoster Row; 65, St. Paul's Churchyard; and 164, Piccadilly: | and sold by the Booksellers.
  12°. Pp. viii, 326. There is no date, but it was published in 1858. Portrait and two engravings.
  During a visit to England in 1808-10 M. "laid the foundation of the Church of England mission to N.Z., pp. 54-9. In his memorial he laid great stress upon the necessity of civilization [=commerce and the arts] going first as the pioneer of the gospel" (p. 56), a view which was not adopted. His seven visits to N.Z. are described in chs. vi-xii, which contain many accounts of the natives (as at pp. 180-3, 217-26), and progress of the missions.
  Founded on Marsden's hitherto unpublished correspondence and other MSS. Reviewed in the *Christian Observer,* xlv. 796, lviii. 794. Marsden's missionary visits to N.Z. *ibid.* xlvi. 10, 75, 145.

*Neu-Seeland, ein günstiges Auswanderung-Gebiet. *Petermann's Mitth.*, 1858, p. 478.

*Palacky, Dr. Joh.   Zur Statistik von Neu-Seeland.   *Zeitschrift für allg. Erdkunde*, N.F., iv. 237–9 (1858).

Shaw, J.   A Gallop | to | the Antipodes, | returning | overland through India. | By | Dr. John Shaw, | Fellow of the Geological and Linnæan Societies of London, and the Botanical of Edinburgh. | Author of " Rambles in the United States, Canada, and the West Indies;" " A Tramp to the Diggings;" " Travel, and Recollections of Travel," &c. | —— | London : | J. F. Hope, 16, Great Marlborough Street. | 1858.
    p. 8°.   Pp. iv, 392.
    <small>Chs. vii. to xiii. relate to N.Z.—Queen Charlotte's Sound, Wairau, Nelson, Wanganui, Wellington; aborigines, pp. 192–8. Habits and manners of the settlers, pp. 199–206. Politics, pp. 206–15.</small>

*Sketches in New Zealand.   *Fraser's Magazine*, lix. 159.

Stones, W.   New Zealand, | (the Land of Promise) | and its Resources. | Seal | *To this Essay the Council of the Society of Arts awarded* | *the Silver Medal*. | By | William Stones. London : | Algar and Street, Clement's Lane, City, Australian and New | Zealand Gazette Office; P. S. King, Parliament Street, | Westminster, of whom all Parliamentary Documents relating to New Zealand may be obtained. | Price 4d.   Post Free, 5d.
    fcp. 8°.   Pp. viii, 80.
    <small>The title-page of another copy is somewhat different, and bears the date, 1858.
" The Council of the Society of Arts, which is in union with several hundreds of the Mechanics' and Literary Institutions throughout Great Britain, having in view the desirableness of circulating correct information regarding the British Colonies, invited the Author . . . to assist in forwarding this object by contributing a paper on New Zealand.   The portion of the present work entitled 'New Zealand and its Resources,' is the result of that invitation.   It was read by the Author on the 24th February, 1858, before the Society of Arts, and published in their Journal on the 26th February. . . .   Mr. Stones . . . has further written the various addenda descriptive of each particular settlement, and compiled the Tables of Statistics appended . . . ."   *Preface*, signed Shaw, Savill & Co.</small>

*Stones, W.   My First Voyage, a Book for Youth.   London : Simpkin, Marshall & Co.
    Date unknown.   Illus.
    <small>There " are descriptions of the countries seen upon the voyage, and especially of that to which they are bound, N.Z., and its past and present condition, occupying four chapters of the seventeen. . . . ."—*Art Journal*.</small>

Thomson, J. T.   Sketch of the | Province of Otago. | A Lecture, | (Being one of the series delivered at Dunedin), | by | J. T. Thomson, Esq., F.R.G.S. &c. ; | C.E., and Chief Surveyor. | Presented to the Subscribers to the " Colonist." | July, MDCCCLVIII.
    8°.   Pp. 16.   Printed by W. Lambert, " Otago Colonist " Office, Dunedin.

*Thomson, J. T.   Survey of the southern districts of Otago.   *Journal, Royal Geographical Society*, xxviii. 298.

Tucker, —.   The | Southern Cross | and | Southern Crown ; | or, | The Gospel in New Zealand. | By Miss Tucker, | author of " The Rainbow in the North," " Abbeokuta," | etc. | Fourth edition. | London : | James Nisbet and Co., 21, Berners Street. | 1858.
    12°.   Pp. viii, 263.   Map and illus.
    <small>Chs. iv to xxi describe Marsden's seven visits and the history of the Church Mission to 1858.   The authorities are not always stated, but some details are from an</small>

Tucker, —.—*continued.*
account by "Col. Jacob, of the Bombay Army, who visited N.Z. in 1833." The periodicals published by the C.M.S. seem to have been much used. Missionaries' private letters were also read.

Young, R. The Southern World : | Journal of a Deputation | from the | Wesleyan Conference | to New Zealand and Polynesia. | By the Rev. Robert Young. | Fourth edition, revised. | London : | Published by John Mason, 14, City-Road ; | sold at 66, Paternoster-Row. | 1858.
p. 8°. Pp. viii, 224.
Mission at Bay of Islands and Waingaroa in 1853, pp. 5–72. List of books in Maori, pp. 9–11. Whiteley's opinions on effect of missions (pp. 15–6) and colonization (pp. 16–8) on Maoris, Maori characteristics (pp. 18–20), causes of decrease of native population (pp. 20–2), and number of natives, p. 23. Conversation with chief on similar topics, pp. 30–4. Maori letters, pp. 40–4, 56–7. Discourses of native Christians, pp. 49–52.

1859.

* **Ausflug** nach Mangatawhiri und an den Waikato (Neu-Seeland). Mitth. der Wiener Geogr. Ges., iii. p. 65.

? **Busby,** James. The Preemptive Land Claims. 1859.
Map and illus.

Canterbury Papers. New Series. [London, 1859.]
No. 1, March, 1859 : Brief Account of the Province of Canterbury in 1858. No. 2, Oct. 1859 : Progress of the Settlement.
Issued in London by the Provincial Government.

Fenton, Francis Dart. Observations | on the state of the | Aboriginal Inhabitants of New Zealand. | By | F. D. Fenton, | the Compiler of the Statistical Tables of the Maori Population. | —— | Auckland : | Printed by W. C. Wilson, for the New Zealand Government, | at the Printing Office, Shortland Crescent, Auckland. | 1859.
f°.
1. General table. 2. Memorandums, pp. 1–3. Tables, statements and summary. Observations, pp. 21–44. Table of affinity of sundry chiefs.
Also in *Journal of Statistical Society,* xxiii. 508.

Fuller, F. Five Years' Residence | in | New Zealand ; | or, | Observations on Colonization. | By Francis Fuller, Esq., | (late Captain 59th Regiment), | A Resident in the Province of Canterbury. | Williams & Norgate, | 14, Henrietta Street, Covent Garden, London ; | and | 20, South Frederick Street, Edinburgh. | 1859.
p. 8°. Pp. xvi, 266.
Class of families who colonize ; religious influence ; preliminary work of establishing colonies ; price of land ; small capitalists in New Zealand ; commercial matters ; farming ; squatting ; employers and employed ; early troubles of Canterbury ; political. Chiefly founded on Canterbury experience.
What seems to be the autobiography of the writer is related at pp. 32–42.

* **Gill,** S. G. Rambles in New Zealand. London : W. H. Smith. 1859.
Davis.

? **Hamel,** Brumo L. Album of Photographic Views, taken by Dr. Hochstetter's Expedition. Auckland. 1859.
Davis.

* **Hochstetter,** Ferdinand. Bericht über geolog. Untersuchungen in der Provinz Auckland. Sitzungsber. der mathem.-naturw. Classe der kaiserl. Akademie der Wissenschaften zu Wien, xxxvii. 123.

Hochstetter, F. Lecture on the geology of the Province of Auckland. *Ibid.* pp. 162–74.

Hochstetter, F.—*continued.*
Primary formation, pp. 164-5. Secondary, p. 165. Tertiary, pp. 165-7, N.Z. brown coal, pp. 167-9. Volcanic formations and phenomena, pp. 169-71 (with Dyson's account of his ascent of Tongariro, and Burn's and Drury's accounts of White Island). Hot springs, pp. 171-3. Auckland volcanic district, pp. 173-4.
Reprinted in Hochstetter and Petermann, *Geology of New Zealand*, Auckland, 1864, pp. 8-43.

Hochstetter, F. Lecture on the geology of the Province of Nelson. *Ibid.* pp. 269-81.
i. Physical features, pp. 270-1. ii. Geological features, pp. 271-80: 1. Primitive formation of the western ranges, pp. 271-2; gold, pp. 272-4. 2. Primary formations in the eastern ranges, pp. 274-6; copper, pp. 275-6. 3. Secondary formations, pp. 276-7; Pakawa coalfield, pp. 276-7. 4. Tertiary formations, pp. 276-9; tertiary formation of Blind Bay, pp. 278-9. 5. Volcanic formations, pp. 279-80. General remarks, pp. 280-1.
Reprinted in *Ibid.* pp. 77-108.

Hochstetter, F. Report of a geological exploration of the coalfields in the Drury and Hunua district, in the Province of Auckland. *New Zealand Gazette* for 1859, pp. 9-12.

***Hochstetter**, F. Ueber die Vulkane Neu-Seelands. *Ausland*, 1859, no. 46.

***Hursthouse**, Charles. The New Zealand Land Question : a Letter to the Hon. C. W. Richmond, Colonial Treasurer of New Zealand. London, 1859. 12°.

Jacobs, Alfred. Les Européens dans l'Océanie.—Nos Antipodes, la Tasmanie et la Nouvelle-Zélande. *Revue des Deux Mondes*, Mars 15, 1859, pp. 323-49.
N.Z. pp. 337-49. A general sketch of the past history, and the position in 1859.

Lyttelton, George William, *Lord*. New Zealand | and the | Canterbury Colony. | By | Lord Lyttelton. | Read at Hagley, January 11, 1859. | London : | Edward Stanford, 6, Charing Cross. | 1859.
large cr. 8°. Pp. 40.
Lecture on the principle of the Canterbury scheme, with a sketch of its successful results.

Major, R. H. Early Voyages | to | Terra Australis, | now called | Australia : | a collection of documents, | and | extracts from early manuscript maps, | illustrative of the history of discovery | on the coasts of that vast island, | from the beginning of the sixteenth century | to the time of Captain Cook. | Edited, with an Introduction, by | R. H. Major, Esq., F.S.A. | —— | London : | Printed for the Hakluyt Society. | M.DCCC.LIX.
8°. cxix, 200+18 pp. Maps.
Mr. Major gives in his Introduction and also in his *Discoveries of Prince Henry the Navigator* (London, 1877) an account of seven manuscript maps, five in England and two in France, which show that Australia and N.Z. had been discovered very much earlier than 1542, the date of one of these maps, by Portuguese or other discoverers, but exactly when or by whom is unknown.
A. Sutherland, in *Melbourne Review*, v. 80-6, discusses Major's conclusion, and argues that the maps represent no real discovery, and were based on no real observations.
Four of the maps in question have now (1886) been reproduced from the originals in the British Museum.

New Zealand—its Progress and Resources. *Quarterly Review*, cvi. 330-68.
A general account of the Natives and of the progress of settlement. The eulogy of Sir G. Grey, pp. 348-51, seems to have been translated in the *Revue Britannique*: see *Quatrefages, Polynésiens*, p. 115 note, where the date 1857 is apparently a mistake for 1859.

***Pompallier**, *Bishop*. Prose et poésie Chretienne en Néo-Zélandais avec la traduction française en regard. Paris : Maisonneuve et Leclerck. 1859.

* Die Provinz Otago in Neu-Seeland. *Ausland*, 1859, no. 45.

*Rochfort, J. Expedition to the west coast. *Jour. R. G. Society*, xxxii. 292. 1859.

Hints to Colonists: A Series of Letters, | Intended Chiefly for Newcomers, | and originally addressed to the "New-Zealander" | Newspaper, | By "Uncle John." | Revised, and re-published by request. | New Zealand.—Colonizing.—Character in the Colonies.—The | Morals of a People.—To New Colonists, 1, 2.—To Old Colonists.—The "Caduceus."—The Land Grants.—Intending | Emigrants. | Auckland: | Published by W. C. Wilson, Shortland-Street, | 1859.

*Swainson, W. New Zealand and its Colonization. London, 1859. 8°.

Thomson, Arthur S., *M.D.* (surgeon-major 58th Regiment). The Story | of | New Zealand: | Past and Present—Savage and Civilized. | In Two Volumes. | London: | John Murray, Albemarle Street. | 1859.

p. 8°. Vol. i: pp. x, 331 ; ii : pp. viii, 368. Illustrated.

Vol. I. Part i.—The country and its native inhabitants. Ch. i. Physical geography (pp. 3-14), flora (pp. 14-20), fauna (pp. 20-35). ii. Climate. iii. Migration. iv. Physical (pp. 60-74), mental (pp. 80-4) and moral (pp. 84-7) characters; tattooing and disfigurements (pp. 74-9); language (pp. 79-80). v. Tribes (pp. 88-93); ranks, land-laws and government (pp. 94-100); tapu (pp. 100-6). vi. Mythology and superstitions. vii. War (pp. 122-41); cannibalism (pp. 141-8); slavery (pp. 149-51). viii. Food and husbandry. ix. Literature. x. Marriage (pp. 176-84); funeral rites (pp. 185-8); feasts (pp. 189-90); pastimes (pp. 190-8); knowledge (pp. 198-200, 203); salutations (pp. 200-1); ornaments (pp. 201-2); arts (pp. 202-7); standard of measurement (p. 207); houses (pp. 207-8); habits (pp. 208-10). xi. Diseases.

Vol. I. Part ii.—History of discovery by Europeans. Ch. i. Until 1810. ii. 1810 to 1838. iii. Pioneers of civilisation. iv. Introduction of Christianity.

Vol. II. Part ii. cont^d.—v. Commencement of colonisation, 1839 to 1842. vi. N.Z. in 1842. vii. Shortland's rule, 1842-3. viii. FitzRoy's, 1843-5. ix. Grey's, 1845-53. x. Wynyard's, 1854-5. xi. Browne's, 1855-9.

Vol. II. Part iii.—Decrease of the Maoris. Ch. i. Are they decreasing? ii. Progress of civilisation among them and means to promote it. iii. Hints to emigrants.

Appendix ii. 319-38: 25 tables of statistics.

Bibliography, ii. 341-62: describes "90 volumes, 200 pamphlets, and nearly a hundred-weight of parliamentary papers."

"During eleven years' residence I saw much of the country; held intercourse with representative men; sojourned for nine months among the aborigines in the interior; was permitted . . . to consult many unpublished official documents . . ."—*Preface.*

Reviewed in *Ausland*, 1860, no. 19; and in the *Christian Observer*, lx. 452. 1860.

1860.

*Arthur Thomson's Geschichte der Unterverfassung von Neu-Seeland. *Ausland*, 1860, no. 19.

Bennett, G. Gatherings of a Naturalist | in | Australasia : | being | observations principally on the | Animal and Vegetable Productions | of | New South Wales, New Zealand, | and some of the | Austral Islands. | By | George Bennett, M.D., F.L.S., F.Z.S., | Fellow of the Royal College of Surgeons of England ; | Member of the Medical Faculty of the University of Sydney, New South Wales ; | and | Author of "Wanderings in New South Wales, Singapore, and China." | London : | John Van Voorst, Paternoster Row. | MDCCCLX.

8°. Pp. xii, 456. Illus.

Ch. xxii gives an account of medicinal remedies in Polynesia, flax and flax-dyeing, &c.

Browne, *Rev.* E. Harold. The case of the war in New Zealand. From authentic documents. Cambridge. 1860.
    8°. Pp. 51.
        Brother of Governor Browne. Afterwards Bishop of Ely.
        Preface, pp. 5–6. Section I. History of events, pp. 7–19. Ii. Principles, pp. 20–46. Notes, pp. 47–51.

Buddle, *Rev.* Thomas. The Maori King movement in New Zealand, with a full report of the native meetings held at Waikato, April and May, 1860. Auckland, 1860.
    8°. Pp. 72.
        Origin, pp. 3–15. Objects, pp. 16–22. Professed principles of action, pp. 23–6. Progress, pp. 27–62. Results, pp. 62–7. Probable future, pp. 67–71. Postscript, p. 71.

Busby, James. Illustrations | of the | System called Responsible Government. | In a letter to His Excellency, | Colonel Gore Browne, C.B., | Governor-in-Chief &c., &c., &c. | By | James Busby, Esq. | Auckland : | Printed by W. C. Wilson, Shortland-Street, | 1860.
    8°. Pp. 42, vi.
        Mr. Busby claimed 40,000 to 50,000 acres; the Commissioners granted him 2,023. On p. vi is a list of Busby's publications.

Busby, J. Remarks | upon a pamphlet | entitled | " The Taranaki Question, by Sir William | Martin | D.C.L., late Chief Justice of | New Zealand ;" | by | James Busby, Esq. | formerly H.M. Resident in New Zealand. | Auckland : | printed by Philip Kunst, " Southern Cross " office. | 1860.
    8°. Pp. 114. Reprinted in Appendix to Journals, House of Representatives, E. 2.
        " The draft of the Treaty [of Waitangi] prepared by me was adopted by Captain Hobson without any other alteration than a transposition of certain sentences, which did not in any degree affect the sense " (p. 4). Mr. Busby had been Resident for seven years prior to 1840.
        See reply by G. Clarke, 1861.
        Busby's appointment and arrival are described in *Rusden*, I. 160–70.

*****Busby**, J. The Right of a British Colonist to the Protection of the Queen and Parliament of England: a letter to the Duke of Newcastle. Auckland. 1860.
    Pp. 12.

* Dr. Hochstetter's Karten von Neu-Seeland. (Nach einem Vortrag in der k.k. geogr. Ges. zu Wien, Feb. 7, 1860.) *Zeit. f. allg. Erdk.*, N.F., viii. 263–5.

Fenton, F. D. Native race of New Zealand. *Journal of the Statistical Society*, xxiii. 508.
    See 1859.

*****Fox**, William. The War in New Zealand. London: Williams and Norgate. 1860.
    cr. 8°.
        General description of New Zealand, constitutional, statistical, geographical; and some notes on the aborigines, their number, civilization, and character, and the effect of missionary influence upon them.

* Goldfelder und fossile Knochen in Neu-Seeland. *Ausland*, 1860, no. 14.

*****Haast**, J. Dr. Ferdinand Hochstetter's Reise durch die nördliche Insel Neu-Seelands, 5 März bis 24 Mai, 1859. *Petermann's Mitth.*, 1860, p. 107.

Heaphy, Charles. On the volcanic country of Auckland. *Quarterly Journal of the Geological Society*, 1860, xvi. 242–52.
    Reprinted in *Southern Monthly Magazine*, i. 118–22.

* **Hadfield**, *Archdeacon* Octavius. One of England's little wars. A letter to the Right Hon. the Duke of Newcastle, Secretary of State for the Colonies. London [1860 ?].

Martin, *Sir* W. The | Taranaki question. | By | Sir W. Martin, D.C.L., | late Chief Justice of New Zealand. | Auckland : | printed at the Melanesian press. | 1860.

    8°. Pp. 152.

i. Native tenure of land, pp. 1-10. ii. Waitara purchase, pp. 10-17. iii. The points in dispute, pp. 17-44. iv. The investigation, pp. 44-63. v. Resort to force, pp. 63-81. vi. The consequences, pp. 81-130. Appendix A. State of Taranaki tribes, pp. 131-6. B. Conclusion of the Waikato Committee on the King Movement, pp. 137-9. C. Original text of Maori letters, pp. 140-152.

"The following Remarks are printed for circulation among Members of the Imperial Parliament and Members of the General Assembly of New Zealand."—*On page facing Contents.*

The pamphlet is reproduced in the Appendix to the Journals of the House of Representatives, 1860, E-No. 2.

See Rusden, *History of N.Z.*, ii. 28.

* Mittheilungen aus Neu-Seeland. *Ausland*, 1860, no. 4.

* Mythology of New Zealand. *Christian Remembrancer*, xxxi. 430. 1860.

* Die neue Aufstand der Maori auf Neu-Seeland. *Ausland*, 1860.

* New Zealand. *London Quarterly Review*, xv. 519; *Tait's Magazine*, N.S., xxvii. 406.

* New Zealand and its affairs, past and present. *Christian Remembrancer*, xlvii. 427. 1860.

* Notizen über Australien und Neu-Seeland. *Ausland*, 1860, no. 46.

Proceedings | of the | Kohimarama Conference, | Comprising nos. 13 to 18 of the "Maori Messenger." | (Edited by the Secretary of the Conference.) | Auckland : | Printed by W. C. Wilson for the New Zealand Government.

    4°. From July 14 to Nov. 30, 1860.

Gives a list of chiefs at the Conference, "with the names of their respective tribes, and their several places of abode;" address of Governor Browne and messages from him; speeches of Mr. Donald McLean, and of chiefs; replies (with songs) from the various tribes to the Governor's address; Chief Justice Martin's rules for the administration of justice; Potatau's speech to his Council; leading articles.

The Conference commenced on July 10, 1860, and was formally dismissed on Aug. 11. It was summoned to afford the chiefs "an opportunity of discussing various matters connected with the welfare and advancement of the two races dwelling in New Zealand." The Governor invited special attention to the King movement. Ex-Chief Justice Martin's rules for the administration of justice; the Waitara purchase and the origin of the war at Taranaki; Maori land-customs; the Treaty of Waitangi; and, generally, the relations between the Maoris and the colonists were discussed. The resolutions adopted by the Conference are printed in no. 16.

Rusden describes the meeting, ii. 7-10. Minutes of the proceedings are in the Appendix to the Journals H. of R., 1860, E 9.

Ridgway, A. F. Voices from Auckland, | New Zealand. | Reliable information | for | Intending Emigrants to that Province ; | to which are added the latest | Waste Land Regulations, | with explanatory notes. | Compiled by | Alex. F. Ridgway & Sons, | General Agents to the | Provincial Government of Auckland. | London : | Alex. F. Ridgway & Sons, 40, Leicester Square, London—W.C. | 1860. | Price Sixpence.

    8°. Pp. xii, 115.

Extracts from *Swainson*, *New-Zealander*, *Illustrated London News*, Uncle John's *Hints*, *Taylor*, letters from Immigration Agent and from settlers. Notes about the Nova Scotians at Waipu, pp. 70-6.

Taranaki. [Papers of great importance on the land question and the war of 1860–1 appear in the Journals, House of Representatives, 1860 and 1861, Appendix E.]

Tasman, Abel Jansz. Journal | van | de Reis naer het onbekende | Zuidland, | in den Jare 1642, | door Abel Jansz Tasman, | met de Schepen | Heemskerck en de Zeehaen. | Medegedeeld en met eenige Aanteekeningen voorzien, | door Jacob Swart, | —— | Met eene Kaart. | Te Amsterdam, | bij de Wed. G. Hulst van Keulen. | 1860.

    8°. Pp. viii, 189.

    Swart's preface, pp. v–vi. Introduction, pp. 1–5. Letter of Authonie van Diemen, pp. 6–8. Instructions to Tasman, pp. 9–32. Instructions to Pool, pp. 32–7. Tasman's Journal, pp. 38–182. Observations on the map of Tasman's voyage, pp. 182–6; on the voyage, pp. 186–9.

    N.Z., pp. 83–6. Tasman's observations are summarised in Tylor, *Researches into the early history of mankind*, ed. 2, pp. 103–4.

* **Thomson's** Story of New Zealand. *Christian Observer*, lx. 452. 1860.

1861.

* **Aylmer,** I. E. Difficulty in New Zealand. *Once a Week*, v. 348.

Bowen, C. C. Poems | by | Charles C. Bowen. Christchurch, New Zealand. | Published at the Union Office, Gloucester Street. | MDCCCLXI.

    12°. Pp. 190.

    "The battle of the free;" "Moonlight in New Zealand;" "Change not the name"—relate to N.Z.

Brodie, Walter. New Zealand and the Constitution Act. Reasons against the re-appointment of Sir George Gray [sic], K.T. [sic].

    Pp. 32. [London, 1861?]

* **Clarke,** G. Remarks on a pamphlet by J. Busby, Esq., commenting upon a pamphlet entitled ' The Taranaki Question,' by Sir W. Martin, D.C.L., late Chief Justice of New Zealand. Auckland, 1861.

    "Mr. George Clarke, the lay agent of the Church Missionary Society in New Zealand, and formerly a catechist and gunsmith of some skill, appeared as the Chief Protector of the Aborigines."—E. J. *Wakefield, Adventure*, ii. 47, who goes on to give an account of his doings, pp. 47–53, and of Mr. Clarke junior, ii. 194–5. Mr. Clarke, sen., arrived in N.Z. in 1824 (*First ten years' quarterly papers*, no. 42). The author of the pamphlet is presumably Mr. Clarke, junior.

Crawford, J. C. Remarks | upon | Railways, | suggesting the | Opening of a Timber Trade | in the | Province of Wellington. | By | J. C. Crawford, M.L.C. | Printed at the "Spectator" Office, Wellington, New Zealand. | 1861.

    8°. Pp. 12.

* **Eley,** H. Traditions of the Deluge among the Maoris. *Recreative Science*, ii. 195. 1861.

* **Expeditionen** in den Alpen-Regionen Neu-Seelands. *Petermann's Mith.*, 1861, p. 77.

Gilbert, Thomas. New Zealand | Settlers and Soldiers; | or, | The War in Taranaki; | being | Incidents in the Life of a Settler. | By | Rev. Thomas Gilbert, | formerly Pastor of the General Baptist Church, Ditchling, | Sussex. | London : | A. W. Bennett, 5, Bishopsgate Without; Houlston and Wright, 65, Paternoster Row. | 1861.

    p. 8°. Pp. iv, 220. Six illus.

    A narrative from experience of events in the war of 1860. The publisher appends (pp. 165–220) "extracts from Colonial papers, which give a general outline of the history of the war from the time Mr. Gilbert left Taranaki."

* Gold-diggings of New Zealand. *Colburn's Monthly Magazine*, cxxiv. 219. 1861.

* Haast, J. On the physical geography of New Zealand, principally in reference to the Southern Alps. Proceedings of the Royal Society of Melbourne, 1861.

Haast, J. Report | of a | Topographical and Geological | Exploration | of the | Western Districts of the Nelson Province, | New Zealand. | Undertaken for the Provincial Government by | Julius Haast, Esq. | Published by Authority. | Nelson : Printed by C. and J. Elliott. | 1861.

8°. Pp. viii, 150.

Ch. i. Descriptive narrative of the journey, pp. 1-69. ii. Physical geography, pp. 70-88. iii. Geology, pp. 89-124. iv. Roads, passes, and available land, pp. 125-33. v. Zoology, pp. 134-45. vi. Botany, pp. 146-50.

Hadfield, Octavius. The second year of one of England's little wars. London. [1861.]

8°. Pp. 90.

Occasioned by Prof. Harold Browne's pamphlet.
Notes by Sir W. Martin, pp. 23-8. Miscellaneous notes on Prof. Browne's pamphlet, &c., pp. 29-40. Appendix, pp. 41-90 (mainly letters, but also report of Maori meeting at Whakaairo, pp. 74-9, and Renata's reply to the Superintendent of Hawke's Bay, pp. 79-90).

Hadfield, Octavius. A sequel to " One of England's little wars : " being an account of the real origin of the war in New Zealand, its present stage, and the future prospects of the Colony. London, 1861.

8°. Pp. 16.

* Hartwig, Georg. Die Inseln des grossen Oceans. London, 1861.

Hawtrey, *Rev.* Montague J. G. Justice to New Zealand, honour to England. London, 1861.

12°. Pp. 108.

Letter to the Duke of Newcastle, pp. 5-9. i. On the general principle of exceptional laws, pp. 12-26. ii. Compensation to the New Zealander for the cession of his land *versus* the New Zealand land-league, pp. 27-43. iii. Compensation to the New Zealander for the cession of his sovereignty *versus* the native king movement, pp. 44-79. iv. Amalgamation.—Les Gombettes, pp. 80-92. v. " The real question at issue," pp. 93-108.

* Der Maorikrieg auf Neu-Seeland. *Ausland*, 1861, nos. 3, 10.

Martin, *Sir* W. Remarks | on | " Notes published for the | New Zealand Government," | January, 1861. | and on | Mr. Richmond's memorandum | on the Taranaki question, | December, 1860. | By | Sir W. Martin, D.C.L. | late Chief Justice of New Zealand. | Auckland : | printed at the Melanesian press. | 1861.

8°. Pp. 48 and addendum.

Sir W. Martin states that " the publication of the official *Notes* was followed shortly after by a Notification in the *New Zealand Gazette* (25 Jan. 1861) deprecating public criticism on the conduct and policy of the Government." In deference to the wish of the Government, Sir W. Martin abstains " for the present from giving publicity within the colony to the following pages."

Remarks on Notes, pp. 1-29; on Mr. Richmond's Memorandum, pp. 30-47. Maori letter, p. 48. Addendum, next page.

The notification above referred to was issued after the publication in Maori of portions of Sir W. Martin's pamphlet (*Rusden*, ii. 33-4).

Memorial to His Grace the Secretary of State for the Colonies; together with a memorandum on New Zealand affairs. London: Church Missionary House, 1861.

    8°. Pp. 46.

    Memorial of the Church Missionary Society, pp. v–xl., Memorandum, pp. 1–23:— I. Wiremu Kingi's tribal right in the Waitara a matter for judicial inquiry. II. Te Teira's title alleged to be incomplete. III. The precipitate declaration of war. Ten appendices, pp. 25–46.

Mythology of Polynesia. *Westminster Review*, xxi n.s., lxxvii o.s., pp. 303–39. 1861.

    N.Z., pp. 300–15. From Taylor, Shortland, Thomson, and Grey.

*New Zealand. *All the Year Round*, vi. 180; *Macmillan's Magazine*, iii. 328.

New Zealand. A Vindication of the character of the missionaries and native Christians. London: Church Missionary House, 1861.

    8°. Pp. 35.

    Introduction, pp. 1–2. The services rendered by the missionary body, pp. 2–11. The native character marked by good faith and a desire for law, pp. 11–25. Appendix A. Three letters from Wiremu Kingi to Archdeacon Hadfield, pp. 27–9. B. Extracts from the reports of Mr. Fenton and the Waikato Committee, pp. 30–5.

New Zealand Company. Thirty-sixth Report | of | The Court of Directors | of the | New Zealand Company.

    Pp. 2. No date is given, but it must have been issued in 1861.

    The Report refers to "the outstanding debt on account of the Canterbury Settlement, amounting to £26,587 14s. 8d., without any calculation of interest."

    The last report of the Company. The 12th (London, 1844) is especially important. Most of the first twenty-five appeared in the *N.Z. Journal*.

The New Zealand war of 1860; an inquiry into its origin and justice, together with some remarks on the land question, in relation to the natives. *Copied, with additions, from the "Colonial Intelligencer:" the organ of the Aborigines' Protection Society.* London [1861?].

    8°. Pp. 52.

    Ch. i. Colonisation: the land question and the natives, pp. 3–27. ii. What the missionaries say of the New Zealand war, pp. 27–34. iii. An inquiry into the origin of the war, pp. 34–48. Extract from the Bishop of New Zealand's pastoral letter to the members of the Church of England in New Plymouth, pp. 49–50. Archdeacon Hadfield on the land league, pp. 50–2.

Notes | on | Sir William Martin's pamphlet | entitled the | Taranaki question. | [*Published for the New Zealand Government.*] Auckland, January, 1861.

    8°. Consists of 64 leaves printed on one side only, and without pagination. The title-page is headed—[Revised copy.]

    The *Notes* appear in the Appendix to the Journals of the House of Representatives, 1861, E2 no. 2, with the preface—"Copy of a Memorandum by Mr. Weld.—The following Notes, on Sir William Martin's pamphlet, have been published by the General Government.—FRED. A. WELD."

    Sir W. Martin's pamphlet is criticized page by page.

    "'Notes by the Governor on Sir William Martin's pamphlet' were officially promulgated. . . . From a revised edition the Governor's name was withdrawn." —*Rusden*, ii. 20.

    See notes on authorship of "Notes" in reply to Martin in *Swainson, N.Z. and the war*, pp. 134–9.

Owen, R. On the remains of a pleiosaurian reptile (*Pleiosaurus australis*) from the oolitic formation in the Middle Island of New Zealand. Proceedings of the British Association, 1861, pp. 122–3.

    The remains show that extensive geological range of a species involves wide chronological range, and indicate the existence of jurassic strata.

Paul, R. B. New Zealand, | as it was and as it is. | By | Robert Bateman Paul, M.A., | late Archdeacon of Nelson. | —— | London : | Edward Stanford, 6, Charing Cross. | 1861.
    fcp. 8°. Pp. iii (not numbered), 63+1. Map.
    Generally descriptive.

* Reise der österreichischen Fregatte Novara um die Erde, 1857-59. 3 Bände. Wien, 1861.
    N.Z.: Bd. 3, S. 96-172.

* Reminiscences of a Veteran : Being Personal and Military Adventures in Portugal, Spain, France, Malta, New South Wales, Norfolk Island, New Zealand, Andaman Islands, and India. London: Skeet. 1861.
    8°. 3 vols.—*Davis.*

* Reminiscences of New Zealand. *Fraser's Magazine.* 1861.
    Describes the voyage of the *John Wycliffe* to Otago, &c.

[**Richmond**, C. W.] Memorandum | by | Mr. Richmond | in reply to | a pamphlet by Sir W. Martin, D.C.L., | on | the Taranaki question. | Auckland : | 1861.
    In Appendix to Journals of House of Representatives, 1861, E-No. 2.
    f°. Pp. 27. Signed—C. W. Richmond.
    The divisions are those of Sir W. Martin's first pamphlet.
    "Mr. Richmond's eagerness in the cause removed all doubt as to the moving spirit in the 'Notes,' for he wrote a separate ' Memorandum' in which whole sentences were word by word the same as in the 'Notes.'"—*Itusden*, ii. 29. See also ii 29-32.

* **Schmarda**, L. Reise um die Erde, 1853-67. 3 Bände. Braunschweig, 1861.
    N.Z.: Bd. 2, S. 180-228.

Sclater, Philip Lutley, *and* **Hochstetter**, Ferdinand *von*. Report on the present state of our knowledge of the birds of the genus *Apteryx* living in New Zealand. *Report of British Association,* 1861, pp. 176-8.
    1. Apteryx australis. 2. A. owenii. 3. A. mantelli. 4. A. maxima.

Taranaki : | a Tale of the War. | With | a Description of the Province | previous to and during the war; | also | An Account | (chiefly taken from the despatches) | of the | Principal Contests with the Natives | during that eventful period. | Auckland : | Printed and published by W. C. Wilson. | 1861.
    fcp. 8°. Pp. 128.
    War of 1860-61. ". . . our object is merely, from individual experience, to write a story, pleasing, beneficial, and truthful for our readers, that they may be led therefrom to form not only a correct impression of the war, but see the real cause in its proper light, of its origin and continuance " (p. 10).
    Adversely reviewed in *Chapman's New Zealand Magazine*, i. 80-4.

White, John. Lectures | on | Maori Customs and Superstitions, | Delivered in the Mechanics' Institute, Auckland, | by | John White, Esq. | Laid on the table of the House of Representatives August 21st, 1861, and ordered to be printed. [Appendix to the Journals of the House of Representatives, 1861, E-No. 7.]
    f°. Pp. 48.
    Lecture i.—1. Legends relating to the origin of the Maoris, their cosmogony, myth of Maui, their migration, principal deities and superstitions, ceremonies—religious and other, initiation, tattooing, &c. 2. Priestcraft and witchcraft (with ceremonies and incantations), war and its rites. Lecture ii.—1. Laws and customs in relation to land. 2. Location of tribes, mana of chiefs.
    There are many translations of traditional poetry.
    The lectures were reprinted in Gudgeon's *History and doings of the Maoris*, 1885.

1862.

Chapman's | New Zealand | Monthly | Magazine | Literary, Scientific, and Miscellaneous. Vol. I. | New Zealand | Published by G. T. Chapman, | Bookseller and Stationer | Queen Street | Auckland.

8°. Pp. xvi, 240. Published in August, September, October, November, and December, 1862.

<small>Sketches of past generation of Maoris, pp. 4, 193, by C. Heaphy. History of N.Z., pp. 23 (reprint of Tasman's Journal), 85, 132, 185, 236 (Cook's journal). Maori tale, p. 70. First experiences, pp. 75, 137, 227. Trees and woods of N.Z., p. 150. Visit to greenstone country, pp. 107, 166. Geology of N.Z., by Rev. R. Taylor, pp. 176-85. Puke Hina, a legend of Mount Eden (as recited to C. Heaphy), p. 193. Among the Maoris, p. 211. Geological age of N.Z., by R. Taylor, pp. 216-25.</small>

Esquiros, Alphonse. L'Angleterre et la vie anglaise, xviii. *Revue des Deux Mondes*, seconde période, t. xlii. 783-7.

<small>A pathetic description of a visit to an emigrant ship for N.Z. at the West India Docks. See translation under 1863.</small>

FitzGerald, J. E. The | Native Policy | of New Zealand. | A Speech delivered in the House of Representatives, | of New Zealand, | August 6, 1862, | by | James Edward FitzGerald | Printed by Mackenzie and Muir, Wellington, N.Z.

8°. Pp. 36.

Flanagan, Roderick. The | History of New South Wales; | with an Account of | Van Diemen's Land [Tasmania] ; | New Zealand, Port Phillip [Victoria], | Moreton Bay, | and other Australasian Settlements. Comprising a Complete View of the | Progress and Prospects of Gold Mining in Australia. | The whole compiled from official and other authentic | and original sources. | By | Roderick Flanagan, | Member of the Australian Literary Institute, and of the Philosophical Society | of New South Wales. | —— | —— | London: | Sampson Low, Son, & Co., 47, Ludgate Hill. | 1862.

8°. 2 vols. Pp. xvi, 544 ; x, 576.

<small>Vol. ii.: pp. 113-7 describe the war in N.Z. in 1845. At p. 118 is described a public meeting in Sydney, promoted by gentlemen connected with N.Z. and addressed by a sufferer from the evacuation of Kororarika. A resolution was adopted advising the despatch of troops and steamers.</small>

* **Fyfe**, J. H. Census of New Zealand. *Once a Week*, viii. 13.

* Die Goldwäschereien auf Neu-Seeland. *Ausland*, 1862, no. 4.

Grayling, W. I. The | War in Taranaki, | During the Years | 1860-61. | By | W. I. Grayling, | of the | Taranaki Volunteer Rifles. | New Plymouth : | G. W. Woon, "Herald" Office, Devon Street. | 1862.

8°. Pp. vi, 112, but continuous (vi+106). Illustrations, plan and map.

<small>General history, pp. 13-76. Explanation of plans, pp. 78-88. Killed and wounded, pp. 89-93. Documents, pp. 94-108. List of settlers whose homesteads were burned, pp. 108-12.</small>

* Haast's Erforschung der Alpen Neu-Seelands. *Peterm. Mith.*, 1862, p. 36.

* Handbook of Otago and Southland, New Zealand. London: F. Algar. 1862.

8°. Pp. 16. Map.—*Davis*.

* **Hochstetter**, F. *von*. Geographische Skizze von Neu-Seeland. *Peterm. Mith.*, 1862, p. 367.

* **Hochstetter**, F. *von*. Der Isthmus von Auckland in Neuseeland. *Ibid.*, 1862, p. 81.

* **Hochstetter**, F. von. Rotomahana oder der warme See in der Provinz Auckland auf der Nordinsel von Neu-Seeland. *Ibid.*, 1862, p. 263.

Hodder, Edwin. Memories | of | New Zealand Life. | By | Edwin Hodder. | London : | Longman, Green, Longman and Roberts. | 1862.
    cr. 8°. Pp. viii, 232.
> Nelson, p. 29. Colonial society, p. 49. Six weeks at the diggings [Massacre Bay], p. 63. Incidents of daily life, p. 85. Summer holiday ramble, p. 107. Trip to Wellington, p. 119. On the ranges, p. 137. In the bush, p. 153. Exploring, p. 168. Taranaki, p. 192. Taranaki war [of 1860], p. 205. Appendix A. Nelson gold-fields, p. 183. B. Taranaki war—battle of Mahoetahi, p. 227. C. Taranaki iron-sand, p. 229. D. Moa's egg and footprints, pp. 231-2.

Lindsay, W. Lauder. On the geology of the goldfields of Otago, New Zealand. Proceedings of British Association, 1862 : *Report*, pp. 77–80.
> Results of a personal examination between Oct. 1861 and Jan. 1862. Has three tables of comparative produce of three fields.

Lindsay, W. L. On the geology of the gold-fields of Auckland, New Zealand. *Ibid.*, pp. 80–2.
> Results of a personal examination in Feb. 1862.

Lindsay, W. L. On the toot-poison of New Zealand. Proceedings of the British Association, 1862. *Report* (Notices and abstracts), pp. 98–100.— Toot plant and poison of New Zealand : *British and Foreign Medico-Chirurgical Review*, July 1865 ; *Seemann's Journal of Botany*, vol. i., p. 247.
> Class, portion poisonous, peculiarities, remedies, genus of plant.

Lindsay, W. L. The Place and Power | of | Natural History | in | Colonisation ; | with Special Reference to Otago : | being portions of a lecture prepared for, and | at the request of the | " Young Men's Christian Association " of Dunedin. | By | W. Lauder Lindsay, M.D., | F.R.S. Edin., F.L.S., & F.R.G.S., London, &c. | Dunedin : | Printed for the Association, by John Dick, " Colonist " Office, | Stafford-Street. | MDCCCLXII.
    8°. Pp. 29 and advertisement.
> Geology of Otago, pp. 10-8. Museum of local natural history, pp. 18-24.
> "Dr. Lauder Lindsay is an eminent Naturalist, who has visited our shores in the pursuit of health, and has devoted such portions of his time as his health would admit of to the prosecution of Geological and Botanical researches, principally in the neighbourhood of Dunedin."—*R. Gillies, preface* to lecture. The lecture was apparently not delivered.

Marjouram, *Sergeant* W. : see **White**.

* [**Marshman**, John.] Canterbury, New Zealand, in 1862. London, 1862.
> See Marshman, 1864.

* **Maunsell** [Archdeacon ?]. Die Fortschritte der Maori in der Civilisation. *Ausland*, 1862, no. 23.

New Zealand. *National Review*, vol. xv. 519–52. Oct. 1862.
> General—resting mainly on Thomson. Quotes from Rev. Walter Lawry the expression of the belief that whites and Maoris will blend into "a fine new race of civilized mixed people."

* **New Zealand** and its Gold Fields. *Leisure Hour*, xi. 422, 537.

Note on the coexistence of Man with the Dinornis in New Zealand. *Natural History Review*, vii. 343.

* **Otago** : its Gold Fields and Resources. Melbourne, 1862.
> Pamphlet.—*Davis*.

* **Politische** Eintheilung und Bevölkerung im Neu-Seeland im December, 1861. *Peterm. Mith.*, 1862, p. 263.

[**Richardson**, *Sir* J. L. C.] Sketch | of | Otago, New Zealand, | as a Field of | British Emigration. | With illustrations. | Edinburgh : Bell and Bradfute. | London : F. Algar, and George Street. | Glasgow : John Smith & Son. | Aberdeen : S. Maclean. | 1862.

    8°. Pp. iv, 80. Coloured frontispiece (which has a slightly different title), map and 3 illus.—all coloured.

* **Rochfort**, J. Journal of Two Expeditions to the West Coast of the Middle Island of New Zealand in the year 1859. By John Rochfort, Esq., of Nelson, Surveyor. *Journal, Royal Geographical Society*, xxxii. 294.

[**Russell**, John.] Some Account | of a | Singular Expedient employed by Providence | to throw Light upon | the Present Complications | of the | Government of New Zealand. | —— | Sydney : | Printed by F. White, William Street. | 1862.

    12°. Pp. 16.

    Personal. The writer refers to a book, *Footsteps unknown*, published in 1862. The "first thoughts" he "published in N.Z. are those dated September, 1856." He wrote something else in 1859: see p. 8. "There is a battle between the writer and the Queen's Government in N.Z." (p. 3), and the three publications named are engagements in it.

Swainson, W. New Zealand | and | the War. | By | William Swainson, Esq., | Formerly Attorney-General for New Zealand, | Author of | "New Zealand and its Colonization," etc. | London : | Smith, Elder and Co., 65, Cornhill. | M.DCCC.LXII.

    p. 8°. Pp. vii, 199.

    Ch. i. Generally descriptive of the country, the political Constitution, and (pp. 12–18) the Church Constitution, Maori land-leagues (pp. 18–24), Maori-king movement (pp. 25–38, from accounts of W. Thompson and Renata). ii. Before the outbreak Maori land-tenure; cause of the outbreak. iii, iv. Waitara. iv, v. Occupation of Waitara. vi. Debates and pamphlets. vii. War. viii. Right and wrong of it.

White, W. Memorials | of | Sergeant William Marjouram, | Royal Artillery ; | including Six Years' Service in New Zealand, | during the late Maori War. | Edited by | Sergeant William White, Royal Artillery. | With a Preface | by the Author of "Memorials of Captain Hedley Vicars." | Third Edition. | London : | James Nisbet and Co., 21 Berners Street. | M.DCCC.LXII.

    cr. 8°. Pp. xx, 382. Portrait.

    Ch. v. New Zealand (New Plymouth, 1855–6). vi. Disturbances (Taranaki, 1858). vii. Tempest. viii. Sunshine and harvest. ix. Progress. x. Anxieties. xi. Incidents. xii. A chequered path. xiii. War (Taranaki, 1860). xiv. The conflict deepens. xv. Camp life. xvi. Maori tactics. xvii. Gloomy anticipations. xviii. A sorrowful story. xix. Progress of events. xx. Maori warfare. xxi. Retrospect. xxii. Health declines. xxiii. Auckland.

    Mainly extracts from Marjouram's diary, describing evangelizing work among the soldiers, with incidental accounts of native troubles.

    The first edition was published in 1861.

1863.

Alexander, *Sir* J. E. Incidents | of | The Maori War. | New Zealand, | In 1860–61. | By | Colonel Sir James E. Alexander, | Knt. K.C.L.S., F.R.G.S., and R.A.S. | Author of "A Campaign in Cafferland," "Explorations in Africa, | America," &c. | —— | London : | Richard Bentley, New Burlington Street. | Publisher in Ordinary to Her Majesty. | 1863.

    cr. 8°. Pp. vi, 425.

    Ch. ii. The Maories in 1800. iii. Taranaki and the T. question. iv. Beginning of hostilities. v, vi, vii. Military operations. viii, ix. Kohimarama Conference; liberality of Victoria, and of Canterbury; continuance of operations. x–xv. Operations. xvi. Illustrations of Maori character during the war. xviii. N.Z. generally. Appendix, pp. 415–25 : Armstrong gun at Taranaki.

* Among the Maoris. *All the Year Round,* x. 309. 1863.

Butler, Samuel. A First Year | in | Canterbury Settlement. | By | Samuel Butler. | London : | Longman, Green, Longman, Roberts, & Green. | 1863.
    p. 8°. Pp. x, 162. Map.
    <small>Pastoral enterprise in Canterbury in 1860.</small>

Carey, —. Narrative | of | the Late War | in | New Zealand. | By | Lieutenant-Colonel Carey, C.B. | Deputy-Adjutant-General | London | Richard Bentley | —— | 1863.
    p. 8°. Pp. v, 199. One coloured illustration.
    <small>A " brief narrative of the events of the . . war of 1860–61, in the Taranaki district, so far as the military operations under Major-General Pratt are concerned."</small>

* Die deutschen Ansiedler in Nelson und ihre Schicksale. *Globus,* iv. 93 (1863).

Esquiros, A. The | English at Home. | Essays from the "Revue des Deux Mondes." | Third series. | By | Alphonse Esquiros, | author of the "Dutch at Home," etc. | Translated by | Sir Lascelles Wraxall, Bart. | London : | Chapman and Hall, 193, Piccadilly. | MDCCCLXIII.
    12°.
    <small>At pp. 166–74 is a description of a visit to an emigrant ship bound for N.Z.</small>

* Gebirge u. Vulkane auf Neuseeland. *Globus,* iv., 59 (1863).

* **Godley**, J. R. Letters from John Robert Godley to C. B. Adderley, 1839–61. London : 1863.
    8°. Portrait.—*Davis.*

Godley, J. R. A | Selection from the | Writings and Speeches | of | John Robert Godley. | Collected and edited by | James Edward FitzGerald. | —— | New Zealand : | Press Office, Christchurch. | 1863.
    8°. Pp. viii, 330.
    <small>Memoir, pp. 1–32. On the government of colonies (a letter to Mr. Gladstone written at Plymouth the night before Mr. Godley sailed for New Zealand [Dec. 12, 1849], and originally published in the form of a pamphlet in London immediately after his departure), pp. 33–42.</small>

* **Haast**, J. On the coal measures and lignitiferous beds of the river Kowai, Province of Canterbury. Christchurch. 1863.

* J. Haast's Forschungen in den Alpen Neu-Seelands. *Peterm. Mitt.,* 1863, p. 214.

Hector, J. Geological expedition to the west coast of Otago. *Otago Provincial Government Gazette,* Nov. 5, 1863, vi. 435–68. With sketch map.

Heywood, B. A. A | Vacation Tour | at the | Antipodes, | through Victoria, Tasmania, New South Wales, | Queensland, and New Zealand, | in 1861-1862. | By | B. A. Heywood, M.A., | Trinity College Cambridge. | London : | Longman, Green, Longman, Roberts, & Green. | 1863.
    p. 8°. Pp. viii, 251. 8 illustrations, and two ancient maps—one Tasman's Chart.
    <small>Ch. iii, pp. 134–231, relates to N.Z.; it describes, with historical references, a tour through both islands in 1861-2. There are views of the Tasman and Great Godley Glaciers, Dunedin, Gabriel's Gully, Potatau's pah. Provincial statistics for 1861, p. 250.</small>

* **Hochstetter**, F. *von,* u. **Petermann**, A. Geologisch-topographischer Atlas von Neu-Seeland. Sechs Karten, hauptsächlich Gebiete der Provinzen Auckland und Nelson umfassend, mit kurzen Erläuterungen. Gotha. 1863.
    <small>Erl. i. Bemerkung über die kartographische Kenntniss von Neu-Seeland (Petermann).
    See 1864.</small>

Hochstetter, F. *von.* Neu-Seeland | von | Dr. Ferdinand von Hochstetter. | Mit 2 Karten, 6 Farbenstahlstichen, 9 grossen Holzschnitten und 80 in den Text gedruckten | Holzschnitten. | Stuttgart. | Cotta'scher Verlag. | 1863.
 4°. Pp. xx, 555.

   Vorwort, pp. vii-ix.—Inhalt:—i. Neun monate auf Neu-Seeland. ii. Physisch-geographische skizze von Neu-Seeland. iii. Traditionen u. mythen. iv. Geschichtliches und politisches. v. Isthmus von Auckland, einst u. jetzt. vi. Norduter. vii. Ausflug nach dem Manukau-Hafen u. der Mündung des Waikato-flusses. viii. Kauri-wälder. ix. Am untern Waikato, von Auckland über Mangatawhiri zum Taupiri. x. Waipa u. die Westküste. xi. Vom Waipa durch den Mokau- u. Tuhua-district nach dem Taupo-see. xii. Taupo-see, Tongariro u. Ruapahu. xiii. Ngawhas u. puias; kochbrunnen, solfataren u. fumarolen. xiv. Ostküste bei Maketu u. Tauranga, u. Rückreise nach Auckland. xv. Nelson. xvi. Südlichen Alpen. xvii. Kohlen. xviii. Gold. xix. Planzenwelt. xx. Thierwelt. xxi. Kiwi u. moa. xxii. Eingeboren. xxiii. Das Maori-königthum u. der Maori-krieg. xxiv. Maori prosa u. poesie. (Anhang: —A. Aus der mythologie: Die trennung des himmels u. der erde, pp. 511-2. B. Ein mährchen: Kohuki u. seine zwei frauen, pp. 512-7.† C. Fabeln, p. 517. D. Sprich-wörter. E. Lieder u. gesänge, pp. 519-26. F. Ansprachen, pp. 526-30. G. Briefe, pp. 530-2.)—Statistischen verhältnisse, pp. 533-45.—Literatur, pp. 547-55.

* **Hochstetter,** F. *von.* Die Provinz Nelson auf der Südinsel von Neu-Seeland. *Peterm. Mitt.*, 1863, p. 13.

* **Ironside,** *Rev.* S. New Zealand and its aborigines. Sydney. 1863.

* **Latest** from New Zealand, 1863. *London Quarterly Review,* xxi. 437. 1863.

* **Life** in New Zealand. *Eclectic Review,* cxix. 205. 1863.

* **Lindsay,** W. Lauder. Illustrations of the geology and mineralogy of New Zealand. *Programme of conversazione of Royal Society of Edinburgh,* Feb. 1863.

Maning, Frederick Edward. Old New Zealand: being incidents of | Native Customs and Character in the | Old Times. | By | A Pakeha Maori. | London: | Smith, Elder and Co., 65, Cornhill. | M.DCCC.LXIII.
 p. 8°. Pp. viii, 216. Published simultaneously with an Auckland edition by R. J. Creighton and A. Scales, with the title—Old N.Z.: a Tale of the Good Old Times.

 "... the descriptions of Maori life and manners of past times, found in these sketches, owe nothing to fiction. The different scenes and incidents are given exactly as they occurred, and all the persons described are real persons. Contact with the British settlers has of late years effected a marked and rapid change in the manners and mode of life of the natives, and the Maori of the present day are as unlike what they were when I first saw them as they are still unlike a civilized people or British subjects."—*Preface.*

 The *vie intime* of the Maoris described by a naturalised Maori; the life of a pakeha among the Maoris; reception of returning tribe; war dance; Maori hospitality; mourning-mutilations; muru; purchase of land; Maori freebooters; character of the Maori; tapu and its inconveniences; war customs; tohungas, oracles, priestcraft, and necromancy; suicide; tapu; relations of pakeha to his rangatira; hill forts; decrease of population and its causes; death of a chief; and mana.
 There is a Glossary, pp. 213-6.
 The book was reprinted in 1876, with a preface by Lord Pembroke. It was translated (wholly or in part) into Danish by Bishop D. G. Monrad—Gamle Ny-Zeeland; udgivet af D. G. Monrad—respecting whom see Journals of House of Representatives, 1867, second session, Appendix, H.-10, p. 2. From this version it was rendered into German—Das alte Neuseeland von D. G. Monrad. Aus dem Dänischen. Deutsch von Dr. August W. Peter.
 Sketches of Maori history by Maning appear in *Important Judgments in the Native Land Court:* see 1879.

Moser, T. Mahoe leaves, being a selection of sketches of New Zealand, and other matters concerning them, by Thomas Moser. *Wellington Independent,* Oct. 4, 11, 21, 23, Nov. 1, 8, 13, 1862; Jan. 10, 24, 1863.
 Reprinted in 1868, q.v.

---

† The English version is in *Chapman's New Zealand Monthly Magazine,* pp. 70-4.

* New Zealand—past, present, and future. *Temple Bar*, xi. 397. 1863.

Pickering, C. The Races of Man ; | and | Their Geographical Distribution. | By Charles Pickering, M.D., | Member of the United States Exploring Expedition. | New edition. | To which is prefixed, | An Analytical Synopsis of the Natural | History of Man. | By John Charles Hall, M.D., | Fellow of the Royal College of Physicians, Edinburgh ; Author of " Facts connected with the Animal Kingdom and Unity of Our Species." | London : | H. G. Bohn, York Street, Covent Garden. | 1863.

    cr. 8°. Pp. xli, 445. Ethnological map, and illustrations ; coloured.

    N.Z., pp. 74-9. Pickering was six weeks in N.Z. in 1840 with the U.S. Ex. Ex. General notes; Maoris treated as belonging to the Malay race. "*Phormium tenax*, the N.Z. flax, according to Clot-Bey and Figari, has been recently introduced into Egypt from the Montpellier Garden " (p. 408).

    A reprint of the seventh volume of the U.S. Exploring Expedition.

Scherzer, K. Narrative | of the | Circumnavigation of the Globe | by the Austrian frigate | Novara, | (Commodore B. von Wullerstorf-Urbair,) | Undertaken by Order of the Imperial Government, | in the years 1857, 1858, and 1859, | under the immediate auspices of His I. and R. Highness | the Archduke Ferdinand Maximilian, | Commander-in-chief of the Austrian navy. | By | Dr. Karl Scherzer, | Member of the Expedition, Author of " Travels in Central America," etc. | London : | Saunders, Otley, and Co., | 66, Brook Street, Hanover Square. | 1863.

    roy. 8°. 3 vols.

    N.Z. : vol. iii., pp. 91-194, 508-18.

    Auckland province, ch. xix., pp. 93-177. Hochstetter's report, pp. 177-94. Appendix III., IV.—Official correspondence of the Governor (Sir T. Gore Browne) and the Commodore relating to the employment of Hochstetter by the Government, pp. 508-10. Appendix V.—Address of the inhabitants of the province of Auckland to Hochstetter, pp. 511-2, and of Nelson, pp. 512-4.

* Silver's Guide to Australasia, and Itinerary to and in the Colonies. London : Silver. 1863.

    Pp. 156. N.Z. : pp. 126-53.—*Davis.*

Smith, Goldwin. The Empire. | A Series of Letters | published in | " The Daily News," 1862, 1863. | By Goldwin Smith. | Oxford and London : John Henry and James Parker. | 1863.

    12°. Pp. xxiv, 306.

    Letter x, Sept. 1862: New Zealand, pp. 147-64. Denounces Imperial expenditure. Copy of Duke of Newcastle's despatch to Sir G. Grey, May 26, 1862.

***Wakefield,** E. J. What Will They Do | in the | General Assembly ? | A pamphlet, | by Edward Jerningham Wakefield. | Price sixpence. | Auckland : | Creighton and Scales, Publishers, | O'Connell Street. | 1863.

    8°. Pp. 37.

    Criticizes Native policy, and suggests measures for extinguishing Native rebellion and preventing its recurrence, and for promoting colonisation in the North Island.

Ward, Crosbie. Letter | to the | Right Honourable | the | Lord Lyttelton, | on the | Relations of Great Britain | with | the Colonists and Aborigines | of | New Zealand. | By | Crosbie Ward, | A Member of the Government and of the House of | Representatives of the Colony. | London : | Edward Stanford, 6, Charing Cross. | 1863.

    sm. p. 8°. Pp. 82.

    Case against the colony, pp. 4-5. Technical responsibility for native government; theory of separate administration, pp. 5-21. Practice of administration in native affairs, pp. 21-9. Moral responsibility for the war, pp. 29-46. Minor charges

Ward, Crosbie—*continued.*
against the colonists, pp. 47-56. Imperial policy towards the colony, pp. 56-65. Future prospects, pp. 65-70. Financial questions, pp. 70-2. Conclusion, pp. 72-4. Note, pp. 75-6. Appendix: address of House of Representatives to the Queen, 1862, pp. 77-82.

1864.

Address of the Aborigines' Protection Society to the native inhabitants of New Zealand. [In English and Maori.] London, 1864.
 8°. Pp. 11.

Barrett, Alfred. The Life | of the | Rev. John Hewgill Bumby. | With | a Brief History | of the | Commencement and Progress | of | the Wesleyan Mission in New-Zealand. | By the | Rev. Alfred Barrett, | author of "Christ in the Storm," "Pastoral | Addresses," &c. | Fourth Edition. | London : | J. Mason, 2, Castle-Street, Finsbury ; | sold at 66, Paternoster-Row. | 1864.
 p. 8°. Pp. vi, Contents, and 254+2. Portrait.
 Early history of Wesleyan mission, pp. 80-124. Mr. Bumby's work, pp. 125-202. Progress of the mission 1842-50, pp. 202-54 ; with long extracts from missionaries' letters and journals.
 The preface is dated Dec. 1851, and the first edition was probably published in 1852.

Carleton, Hugh.] New Zealand. *Westminster Review*, New Series, no. 1., April 1864, pp. 420-72.
 "The colonial history is known only to those who have taken a part in making it. . . . Our present object is to redeem a portion of it from oblivion." The author confines himself to the history of the land-question, which "is substantially the history of the colony."

* Die erste Eisenbahn auf Neu-Seeland. *Peterm. Mitt.*, 1864, p. 153.

* First week in New Zealand. *Good Words*, v. 621. 1864.

* From Auckland to Awamutu. *Fraser's Magazine*, lxx. 407. 1864.

* Geschichte der Entdeckung der Goldlager in Neu-Seeland. *Ausland*, 1864, no. 38.

A Glance at Dunedin. *Chambers's Journal*, xli. 344-6. May 28, 1864.

Gorst, J. E. The | Maori King ; | or, The | Story of our Quarrel | with | the Natives of New Zealand. | By | J. E. Gorst, M.A. | late Fellow of St. John's College, Cambridge, and recently Commissioner | of the Waikato District, New Zealand. | London and Cambridge : | Macmillan and Co. | 1864.
 cr. 8°. Pp. x, Note, 409. Portrait of Te Waharoa and map of Waikato.
 Ch. i. Introductory. ii. The Waikato. iii. The Queen's sovereignty. iv. The revolt. v. Potatau. vi. The Justice on circuit. vii. Taranaki war. viii. Te Waharoa. ix. Interregnum. x. Sir G. Grey. xi. Face to face. xii. The "new institutions." xiii. The Maori kingdom. xiv. Rumours of war. xv. The Awamutu. xvi. Tataraimaka. xvii. Rewi. xviii. Outbreak of war. xix. Invasion of Waikato. xx. Conclusion.

* **Haast,** J. Notes on the Mountains and Glaciers of the Canterbury Province. *Journal, Royal Geographical Society*, xxxiv. 87. 1864.
 Probably identical with next paper.

* **Haast,** J. On the Southern Alps of Canterbury. Proceedings Royal Geographical Society, Feb. 1864.

* **Hector,** J. Expedition to the West Coast of Otago ; with an Account of the Discovery of a Low Pass from Martin's Bay to Lake Wakatipu. By James Hector, Esq. M.D., Provincial Geologist. *Journal, Royal Geographical Society*, xxxiv. 96 ; Pro. R.G.S., viii. 47, ix. 32. 1864-5.

Hochstetter, F. *von, and* **Petermann,** A. Geological and Topographical | Atlas of New Zealand. | By | Dr. Ferdinand von Hochstetter and Dr. A. Petermann. | Six Maps | of the | Provinces of Auckland and Nelson. | Auckland: | Published by T. Delattre, Lower Queen Street. | 1864.

    4°.

       Map 1. N.Z.; by Petermann. 2. Southern part of Auckland Province, showing the routes and surveys; by Hochstetter. 3. Isthmus of Auckland, with its extinct volcanoes; by Hochstetter. 4. Harbours and bays of Aotea and Kawhia; by Hochstetter. 5. Rotomahana and the hot springs; by Hochstetter. 6. Geological map of Nelson; by Hochstetter and Haast.

Hochstetter, F. *von, and* **Petermann,** A. The Geology of New Zealand : in explanation of the Geographical and Topographical Atlas of New Zealand. From the scientific publications of the Novara Expedition. Translated by C. F. Fischer. Also, Lectures by Dr. F. Hochstetter delivered in New Zealand. Auckland, 1864.

    8°. Pp. 113.

       1. Petermann, A. Observations upon the chartography of N.Z., pp. 3-8. 2. Hochstetter, F. Geology of Auckland, pp. 8-43. 3. Hochstetter, F. Explanations of the maps, pp. 43-77, 108-13. 4. Hochstetter, F. Geology of Nelson, pp. 77-108. (2 and 4 are reprints of lectures published in the *N.Z. Gazette*: see *antea*, 1859.)

Hooker, J. D. Handbook | of the | New Zealand Flora : | a Systematic Description | of the | Native Plants | of | New Zealand | and the | Chatham, Kermadec's, Lord Auckland's, Campbell's, | and Macquarrie's Islands. | By J. D. Hooker, M.D., F.R.S. L.S. & G.S., | and Honorary Member of the Philosophical Institute of Canterbury, New Zealand. | Published under the authority of the Government of | New Zealand. | London : Lovell Reeve & Co., 5, Henrietta Street, Covent Garden. | 1864.

    This is the title-page of Part I, pp. 1-392. Part II, pp. 393-798, with a similar title-page, was published in 1867.

    8°. Pp. lxviii, 798.

       The Preface (pp. 7*-15*) recapitulates the history of botanical exploration in N.Z. Outlines of Botany, to accompany the Colonial floras (from Bentham's 'Flora Australiensis'), pp. i-xl. Classifications of orders and genera (pp. xli-lxviii) : 1. Key to the natural orders, etc., of flowering plants ; 2. Key to the genera of N.Z. flowering plants, arranged under the Linnæan classes ; 3. Classification of the N.Z. natural orders, according to the natural system. At pp. 757-63 is—A list of the principal naturalized, or apparently naturalized, plants of N.Z. And at pp. 764-9 an—Alphabetical list of native and vernacular names.

Hooker, J. D. [List of plants in the Kermadec Islands.] *Linnæan Society's Journal, Botany*, i. 125. 1864.

* How we live at Awamutu. *Fraser's Magazine*, lxx. 606. 1864.

The last of the Moas. *Chambers's Journal*, xli. 115. 1864.

***McKerrow,** J. Reconnaissance Survey of the Lake-districts of Otago and Southland. *Journal, Royal Geographical Society*, xxxiv. 56. 1864.

* [**Maning,** F. E.] History of the War in the North against the Chief Heke, in the year 1845. Told by an old Chief of the Ngapuhi tribe. · By Pakeha Maori. Auckland : Creighton & Scales. 1864.

    8°. Pp. 113.—*Davis.* See 1876.

[**Marshman,** John.] Canterbury, | New Zealand, | in 1864. | Published with the approval of the | Provincial Government. | English Agent,—Henry Selfe Selfe, Esq. | Emigration Agent,—John Marshman. | London : | G.

[**Marshman,** John]—*continued.*
Street, "New Zealand Examiner" Office, | 30, Cornhill, E.C. | Price Sixpence.
  cr. 8°. Pp. iv, 63. Map.

   A reprint of a pamphlet, *Canterbury in 1862;* corrected from observations and inquiries made during a visit in spring, 1864.
   Description of Canterbury. Climate, natural productions. Settlement, &c. Inland communication. Land regulations. Agriculture. Sheep farming. General observations. Emigration. Stock, markets, rates of wages. Statistics, 1854-63. Customs duties.

* **Maunoir,** —. La Nouvelle-Zélande, colonie anglaise. *In* Bulletins de la Société de Géographie (of Paris). [Date unknown, but not later than 1864.]
  Referred to in Quatrefages (*Polynésiens,* pp. 112-3), who describes the author as Secretary of that Society.

Muter, *Mrs.* D. D. Travels and Adventures | of | an Officer's Wife | in | India, China, and New Zealand. | By | Mrs. Muter, | Wife of Lieut.-Colonel D. D. Muter, | Thirteenth (Prince Albert's) Light Infantry. | In two volumes. | —— | London: | Hurst and Blackett, Publishers, | —— | 13, Great Marlborough Street. | 1864.
  p. 8°. Vol. ii.: pp. vi, 314.

   Chs. xi-xv, pp. 201-310, describe a visit to N.Z., apparently in 1862. Outspoken ideas on New Zealand settlements, and the manners and habits of the settlers.

* Die neuesten Explorationen in Neu-Seeland. *Ausland,* 1864, no. 23.

* Die Neu-Seelandische Provinz Southland. *Peterm. Mitt.,* 1864, p. 34.

The New Zealand Government | and the | Maori war of 1863-64, | with Especial Reference to the | Confiscation of Native Lands, | and the Colonial Ministry's Defence | of their War Policy. | Published for the Aborigines' Protection Society. | By William Tweedie, 335, Strand. | 1864.
  8°. Pp. 38.

   A reply to the N.Z. ministerial memorandum reprinted at pp. 25-9. An appendix contains — Address to Governor Grey (pp. 22-3, bearing over 70 signatures); the Governor's reply, pp. 23-4; memorandum by Sir W. Fox, pp. 25-9; despatch of Mr. Cardwell, pp. 31-8.
   Criticized in *Southern Monthly Magazine,* iv. 27-33.
   "The Aborigines' Protection Society was founded by the late Sir Thomas Fowell Buxton, and for a period of nearly twenty-eight years the society has been unceasing in its efforts to elevate the social and political condition of the native inhabitants of the British colonies, and to defend them against injustice and oppression."—*Advertisement.*

The | New Zealand Handbook. | Tenth Edition. | London: | Willis, Gann, & Co., Crosby Square. | 1864.
  fcp. 8°. Prefaces (4 pp.), Contents, and 132 pp. Map.

   Discovery, rise, and progress of New Zealand; products; soil; Government; laws; land regulations; institutions; market prices; gold-diggings; pasture; farm; employment.
   "Nearly 40,000 copies . . . have already been called for, and it has been translated into German and Welsh."—*Title-page.*

Origin of the New Zealand war; and who are responsible for the payment of all expenses arising therefrom. By Veritas. Printed for private circulation. [London, 1864.]
  8°. Pp. 16.

Protest against the confiscation of native lands in New Zealand. The report of a debate in the Legislative Council of the Colony, together with the memorial of the Aborigines' Protection Society and other documents. London, 1864.
  8°. Pp. 20.

   Note, p. 3. Confiscation Act, pp. 4-7. Report, pp. 7-17. Memorial, pp. 17-19.

Quatrefages, A. *de.* Histoire naturelle de l'homme.—Les Polynésiens et leurs migrations. *Revue des Deux Mondes*, Fév. 1 and 15, 1864, séconde période, tome xlix., 521-47, 858-901.

>I. Caractères physiques et moraux des Polyuésiens, Fév. 1. i. Caractères physiques, pp. 522-31. ii. Caractères intellectuels, pp. 531-40. iii. Caractères religieux et moraux, pp. 540-7. II. Origine et migrations des Polynésiens. i. Possibilité des migrations de l'ouest à l'est. Examples isolés. Carte de Tupaia. Pp. 861-71. ii. Colonisation de la N.Z. par la race polynésienne, pp. 871-85. iii. Centre de formation et migration des diverses tribes polynésieunes, pp. 886-95. iv. Date des migrations, pp. 806-901.

>The Polynesian race (which is one race) has the characteristics alike of the white, yellow, and black races: the yellow appears in the colour; the black in the features and shape of the cranium; the white is the dominant element. The Polynesians came from the eastern archipelagoes of Asia, where we still find the mother-race. They settled at first in Samoa and Tonga, and then passed to other archipelagoes. Some of the islands they found deserted, others occupied by a dark race. Whether remaining pure, or allied to these wandering negro tribes, they formed secondary centres whence have sprung new colonies. None of these migrations belongs to prehistoric times; some of the chief of them occurred a few years before or after the Christian era; others are more recent, and some are entirely modern.

>Quatrefages refers to a work by Maunoir in the *Bulletins de la Société de Géographie*, apparently on N.Z.

>See later the author's *Les Polynésiens et leurs migrations*, 1866.

Reise | der | Oesterreichischen Fregatte Novara | um die Erde | in den Jahren 1857, 1858, 1859 | unter den Befehlen des Commodore | B. von Wüllerstorf-Urbair. | Geologischer Theil. | Erster Band: | Erste Abtheilung, Geologie von Neu-Seeland. | Zweite Abtheilung, Paläontologie von Neu-Seeland. | Herausgegeben in Allerhöchsten Auftrage unter der Leitung der kaiserlichen Akademie der Wissenschaften. | Wien | Aus der kaiserlich-königlichen Hof- und Staatsdruckerei. | 1864 | In Commission bei Karl Gerold's Sohn.

Erste Abtheilung: | Geologie von Neu-Seeland :—

Hochstetter, Ferdinand *von.* Geologie von Neu-Seeland. | Beiträge zur Geologie | der | Provinzen Auckland und Nelson, | von | Dr. Ferdinand von Hochstetter | [here follow his titles] | Mit 6 geologischen | Karten in Farbendruck, | 6 Lithographien, | 1 Kupferstich, | 1 Photographie | und 66 Holzschnitten.

>roy. 4°. Pp. xlvii, 274.

>Historische Einleitung (p. xvii.) und Literatur, p. xxiv. Neu-Seeland: allgemeine Uebersicht, p. xxvii; Uebersicht der auf Neu-Seeland auftretenden Formationen und Formationsglieder iu chronologischer Reihenfolge, pp. xxxiv-xlvii.

>Nord-Insel (pp. 1-194): südöstliche Theil, pp. 1-6; nordwestliche Theil, pp. 8-18; mittlere Theil, pp. 18-185. Anhang: Vorzeichniss von Höhen im südlichen Theile der Provinz Auckland, pp. 187-92. Wasser-Temperaturen, pp. 193-4.

>Süd-Insel, pp. 195-268. Anhang: Maori-Wörter zur Bezeichnung von Gesteinen, Mineralien, Erdarten, heissen Quellen, u.s.w., pp. 269-74.

Zweite Abtheilung:—

Paläontologie von Neu-Seeland. | Beiträge zur Kenntniss | der | Fossilen Flora und Fauna der Provinzen Auckland und Nelson | von Prof. Dr. Unger, Prof. Dr. Karl Zittel, Prof. E. Suess, Felix Karrer, Dr. Ferdinand | Stoliczka, Dr. Guido Stache, Dr. Gustav Jaeger. Redigirt | von Ferdinand von Hochstetter, Dr. Moriz Hörnes und Franz Ritter von Hauer. | Mit 26 lithographirten Tafeln.

>roy. 4°. Pp. vii, 318.

>i. Unger, F. Fossile Pflanzenreste, mit 5 Tafeln (i-v), pp. 1-13. ii. Zittel, K. A. Fossile Mollusken und Echinodermen, mit 10 Tafeln (vi-xv), pp. 15-58. iii. Karrer, F. Die Foraminiferen-Fauna des tertiären Grunsandsteines der Orakei-Bay bei Auckland, mit 1 Tafel (xvi), pp. 60-86. iv. Stoliczka, F. Fossile Bryozoen aus dem tertiären Grünsandsteine der Orakei-Bay bei Auckland, mit 4 Tafeln (xvii-xx), pp. 87-158.

Paläontologie von Neu-Seeland—*continued.*
> v. Stache, G. Die Foraminiferen der tertiären Mergel des Whaingaroa-Hafens (Prov. Auckland), mit 4 Tafeln (xxi-xxiv), pp. 159-304. vi. Jaeger, G. Bericht über einen fast vollständigen Schädel von *Palapteryx*, mit 2 Tafeln (xxv-xxvi), pp. 305-18.

*Sewell, H. The New Zealand Rebellion | A Letter | from Henry .Sewell, Esq., | late Attorney-General of New Zealand, | to the | Right Hon. Lord Lyttelton. | London and Cambridge: | Macmillan and Co. 1864.
> 8°. Pp. 56.
> Historical review from the outbreak of war in 1860; King movement; law of the question, and legal opinions; political and military measures; letters from chiefs and officials; Potatau's proclamation; three Acts of the Assembly, and parliamentary events.

The Southern Monthly | Magazine. | Vol. I. March, 1863. Illus. Auckland: Creighton and Scales, Queen Street. | M.DCCC.LXIV.
> 8°. Pp. iv, 711, errata. Illus.
> The Assembly, p. 337; colonial experience, pp. 36, 58, 113, 168, 218; convict discipline for New Zealand, p. 272; ethics of our colonisation, p. 547; gold discoveries in New Zealand, p. 664; a lament, p. 309; Maori courage, p. 243; Mere-Mere, p. 419; Native institutions, p. 25; pakeha war-song, p. 342; responsibility of colonists, p. 310; the Waitara and the Native question, pp. 209, 402; Native watch-chants, pp. 171, 381.
> Vols. ii, iii, and (in March, 1865) no. 1 of iv were published, with a few N.Z. articles.

Taylor, R. The Age of New Zealand: | by the | Rev. R. Taylor, M.A., F.G.S., | Author of | "New Zealand and its Inhabitants." | Auckland: | Geo. T. Chapman, Bookseller and Stationer, Queen-Street.
> 8°. Pp. 26. No date, but after 1864.
> Of "all the surface of our planet, this is probably the oldest portion, and still preserves, with little change, its primeval condition, from its not having been submerged with the rest of the grand southern continent" (p. 24).

*Travers, W. T. L. [On the flora of Canterbury, Nelson, and Marlborough.] *Natural History Review*, January, 1864.
> Many new plants. "His observations on the spread of introduced plants are extremely interesting."—J. HOOKER, *Handbook*, p. 12*.

Weld, F. A. Hints | to | Intending Sheep-Farmers, | in | New Zealand. | By | Fred. A. Weld, Esq., | of Flaxbourne, New Zealand, | Member of the House of Representatives, etc. etc. | With an Appendix | containing an | Epitome of the Land Regulations, | of the Different Provinces. | Fourth edition. | London : | Edward Stanford, 6, Charing Cross. | 1864.
> 12°. Pp. 40.
> Altered and enlarged from the little pamphlet of 1851; second ed., 1853.
> There is a biographical sketch of Weld in Cox, *Men of mark*, &c.

*Whitcombe's Reise durch die südlichen Alpen von Neu-Seeland und die . . . Umstände seines Todes. *Petermn. Mitt.*, 1864, p. 216.

1865.

Alexander, *Sir* James E. Notes on the Maories of New Zealand, with suggestions for their pacification and preservation. Printed and published for the Aborigines' Protection Society. London, 1865.
> Pp. 7.

B, P. C. A chapter on Pai Marire, the new religion of the Maoris. *Fraser's Magazine*, Oct. 1865.
> See next entry.

B, P. C. Pai Marire, the new religion of the Maoris. By an Army Chaplain. *Good Words*, Oct. 1, 1865, pp. 726-32.
> A revival of the old religion, effected through the influence of the native priests. Account of the murder of Volkner.

* Bevölkerungsstatistik Neu-Seelands. *Ausland*, 1865, no. 7.

Buller, Walter Lawry. New Zealand Exhibition, 1865. | Essay | on the | Ornithology | of | New Zealand. | By | Walter Buller, Esq. F.L.S. | —— | Printed for the Commissioners, | by Fergusson and Mitchell, Dunedin, Otago, N.Z. | MDCCCLXV.
    roy. 8°. Pp. 20.

* **Carter**, S. D. Life in New Zealand. *Hours at Home*, New York, ii. 426. 1865.

Coleman, J. N. A Memoir | of the | Rev. Richard Davis, | for thirty-nine years a missionary in New Zealand. | By the | Rev. John Noble Coleman, M.A. | late Incumbent of Ventnor. | London : | James Nisbet and Co., Berners Street. | 1865.
    p. 8°. Pp. xii, 457.
    Ch. iv. Appointment as missionary of the Church Society, and settlement. Ch. v. Missionary operations from 1824 to 1828. Ch. vi. To 1831. Ch. vii. To 1837. Ch. viii. To 1843. Ch. ix. To 1852. Ch. x. To 1863. Appendix II. contains a report of a conference between missionaries and chiefs, and letters from Natives.
    Stationed at Bay of Islands. "His missionary operations exhibit a graphic portraiture of the New Zealanders in their cannibalism and savage barbarism. . . . They present an accurate delineation of the population of the Northern Island, and of the progress of the Church Mission therein, from 1824 to 1863."—*Preface*.

Colenso, W. New Zealand Exhibition, 1865. | Essay | on the Botany | of the | North Island of New Zealand. | By William Colenso, M.G.A. F.L.S., | Napier. | —— | Printed for the Commissioners, | by Fergusson and Mitchell, Dunedin, Otago, N.Z. | MDCCCLXV.
    roy. 8°. Pp. 58.
    §1. Preliminary, pp. 1-3. §2. Geographic, pp. 3-29. §3. Economic, pp. 29-54. Notes, pp. 55-6. Table of strength and weight of woods, p. 57.
    The Rev. W. Colenso, "during many successive years, has collected throughout the whole length of the Northern Island, with great care and skill, discovering more new and interesting plants (especially on the Ruahine Range, Tongariro, Hikurangi, etc.) than any botanist since Banks and Solander." The above work "is full of interesting matter, which the author alone was able to supply, especially regarding the altitudinal and latitudinal ranges of the species."—*Hooker*.

Crawford, J. C. New Zealand Exhibition, 1865. | Essay | on the | Geology of the North Island | by | Hon. J. Coutts Crawford, M.L.C., F.G.S. | —— | Printed for the Commissioners, | by Fergusson and Mitchell, Dunedin, Otago, N.Z. | MDCCCLXV.
    roy. 8°. Pp. 27.
    At pp. 1-2 is a sketch of the geological exploration of the North Island.

* Ferdinand von Hochstetter über den Bau der Vulkane auf Neu-Seeland. *Ausland*, 1865, no. 3.

FitzGerald, J. E. Letters on the Present | State of Maori Affairs. | He Pukapuka Whakaatu i nga Korero mo nga | Ritenga Maori o | Tenei Takiwa. | Christchurch : | Printed at the " Press " Office, | Cashel Street. | 1865.
    12°. Pp. 47.
    A letter from Aterea Puna, "for all the tribes," is in Maori at pp. 3-8, and in English at pp. 27-34.

Flora of New Zealand. *Journal of Science*, ii. 162. 1865.

Fox, William. The revolt in New Zealand. A series of letters addressed to the Rev. George Townshend Fox. London [1865].
    8°. Pp. vi, 37.
    Preface by G. T. Fox, pp. iii-vi.

* **Gorst**, J. E. Conquests in New Zealand. *Macmillan's Magazine*, xii. 168. 1865.

[**Hope**, *Captain.*] Thirty years' policy in New Zealand. *Blackwood's Magazine*, xcvii. 739–53. June, 1865.

> Systematic colonisation should have begun with Canterbury and Otago. The author of the article (commander of a ship-of-war on the Pacific Station) is given on the authority of Sir G. Grey.

Howitt, William. The | History of Discovery | in | Australia, Tasmania, | and | New Zealand, | from the Earliest Date to the Present Day. | By | William Howitt, | Author of "Two Years in Victoria," etc. etc. | With Maps of the Recent Explorations from Official Sources. | In Two Volumes. | —— | London : | Longman, Green, Longman, Roberts, and Green, | Paternoster Row. | MDCCCLXV.

> 8°. Vol. ii : pp. 461. Map of N.Z.
>
> Ch. xxi. Incidents of discovery and settlement in New Zealand, ii. 398–417; the survey of the coasts, ii. 398–9; discovery in the North Island, ii. 399–417. Ch. xxii. Discovery of the insularity of the South Island, ii. 418; settlement of the Middle Island, ii. 418–9; settlement of Canterbury, ii. 419–22; discoveries in the Middle Island continued, ii. 422–6. Ch. xxiii. Dobson's discovery of a route over the mountains to the west coast of the Middle Island, ii. 427–30. Rochfort's surveys, ii. 430–2; Haast's explorations of the mountainous regions, and the rivers of the Middle Island, ii. 432–8. Ch. xxiv. Opening communication with the west coast, pp. 439–58; remarks on the Maories, pp. 458–61.

Hursthouse, C. England's New Zealand war, | Second Edition, | by | Charles Hursthouse. | London :— | Edward Stanford, 6, Charing Cross, S.W. | Price Sixpence.

> cr. 8°. Pp. 90.
>
> A reprint of Letter i, below : pp. 1–71. Additional remarks, &c., pp. 71–5. Notes, pp. 76–90.

Hursthouse, C. Letters | on | New Zealand Subjects | by | Charles Hursthouse. | 1. The New Zealand War. | 2. New Zealand's "Home Minister." | 3. "Maori Emigrants." | London :— | Edward Stanford, 6, Charing Cross, S.W. | Price Sixpence.

> cr. 8°. Pp. 85. [1865.]
>
> Letter i is nominally addressed to the *Times*, from London, 1865 (pp. 1–71): it is a general review of the policy of the Home Government to the colony, of that of the Colonial Government to the Maoris, and the cause of the war. Letter ii (pp. 72–80) recommends the appointment of an annual colonial Resident in London. iii (pp. 81–5) recommends the Chatham Islands as a fit place for the settlement of disaffected natives.

* **Lindsay**, W. Lauder. Contributions to the flora of Otago. *Transactions of Botanical Society of Edinburgh*, vol. viii., p. 250 (1865); *Proceedings of Royal Society of Edinburgh*, vol. v., p. 434.

Lindsay, W. L. On the relations of the southern to the northern flora of New Zealand. Proceedings of British Association, 1865. *Report* (Notices and abstracts), pp. 82–3.

Lubbock, J. Pre-historic times, | as illustrated by | Ancient Remains, | and the | Manners and Customs of Modern Savages. | By | John Lubbock, F.R.S., Vice-President of the Linnæan Society; Fellow of the Geographical, Zoological, and other Societies; and President of the Ethnological Society. | —— | Williams and Norgate, | 14, Henrietta Street, Covent Garden, London ; | and | 20, South Frederick Street, Edinburgh. | 1865.

> 8°.
>
> A general account of the Maoris, compiled from Dieffenbach, D'Urville, &c., is given at pp. 365–72.

Ludlam, A. New Zealand Exhibition. | Essay | on the | Cultivation and Acclimatization | of | Trees and Plants, | by | A. Ludlam, | Newry, Hutt Valley, Wellington. | —— | Printed for the Commissioners, | by Fergusson and Mitchell, Dunedin, Otago, N.Z. | MDCCCLXV.
    roy. 8°. Pp. 23.
    Mentions experiments in cultivation and acclimatisation.

Lusk, Hugh. Maori Mahommedanism. *Fortnightly Review,* ii. 731–7. 1865.
    Rise and spread of Hauhauism.

Maori Sketches. *Cornhill Magazine,* xii. 498–512. Oct. 1865.
    Founded on Maning's *Old New Zealand.*

* Die Maoris und der Engländer auf Neuseeland. *Globus,* ix., p. 1 (1865).

The | Middle Island | New Zealand, | or | A Short Account of the Present State | of the | Different Settlements. | By an Old Colonist. | *Price Sixpence.* | London : | T. W. Nicholson, 3 & 4, Bell Yard, Gracechurch Street | 1865.
    8°. Pp. 17.
    At pp. 11–16 there is—An approximate outlay of a N.Z. land and stock investment company for the first year.

The Murder | of the | Rev. C. S. Volkner, | in | New Zealand. | London : | Church Missionary House, Salisbury Square. | MDCCCLXV.
    8°. Pp. 32.
    1. Murder of the Rev. C. S. Volkner. 2. Diary of S. A. Levy, pp. 4–7. 3. Journal of Rev. T. S. Grace, pp. 8–18. 4. Minutes of Missionary Conference held at Auckland after the release of Mr. Grace, pp. 18–19. 5. Journal and letters of Bishop of Waiapu, pp. 19–30. 6. Remarks of the Committee, pp. 30–2.

* Die neuentdeckten Canterbury-Goldfelder auf der Süd-Insel von Neu-Seeland. *Ausland,* 1865, no. 39.

Remarks | on the | Credit of New Zealand | and the | Honour of Great Britain. | London : | Rees & Collin, 38, Gracechurch Street, E.C., | 1865.
    roy. 8°. Pp. 38.
    Strictures on the policy of the Weld-FitzGerald Ministry; Waitara war caused by southern pressure.

Second-class to New Zealand and back. *Chambers's Journal,* xlii. 765–8, 781–4. Dec. 2 and 9, 1865.

Shortland, E. New Zealand Exhibition, 1865. | A | Short Sketch | of the | Maori Races, | by | Edward Shortland, Esq. | —— | Printed for the Commissioners, | by Fergusson and Mitchell, Dunedin, Otago, N.Z. | MDCCCLXV.
    roy. 8°. Pp. 11.
    The Maoris are a mixed race of pure Indians and Papuans, who were blended in the Indian archipelago, whence they migrated to the Sandwich Islands.

* Sitten- u. Rechtsansichten der Maori. *Ausland,* 1865, no. 43.

1866.

* The Auckland Isles. *Every Saturday,* Boston, i. 417. 1866.

B., P. C. Two years' experience of the Maoris. By an Army Chaplain, P.C.B. *Good Words,* vii. 696. 1866.

* **Bayliss,** Daniel. A glimpse of shepherd life in New Zealand. *Good Words,* vii. 620–2. Sept. 1866.
    In the North Island.

Busby, J. Our Colonial Empire | and the Case of | New Zealand. | By James Busby, | Her Majesty's Resident at New Zealand from 1832 to 1840, | and a Settler there since that Period. | Williams and Norgate, 14 Henrietta Street, Covent Garden, London; and | 20, South Frederick Street, Edinburgh.
    8°. Pp. xii, 194. There is no date, but it was published in 1866.

> "It is the object of the following pages to explain and illustrate the true relations of British Colonies to the mother country." He traces the Native disturbances in N.Z. to "the system called responsible government," and praises the old form of colonial government. Part ii is on the land question (pp. 91-178). An appendix (pp. 179-94) contains official documents.
> The book partly reproduces a paper read by Mr. Busby before the Social Science Association in 1864: see *Transactions*, pp. 603-12.

A Campaign | on the | West Coast of New Zealand, | comprising the western portion of the | Provinces of Wellington and Taranaki, | by | European and Colonial Forces, | under the command of | Major-General Chute, | during the months of January and February, 1866. | Wanganui, New Zealand : | Printed and published at the 'Times' Office, Ridgway Street. | 1866.
    8°. Pp. 47.

* Cast away on the Auckland Islands: A Narrative of the Wreck of the *Grafton*, and of the Escape of the Crew after Twenty Months' Suffering. From the Private Journals of Captain Thomas Musgrove. Edited by J. J. Shillinglaw, F.G.S. London: Lockwood. 1866.
    8°. Pp. 174.

* Catalogue | of Books relating to New Zealand | recently added to the | Library of the | General Assembly, | New Zealand. | —— | London : | F. Guillaume and Co., Colonial Booksellers, | 42, Chester Square. | 1866.
    p. 8°. Pp. 22.

Colonial policy in the government of coloured races. *North British Review*, vol. xliv. June, 1866.

> N.Z., pp. 403-8. "The embarrassments which may beset the Queen's representatives in working out the theory of responsible government . . . have received their most recent and most remarkable illustration in N.Z."

Fox, W. The | War in New Zealand. | By | William Fox, A.M., Oxon, | late Colonial Secretary and Native Minister of the Colony. | —— | With two maps and a plan. | London : | Smith, Elder and Co., 65, Cornhill. | 1866.
    cr. 8°. Pp. xvi, 268.

> Ch. i. Introductory. ii. Origin. iii. Purchase of Waitara, hostilities (1860-1) and truce. iv. Attempts at pacific solution. v. Origin of war. vi. Waikato country. vii. Waikato campaign. viii. Tauranga campaign. ix. Events in Taranaki. x. Negotiations. xi. Escape of prisoners. xii. Wanganui and Taranaki campaign of 1865. xiii. Differences between Gov. Grey and Gen. Cameron. xiv. Wanganui river and interior. xv. Campaign on east coast. Conclusion. Relations between Imperial and Colonial Governments. Notes, pp. 263-8.
> "I have been a colonist of N.Z. almost from its foundation as a colony. I have been a Member of the Legislature for many years, and during a great part of the present struggle I filled the offices of Colonial Secretary and Native Minister.' I have probably had better opportunities of obtaining accurate information, and observing current events in the colony, than any other person. . . . In describing the operations of the military campaigns, I have relied for the main facts chiefly on the despatches of General Cameron, or of his subordinate officers who may have reported to him. I have also referred to the cotemporary reports of the correspondents of the local newspapers. . . . 'I am myself acquainted, more or less, with all the country in which operations were carried on, and as regards the Northern campaigns I have visited all the places where the principal engagements occurred, many of them several times, and most of them in the company of officers who were in the engagements, and described them to me on the spot."—*Preface.*
> In the Appendix Note A should be C, and Note C should be A.

A full history of the Maungatapu murders: including a narrative of the events preceding the murders; confessions of Sullivan and Burgess; a corrected report of the trial; detailed particulars of the remarkable execution of Burgess, Kelly, and Levy; and lives of the murderers; with portraits, and plans and sections of the road. Nelson, 1866.
  8°.

Hadfield, Octavius. Ahab's Crimes | and the | Maungatapu Murders | treated on the Principles | of the | New School of Morals and Religion. | By the Right Reverend the Bishop of Wellington | Auckland: | Printed at the Cathedral Press. | MDCCCLXVI.
  p. 8°. Pp. 14.

Hector, J. Geological Survey of New Zealand. | First | General Report | on the | Coal Deposits | of | New Zealand: | by James Hector, M.D., F.R.S. | Director. | Published by command. | New Zealand: | By authority: George Didsbury, Government Printer, Wellington. | 1866.
  roy. 8°. Pp. 46.
  Has a list of principal special reports on the coal deposits of N.Z. which have appeared in Government Gazettes, &c.

  The Progress Reports of the Geological Survey during 1866-7 were published in 1868, and are now continuous. Partially independent reports by Captain Hutton on the geology of the Lower Waikato district and the Thames goldfields were made in 1867.
  The Meteorological Report for 1868 embraces an abstract of all prior meteorological returns.

[**Henderson**, *Capt.*] Otago, | and the | Middle Island, | New Zealand. | A Warning to Emigrants. | By Aliquis. | ——— | Melbourne: | George Robertson, 69 Elizabeth Street. | ——— | 1866.
  cr. 8°. Pp. 56.
  Pp. 17-47, history of a squabble.

***Hoyle**, F. W. Fragments of a journal saved from shipwreck. By an Old Kensingtonian. London, 1868.
  12°.
  With account of a journey across N.Z. in 1866.

Hunt, Fred. Twenty-five Years' Experience | in | New Zealand | and | the Chatham Islands. | An Autobiography. | By | Frederick Hunt. | Edited by John Amery. | Second edition. | ——— | Wellington: William Lyon, Willis Street. | ——— | 1866.
  8°. Pp. 64.
  Hunt was in Wellington from 1840. Life in a Maori district, chs. ii, iii, iv, ix, x. At the Chathams, chs. v-viii, xi-xiv. The Morioris are described in ch. vii.
  "The words, with some few exceptions, are" Hunt's: the pamphlet was written by Amery.

Hursthouse, C. A Letter | to the | Hon. E. W. Stafford, | "Premier" of New Zealand, | on the | "*Desirableness,*" *and the* "*Practicability,*" *of* | *making New Zealand a more popular Emigration* | *Field in the Mother Country*. | By | Charles Hursthouse. | London: | Printed by G. Witt, 7, Earl's Court, Leicester Square.
  cr. 8°. Pp. 21.
  Letter is dated 1866.

Illustrated Narrative | of the | Dreadful Murders | on the | Maungatapu Mountain, | and track between the | Wakamarina River and Nelson, | in the Province of Nelson, New Zealand. | Five Men foully Murdered by Bush-

Illustrated Narrative—*continued.*
rangers. | Capture of the Four Murderers. | Trial, Conviction and Execution. | Statement of Sullivan, the Approver. | Confession of " Burgess, the Murderer." | — Life of Burgess, Written by Himself, | also | Other Particulars in the Lives, | and | Photographic Portraits of the Murderers, | and a Lithographic Plan of the District. | Printed and published by | Nation & Luckie, " Colonist " Office, Nelson, N.Z. | 1866.
roy. 8°. Pp. iv, 113.

* Die Industrie der Maoris auf der allgemeinen Ausstellung in Auckland. *Ausland*, 1866, no. 51.

* **Jacox**, F. The coming man from New Zealand. *Colburn's Monthly Magazine*, cxxxviii. 282. 1866.

* **Lindsay**, W. Lauder. Observations on New Zealand Lichens. Trans. Linn. Soc., vol. xxv., pp. 493–560. Plates lx.–lxiii. ; 146 figures. Read June 7, 1866.
4°.

Mr. Secretary Cardwell and the right of petition. [No place of publication, and no date, but probably 1866.]
8°. Pp. 16.
Correspondence between the London Committee of the Northern Association of New Zealand and the Secretary for the Colonies. Committee proposes that a Committee of the House of Lords should be appointed to consider the petitions from Auckland province to be erected into a separate Government.

* Neuseeland in geographischer Hinsicht. *Unsere Zeit*, 1866, Heft 8, p. 19.

* **Quatrefages**, A. *de.* Les | Polynésiens | et | Leurs Migrations. Par | A. de Quatrefages | Membre de l'Institut (Académie des Sciences), | Professeur au Muséum. | Ouvrage accompagné de 4 cartes gravées. | Première Partie. | Caractères | généraux de la race polynésienne. | Seconde Partie. | Origine et migrations des Polynésiens. | Paris. | Arthur Bertrand, Editeur | Libraire de la Société de Géographie | 21, rue Hautefeuille. [1866.]
4°. Pp. 200.
Ch. iv of part ii, pp. 112-35, is on the colonisation of N.Z. by the Polynesian races. The author's general conclusions are stated above, 1864. The Maoris are a mixed race consisting of a small number of original Melanesian immigrants blended with brown immigrants from the Sandwich Islands.
Plate iv. is Hale's chart of the Polynesian migrations.

Review | of the | position of Southland | compiled from a debate on the causes which led to the | financial embarrassments of Southland, | and consequent | stoppage of railway works. | By an old colonist. | —— | Dedicated to the Members of the General Assembly, New Zealand. | 1866: | Reynolds and Co., General Printers, Esk-Street, Invercargill, Southland, N.Z.
8°. Pp. 20.
Report of debate in Council of province of Southland, March 20, 1866. Correspondence between Superintendent of Southland, Colonial Secretary, and others.

Supplement to the Review of the Position of Southland. Wellington. 1866.

* Telegraphen-Linien in Neu-Seeland. *Peterm. Mitt.*, 1866, p. 392.

Travers, W. T. L., on the Destruction of the Aborigines of Chatham Island. Read March 7, 1865. Transactions of Ethnological Society of London, Vol. IV., New Series, pp. 352–60.
General description of Morioris, pp. 352-5. Flora, pp. 356-7, 359-60. Soil, p. 357. Fauna, p. 358.
Subsequent papers by W. T. L. and H. H. Travers on the Chatham Islands are in the Transactions, N.Z. Institute.

Wilson, J. A. The | Story of Te Waharoa. | In Three Parts. | A Chapter in Early New Zealand History. | By John Alexander Wilson. | Auckland : | Printed and published at the Daily Southern Cross Office, | Queen-Street. | 1866.
 p. 8°. Pp. 63.

Part i : Early history of Maoris. ii : Maori characteristics prior to 1834; advent and influence of missionaries. iii : Maori history at the Lake district, 1835-6.

The only evidence accepted has been derived from missionaries, pakeha-Maoris, and Maoris who were acquainted with Te Waharoa.

The author is also writer of the pamphlet, "How I lost my judgeship." In it, p. 62, he implies that he is "in possession of a considerable mass of information regarding the history of the Maori tribes from their arrival in New Zealand. As a matter of fact I have, since I published the story of Te Waharoa thirteen years ago, which story was the first step taken in this direction, made it a recreation and a study to collect first hand from the best native sources the histories we are anxious to preserve, and some day when I consider my labours complete I hope to publish their result."

1867.

Blair, W. N. The cold lakes of New Zealand. *Scottish Geographical Magazine,* vol. iii, no. ii, pp. 577–88, Nov. 1867. Edinburgh : T. and A. Constable.

Describes the physical aspect of the southern lakes.

Broadfoot, A. New Zealand, | its | Banking and Currency : | being | A letter to His Excellency Sir G. Grey, K.C.B., | Governor of New Zealand, &c. &c. &c. ; | and | the Honorable the Members of the General | Assembly, | by | Alexander Broadfoot. | Christchurch : | Published by A. J. Stevens, High Street. | 1867.
 8°. Pp. 36.

Suggests the establishment of a National Bank, performing functions similar to those of the Bank of England; with prospectus.

Buchanan, J. Botanical Notes | on | the Kaikoura Mountains | and | Mount Egmont. | By John Buchanan, | N.Z. Geological Survey. | Wellington. | By authority : George Didsbury, Government Printer. | 1867.
 roy. 8°. Pp. 16.

*Christianity among the New Zealanders. *Eclectic Review,* cxxv. 443.

Probably a review of *Williams,* below.

Golder, W. The | New Zealand Survey ; | A Poem in Five Cantoes. | With Notes illustrative of New Zealand Progress | and future Prospects. | Also, The Crystal Palace of 1851 ; A Poem in Two Cantoes. | With other Poems and Lyrics. | By | W. Golder, | Author of "New Zealand Minstrelsy," " Pigeons' | Parliament," etc., etc. | O Nature! by impassioned hearts alone | Thy genuine charms are felt.—Pringle. | Wellington : Printed by J. C. Stoddart and Co., for the Author. | 1867.
 fcp. 8°. Title-page, dedication, preface, prospectus, contents, 8 pp. unnumbered; 170 pp.

N.Z. survey, 5 cantos, pp. 1–67, poetically describing the country within a radius of 60 miles from Wellington; notes, pp. 68–72. Ode on Manawatu, p. 83. Paikakariki —a sonnet, p. 84. Signs of the times in 1853 : a quaint epistle on the introduction of the N.Z. Constitution, pp. 116–33. Electioneering, p. 135. Poems on deaths of W. Swainson (pp. 137–43), G. Copeland (pp. 143–4), and Dr. Logan (pp. 144–6).

*Die Goldfelder an der Westküste der Provinz Canterbury, Neu-Seeland, und die neuesten Arbeiten von Dr. Julius Haast daselbst. *Peterm. Mitt.*, 1867, p. 135.

* **Haast,** Julius. Altitude Sections of the principal Routes between the East and West Coasts of the Province of Canterbury, across the Southern Alps. *Journal of the Royal Geographical Society*, xxxvii. 328.
    Probably identical with Appendix 1 to following publication, pp. 59-60, 63-8.

Haast, J. Report | on | The Headwaters | of | The River Rakaia, | with Twenty Illustrations | and Two Appendixes, by | Julius Haast, Ph.D., F.L.S., F.G.S., &c., Provincial Geologist. | Christchurch : | Printed, under the authority of the Provincial Government of the Province of Canterbury, | at the 'Press' Office, Cashel-street, | by James Edward FitzGerald, official printer for the time being to the said Government. | 1866.

f°. Pp. 71+1. Topographical map and illus. There is a third appendix—an advertisement, dated April 15, 1867. The Report was not published till 1867.

* **Hochstetter,** F. *von.* Der Franz-Joseph-Gletscher in den südlichen Alpen Neu-Seelands. *Ausland,* 1867; *Mittheil. der Geogr. Ges. zu Wien,* x. 57. 1866-7.

Hochstetter, F. *von.* New Zealand | its Physical Geography, Geology and Natural History | with special reference | to the Results of Government Expeditions in the Provinces of | Auckland and Nelson | By | Dr. Ferdinand Hochstetter, | Professor of Mineralogy and Geology at the Polytechnic Institution of Vienna, late member of the Austrian | Novara Expedition, President of the J. R. Geographical Society of Vienna, | Honorary Member of the | New Zealand Society at Wellington, | and of the Philosophical Institute of Canterbury, N.Z., etc. etc. | Translated from the German original published in 1863 | by Edward Sauter, A.M., Principal Little Rock Academy, Arkansas. | With additions up to 1866 by the author. | Illustrated with two maps, seven plates in tints, ten large woodcuts page-size, and ninety-three wood-engravings in the text. | Stuttgart, J. G. Cotta. 1867.

4°. Pp. xvi, 515.
Preface to German edition, pp. iii-v. Preface to English edition, pp. vi-vii. Contents, pp. ix-xvi. Ch. i. Nine months in N.Z., pp. 1-32. ii. N.Z.: sketch of its physical structure, pp. 33-45. iii. Geology and palæontology, pp. 46-73 (history of geological and palæontological explorations, pp. 46-50 ; synoptical view of the geological formations and strata in chronological succession, pp. 55-68 ; list of earthquakes, 1856-8, p. 73). iv. Mineral riches, pp. 74-92 (analytical tables of coal, pp. 91-2). v. Gold, pp. 93-121 (history of discovery ; appendix by Haast: list of ores and minerals in Canterbury ; and summary of gold exported). vi. Flora, pp. 123-38 (an appendix has list of flowering alpine plants and of ferns, &c., by Haast, pp. 136-8). vii. Kauri and Harakeke: pine and flax-plant, pp. 139-59 (an appendix gives from Taylor a list of chief vegetable products available as food, pp. 157-8, and a table of chief timber-trees, p. 159). viii. Fauna, pp. 160-72. ix. Kiwi and Moa, pp. 173-98 (appendix, p. 198, compares dimensions of moa with those of ostrich, emu, and kiwi). x. Maoris, pp. 199-222 (appendix, pp. 222-4, contains "the story of Te Uira"). xi. Isthmus of Auckland, pp. 225-45. xii. North Shore, pp. 246-57. xiii. Round the Manukau harbour and to the mouth of the Waikato river, pp. 258-81. xiv. On the lower Waikato ; from Auckland to Tanpiri, pp. 282-304. xv. Waipa and the west coast, pp. 305-32. xvi. From the Waipa through the Mokau and Tuhua districts to Lake Taupo, pp. 333-59. xvii. Lake Taupo, Tongariro and Ruapehu, pp. 360-88. xviii. Ngawhas and puias ; boiling springs, solfataras and fumaroles, pp. 389-434 (appendix, pp. 434-5, contains analyses of hot springs). xix. East Coast from Maketu to Tauranga, and return to Auckland, pp. 436-58 (appendix has table of altitudes in southern part of the Province of Auckland, pp. 458-62). xx. Nelson. xxi. Southern Alps, pp. 478-511 (appendix: Otira road, pp. 511-5).

"The English edition, as here presented, is not a mere translation of the German original. A great portion of the matter in the German work, such as the chapters on the History of Colonisation, on the Maori war, on the Maori poetry, and on the sta-

Hochstetter, F. *von—continued.*
tistics of New Zealand, was intended exclusively for German readers, to whom the numerous English works on New Zealand, treating at length upon these subjects, are often inaccessible. In these subjects I could have offered nothing new to the English public. I have therefore entirely omitted them in the English edition, and have instead rewritten and enlarged the chapters on the Physical Geography and Geology. In the same way, also, the chapter on the Southern Alps had, in consequence of the discoveries and explorations of the latter years, to be entirely rewritten, and likewise in the other chapters additions up to the year 1866 have been made. Also the sequence of chapters has been altered in the English edition. . . . A number of the former illustrations have likewise been replaced here by new ones."—*Preface to the English edition.*
    An English edition was published by Williams and Norgate in 1868.

* **Lindsay,** W. Lauder. Protophytæ of New Zealand. *Quarterly Journal of Microscopical Science,* April, 1867.

M., J. K. The Mary Ira. | Being | the Narrative Journal of a Yachting | Expedition from Auckland to the | South Sea Islands, | and | A Pedestrian Tour in a New District of New Zealand Bush. | *Illustrated with Sketches taken on the spot.* | By | J.K.M. | London : | T. Cautley Newby, Publisher, | 30, Welbeck Street, Cavendish Square. | 1867.
    p. 8°. Pp. ii, 324.
    Chs. ii and iii describe the "tour;" the district was Waikari.

* **[Morison,** J.] Australia as it is : or facts and features, sketches and incidents of Australia and Australian life, with notices of New Zealand. By a clergyman thirteen years resident in the interior of New South Wales. London : 1867.
    8°. Pp. xiii, 286. From Halkett and Laing's *Dictionary of anonymous and pseudonymous literature.*

A New Field for Agricultural and Pastoral Pursuits ; being a Description of the Province of Southland. London. 1867.
    Prize pamphlet.—*Davis.*

Pyke, Vincent. Lost at the gold-fields. *Chambers's Journal,* 1867, and *Southern Mercury,* June 11, 1875.
    A story written in "the Lowland Scotch idiom." "The circumstances narrated are . . . only true in all the more essential particulars."

Taylor, R. Wanganui, | its Past, Present, and Future. | A Lecture | delivered by | The Rev. R. Taylor, M.A., | in the | Oddfellows' Hall, Wanganui, | on the 6th February, 1867. | Previous to his return to England, after a residence of twenty-four years in this | town and district. | Wanganui : | Printed at the Times office, Ridgway-Street. | 1867.
    8°. Pp. 16.

Thomson, *Mrs.* Charles. Twelve Years | in | Canterbury, New Zealand, | with | Visits to the Other Provinces, | and | Reminiscences of the Route Home | through | Australia, etc. | (From a Lady's Journal.) | By Mrs. Charles Thomson. | London : | Sampson Low, Son, and Marston, | Milton House, Ludgate Hill.
    sm. cr. 8°. Pp. xiv, 226. The title bears no date, but it appears in the English Catalogue as having been published in July, 1867.
    The first five chapters (pp. 1-106) relate to N.Z. Ch. i. Twelve years in Canterbury. ii. to v. Dunedin, Wellington, Taranaki, and Auckland.

[Thomson, J. Turnbull.] Rambles | with a | Philosopher ; | or, Views at the Antipodes. | By | An Otagonian, | 1867. | —— | Dunedin : Printed and

[**Thomson**, J. Turnbull]—*continued*.
  published by Mills, Dick & Co., | and sold by the Booksellers. | MDCCCLXVII.
  p. 8°. Pp. xi, 250.
  Sketches of life in Otago before the "Diggings"—life in Dunedin, in villages, and pioneer settlers' life up country, with incidental sketches of Maoris. In the form of a journey on horseback through Otago, with conversations and reflections of a semi-philosophical character. According to Marcus Clarke, "it contains genuine humour, quaint comparison, and philosophic speculation of a high order."

Williams, W. Christianity | among the New Zealanders. | By | the Right Rev. William Williams, D.C.L. | Bishop of Waiapu. | With six illustrations. | Seeley, Jackson, and Halliday, 54 Fleet Street, | London. MDCCCLXVII.
  cr. 8°. Pp. vi+ii, 384.
  A history of the Church of England mission from the time of Marsden, with much information about the Natives. Ch. xvi: Heke's war. Chronological résumé of N.Z. affairs, pp. 381-4.
  Bishop W. derived his "information from the publications of the Church Missionary Society, and much also from personal observation" (*Preface*).

1868.

Bowden, T. A. A Memorial | upon | Colonial Education | addressed | (in the form of a letter) | to William Fox, Esq., M.A., M.H.R., | by | Thomas A. Bowden, B.A., | Inspector of Public Schools, | Province of Wellington. | Wellington : | Printed by T. McKenzie, "Independent" Office, Willis Street. | 1868.
  8°. Pp. 12.
  A scheme of Colonial education.

Bowen, *Sir* G. F. Inaugural Address of Governor Sir George F. Bowen, G.C.M.G., as its first President. Delivered to the Members of the New Zealand Institute, August 4, 1868.
  Published at Wellington, and in Trans., N.Z. Institute, i. 1-9.

***Broome**, [*Sir*] Frederick Napier. Poems from New Zealand. London: Houlston. 1868.
  p. 8°.

Description | of the | Outlying Islands South and East of New Zealand, | viz. | Auckland, Campbell, Antipodes, Bounty, | and the | Chatham Islands. | Published by order of the Lords Commissioners of the Admiralty. | London : | Printed for the Hydrographic Office, Admiralty ; | and sold by | J. D. Potter, *Agent for the Admiralty Charts*, | 31 Poultry, and 11 King Street, Tower Hill. | 1868.
  roy. 8°. Pp. 26.

Fox, W. The Rangitikei-Manawatu purchase. | Speeches | of | William Fox, Esq., | counsel for the Crown, | before the | Native Lands Court, | at Otaki : March and April, 1868. | Together with other documents. | New Zealand : | Published by William Lyon, Willis Street, Wellington. | 1868.
  8°. Pp. 36.
  Mr. Fox's two speeches, pp. 5-32. Judgment, pp. 33-4. Extract from speech of Superintendent, pp. 35-6.

***Haast**, J. Reise von Christchurch auf Neu-Seeland nach den Goldfeldern der Westküste, in Jahre 1865. *Mittheil. der k. k. geogr. Ges. in Wien*, N.F., 1868, pp. 132-189.

* **Haast's** neueste Forschungen in den Neu-Seeländischen Alpen, März u. April, 1868. *Peterm. Mitt.*, 1868, p. 349.

* **Haynes**, S. L. A Ramble in the New Zealand Bush. London, 1868.

The History of Local Government in New Zealand. *Timaru Herald* Office, Timaru, 1868.

> Reprinted from the *Timaru Herald*, where articles answering to the title appear in nos. for Jan. 25, 29, Feb. 5, 19, 22, 28, March 4, 7, 11, 18, of that year.

* Life in New Zealand. *Once a Week*, xx. 471.

Lindsay, W. Lauder. Contributions | to | New Zealand Botany. | By | W. Lauder Lindsay, M.D., | —— | Williams & Norgate, | London and Edinburgh. | 1868.

> 4°. Pp. 102. 4 coloured plates.
>
> i. Introduction [personal]. ii. History of botanical research in Otago. iii. Localities and circumstances of author's plant-collections in Otago. iv. Projected florula of Otago. v. Colonial sections in national herbaria. vi. Comparative study of cultivated forms. vii. Determination of species.. viii. Climatology of Otago. ix. Physical geography and geology of Otago. x. Enumeration of plants collected. xi. Continuity of variation in relation to the limitation of species. xii. Observations of genera and species. xiii. Bibliographical references. xiv. Plates and their explanation. xv. Index.

Lindsay, W. L. On the conservation of forests in our Colonies. Proceedings of British Association, 1867. *Report* (Notices and abstracts), pp. 85–7. London, 1868. *Seemann's Journal of Botany*, vol. vi.

> Urges the establishment of Boards or Inspectors. Describes destructive agencies and results likely to accrue from acclimatisation-experiments.

Lindsay, W. L. On the obstacles to the utilization of New Zealand flax. Proceedings of British Association, 1867. *Report* (Notices and abstracts), pp. 141–3. *Seemann's Journal of Botany*, v. 341.

> Inadequate supply, scarcity and high value of labour, want of suitable processes.

Lyttelton, *Lord*. Two Lectures | on a Visit to the | Canterbury Colony | in 1867–68. | 1.—The Voyage. | 2.—The Colony. | By | Lord Lyttelton. | Stourbridge : | T. Mark, Printer and Publisher, High Street. | London : | Simpkin, Marshall, & Co. | 1868.

> 8°. Pp. 38.
>
> A familiar description of the Settlement of Canterbury, its society, &c.

* New Zealand and its gold fields. *Blackwood*, cv. 298. 1868.

[**Pyke**, Vincent.] The | Province of Otago, | in | New Zealand : | its | Progress, Present Condition, | Resources, and Prospects. | Published by Authority of [The Provincial Government. | Dunedin, Otago, New Zealand. | 1868.

> 8°. Pp. iv, 70. Six illus. and map.
>
> Ch. i. Descriptive. ii. Rivers and harbours. iii. Towns. iv. Historical sketch. v. Climate. vi. Land. vii. Goldfields. viii. Land-laws. ix. Animals and products. x. Government. xi. Public institutions. xii. Labour and cost of living. xiii. Trades, manufactures, and commerce. xiv. Conclusion.

* **Saunders**, A. New Zealand, its climate and soil. London, 1868.
> Pamphlet.

* **Taylor**, Richard. The Past and Present of New Zealand, with its Prospects for the Future. With numerous illustrations. By the Rev. Richard Taylor, M.A., F.G.S. London : W. Macintosh. Wanganui : H. I. Jones. 1868.

> 8°. Pp. 331.
>
> See notices of the book on a leaf appended to *Te Ika a Maui*, second edition.

Wakefield, E. G. The | Founders of Canterbury. | Volume I. | Being Letters from the late | Edward Gibbon Wakefield | to the late | John Robert Godley, |

Wakefield, E. G.—*continued*.
and to other well-known helpers in the | foundation | of the | Settlement of Canterbury | in | New Zealand. | Published by Stevens and Co., High Street, Christchurch, | New Zealand. | 1868.
8°. Pp. xvi, 352.
Editor's preface (by E. Jerningham Wakefield) contains (pp. iii-xlii) a sketch of E. Gibbon Wakefield's connection with N.Z.
The correspondence extends from Nov. 1847 to Oct. 1850. A second volume—"to consist principally of letters from leading colonizers to " E. G. Wakefield—was never published. The letters relate chiefly to the Canterbury settlement.. Letters at pp. 31-47 refer to E. G. Wakefield's book on Colonization, which he describes (after Godley) as his "Mrs. Harris;" to the Canterbury Papers, pp. 200, 203, 206-7.
There is a long letter from W. to Gladstone in the *N.Z. Journal*, vii. 126-30, on the government and colonization of N.Z.

Williams, Thomas C. The Manawatu purchase completed; or, The treaty of Waitangi broken. London. 1868.
8°. Pp. 72.

1869.

Adderley, C. B. Review | of | "The Colonial Policy | of Lord J. Russell's Administration," | By Earl Grey, 1853; | and of | Subsequent Colonial History. | By the | Rt. Hon. C. B. Adderley, M.P. | London : | Edward Stanford, 6 and 7, Charing Cross, S.W. | 1869.
8°. Pp. vi (not numbered), 423.
The part relating to N.Z. is at pp. 129-62. A general criticism of Grey's account, continuing the narrative to 1868; with extracts from Gladstone's speech on the Constitution Act of 1852.
Reviewed in the *Edinburgh*, cxxx. 113-22 : see 1870.

An Appeal | to the | Men of New Zealand. | By Fémmina. | Nelson : | Published by J. Hounsell, Bookseller and Stationer. | 1869.
8°. Pp. 13.
An argument for female suffrage.

*****Bourne**, H. R. Fox. The Story of Our Colonies; with Sketches of their present Condition. London : Hogg. 1869.
12°. Pp. 411.

Bowden, Thomas A. Manual | of | New Zealand Geography, | With Maps and Examination Questions; | by | Thomas A. Bowden, B.A., | Inspector of Provincial Schools and Mathematical Master of | Wellington Grammar School, assisted by | James Hector, M.D., F.R.S., | Geologist to the New Zealand Government. | In Two Parts. | Part I.—Containing the General Geography of the Colony, with a Sketch of its History and Productions. | Part II.—Containing a Descriptive Account of each Province or Principal Division. | London : | George Philip and Son, 32, Fleet Street. | Liverpool : | Caxton Buildings, South John Street. | Wellington, New Zealand : Edward Greaves Smith. | —— | 1869.
12°. Pp. x, 143. 10 maps.
Introductory chapter on the geological structure of N.Z. by Dr. Hector, pp. 49-56.

*****Broome**, Frederick Napier. The crisis in New Zealand. *Macmillan's Magazine*, xx. 417.

Buller, Rev. J. The Maori War. | A Lecture | delivered at the Rooms of the Young Men's Christian Association, on Friday Evening, June 25, 1869. | By the | Rev. James Buller, | Thirty-three Years Missionary in New Zea-

Buller, Rev. J.—*continued.*
land. | Reprinted from "The Daily Southern Cross." | Auckland: | Printed by Charles Williamson, O'Connell Street. | 1869.
    sm. 4°. Pp. 9, double columns.
        Moral aspect of the war. Defence of the missionaries. Imperial Government responsible for the war. Vigorous dealing with the Maoris needed.

*****Busby,** J. The Case of Mr. Busby: Address in the House of Representatives, 30th July, 1869. By J. Busby. Auckland: W. Atkin.
    Pp. 35, with Appendix.—*Davis.*

***** Census von Neu-Seeland, 19 December, 1867. *Petcrm. Mitt.*, 1869, p. 72.

Colenso, W. On the Maori Races of New Zealand. Transactions of New Zealand Institute, 1868. Vol. i: 1869, 76 pp.: separately paged.
        §§ 1–9. Physical characteristics. 10–17. Industry. 18. Domestic. 19. Rank. 20. Property. 27–35. Intellectual and moral characteristics and sentiments. 36–9. Religion. 40–43, 48–9. Language. 44–7. Literature. 50, 53. Ethnology. 51. Antiquity in N.Z. 54–8. External history. 59–64. Domestic history. 65–6. Future. Table of Native population, North Island, with names of tribes and boundaries.

Dilke, C. W. Greater Britain: | a Record of Travel | in | English-Speaking Countries | during | 1866 and 1867. | By Charles Wentworth Dilke, M.P. | In two volumes.—Vol. I. | With maps and illustrations. | Second edition. London : | Macmillan and Co. | 1869.
    8°. View from the Buller and sketch-map.
        The part relating to N.Z. is at pp. 330–404. Life at the Westland gold-diggings in 1866, pp. 330–46. Polynesians generally, pp. 347–54 (Maories were Malays; resemble Red Indians). A runanga, pp. 355–78. Maories generally, pp. 379–89. Their gradual disappearance, pp. 390–7. The future of N.Z., pp. 398–402.

Dobson, Edward. On the public works of the Province of Canterbury. Read before Institution of Civil Engineers, Dec. 7, 1869. Abstract in *Nature*, i. 199–200. Apparently identical with a paper in the Trans. N.Z. Institute, i. 181–202.
        A history of the Public Works Department of Canterbury from its establishment in 1854 to the completion of the railways in 1868.

Hamilton, A. On the | Economic Progress | of | New Zealand. | A Paper read before | The Section for Economic Science and Statistics | of the | British Association, | *At Exeter*, 24*th August*, 1869. | By Archibald Hamilton, Esq. | London : | Harrison and Sons, St. Martin's Lane, | Printers in Ordinary to Her Majesty. | 1869.
    8°. Pp. 18. The paging is pp. 293–307, being that of the *Journal of the Statistical Society*, vol. xxxii., Sept. 1869.
        In a preface the writer states that he has never been in N.Z. Sir G. Grey's speech (which is also given in *Scientific Opinion*, ii. 303–4) is appended. An abstract of the paper is in the Report of the British Association, 1869, pp. 192–3.

***** History and Description of Thames Goldfields; with authentic Statistics. By an old Californian Miner. Auckland. 1869.
    Pamphlet.—*Davis.*

[Hawthorne, James.] A | Dark Chapter | from | New Zealand History. | By a Poverty Bay Survivor. | "*Solitudinem faciunt, pacem appellant.*" | 1869. | Printed and published by James Wood, at his Printing | Office, Tennyson-Street, Napier, Hawke's Bay.
    cr. 8°. Pp. 41.
        An account of the massacre by Te Kooti, its antecedents, and the subsequent campaign.
        The authorship is acknowledged in a private letter.

***Hursthouse**, C. F. The Case of New Zealand. Walton: Lewes, 1869.
Pamphlet.

Hursthouse, Charles Flinders. "New Zealand wars." A letter to the Times. Ed. 2. London [1869].
cr. 8°. Pp. 3+27.

Maori life. *Once a Week*, June 12, 1869, pp. 471–4. Four illus.
From personal experience.

Potts, T. H. Notes | on the | Breeding Habits | of | New Zealand Birds. | By T. H. Potts. | Read before the Wellington Philosophical Society, July 17, 1869. | Wellington: James Hughes, Printer, Lambton Quay.
roy. 8°. Pp. 39, and continued (by papers read in 1870) to 110 pp. Illus.

Sadler, W. E. Roving Diggers to become Colonial Settlers: How? An Essay. By William Edmund Sadler. Auckland: Atkin. 1869.
8°. Pp. 32.—*Davis*.

Scoffern, John, *M.B.* The Maories. *Belgravia*, x. 96–103. Nov. 1869.
General remarks.

Sewell, Henry. The | Case of New Zealand, | and | Our Colonial Policy. | A Letter | from Henry Sewell, Esq. | (formerly Colonial Secretary and late Attorney-General of New Zealand), | to Edward Wilson, Esq., Victoria. | London: | Bell and Daldy, York Street, Covent Garden. | 1869.
8°. Pp. 30.
Occasioned by Lord Granville's despatch announcing the withdrawal of the troops. Reviews the history of the management of Native affairs and its transference to the Ministry.

***Strelitz**. Aus dem Tagebuch eines Goldgräbers in Neuseeland in den Jahren 1863–67. *Ausland*, 1869, nos. 31, 36.

***Strelitz**. Eine Reise von Australien nach Neuseeland zur Zeit der Goldperiode. *Post* [a newspaper], 1869, no. 643.

Transactions | and | Proceedings | of the | New Zealand Institute, | 1868. | Vol. I. | Edited and published under the authority of the Board of | Governors of the Institute, | By | James Hector, M.D., F.R.S. | Issued May, 1869. | Wellington: | James Hughes, Printer, Lambton Quay.
8°.
The Transactions of the Institute have been issued annually since 1869, and contain a mass of materials on the physical geography, geology, and natural history of New Zealand, and on the Maoris—their race, language, and religion. A full Index to the first seventeen volumes was issued in 1880.
The present volume reprints the six Exhibition essays published in 1865, and adds one by Colenso on the Maori races.

Weld, F. A. Notes | on | New Zealand affairs: | comprising | A Sketch of its Political History, | in reference especially to | The Native Question; | its present position—the policy for the future, | with a few general remarks upon the | relations of England to her colonies. | By Fred. A[loysius] Weld, Esq. | late Prime Minister of that Colony. | London: | Edward Stanford, 6 & 7, Charing Cross, S.W. | 1869.
8°. Pp. 83.
"I propose to give a very slight sketch of the history of the Colony, and to add some geographical and statistical information—to touch upon its political position—to point out the nature and causes of the present insurrection—and to conclude by offering a few remarks and suggestions" (p. 4). Mr. Weld gives an account of his own Ministry and its policy at pp. 23–46.
There is a sketch of Mr. (now Sir F.) Weld in Estcourt's *Pillars of the Empire*, pp. 333–9. His policy is described in *Rusden*, ii. 264–5.

Wilmer, G. The Lowing Herd; and Zealandia. By G. Wilmer. Riccarton. 1869.
    12°. Pp. 16.
    Two poems, describing in blank verse the shooting of wild cattle.

Wilson, G. H. Ekino | and | Other Poems. | — — | Wellington : | Published by Wm. Lyon, Willis-street. | MDCCCLXIX.
    12°. Pp. vi (not numbered), 96.
    Poems on Maori legend and history, scenery and life.

1870.

Barker, Mary Anne, *Lady.* Station Life | in | New Zealand. | By | Lady Barker. | London : | Macmillan and Co. | 1870.
    cr. 8°. Pp. xi, 238. One illus.
    Narrative (in the form of letters) of residence, work, and expeditions in the inland portion of Canterbury in 1865-68. The book was reviewed in *Chambers's Journal,* Feb. 4, 1871, pp. 73-6, and translated into German—Stationsleben auf Neu-Seeland. Coburg : Sendelbach, 1875. 8°.

*****Bates,** J. C. New Zealand. *Scribner's Magazine,* i. 529, 577. 1870.

Braim, Thomas Henry. New Homes : | the Rise, Progress, Present Position, | and future Prospects | of each of the | Australian Colonies and New Zealand, | regarded as | Homes for all Classes of Emigrants. | By | Thomas Henry Braim, D.D., F.R.G.S., | &c., &c., &c., | late Archdeacon, Diocese of Melbourne, and now Rector of | Bishop's Caundle, Sherborne, and Chaplain to the Most Noble the Marquis of Lothian. | Profusely Illustrated. | — — | London : | Bull, Simmons & Co., 9, Wigmore Street. | 1870.
    cr. 8°. Pp. vii, 411.
    Ch. vii, pp. 363-97, describes New Zealand at second-hand.

Chapman's Centenary Memorial | of | Captain Cook's | Description of | New Zealand | One Hundred Years Ago | New Zealand | Geo. T. Chapman, publisher | Queen Street, Auckland | 1870.
    sm. 4°. Pp. xx, 164. Cook's charts of N.Z., Tolago Bay, Cook's Strait, R. Thames and Mercury Bay, and Bay of Islands ; charts of 1601 and 1620 ; chart showing all known of Pacific in 1579 ; Tasman's chart of N.Z. of 1642 ; and Kitchen's chart of 1772. 27 illustrations, many from original sketches.
    Consolidated extracts of all that relates to New Zealand in Cook's Voyages, with introductory sketch of discovery of islands, narratives of Maoris who remember Cook, notes and illustrations of places considered remarkable by Cook, or made remarkable by incidents in which he was a performer.
    Introduction, pp. ix.-xx. Cook's voyages, pp. 21-2. First voyage round N.Z., pp. 23-106. Notes on the habits and customs of the Maori, pp. 107-11. Cook's second voyage, pp. 125-44. Cook's third voyage, pp. 145-53. Life of Cook, pp. 154-6, from *Rev.* Gideon Smales, "Whitby authors." First English vessel in the Waitemata (from Cruise), pp. 157-8. Geographical discovery in connection with the history of N.Z., as shown in our Charts of Progressive Discovery, pp. 159-60.
    "An interesting volume might be made of all that is related respecting N.Z. in Cook's several voyages."—*N.Z. Journal,* Oct. 2, 1841.

***** **Christianity** among the New Zealanders. *Christian Observer,* lxx. 374. 1870.

***** **Clarke,** G. M. The resources of New Zealand. *Overland Monthly,* San Francisco, vi. 250. 1870.

Denison, *Sir* W. Varieties | of Vice-Regal Life. | By | Sir William Denison, K.C.B. | late Governor-General of the Australian Colonies | and Governor

Denison, Sir W.—*continued.*
of Madras. | In two volumes. | —— | London: Longmans, Green, and Co. | 1870.
8°.
New Zealand, ii. 1-24. Remarks on responsible government; correspondence between the author, the Duke of Newcastle, and Governor Gore Browne.

* **Engler,** L. Der Golddistrict Shortland in Neu-Seeland. *Aus allen Welttheilen*, 1870, no. 40.

* **FitzGerald,** J. E. The self-reliant policy in New Zealand. London, 1870.
8°. Pamphlet.

* Die Goldfelder an der Thames in Neu-Seeland. *Peterm. Mitt.*, 1870, p. 110.

Grey, Sir George. [A communication on recent date of the moa in the Transactions of Zoological Society.]

* **Haast,** Julius. Notes to accompany the Topographical Map of the Southern Alps, in the Province of Canterbury. *Journal of the Royal Geographical Society*, xl. 433. 1870.

* **Hadfield,** *Bishop* O. [A paper in the *Journal of Ethnological Society*, of London. 1870.]

Hursthouse, Charles Flinders. Australasian Independence. Remarks in favour of the Six Australasian Colonies, &c. &c. London:—Edward Stanford, 6 & 7, Charing Cross. 1870.
8°. Pp. 24.
The "case of New Zealand" is argued at pp. 12-14, and "Maori prowess" discussed at pp. 20-2.

* **Hutton,** F. W. A Lecture on the Manufacture of New Zealand Flax, delivered before the Auckland Institute, July 12, 1870. By Captain F. W. Hutton, F.G.S. Auckland. Printed by Charles Williamson, O'Connell Street. 1870.
sm. 4°. Pp. 17, double columns.

* Jahresbericht des Norddeutschen Bundesconsuls zu Wellington, Neu-Seeland, für das Jahr 1869. *Preuss. Handelsarchiv*, 1870, no. 39.

* **Lang,** J. D. The Coming Event; or, Freedom and Independence for the Seven United Provinces of Australia. By John Dunmore Lang, D.D., A.M. Sydney. 1870.
See extracts from it in E. J. Wakefield's *Taxes in N.Z.*, 1878, pp. 30-2.

Meade, Herbert. A Ride | through the Disturbed Districts of | New Zealand; | together with some Account of the | South Sea Islands. | Being Selections from the Journals and Letters of | Lieut. the Hon. Herbert Meade, R.N. | Edited by his Brother. | —— | *With Maps and Illustrations from the Author's Sketches.* | London: | John Murray, Albemarle Street. | 1870.
8°. Pp. xi, 375. Eight illus. of N.Z. scenes and a map of the Hot Lakes district.
Chs. i-vi, pp. 1-170, describe a visit to Tauranga, Taupo, and the Lakes in 1864, when he was captured by the Kingites; Pai Marire worship and tenets; Volkner's murder; and natives generally. The book is of more than average literary merit. A letter from Sir G. Grey is embodied in the Preface.

* **Meinicke.** Die Alpen Neu-Seelands. *Aus allen Welttheilen*, 1870, no. 40 f.

New Zealand Institute. *Nature*, ii. 160. 1870.

Sir Charles Adderley on colonial policy. *Edinburgh Review*, cxxxi. 98. Jan. 1870.
    N.Z.: pp. 113-20. The affairs of N.Z. illustrate the evil consequences (1) of the imprudent interference of the mother-country, (2) of disposition of colony to claim that interference when withdrawn. Defence of Lord Granville.

Taylor, *Rev.* R. Maori and English | Dictionary. | New and enlarged edition | of | " *A Leaf from the Natural History of New Zealand, or a Vocabulary* | *of its different Productions, &c., with their Native Names.*" | By | Rev. Richard Taylor, M.A., F.G.S., | Author of " New Zealand and its Inhabitants," " The Past, | Present, and Future of New Zealand," etc. | New Zealand | George T. Chapman, Publisher | Queen Street | Auckland.
    12°. Pp. 120, with 6 pp. (unnumbered) of title-page, preface, contents, and sub-title-page. 1870.
    Mr. Taylor made a number of corrections and additions to the "Leaf," and sent it from Whanganui in Jan. 1867. "Since that time three gentlemen well acquainted with the native [sic] history, &c., of New Zealand have gone carefully over the work, making numerous additions and improvements. . . ."—*Preface*.
    Part I.—*Natural history*:—Plants indigenous to N.Z. available for food, medicine, and other economic purposes, pp. 1-12. Animals, pp. 13-4. Reptiles, pp. 14-5. Insects, pp. 15-6. Birds, pp. 17-23. Fish, pp. 23-8. Shells, pp. 28-9. Trees, pp. 30-5. Ferns, pp. 35-6. Shrubs, pp. 36-9. Flowers, plants, &c., pp. 30-43. Creeping, climbing, and parasitic plants, pp. 43-5. Grasses, pp. 45-6. Seaweed, p. 47. Mosses, &c., pp. 47-8. Kumara, &c., pp. 48-50. Stones, earth, &c., pp. 50-2. Parts of trees, pp. 52-3. Parts of fish, birds, &c., pp. 53-4.
    Part II.—*Religion, traditions, and habits and customs*:—Religion, pp. 57-60. Original canoes, pp. 60-70. Parts of the body, pp. 70-4. General names, pp. 74-6. List of principal tribes, with localities, pp. 76-7. War, murder, &c., p. 77. Fortifications, p. 78. Tattooing, pp. 78-9. Salutations, p. 79.
    Part III.—Time, pp. 83-5. Heavens, stars, &c., pp. 85-6. Elements, pp. 86-7. Water, pp. 87-9. Winds, p. 89. Land, pp. 90-1. Manufactured substances, apparel, &c., pp. 91-4. Canoe, pp. 94-6. Houses, &c., pp. 96-9. Implements, pp. 99-103. Games and amusements, pp. 103-5. Proverbs, pp. 105-6.
    Part IV.—Pharmacopœia, pp. 109-11. Diseases, pp. 112-7. Tradition, pp. 117-20.

Taylor, *Rev.* R. Te Ika a Maui; | or, | New Zealand and its Inhabitants. | Illustrating the | Origin, Manners, Customs, Mythology, Religion, Rites, | Songs, Proverbs, Tables, and Language of the Maori | and Polynesian Races in General; | together with the Geology, Natural History, Productions, and Climate | of the Country. | *Second edition*. | With numerous Illustrations. | By the | Rev. Richard Taylor, M.A., F.G.S. | *A Missionary in New Zealand for more than Thirty Years.* | London : | William Macintosh, 24, Paternoster Row; | and | H. Ireson Jones, Wanganui, New Zealand. | MDCCCLXX.
    Pp. xv, 731. Many illustrations, from sketches by the author.
    ". . . While all relating to the Maori and his myths, &c., which appeared in the former work has been retained in this, so much new matter is added, and so many other subjects introduced, that, to a certain extent, it may be regarded as a new Work. . . . The present Work may be viewed as a digest of a mass of notes made by the author during a residence of more than thirty years in those parts. . . ."—*Extract from preface to Second Edition*.
    Ch. i. Introduction. ii. Two Polynesian races. iii. Our race and its origin. iv. Civilization. v. Religion. vi, vii. Mythology. viii. Tapu. ix. Whare-kura (ancient temple, pp. 174-80); religious rites (pp. 180-5); infant baptism (pp. 185-6); war ceremonies (pp. 186-96). x. Fishing ceremonies (pp. 197-201); manner of hunting the rat (pp. 201-3); witchcraft (pp. 203-5) and divination—*niu* (pp. 205-6); karakias (festivals, p. 207); cursing (pp. 208-9); kura—sacred colour (pp. 209-10). xi. Images. xii, xiii. Funeral rites. xiv, xv. Traditions and legends. xvi. Proverbs (pp. 293-302); fables (pp. 302-5). xvii. Songs (pp. 306-14); mottoes (pp. 315-6). xviii. Personal ornaments (pp. 317-20); tattoo (pp. 320-3); embalming (pp. 324-5); names (pp. 325-31); degrees of consanguinity (pp. 331-2). xix. Dreams (pp. 333-5); marriage (pp. 335-9); eating (pp. 339-42); feasts (pp. 342-3); night speaking (pp. 343-4). xx. Amusements (pp. 345-50);

Taylor, Rev. R.—*continued.*
chiefs (pp. 350-55); tenure of land (pp. 355-0); barter (pp. 359-00). xxi. Seasons (pp. 361-3); constellations (pp. 363-4); time (pp. 364-6); fire (pp. 367-71); measures (p. 371). xxii. Language. xxiii. Origin, as traced by language; table of tribes and population of N.Z. (p. 411). xxiv. Maori middens. xxv. Age of N.Z. xxvi. Geology; visit to Rotomahana (pp. 464-9). xxix. Means of support (pp. 493-500); houses (pp. 500-2); native ovens (pp. 503-4);]pua bread (pp. 504-8). xxx. Hongi (pp. 509-17); Tareha (pp. 517-19); Te Heuheu (pp. 520-5). xxxi. Te Rauparaha and Rangihaeata (pp. 526-44). xxxii. Hone Heke (pp. 545-51) and other chiefs. xxxiii. Samuel Marsden. xxxiv, xxxv. Natural history. xxxvi. Miscellaneous and (pp. 665-8) climate. xxxvii. Botany. xxxviii. Chronology.

The traditions reported by Taylor had not, he says, been previously collected.—*Preface to first ed.*

Taylor, William. The Education of the People. | Ten Letters | addressed to | his Honour T. B. Gillies, Esq., | Superintendent of the Province of Auckland, New Zealand. | With | Notes and Appendices. | By | William Taylor, | Head Master of St. Matthew's School, Auckland. | Auckland : | Published by E. Wayte, Bookseller and Stationer, Queen Street. | 1870.

8°. Pp. 32.

Letter iv is on the Act of 1869 and v on that of 1857, the re-enactment of which is recommended.

* Twenty Months in Southland, 1867-69. By a Tasmanian. Hobart Town. 1870. Pamphlet.—*Davis.*

Whitworth, R. P. Martin's Bay Settlement, | West Coast of Otago, New Zealand. | Narrative of a Voyage from Dunedin to Martin's Bay, | and of a Return Journey Overland, | with Maps of the Country, and the Land Regulations. | By R. P. Whitworth, | Special Correspondent of the "Otago Daily Times." | Price One Shilling. | Dunedin : | Printed at the "Otago Daily Times" Office, Princes Street. | 1870.

8°. Pp. 64.

Wood, J. G. The | Natural | History of Man; | being | an Account of the Manners and Customs of the | Uncivilized Races of Men. | With new designs | by Zwecker, Angas, Danby, Handley, etc. etc. | Engraved by the brothers Dalziel. | Australia, New Zealand, Polynesia, America, Asia, | and Ancient Europe. | London : | George Routledge and Sons, The Broadway, Ludgate. | New York : 416, Broome Street. | 1870.

imp. 8°. Pp. viii, 864. Illus.

A general account of the Maoris—their dress, domestic life, food and cookery, war, canoes, religion, tapu, funeral ceremonies, and architecture—is given at pp. 106-202. There are many illustrations, chiefly from *Angas*, but some are of weapons and instruments in Mr. Wood's own collection.

The writer is "indebted for much information about the country" to Mr. A. Christie, and there are descriptions of articles from personal examination; but the book is mainly a compilation, though from good sources.

1871.

* **Barclay,** P. The Word of Christ in New Zealand. London : Whittaker. 1871.

p. 8°.—*Davis.*

Canterbury Flax Association: Information relative to the Utilization of the Phormium Tenax, &c. Christchurch : Printed by Jones and Tombs, Cathedral Square; and Auckland. 1871.

8°. Pp. 76.

The Case | of | Messrs. | Lundon and Whitaker. | Narrative of Facts connected therewith, | and | consideration of the law thereon. | Auckland : | printed at the " Herald " office, 10, Wyndham-street. | 1871.
    8°. Pp. 29.
    Petition, pp. 3–8, of J. Lundon and F. A. Whitaker. Origin of the case, pp. 8–11. State of the law at the time, pp. 11–14. Actions pending in the Supreme Court, pp. 14–5. Action taken by Mr. Graham before the Assembly, pp. 15–16. Action taken by O'Keefe and others, pp. 16–21. Final passing of the Native Lands Bill, 1869, and the legal effect of clauses 8 and 9, pp. 21–4. Trial under Native Lands Bill, 1800, and its termination, pp. 24–5. Conclusion, pp. 26–7. Appendix : declaration of J. de Hirsch, pp. 28–9.
    Private controversy on title to certain lands. Replied to by J. de Hirsch : see below.

Colenso, W. Fiat Justitia. | Being a Few Thoughts Respecting the Maori Prisoner | Kereopa, | now in Napier Gaol, awaiting his Trial for Murder. | —— | By W. Colenso. | " *Audi alteram partem.*" | Napier : | Printed by Dinwiddie, Morrison, and Co. Herald Office. | 1871.
    roy. 8°. Pp. 23.
    Two letters to the *Hawke's Bay Herald* mainly on the Hauhau movement; a speech by Bishop Selwyn in the House of Lords, pp. 21–2; Te Kooti's "Hau-Hau" prayers, p. 23.
    Historical articles relating to Te Kooti appeared in the *N.Z. Times*, March, 1889.

* **Cooper,** H. T. The lake district of New Zealand. *Victoria Magazine,* xvii. 516. 1871.

Gillies, Thomas Bannatyne. "Our System of Government." A Lecture by His Honor T. B. Gillies, Esq. Reprinted from the *Morning News*. On July 7, 1871.
    sq. 8°. Pp. 12.

* **Haast,** J. Die Thermen der Hanmer-Ebene in Neu-Seeland. *Peterm. Mitt.*, 1871, p. 95.

* **Hector,** J. Neue Moa-Funde in Neuseeland. *Globus,* xx. 60 (1871).

Hector, J. On recent Moa remains in New Zealand. *Nature,* iv. 184–6, 221. 1871.
    In support of the view that the Moa survived to very recent times. Translated in *Globus,* above.

Hirsch, James de. [Pamphlet, of which first four pages with title-page are wanting. Dated Grahamstown, 31st August, 1871.]
    8°. Pp. 25, with appendix, pp. 26–8, and plans.
    Reply, section by section, to Whitaker and Lundon's pamphlet.

Hursthouse, C. Remarks | on | " New Zealand Immigration :" | addressed, with permission, to the | Hon. William Fox, M.H.R. | By Charles Hursthouse. | Respectfully presented to the Hon. Members of the General Assembly, and to the | New Zealand Press, in the hope of awakening public attention to the necessity | of some change of Policy in the vital matter to which they relate. | —— | New Plymouth :—R. Pheney. | 1871.
    8°. Pp. 15.
    Proposes (1) one uniform system of land-regulations for whole colony, and (2) establishment in London of an Immigration and Colonization Agency.
    At pp. 14–5 is a letter from Carlyle, who still persuades himself " that the Government will before long find itself compelled to attempt, in concert with its colonies, some suitable *National System of Emigration,*" &c.

Hutton, F. W. Geological Survey of New Zealand. | Catalogue | of the | Birds of New Zealand, | with | Diagnoses of the Species. | By | Frederick

Hutton, F. W.—*continued*.
Wollaston Hutton, F.G.S., | Assistant Geologist. | Published by command. | New Zealand. | James Hughes, Printer, Lambton Quay, Wellington. | 1871.
roy. 8°. Pp. x, 85.
Birds of N.Z., pp. 1-54. Birds introduced by European settlers, pp. 55-69. Critical notes, pp. 71-81. Bibliography, pp. viii-ix.

Macfarlane, J. S. Craig's troubles ; | or, Our Antipodean Courts and Laws. | —— | Auckland : | Printed by Reed and Brett, "Evening Star" Office, Queen-street. | 1871.
8°. Pp. 23. Appendix 1.
The preface is: "As Mr. Craig's troubles at Whaugapoua have assumed an aspect of public importance, I take this method of publishing them for general information. —J. S. MACFARLANE, Auckland, 14th August, 1871."
A "painful and peculiar case" stated to show that Natives may ignore bargains made, payments received, and agreements signed, and be encouraged in so doing by the Courts.

* **Manning, J.** The Maoris of New Zealand. *Overland Monthly*, San Francisco, vii. 48. 1871.

* **Moister,** *Rev.* W. History of Wesleyan Missions. 1871.

* **Money,** Charles L. Knocking about in New Zealand. Melbourne. 1871.
cr. 8°.
A cadet's reminiscences of Canterbury, Westland diggings, colonial forces, war at Patea, Von Tempsky, McDonnell, &c.

Mr. Robert Graham's | Remarks on | a Pamphlet | published by | Messrs. Whitaker and Lundon. | (*For distribution among the Members of the House of Representatives.*) | Auckland : | Printed by Jones and Tombs, Wellesley-street, Auckland. | 1871.
8°. Pp. 10 and appendix, p. 11.
See the pamphlet above, Case, &c.

A New Zealand Station. *Chambers's Journal*, xlviii. 73-6. Feb. 4, 1871.
A review of Lady Barker's *Station Life in N.Z.*

* **Nöggerath,** ——. Die Tuf- oder Explorationskrater auf Neuseeland verglichen mit den ähnlichen Erscheinungen in der Eifel und im Laacher-Seegebiet. *Ausland*, 1871, no. 48.

Parliamentary | Skits and Sketches, | by | Silver Pen. | Dedicated to the | Members of the House of Representatives, | By the Authoress. | Wellington : | Printed by T. McKenzie, at his Steam Printing Office. | MDCCCLXXI.
fcp. 8°. Pp. 26.
A second series appeared in 1872, pp. 31.

Tylor, Edward Burnett. Primitive Culture : | Researches into the Development of Mythology, Philosophy, | Religion, Art, and Custom. | By | Edward B. Tylor, | author of " Researches into the early history of mankind, &c." | —— | In two volumes. | London : | John Murray, Albemarle Street. | 1871.
Only incidental references to N.Z. occur. In i., pp. 302-4, Tylor gives an account of the Maui-myth, upon which he says: "I have to thank Sir G. Grey for a more explicit and mythologically more consistent translation of the story of Maui's entrance into the womb of Hine-nui-te-po and her crushing him to death between her thighs, than is given in his English version." He adds: "I have had inquiry made in " N.Z. on a particular point, "and have received a perfect confirmation of the interpretation of the legend of the death of Maui, as being a nature-myth of the setting sun" (i. 304). See also i. 309-11, 325, ii. 242-3, 253. References to the literature of the Maui-myth are given by Tylor, i. 311. Add—Wade, *Journey*, 1842, pp. 87-96, and A. Lang, in *Princeton Review*, July 1884, pp. 64-6.

Williams, W. A | Dictionary | of the | New Zealand Language ; | to which is added | A Selection of Colloquial Sentences. | By the Right Reverend | William Williams, D.C.L. | Bishop of Waiapu, New Zealand. | Third Edition, | with numerous additions and corrections and | an introduction | by the Venerable | W. L. Williams, B.A. | Archdeacon of Waiapu. | —— | Williams and Norgate, | 14, Henrietta Street, Covent Garden, London ; | and 20, South Frederick Street, Edinburgh. | 1871.

8°. Pp. xvi (grammatical introduction), 267.

"The principal feature in this edition of the Maori Dictionary, which calls for special notice, is the arrangement of the words." Words with reduplicated syllables are grouped under the simple forms. The "additions amount to upwards of 1200 genuine Maori words, without reckoning the reduplicated forms, the causatives with ' *whaka,*' or the derivative nouns. The large number of corrections and additions and the alteration in the general plan of the work have involved the necessity of re-writing the whole." The Concise Grammar has been omitted. "The failure of the attempt to get this book printed in N.Z. involved the necessity of sending it home . . .; hence the deplorable number of typographical errors. . . ." See also 1844 and 1852.

* **Wissenschaftliche Forschungen in Neu-Seeland.** *Ausland,* 1871, no. 15.

1872.

Baden-Powell, G. S. New Homes | for the.| Old Country. | A Personal Experience | of the | Political and Domestic Life, the Industries, | and the Natural History | of | Australia and New Zealand. | By | George S. Baden-Powell. | —— | With forty-six illustrations. | London : | Richard Bentley and Son. | —— | 1872.

8°. Pp. xx, 512.

N.Z., local, pp. 70-82. Social, pp. 83-9. Both descriptive. Ch. 44 is on moas and wekas. Ch. 23 is partly on N.Z. flax.

Barclay, P. Notes | on | New Zealand. | For the Use of Emigrants. | By the Rev. P. Barclay, M.A. | formerly Minister at Napier, New Zealand. | With a Map. | London : | G. Street, 30 Cornhill, E.C. | John Menzies & Co., Edinburgh and Glasgow. | 1872. | Price Twopence.

8°. Pp. 30.

Discovery and settlement, size and position, natives, general description, mineral wealth, animal and vegetable productions, prospects for colonists, schools and churches. Statistical appendix.

"A good summary of facts, for the use of intending emigrants."—*W. Chambers,* in *Chambers's Journal,* Sept. 6, 1873.

Barker, Mary Anne, *Lady.* A Christmas Cake | in Four Quarters. | By Lady Barker, | Author of " Stories About . . ," " Station Life in New Zealand," etc. | —— | With Illustrations. | London : | Macmillan and Co. | 1872.

cr. 8°. Pp. vi (not numbered), 304.

Christmas-day in New Zealand, pp. 239-304.

Domett, A. Ranolf and Amohia : | a South-Sea Day-Dream. | By | Alfred Domett. | London : | Smith, Elder & Co., 15, Waterloo Place. | 1872.

p. 8°. Pp. 511.

At pp. 97, 153, 158, 245, 354, 374, 379, 407, 412, are paraphrases of songs, chiefly in Sir G. Grey's collection. Notes on Maori customs, &c., pp. 480-503. The contents are given under the new edition, *ann.* 1883.

"I do not know whether there is truth in the story that this writer is the 'Waring' of Mr. Browning's poem, returned from the Antipodes with this to show for himself. But to the Antipodes the writer has been, and his poem is a sort of New Zealand *Atala,* without the Christianity, the self-denial, and the tragic end. . . . The New Zealand landscape of Mr. Domett is as new as was Chateaubriand's description

Domett, A.—*continued.*
of Virgin America in his day. . . ."—*Sidney Colvin, Fortnightly Review,* N.S., xii. 753-0.
" Waring " is in *The Poetical Works of Robert Browning,* vol. i., pp. 215-24, ed. 4, 1865.
There is an article by J. Mortimer on Robert Browning's " Waring " in the *Manchester Quarterly,* Jan. 1888.

***Engler,** L. Neuseelands Wälder, ihre Nutzhölzer. *Aus allen Welttheilen,* iii. 59, 70 (1872).

Figuier, L. The | Human Race. | By | Louis Figuier. | Illustrated by | two hundred and forty-three engravings on wood, | and eight chromolithographs. | London : | Chapman and Hall, 193, Piccadilly. | 1872.
8°. N.Z.: pp. 381-8. A compilation ; from the French.

Fishes of New Zealand. | Catalogue with Diagnoses of the Species | by | Frederick Wollaston Hutton, F.G.S. | Assistant Geologist. | Notes on the Edible Fishes | by | James Hector, M.D., F.R.S. | Director | With twelve plates | New Zealand | James Hughes, Printer, Lambton Quay, Wellington. | 1872.
roy. 8°. Pp. xvi, 133, ii, 12 plates, and iii pp.
Bibliography, p. xvi.

Gibb, Sir Duncan. A pata-patoo from New Zealand. Proc. Brit. Ass. 1872, Abstract in *Report,* ii. 185-6.

Hector, J. Notes on the Edible Fishes, 1872. *In* Fishes of New Zealand, above.

Hutton, F. W. Catalogue | of the | Echinodermata | of New Zealand, | with Diagnoses of the Species. | By Frederick Wollaston Hutton, F.G.S., C.M.Z.S. | Assistant Geologist. | New Zealand. | James Hughes, Printer, Lambton Quay, Wellington. | 1872.
roy. 8°. Pp. vi, 20.

Hutton, F. W. Catalogue of Fishes, 1872: see Fishes, above.

K., J. H. Henry Ancrum. | A Tale of the last | War in New Zealand. | By | J. H. K. | In two volumes | —— | —— | London : | Tinsley Brothers, 18, Catherine Street, Strand. | 1872.
cr. 8°. Vol. i : 244 pp. ; vol. ii : 261 pp.
" The object of ' Henry Ancrum ' is to give to the general reader some knowledge of N.Z., of its short history, of its last war, and of the character of that most interesting race the Maori, in the popular form of a novel."—*Preface.*

***Ogilby,** J. P. Facts about New Zealand. *Overland Monthly,* ix. 247. San Francisco, 1872.

Travers, William Thomas Locke. Some Chapters | in | the Life and Times | of | Te Rauparaha, | Chief of the Ngatitoa. | By W. T. L. Travers, F.L.S. | New Zealand. | James Hughes, Printer, Lambton Quay, Wellington. | 1872.
roy. 8°. Pp. 77.
Ch. i. Customs of Maoris in relation to ownership of land and to war. ii. Early voyages. Primitive population ; causes of its decrease ; early wars. iii. Ngatitoa tribe. Early life of R.: raid upon the South. iv. Migration of tribe. v. Warlike expeditions. vi. Conquest of Middle Island. vii. Defeat of Ngatiruanui. Capture. Death.
Mr. Travers states (p. 29 and p. 63) that he has "obtained a large amount of information respecting the career of " R. from Tamihana Te Rauparaha. He gives R.'s " own view of the disastrous affair at the Wairau in 1843, and of its results as related to me by his son " (pp. 75-6), and of his capture at Porirua (pp. 76-7).
Rusden goes over part of the same ground, availing himself of portions of Travers's narrative, " but checking them by means of evidence adduced in courts of law " (i. 47, *note*). See also i. 49, *note.*

Turner, J. G. The Pioneer Missionary : | Life of the | Rev. Nathaniel Turner, | Missionary in New Zealand, Tonga and | Australia. By his son, | the Rev. J. G. Turner, | of the Australasian Conference. | With a portrait. | Melbourne : George Robertson ; | and the Wesleyan Book Depots at Sydney | and Melbourne. | Also Wesleyan Conference Office, Castle Street, City Road, | and 66, Paternoster Row, London. | 1872.
 cr. 8°. Pp. viii, 335.

 Turner was a missionary at the Bay of Islands 1823-27, 1835-39. Chs. v-ix describe the work of the first period ; ch. xiii, that of the latter. Ch. xiv describes the ruin that has overtaken the Wesleyan missionary stations ; missions a partial failure.

 Materials were derived from an autobiography, Turner's reports and letters, and J. Buller's letters.

Ward, R. Life | among the | Maories of New Zealand. | Being a description of | Missionary, Colonial, and Military | Achievements. | By the | Rev. Robert Ward, | *Twenty-six Years a Resident in the North Island.* | Edited by | Rev. Thomas Lowe and Rev. William Whitby. | —— | —— | London : | G. Lamb, Sutton Street, Commercial Road, E. | Canada : W. Rowe, Toronto. | —— | 1872.
 cr. 8°. Pp. x, 472.

 Ch. i. Discovery. ii. Country. iii. Natural productions. iv. Maories. v, vi. Missions. vii-ix. Commencement and growth of colony. x. Country life. xi. Town life. xii. Religious aspect. xiii-xxv describe King-movement, Taranaki and Waikato wars, Tauranga campaign, Pai Marire and war with Hau Haus. Comes down to 1870.

1873.

Alexander, Sir J. E. Bush Fighting. | Illustrated by | Remarkable Actions and Incidents | of | The Maori War in New Zealand. | By | Major-General Sir James Edw. Alexander, K.C.L.S., F.R.S.E., | Author of " A Campaign in Caffreland," " Explorations in Africa and America," etc. | With a map, plans, and woodcuts. | London : | Sampson Low, Marston, Low, and Searle, | Crown Buildings, 188 Fleet Street. | 1873.
 8°. Pp. xvi, 326. 17 illustrations and a map.

 "As no other military or naval man . . . had given a detailed account of the last operations in New Zealand, I undertook the task. . . . I have introduced the name of every officer, non-commissioned officer, or private sentinel, soldier, or seaman I could discover, who is mentioned in any dispatch or report of a creditable action. I was liberally allowed by the Military and Naval authorities free access to all the documents at the Horse Guards and Admiralty relating to the Maori War. . . ."—*Preface.*

 An account of the war from May, 1863, to Feb. 1866.

 Appendix I. N.Z. statistics. II, III. Return of killed and wounded. IV. Criticisms on the services of the military in N.Z. V. Escape of prisoners in Wellington harbour.

Annual Record | of | Science and Industry | for 1873. | Edited by | Spencer F. Baird, | with the assistance of eminent men of science. | New York : | Harper & Brothers, Publishers, Franklin Square. | 1874.
 p. 8°. See also later vols.

 1873. Transporting salmon-eggs to N.Z., p. 445. Naturalization of trout in N.Z., p. 447. Arrival of salmon-eggs in N.Z., p. 402.

 1876. Renewed attempt to send salmon-eggs to N.Z., p. 407.

Buller, W. L. A History | of the | Birds of New Zealand. | By | Walter Lawry Buller, Sc.D. | (Resident Magistrate of Wanganui, N.Z.), | Fellow of the Linnean Society, of the Geological Society, and | of the Royal Geographical Society, Corresponding Member of the Zoological Society, |

Buller, W. L.—*continued.*
Member of the British Ornithologists' Union, | etc., etc., etc. | London : | John Van Voorst, 1 Paternoster Row. | 1873.
roy. 4°. Pp. xxiii, 384.

The work comprises an introductory treatise on the ornithology of N.Z., pp. xiii–xxiii; a concise diagnosis of each bird in Latin and English, synoptical lists of the nomenclature, and a popular history and description of all the known species; together with coloured lithographs by Keulemans of all the more interesting and characteristic forms, including about 70 figures of N.Z. birds.
Reviewed by F. W. Hutton, *New Zealand Magazine*, I. 94–100.
Vol. I of a new edition was published in 1888.

Butler, S. Erewhon | or | Over the Range | by | Samuel Butler | —— | —— |
Fifth Edition | London | Trübner & Co., Ludgate Hill | 1873.
cr. 8°. Pp. xii, 244.

The first four or five chapters of this *voyage imaginaire* evidently describe scenes and station-life in Canterbury.
The first edition seems to have appeared in 1871; it was reprinted from *The Press*, Christchurch.

Chambers, W. A word about Otago. *Chambers's Journal*, I. 573–5. Sept. 6, 1873.

*__Christmann__, Fr., *u.* Oberländer, Richard. Oceanien. 1. Theil : Neu-Seeland. Das Grossbritannien der Südsee. Von Fr. Christmann. Leipzig. 1873.
gr. 8°.

The Effect | of | the Native Lands Acts | upon the | Colonization of the North Island | of | New Zealand. | Wellington : | printed by J. Hughes, Lambton Quay. | 1873.
8°. Pp. 16. Appendix, 2 pp.

Denounces land-sharking and recommends resumption of pre-emptive right.

*__Engler__, L. Ein Besuch bei den heissen Quellen Neuseelands. *Aus allen Welttheilen*, v. 1 (1873).

*__Harrison__, W. G. New Zealand. *Overland Monthly*, xi. 519; xii. 55, 103. 1873.

Hawke's Bay | Native Lands Alienation Commission. | Report of the inquiry | into | the Heretaunga purchase. | 5th March to 12th April, 1873. | Napier : printed by T. B. Harding, Hastings-street. | 1873.
8°. Pp. 290.

The inquiry arose out of complaints preferred by natives that their lands had been wrongfully taken or insufficiently paid for.

Henderson, J. The proposal made by Messrs. John Brogden and Sons to entrust to a company the construction and management of the public railways in New Zealand, stated and explained by John Henderson. Wellington, 1873.
8°. Pp. 66.

Appendix i. Correspondence with Mr. James Brogden relative to the formation of a company for the construction of railways in New Zealand, pp. 29–38. ii. Evidence and opinions relating to the construction of railways by companies. iii. N.Z. statistics.

Horne, Richard Hengist. Australia and New Zealand. *Contemporary Review*, xxii. 699–730. 1873.

The N.Z. part, pp. 725–9, is, like the rest, a review of A. Trollope's *Australia and New Zealand*.

Hutton, F. W.. Catalogue | of the | Land Mollusca | of | New Zealand, | with Descriptions of the Species. | Collected from Various Authors. | —— | New Zealand : | James Hughes, Printer, Lambton Quay, Wellington. | 1873.
  roy. 8°. Pp. vi (not numbered), xxvii.
   The Natural History catalogues are publications of the Colonial Museum and Geological Survey Department.

Hutton, F. W. Catalogue | of the | Marine Mollusca | of | New Zealand, | with Diagnoses of the Species, | by | Frederick Wollaston Hutton, F.G.S., C.M.Z.S., | Assistant Geologist. | —— | Wellington. | By authority: G. Didsbury, Government Printer. | 1873.
  roy. 8°. Pp. xx, 116. Illus.

Hutton, F. W. Catalogue | of the | Tertiary Mollusca and Echinodermata | of | New Zealand, | in the Collection of the Colonial Museum, | by | Frederick Wollaston Hutton, F.G.S., C.M.Z.S., Assistant Geologist. | —— | Wellington. | By authority: G. Didsbury, Government Printer. | 1873.
  roy. 8°. Pp. xvi, 48.

Kennedy, Alexander. New Zealand. | By | Alexander Kennedy | formerly | Manager of the Union Bank of Australia, at Auckland, New Zealand, | and subsequently for some years General Manager and | Inspector of the Bank of New Zealand | London | Longmans, Green, and Co. | 1873.
  cr. 8°. Pp. x, 171. Map.
   Description of islands, their natural history and productions; narrative of a residence in Auckland Province from 1840 to 1872, with a history of principal events; characterizes leading men during that period.

Lang, J. D. New Zealand in 1839. [Same title-page as edition of 1839, down to "Inhabitants."] With a Preface and Appendix for 1873. | By | John Dunmore Lang, | D.D. A.M. | Minister of the Scots Church, Sydney; and recently, and for many years, one of the representatives | of the City of Sydney, | in the Parliament of N.S. Wales; | Hon. Member of the African Institute of France; | of the American Oriental Society; | and of the Literary Society of Olinda, in the Brazils. | London : Smith, Elder and Co., 1839. | Sydney. Republished 1873.
   Prefatory Notice, pp. iii-v. Pamphlet was written on ship-board to embody result of observations and enquiries during accidental detention at Bay of Islands in Jan. and Feb. 1839. Published 7th or 8th July, 1839. Appendix for 1873, pp. 87-96, mainly on land-purchases prior to 1840.
   See first edition under 1839.

MacKay, Alexander. A Compendium | of | Official Documents | Relative to | Native Affairs | in the | South Island. | Compiled by | Alexander MacKay, Native Commissioner. | Wellington, New Zealand.
  f°. 2 vols., pp. 339, 401. With plans. Vol. i. is dated 1873; vol. ii. 1872.
   Mainly a collection of documents connected with the extinction of the Native title in lands in the South Island.
   Introductory chapter: Part i. Epitome of the early history of New Zealand, from the date of its discovery to the promulgation of the Constitution Act, in January, 1853, pp. 1-27.—Part ii. Narrative of the principal subjects included in the work, pp. 1-36.—Part iii. Traditional history of the Natives of the South Island up to the time of their conquest by the northern tribes under Te Rauparaha, pp. 37-53.
   "The accounts of the condition of the Natives in early times are derived from information gathered by Dr. Shortland (formerly Native Secretary), the Hon. Mr. Mantell, Mr. James MacKay, junior, the Rev. J. W. Stack, and from a variety of documents."—*Introduction.*
   Mr. Mantell's report on the geology of a portion of the South Island, i. 223-7.
   There is much information on the state of the Natives in both volumes.

P

*The Maoris of New Zealand. *St. James's Magazine*, xxxii. 558. 1873.

Martens, E. *von.* Critical list | of the | Mollusca of New Zealand | contained in European collections, | with references to descriptions and synonyms. | by | Edouard Von Martens, C.M., M.D., C.M.Z.S. | —— | New Zealand : | James Hughes, Printer, Lambton Quay, Wellington. | 1873.
    roy. 8°. Pp. iv, 3, v, 7–51, viii.
    The Introduction describes the principal contributions to a scientific knowledge of N.Z. Mollusca. Supplement to Hutton's Catalogue, above.

***Quatrefages**, A. *de.* Sur les races Moriori (Iles Chatham) et Maori (Nouvelle-Zélande). *Revue d'Ethnologie*, 1873.

Roots. *Temple Bar*, xxxvii. 107, 226, 329, 534. 1873.
    Said to be by Lord Pembroke : see new edition, 1888. Dialogues and meditations; scene in N.Z. There are vivid descriptions of scenery, and notices of Maori traits and religion.

Pyke, Vincent. The Story | of | Wild Will Enderby, | told by Vincent Pyke. | —— | Second Edition. | Published by George Robertson, Melbourne, and | R. T. Wheeler, Dunedin. | 1873.
    8°. Pp. vii, 260.
    Describes life on the Otago goldfields.

Raynal, F. E. Les Naufragés | ou | Vingt Mois sur un Récif | des Iles Auckland | Récit Authentique | Par F. E. Raynal | Illustré | de 40 gravures sur bois dessinées par A. de Neuville | et accompagné d'une carte | Troisième Edition | Paris | Librairie Hachette et Cⁱᵉ | Boulevard Saint-Germain, 79 | 1873.
    imp. 8°. Pp. vi (not numbered), 374+1. Map and 40 illus.
    Records the adventures of a small company of shipwrecked seamen on one of the Auckland Isles. Gives accounts of sea-lions.
    The book was translated in 1885.

St. John, J. H. H. Pakeha Rambles | through Maori Lands. | By | Lieut.-Colonel St. John (New Zealand Militia). | Wellington : Printed by Robert Burrett, Molesworth Street. | 1873.
    cr. 8°. Pp. 212.
    Part i. is descriptive of the Natives and their wars from 1830 to 1840, being the narrative of an old Waikato flax-trader; Thames, Lakes, Taupo. Second part, the same localities previously described, revisited in 1871 to 1873, with description of Bay of Plenty, Taupo, Wairoa, and Taranaki.

Trollope, Anthony. Australia | and | New Zealand. | By | Anthony Trollope. | In Two Volumes. | Vol. II. | London : | Chapman and Hall, 193, Piccadilly. | 1873.
    8°.
    N.Z.: pp. 301–494. Ch. xix. Early history. xx, xxi. Otago and Lakes. xxii. Godley. xxiii. Canterbury. xxiv. Marlborough and Nelson. xxv. Maoris. xxvi. Wellington and the Central Government. xxvii. Taranaki. xxviii. Auckland. xxix. Hot Lakes. xxx. Waikato.
    " Personal observations in 1872. Many of the ideas are original and well expressed, but the facts are untrustworthy."—*G.A.L. Catalogue.*
    Sir George Bowen's account of the Sounds, ii. 506–10.

Whitmee, S. J. Mr. Wallace on the ethnology of Polynesia. *Contemporary Review*, xxi. 389–407. 1873.
    The brown Polynesians (intimately related to the Malays) "have migrated from the west to some island or islands in the Pacific; and, from that centre or those centres, have become distributed throughout the numerous islands they now inhabit."

Williams, T. C. A Letter | to | the Right Hon. W. E. Gladstone | being | an Appeal on Behalf | of | the Ngatiraukawa tribe. | By T. C. Williams. | New Zealand : | Printed by J. Hughes, Lambton Quay, Wellington. | 1873.

 roy. 8°. pp. 72, clxi. Map.

  Introduction, pp. 1-3. Letter, pp. 5-66. Despatch from Governor Grey, petition, and memorandums by J. C. Richmond, pp. 67-72.
  Appendix :—Despatches, &c., pp. i-viii. Notes by Travers, pp. viii-xl. Extracts from Wakefield's *Adventure* and Travers's *Te Rauparaha*.
  Son of Rev. Henry Williams (and described by Mr. Fox in a passage quoted, p. 1), who translated and repeated to the natives the Treaty of Waitangi in 1840. Asserts that the N. tribe has been unjustly deprived of its rights in the Rangitikei-Manawatu block. His "case is one of unscrupulous Anglo-Saxon greed and oppression triumphant over peaceable Maori submission." The Wellington newspapers of April, 1887, contained an advertisement in which Mr. W. refuses to subscribe to the Imperial Institute on the ground of the unrepaired injustice to the tribe. The book contains incidental sketches of Maori history.

1874.

Adam, James. Twenty-five Years | of | Emigrant Life in the South | of New Zealand. | By James Adam, | Late Member of the Provincial and Executive Councils, Otago. | Edinburgh : | Bell and Bradfute, Bank Street. | London : George Street, 30 Cornhill. | 1874.

 8°. Pp. iii, 112. Map of Otago. Four illustrations. A second edition appeared in 1876.

  Ch. vii. Lost in the bush (between P. Chalmers and Dunedin). viii. Origin of Otago. ix. House-building. x. Condamine store. xi. Trade. xii. Land difficulties. xiii. Discrepancy of sexes. xiv. Remarkable colonists (Vogel, p. 40 ; Macandrew, pp. 41-4). xv. Politics. xvi. Gold. xvii. Agriculture. xviii. Land on deferred payments. xix. My neighbours. xx. Climate. xxi. Education. xxii. Sheep-farming. xxiii. Industries. xxiv. Aborigines. xxv. Bush. xxvii. Social condition. xxviii. Stewart's Island. xxix. Wages and provisions.—Almost a handbook for intending settlers—replete with facts and figures.
  Mr. Adam arrived in Otago in 1849.

B., W. M. The Narrative | of | Edward Crewe ; | or, | Life in New Zealand. | By W. M. B. | London : | Sampson Low, Marston, Low, & Searle, | —— | 1874.

 cr. 8°. Pp. iv, 288.

  Sketch of Auckland ; rambles amongst the Maoris, and on the coast of N.Z.

Bathgate, Alexander. Colonial Experiences ; | or | Sketches of People and Places in the Province of | Otago, New Zealand. | By | Alexander Bathgate. |. Glasgow : | James Maclehose, 61 St. Vincent Street, | Publisher to the University. | 1874.

 p. 8°. Pp. vii, 286.

  Chs. ii, iii. Dunedin—description and early history. v. Local industries. vi. Domestic servants. viii, ix. Goldfields life. vii, x, xi. Country and country life. xiii. Chinese. xv. Cockatoos and squatters. xvi. Avocations.

* **Beschreibung** einiger Häfen der Nordinsel (Neu-Seeland). Hydrogr. Mittheil., 1874, no. 12.

* **Bridges**, E. T. Emigration to New Zealand. *St. James's Magazine*, xxxv. 286. 1874.

Carleton, Hugh. The Life | of | Henry Williams, | Archdeacon of Waimate. | By Hugh Carleton. | —— | —— | Auckland : | Upton & Co., | 1874.

 8°. 2 vols. Vol. i : pp. 245, xiv. ; vol. ii : pp. 364, lxxxiii. Illustrations (photographs), sketch-maps and portrait.

  The book, which is almost a history of northern N.Z. from 1823 to 1867, abounds with accounts of the natives: Hongi's death (i. 61-62) and biography (i. 62-5, note); battle of Kororareka (i. 76-87); Heke (ii. 12-4, notes) and Heke's war (ii. 35, 76-132, iii-l).

Carleton, Hugh—*continued.*
History of the mission, i. 24 ff., ii. 57-9, and passim. Conflict with the N.Z. Company, i. 236-43. Signing of the Waitangi Treaty, ii. 11-17. Controversy about the land-purchases of the missionaries, ii. 29-5, 159-287, and appendices.
Written from letters of H. and Mrs. Williams, journal, reports, autobiographical papers by H.W.—"Early Recollections" and "Reminiscences," and personal knowledge.

Cawkwell, W. J. Local Industry | and the | New Zealand Government. | By W. J. Cawkwell. | Auckland : | William Atkin, General Printer, High Street. | 1874.
8°, Pp. 27.
An Auckland distiller, who complains that the Government specially legislated to call his industry into existence, and then visited it with uncompromising hostility.

***Dieffenbach**, Ernst. Ferdinand Dieffenbach, der Erforscher Neu-Seelands. *Ausland*, 1874, no. 5.

Evans, C. A Strange Friendship : | a Story of New Zealand. | By C. Evans. | London : | Sampson Low, Marston, Low, & Searle, | Crown Buildings, 188, Fleet Street. | 1874.
cr. 8°. Pp. viii+247.
A love-story, without local colouring.

Evans, C. Over the Hills and Far Away : A Story of New Zealand. London : Sampson Low and Co. 1874.
8°. Pp. 334.—*Davis.*

***Faithfull**, Emily. Emigration to New Zealand. *Victoria Magazine*, xxiv. 189. 1874.

Haast, J. Researches & Excavations | carried on in and near the | Moa Bone Point Cave, Sumner Road, | In the Year 1872, | by | Julius Haast, Ph.D., F.R.S., | —— | —— | Christchurch : | Printed at the " Times " office, Gloucester Street. | MDCCCLXXIV.
sq. 8°. Pp. 22, double columns.
The pamphlet gave rise to an amusing controversy : see speeches in the Legislative Council, Oct. 19, 1875, *N.Z. Hansard*, xix. 546-8, note and letter in *Nature*, xiii. 106, xiv. 90-1.

Johnstone, J. C. Maoria. | A Sketch of the | Manners and Customs of the Aboriginal | Inhabitants of New Zealand. | By | Captain J. C. Johnstone, | Bengal Army. | London : | Chapman and Hall, 193, Piccadilly. [1874.]
p. 8°. Pp. xvi, 199.
A story descriptive of Maori life—pahs and dwellings, childbirth customs, marriage, tattooing, industry, incantations, traditions, superstitions, government, law and justice, war and single combat, &c.

Kennaway, L. J. Crusts. | A Settler's Fare due South. | By | Lawrence J. Kennaway. | London : | Sampson Low, Marston, Low, & Searle, | —— | 1874.
cr. 8°. Pp. 234. Chart of Canterbury, and sketches.
Notes describing a settler's life in Canterbury in the early days; apparently written 1853-63.

***Marryat**, Emilia. Amongst the Maoris. London : Warne. 1874.
12°.—*Davis.*

Merewether, H. A. By Sea and By Land | Being a trip through | Egypt, India, Ceylon, Australia, New | Zealand, and America | All Round the World | By Henry Alworth Merewether | one of Her Majesty's Counsel | —— | London | Macmillan and Co. | 1874.
cr. 8°. Pp. xvi, 343.
A tour through N.Z. is described at pp. 157-93.

Potts, T. H. On Recent Changes | in the | Fauna of New Zealand. | From a paper read before the Philosophical | Institute of Canterbury, | December 12, 1872. | By Thomas H. Potts, F.L.S. | *Reprinted from " The Field."* | Christchurch : | Printed at the "Times" Office, Gloucester Street. | MDCCCLXXIV.

    sq. 8°. Pp. 12.

Purnell, C. W. An | Agrarian Law | for | New Zealand. | By | Charles W. Purnell. | Addressed to the Young Men of the Colony. | Wellington : | Printed for the Author by Robert Burrett, | —— | 1874.

    8°. Pp. 28.

Pyke, Vincent. The Adventures | of | George Washington Pratt. | By | Vincent Pyke, | Author of " Wild Will Enderby." | Price Two Shillings & Sixpence. | Published by | George Robertson, Melbourne : R. T. Wheeler, Dunedin. | 1874.

    8°. Pp. iv (not numbered), 97.

    A continuation of *Wild Will Enderby*. Mining life in Otago.

Rees, W. L. The Coming Crisis : | a Sketch of the | Financial and Political Condition | of | New Zealand, | with the | Causes and Probable Results of that Condition | by | W. L. Rees, | Of the Supreme Courts of Victoria and New Zealand, Barrister-at-law. | Price : one shilling. | Auckland : | Reed and Brett, printers, "Evening Star" Office, Wyndham-Street. | 1874.

    8°. Pp. 49.

    Ch. i. Introductory. ii. Manner of colonization of N.Z. and consequences. iii. Change in the character of the House. iv. Provincialism. v. Vogel. vi. The three resolutions; the compact of 1856. vii. Public works and immigration policy. viii. End of public works and immigration policy. ix. Conclusion.

Spencer, Herbert, *and* **Duncan**, David. Descriptive | Sociology; | or, Groups of | Sociological Facts, | Classified and Arranged | by | Herbert Spencer. | —— | Division I.—Part I.—A. | Types of Lowest Races, Negritto Races, | and Malayo-Polynesian Races. | Compiled and Abstracted | by | Prof. David Duncan. | Williams and Norgate | London and Edinburgh | May, 1874.

    roy. f°.

    The Maoris are described (Table XIII) under 37 headings:—Inorganic, organic, and sociological [social] environments; physical, emotional, and intellectual characters; operative (division of labour) and regulative (industrial government); marital and filial institutions; political integration, civil government, public, military, and ecclesiastical institutions; professions; mutilations, funeral rites, laws of intercourse, habits and customs; æsthetic and moral sentiments, superstitions, knowledge; language; distribution, exchange, and production of commodities; arts; rearing, land-works, habitations, food, clothing, implements, weapons; æsthetic products.

    Extracts from various writers supporting the statements in the Table are classified, pp. 3–61.

Tinné, J. Ernest. The Wonderland of the Antipodes : Sketches of Travel in the North Island of New Zealand. London, 1874.

    small 8°.

    Description of the Rotomahana boiling springs, and the Island of Kawau. Good photographs.

White, John. Te Rou ; | or, The Maori at Home. | A Tale, exhibiting the Social Life, Manners, Habits, | and Customs of the Maori Race in New | Zealand prior to the introduction | of civilisation amongst them. | By | John White, | native interpreter, Auckland ; formerly Resident Magistrate | at Whanganui, and Native Land Purchase Commissioner. | London :

White, John—*continued.*
   Sampson Low, Marston, Low, and Searle, | Crown Buildings, 188 Fleet Street. | 1874.
   cr. 8°. Pp. viii, 343.
   A tale, but not a fiction, exhibiting "everyday life, habits, and character of the pre-civilisation Maori," written from "personal knowledge and observation." Mythical account of origin of Hokianga (ch. i). Council of revenge (ii). Summoning allies to take revenge (iii). Feast of the slain (iv). A love-tale (vi). Attack and capture of a pah (vii). Purification of corpse-bearers (xiv). Cooking a dead slave (xv). Burial and burial rites of those who died in battle (xviii). Debate on power of disembodied spirits (xxii). Evening tales (xxiii). Old priest's death and attendant rites (xxiv).
   Maori poetry—incantations, canoe-songs, war-songs, love-songs, laments, &c.—is given at pp. 12, 18, 31, 33, 34, 36–7, 39–40, 44, 51, 57, 59–60, 61–2, 115, 133, 135, 136, 186, 200–1, 202, 218, 220, 221, 241–2, 207–8, 270, 271, 273, 283.

Wilson, G. H. Ena, | or | The Ancient Maori. | By | George H. Wilson. | London : | Smith, Elder & Co., 15 Waterloo Place. | 1874.
   cr. 8°. Pp. viii, 287.
   A "not altogether fictitious story" "written among the hills, ravines, and forest wilds" of N.Z. Glossarial appendix, pp. 281–7.

Yonge, Charlotte M. Life | of | John Coleridge Patteson | Missionary Bishop *of the* Melanesian Islands | By | Charlotte Mary Yonge | —— | Third Edition, somewhat abridged | In Two Volumes | —— | London | Macmillan and Co. | 1874.
   cr. 8°. Vol. i : pp. xii, 370 ; vol. ii : pp. iv (not numbered), 390. Two portraits and map.
   Chs. vi, viii, ix, x, describe Bishop Patteson's work in N.Z. The book was reviewed in the *Quarterly Review*, cxxxvii. 458 (reprinted in Gladstone, *Gleanings of past years*, ii. 213); by H. James, *Nation*, xx. 244; and in *Christian Observer*, lxxiv. 10. There are articles on the labours of Bishop Patteson, by P. Y. Reid, *Good Words*, xv. 525, 587.

Young, Frederick. New Zealand—past, present, and future. *Proceedings of the Royal Colonial Institute*, v. 180–99. 1874.
   Early history and natural features; Maories; authentic history; N.Z. Company; resources and productions; statistics; emigration.
   Discussion, pp. 199–217, in which Sir C. Clifford, Duke of Manchester, Sir J. Hall, and others took part.

1875.

All About | New Zealand. | Being | a Complete Record | of | Colonial Life. | Glasgow : | Porteous Brothers, West Nile Street, | —— | [1875.]
   8°. Pp. 220.
   i. Free passages, pp. 12-15. ii. Free grants of land, pp. 16–19. iii. Historical, pp. 20–3. iv. Native war, &c., pp. 24–53. v. Geography, topography, and climate, pp. 54–72. vi. The Provinces, pp. 73–173. vii. Government, pp. 174–0. viii. Productions, pp. 180–98. ix. Preparing to emigrate, pp. 199–206. x. How will we find it? pp. 207–20.
   A compilation, with extracts from private letters.

Brown, R. The | Races of Mankind : | being | a Popular Description of the Characteristics, Manners and | Customs of the Principal Varieties of | the Human Family. | By | Robert Brown, M.A., | Ph.D., F.L.S., F.R.G.S., | —— | Vol. II. | —— | Cassell, Petter, and Galpin : | London, Paris, & New York. | [1875.]
   4°. Pp. viii, 320. Many illus.
   The Maoris—their customs, cannibalism, mythology and sorcery, government and present condition—are described under "The Oceanic Group," pp. 12–84.

Fellows, Charles. The financial policy of New Zealand. *Fraser's Magazine,* xi. 74–87. January, 1875.

> Ordinary expenditure defrayed out of loans; unreproductive public works executed; assisted immigration not permanent; interest on debt paid out of loans debt increasing faster than population; probable exodus of colonists.
> Replied to by Sir J. Vogel, below.

Fellows, C. A rejoinder on the debts of New Zealand. *Ibid.*, xi. 384–92. March, 1875.

> A continuation of foregoing, and reply to Sir J. Vogel, below.

Grey, *Sir* G. [Addresses at Auckland at the time of his election as Superintendent.] Auckland, 1875.

> 8°. Pp. 19, double columns.

Hutton, F. W., *and* **Ulrich,** G. H. F. Report | on the | Geology and Gold Fields | of | Otago. | By | F. W. Hutton, F.G.S., C.M.Z.S., | *Provincial Geologist;* | and | G. H. F. Ulrich, F.G.S., | *Consulting Mining Geologist and Engineer;* with Appendices | By J. G. Black, Professor of Chemistry in the Otago University, and J. McKerrow, Chief Surveyor. | Published by order of the Provincial Council of Otago. | Dunedin : | Mills, Dick & Co., Printers, Stafford Street. | 1875.

> 8°. Pp. 245. 11 plates.
>
> Part I.—Geology. Section i. Physical geography. ii. Previous observers. iii. General geological structure. iv. Descriptive geology. v. Historical geology. vi. Surface geology. vii. Economic geology. Appendix A. Bibliography. B. Minerals. C. Fauna. D. Altitudes. E. Analyses.
> Part II.—Gold Fields.
> Noticed in *Nature*, xiv. 146–7.

Jackson, J. R. New Zealand plants suitable for paper-making. *Nature,* xi. 212–13. 1875.

> Founded on T. Kirk's paper, Trans. N.Z. Inst., vi. 55.

* Life and recollections of a New Zealand colonist. 3 vols. 1875.

Macandrew, James, *M.H.R.* Address | to | the People of Otago. | By | His Honor James Macandrew, | *Superintendent of the Province.* | Dunedin : Mills, Dick, and Co., Steam Printers, Stafford Street. | 1875.

> 8°. Pp. 15.
> A plea for the Provinces.

* **Meinicke,** C. E. Die inseln des stillen Oceans. Leipzig : Frohberg, 1875. 2 vols.

> 8°.
> N.Z. Vol. i., pp. 247–358.

Mundy, D. L., *and* **Hochstetter,** F. Rotomahana ; | and | the Boiling Springs | of | New Zealand. | A Photographic Series of Sixteen Views | by D. L. Mundy. | With descriptive notes | by | Ferdinand von Hochstetter, | Professor of the Polytechnic Institution of Vienna. | " O ye Fire and Heat, bless ye the Lord ; | Praise him, and magnify him for ever ! " | London : | Sampson Low, Marston, Low, and Searle, | Crown Buildings, Fleet Street. | 1875.

> roy. f°. Sketch-map and 16 plates—photographs reduced by autotype process. Sketch-map of the district.

A **Native** | on | Abolition. [Imprint torn ; but dated Sept. 21, 1875.]

> 8°. Pp. 10.
> On the abolition of the Provinces.

The Official Handbook | of | New Zealand. | A Collection of Papers | by Experienced Colonists | on | the Colony as a Whole, and on the Several | Provinces. | Edited by Julius Vogel, C.M.G. | ―― | London : | Printed for the Government of New Zealand, by | Wyman & Sons, Great Queen Street, | Lincoln's Inn Fields, W.C. | 1875.

    8°. Pp. 272. Two maps, 7 photographs, and 25 wood-engravings.

    Introduction. Editor.—Discovery and early settlement. Sir W. Fox.—Natives. Sir D. McLean.—Government. W. Gisborne.—Climate and mineral and agricultural resources. Dr. Hector.—Animal and vegetable productions. Mr. Travers.—Some institutions, &c. Mr. Woodward.—Statistics. Messrs. Brown, Batkin, and Seed.—Public Works Department. Mr. Knowles.—Immigration Department. Mr. Haughton.—Official Directory. Mr. Cooper.—Otago. J. McIndoe.—Canterbury. W. M. Maskell.—Westland. J. Driscoll.—Marlborough. A. Maskell.—Nelson. C. Elliott.—Wellington. H. Anderson.—Manchester "Special" Settlement. A. F. Halcombe.—Hawke's Bay. W. W. Carlile.—Taranaki. C. D. Whitcombe.—Auckland. Dr. Kidd and T. W. Leys.

Politics : a contribution to the | Question of the Day. | Reprinted from the | New Zealand Herald, | and respectfully dedicated to an intelligent public, | by | A Provincialist. | Auckland : | Printed at the "Herald" Office, Wyndham Street, Auckland. | MDCCCLXXV.

    8°. Pp. 22+1.

    Ch. ii. Birth of the Constitution. Mr. Gladstone on concurrent jurisdiction (shows the conditions under which the Constitution came into existence). iii. N.Z. and Rhode Island (the Constitution of N.Z. modelled on that of Rhode Island). iv. The land. v. Provisions of the Constitution (compared disadvantageously with that of the U.S.). vi. The future.

    Written by a colonist of 15 years' standing, who had a close acquaintance with Provincial institutions.

The Savings-Bank in the School. | An Economic Experiment | at Ghent, | adapted to | New Zealand | (*From "Macmillan's Magazine"*), | and issued by | the Society for encouraging habits of | thrift | among the young people of the colony | London : | Harrison and Sons, St. Martin's Lane, | Printers in Ordinary to Her Majesty. | 1875.

    8°. Pp. 12.

    The substance of the article is by Mr. J. G. Fitch ; the "adaptation" to New Zealand is at pp. 9, 11-12.

***Scheube**, H. Unter den Schafbaronen Neuseelands. Nach Briefen einer Englischen Dame. *Aus allen Welttheilen*, vi. 102, 134 (1875).

Thomson, J. T. An | Exposition | of | Processes and Results | of the | Survey System | of | Otago. | By | J. T. Thomson, C.E., F.R.G.S. | Dunedin : | Henry Wise and Co., Stationers, Princes Street. | 1875.

    8°. Pp. 19.

    "The peculiar characteristics that I hold to be possessed by the Otago System of Survey consist in its Rapidity and Accuracy. . . . To the above characteristics may be added Elasticity. . . ."—*Preface.*

***Tomlinson**, Harry. Diary of voyage to New Zealand. Laceby, 1875. Pamphlet.

Vogel, Julius. The | Finances of New Zealand | By the | Premier of the Colonial Government | *Reprinted (by permission) from 'Fraser's Magazine,' February, 1875* | London | Longmans, Green, and Co. | 1875.

    8°. Pp. 21. Dated Paris : January 17, 1875.

    A reply to C. Fellows, above.

1876.

Adam, J. Twenty-five Years | of | Emigrant Life in the South | of New Zealand. | By James Adam, | Late Member of the Provincial and Executive

Adams, J.—*continued.*
Councils, Otago. | Second edition. | Edinburgh : | Bell and Bradfute, Bank Street. | London : George Street. | 1876.
8°. Pp. vii, 156.
Contains four chapters additional to first edition, and (in an appendix) nine letters from working-men who have emigrated to various parts of N.Z.

* Bemerkungen über einige Häfen von Neu-Seeland. Annalen d. Hydrographie, iv. 407 (1876).

Clarke, Marcus. Abel Jansen Tasman. A Note. *Melbourne Review,* i. 451-7. October, 1876.
"I have taken the materials for the following brief account of his first voyage from Dalrymple's Voyages to the South Pacific Ocean, London, 1770, collating with Harris's Navigatiarum [*sic*] Bibliotheca, 1774, Thevenot, and the Terra Australis Cognita, published at Edinburgh in 1766" (p. 453).

Correspondence | between | the Hon. the Premier of New Zealand, | and His Honor the Superintendent of Otago, | *Relative to the Proposed Abolition of Provinces.*
8°. Pp. 36.
Correspondence between Mr. Vogel and Mr. Macandrew March 28 to June 9, 1876. Statement of nature of proposed scheme, with a controversy on the position of Otago.

Davis, C. O. The Life and Times | of | Patuone, | The Celebrated Ngapuhi Chief, | by | C. O. Davis. | Auckland : | Printed by | J. H. Field, Steam Printing Office, Albert Street. | 1876.
fcp. 8°. Pp. 141. Photographic portrait.
Eruera Maihi Patuone, chief of the Ngatihao tribe, Hokianga, died at Auckland in 1872, aged about 108 years.
The biography is founded on material derived from Maoris, missionaries, and personal knowledge.

Fox, William. New Zealand. *Proceedings, Royal Colonial Institute,* vii. 247-59.
A Wakefield colony ; wars ; life ; climate ; scenery ; staples ; minerals ; railways ; future.
Discussion, pp. 260-73 : Sir C. Clifford, Sir R. MacDonnell, Col. Thompson, E. Wilson, Dennistoun Wood.

Hector, J. On Certain Early Forms of Stone Implements in use among the Inhabitants of New Zealand. *Journal of Ethnological Society,* 1876.
Of recent origin ; did not belong to pre-historic race. A reply to Haast.

* **Kennedy,** D. Colonial Travel : A Four Years' Tour through Australia, New Zealand, &c. By David Kennedy, Scotch Vocalist. Edinburgh, 1876.
12°.—*Davis.*

Maning, Frederick Edward. Old New Zealand, | a Tale of the Good Old Times ; | and | a History of the War in the | North against the chief | Heke, in the year | 1845. | Told by an old chief of the Ngapuhi tribe. | By a pakeha Maori. | With an introduction | by the Earl of Pembroke. | London : | Richard Bentley and Son, | Publishers in Ordinary to Her Majesty the Queen, | New Burlington Street. | 1876.
8°. Pp. xxi, 278.
Introduction by Lord Pembroke, pp. ix.-xxi. Preface to original edition, pp. xxiii.-xxiv. History of the war in the North, pp. 181-274. Glossary, pp. 275-8.
The first edition was translated into Danish by Monrad, respecting whom see *Vapereau, Dictionnaire des contemporains.* Monrad's version (*Eldtog*) was rendered into German :—Das alte Neu-Seeland. Aus dem Dänischen. Deutsch von A. W. Peters. Bremen : Kühlmann und Co. 1871. gr. 8°.—Second edition, 1885 : Norden, H. Fischer.
According to the Catalogue of the Grey Collection, Auckland, two editions were published in 1863, and the London edition of 1863 was the third.

Miers, E. J. Catalogue | of the | Stalk- and Sessile-eyed Crustacea | of | New Zealand, | by | Edward J. Miers, F.L.S., | Assistant in the | Zoological Department of the British Museum. | London : | E. W. Janson, Printer, 28, Museum Street, W.C. | 1876.
      roy. 8°. Pp. xii, 136 + 2. 3 plates.

*The **Moa** bird or Dinornis. *Chambers's Journal*, liv. 578. 1877.

The **New Zealand Magazine.** Dunedin, 1876.
    Vol. I has the following articles relating to New Zealand :—
    Bruce, *Rev.* David. The unification of the Colony, pp. 187-200. Davis, J. Upton. Primary education in New Zealand: its history and prospects, pp. 358-65. Eyton, Robt. H. Our representative system, pp. 171-80. Hutton, F. W. Birds of New Zealand (a review of Buller's History of the Birds of New Zealand), pp. 94-100. Macgregor, *Prof.* Duncan. The problem of poverty in New Zealand, pp. 60-75, 207-16, 310-21. Mueller, Friedrich. The Malay race, pp. 417-30. Purnell, C. W. The public estate, pp. 274-92. Rankon, W. H. L. Maori migrations, pp. 221-38. Shaw, John H. National evolution in New Zealand, pp. 151-70. Stout, Robert. Specialization in government, illustrated by the struggle between provincialism and centralism, pp. 76-93.

New Zealand proverbs and legends. *All the Year Round*, May 6, 1876, pp. 175-80.

Piako. | Auckland : | Printed at the "Herald" office, Auckland. | MDCCCLXXVI.
      8°. Pp. 21. Plan.
    Complains of being robbed of his property by the Commissioner at Coromandel : he claimed 180,000 acres, for which he had paid £380.

Polynesian legends and fairy stories. *All the Year Round*, Sept. 23, 1876, pp. 29-35.

Purnell, C. W. Our | Land Laws : | What should be their Basis ? | By | Charles W. Purnell. | 1876. | Dunedin : | Printed at the Evening Star office, Bond Street.
      8°. Pp. 32.
    Advocates land-nationalisation and limited occupancy.

Spry, W. J. J. The Cruise | of Her Majesty's Ship | "Challenger." | Voyages over Many Seas, | Scenes in Many Lands. | By W. J. J. Spry, R.N. | —— | With Map and Illustrations. | London : | Sampson Low, Marston, Searle, and Rivington. | —— | 1876.
      8°.
    N.Z. in 1873, pp. 175-81.

***Tomlinson,** Harry. Farm labourer's report on New Zealand. Laceby, 1876. Pamphlet.

Wallace, A. R. The Geographical | Distribution of Animals, | With a Study of | the Relations of Living and Extinct Faunas | as elucidating the | Past Changes of the Earth's Surface. | By | Alfred Russel Wallace. | —— | With Maps and Illustrations. | In Two Volumes.— | London : | Macmillan and Co. | 1876.
      8°. Pp. xxiv, 503. One plate shows remarkable birds of N.Z.
    The N.Z. sub-region is discussed, i. 449-64. The "fauna, living and extinct, demonstrates the existence of an extensive period of land in the vicinity of Australia, Polynesia, and the Antarctic continent . . . since the period when mammalia had peopled all the great continents" (pp. 461-2).

A **Week** among the Maoris of Lake Taupo. *Cornhill Magazine*, xxxiii. 61-70. 1876.

***White,** J. H. Emigration to New Zealand. Laceby, 1876.
    Pamphlet.

1877.

Barraud, C. D., *and* **Travers**, W. T. L.   New Zealand: | Graphic and Descriptive. | The Illustrations | by | C. D. Barraud. | Edited by | W. T. L. Travers, F.L.S. | London | Sampson Low, Marston, Searle & Rivington. | 1877.

   Atlas f°.
   Map of N.Z.; 25 chromo-lithographs; 19 plain lithographs in 6 plates; and 31 woodcuts.
   Reviewed in the *Saturday Review*, Nov. 10, 1877.

* Ein Blick auf Neuseeland.   *Ausland*, 1877, no. 33 f.

***Broomhall**, J.   A journey in New Zealand. Fragments of the journal of J. B.   London, 1877.
   4°.

Bull, W. J.   Public Works | in | New Zealand : | from 1870 to 1877. | By W. J. Bull, C.E. | —— | Christchurch, N.Z. : | printed by "The Press" Company, Limited. | 1877.
   8°. Pp. 68, 4 lithographed drawings ; and appendix, pp. A54, by H. Czerwonka, C.E., on bridges, bridge-cables, and water-races.
   Ch. i. Government administration.   ii. Construction of works.   iii. Railway management.   iv. General summary.
   Denounces mistakes made in connection with public works in previous seven years.

Campbell-Walker, ——.   State Forestry : its Climatic and Financial Aspect. A Paper read before the New Zealand Institute, Wellington, March 17th, 1877. By Captain Campbell-Walker, F.R.G.S., Staff Corps; Conservator of State Forests, N.Z.
   roy. 8°. Pp. 23.
   Forest-conservancy as applicable to N.Z. Also in the Trans. N.Z. Inst., ix, Appendix. A previous paper on State Forestry is in the same volume, pp. 187-203.

***Cooper**, R.   Land Purchases | on the | East Coast. | A reply | by | Robert Cooper, | settler, Poverty Bay. | —— | Printed at the 'Evening Argus' office, Wellington. | [1877.]
   8°. Pp. 22.
   A personal vindication against charges preferred by a late officer of the Land Purchase Department. Appendix: affidavit, p. 20.

Fac-similes | of the | Declaration of Independence | and the | Treaty of Waitangi. | Wellington. | By authority : | George Didsbury, Government Printer. | 1877.
   fcp. f°. Pp. 14 (printed), 10 fac-similes in photo-lithography, and 1 printed page.
   A preface by H. Hanson Turton gives an account of the documents—(1) Declaration of Independence, (2) original draft of the Treaty by Lieut.-Governor Hobson, and (3) a series of copies of the Treaty as finally adopted, with the chiefs' signatures or marks—either arbitrary signs or some particular part copied from the tattoo of the writer's face. The Treaty, in English and Maori, with official and other accounts of its ratification and signature, are also given in the Preface.

Grey, *Sir* G.   The Policy of the Future | *not* | Class against Class. | A Speech | delivered by | the Hon. Sir George Grey, K.C.B., | Premier of New Zealand, | in the House of Representatives, in reply to the Hon. | Major Atkinson's motion of "No Confidence." | Friday, October 26th, 1877. | Second edition. | Price one penny. | Lyon and Blair, steam printers, Lambton Quay.
   8°. Pp. 11, including preface, &c.
   Republished preliminary to a dissolution.

Gully, J., *and* **Haast**, J. *von*. New Zealand scenery chromo-lithographed after original water-color drawings. By John Gully. With descriptive letterpress by Dr. Julius von Haast. Dunedin, 1877.
    Imp. f°.
        Chromo-lithographs. Bradshaw Sound, Otago. Valley of the Wilkin, from Huddlestone's Run. Waterfall in Thompson's Sound, West Coast. Mitre Peak, Milford Sound. Mount Cook, with the Hooker Glacier. Mount Cook and Mount Tasman, from the west. Wairau Gorge. Waimea plains and cultivated country near Nelson. Valley of the Awatere, with the Inland Kaikouras. New Zealand vegetation; open country. Manawatu Gorge. Up-river scene, Wanganui. Mount Egmont. Ruapehu and Tongariro mountains, from Lake Taupo. N.Z. forest vegetation.

Hamilton, Archibald. On the recent economic progress of New Zealand: a paper read before the Statistical Society of London, 30th January, 1877. London, 1877.
    8°. Pp. 32.
        i. Introduction. Peculiar advantages of the colony. ii. Retrospect. iii. Native policy. iv. Colonial debt, its outlay and comparative pressure. v. Revenue. vi. Expenditure. vii. Railways and roads. viii. Telegraphs. ix. Live stock. x. Wool. xi. Land under cultivation. xii. Exports. xiii. Imports. xiv. Savings banks. xv. Municipalities. xvi. Crown lands. xvii. Land transfers. xviii. Maoris. xix. Population, birthplaces and occupations. xx. Immigration and emigration. xxi. Vital statistics. xxii. Education. xxiii. Conclusion. Appendix, Tables i to vii.

Montégut, Emile. L'Australie d'après les récens voyageurs. III. La Nouvelle-Zélande. *Revue des Deux Mondes*, Oct. 15, 1877, pp. 867–99.
    i. Le passé de la N.Z. La colonisation. ii. Les Maoris. iii. Le présent de la N.Z. Caractère démocratique de la colonie.

Musings on Manning's [*sic*] 'Old New Zealand.' *Temple Bar*, li. 518–35. 1877.
    Contains a translation by Maning of a Maori poem (pp. 534–5) now first published.

* Neuseelands Handel. *Preuss. Handelsarchiv*, 1887, no. 40.

The **New Zealand | Country Journal : | Vol. I. | —— | Edited and Published by the Committee of the Canterbury | Agricultural and Pastoral Association. | 1877 | Christchurch.**
    8°.
        With its successors, contains many articles on natural history of N.Z. Mr. Potts's *Out in the Open* appeared in its pages.

The **New Zealand Magazine**, for 1877. Dunedin, 1877.
        De Lautour, C. A. Technical education, pp. 155–67. FitzGerald, J. E. The New Zealand University, pp. 231–40. Hutton, Prof. F. W. Earthquakes, pp. 336–47. Mackenzie, M. J. S. Free trade in land: a policy of substantial settlement, pp. 380–97. Shand, J. The higher education in New Zealand, pp. 291–3.

Notes | of | a Tour through various parts | of | New Zealand | including | a Visit to the Hot Springs. | By a German Lady. | Price one shilling. | Sydney: | Lee & Ross, Steam Machine Printers, 231 and 233 Castlereagh Street, | eight doors south of Market Street. | 1877.
    sq. 8°. Pp. 31. Reprinted from the *Protestant Standard*.

[**Pratt**, W. T.] Colonial Experiences ; | or, | Incidents and Reminiscences | of | Thirty-four Years in New Zealand. | By | an Old Colonist. | —— | London : | Chapman & Hall, 193, Piccadilly. | 1877.
    cr. 8°. Pp. vii, 288. Map of South Island.
        Settler's life in Nelson from 1843, and afterwards in Wellington and Canterbury; with much about the N.Z. Company and the Canterbury Association.

Purnell, C. W. The | New Zealand | Confederation : | an enquiry into the present state of | political affairs, with suggestions as to the best form of | government for the colony. | By | Chas. W. Purnell, | author of " An

Purnell, C. W.—*continued*.
Agrarian Law for New Zealand," etc. | Dunedin : | E. T. Wheeler, Stafford Street. | 1877. | Price one shilling.
8°. Pp. 32.
Advocates federalisation of the government.

***Russell**, I. C. The giant birds of New Zealand. *American Naturalist*, Salem, xi. 11. 1877.

***Stewart**, G. Vesey. Notes on the Kati-Kati settlement. Omagh, 1877.
Pamphlet.

Treadwell, J. W. New Zealand, June 30, 1877. | True Financial Statement | dedicated to | the Marquis of Normanby, | Governor of this Colony ; | the Legislative Council, the House of Representatives ; also, ad viros et ad profanum vulgus ; | also to | the London Stock Exchange, | by J. W. Treadwell, | formerly of 20 Cornhill, London, stockbroker. | Christchurch : | Printed at the " Press " office, Cashel-street. | 1877.
8°. Pp. 20.
Ch. 1. N.Z. deficit, pp. 5-9. ii. Taxation of workers, and freedom of real and personal estates, pp. 9-12. iii. Land fund misappropriated, pp. 12-3. iv. Railways a loss wrongly charged, p. 13. v. Colonial industry and free trade, pp. 14-6. vi. Representation a farce, pp. 16-8. vii. Budget as it ought to be, p. 19. Conclusion, pp. 19-20.
The author was apparently for six years a member of the House of Representatives : see p. 20.

Vogel, *Sir* Julius. New Zealand and the South Sea Islands, and their relation to the Empire. *Proc. Roy. Col. Inst.*, ix. 164-210. 1877.
Routes to ; seaboard ; description ; Maoris ; political institutions ; statistics ; minerals ; timber and land ; railway-policy and loans ; immigration and land-systems ; South Sea Islands.
Discussion (pp. 210-23) : Sir James Fergusson, Sir R. Torrens, E. B. Cargill.

Vogel, *Sir* J. Some remarks on the resources of New Zealand. *Fraser's Magazine*, N.S., xvi. 134-8. 1877.
A reply to Wilson's article, Australia and New Zealand, q.v.

Wakelin, Richard. History and Politics. | Containing | the Political Recollections | and | Leaves from the Writings | of a New Zealand Journalist, | 1851-1861-1862-1877. | By Richard Wakelin. | Wellington : | Lyon & Blair ; George W. Dutton, | —— | MDCCCLXXVII.
roy. 8°. Pp. iv. (not numbered), 100, double columns.
Twenty chapters on the political history of N.Z. and Wellington Province, 1851-61 : Sir G. Grey's first Governorship ; the Constitution ; Wairarapa—purchase and settlement ; Provincial land legislation ; Dr. Featherston's Superintendency. Reprints of newspaper articles on similar topics, pp. 69-100.

Wedderburn, *Sir* David. Maoris and Kanakas. *Fortnightly Review*, N.S., xxi. 782-802. 1877.
Reflections after a visit in 1874, pp. 782-96.

Wilson, A. J. British trade.—No. X. Australia and New Zealand. *Fraser's Magazine*, N.S., xv. 715-18. 1877.
Reproduced in Wilson's *Resources of modern countries*. The prosperity N.Z. enjoys has followed the expenditure of borrowed money, and will cease with that.

[**Wilson**, J. A. ?] How the | Native Land Court | and | Land Purchase Department | behave | on the East Coast. | A Series of Letters | from an | "Occasional Correspondent " | to | " The Otago Daily Times." | With a preface by " Argus." | Auckland : | William Atkin, General Printer, High Street. | 1877.
8°. Pp. vi, 40.
Written on behalf of J. A. Wilson, formerly Government land purchaser at Gis-

[Wilson, J. A. ?]—*continued.*
borne; who reported that the Native Department connived at alienation of native lands to wealthy private buyers.

1878.

Adams, W. Acton B. The Nelson & West Coast Section | of the | Main Trunk Railway | of New Zealand. | A Letter | to | the Hon. James Macandrew, Minister for Public Works, | by W. Acton B. Adams. | 1878. | Nelson: | R. Lucas and Son, Book and General Printers, Bridge-st. | 1878.
8°. Pp. 15.

*****Bickford,** J. Christian Work in Australia, with Notes of the Settlement and Progress of the Colonies. London, 1878.

Blair, D. The | History of Australasia | from the First Dawn of Discovery in the Southern | Ocean to the Establishment of Self-Government | in the Various Colonies | comprising the | Settlement and History of New South Wales, Victoria, | South Australia, Queensland, Western Australia, | Tasmania, and New Zealand | —— | by | David Blair | Numerous Illustrations and Maps. | Glasgow, Melbourne, and Dunedin | McGready, Thomson, & Niven | 1878.
roy. 4°. Pp. xxvii, 711. Map of N.Z. and 2 tinted illus.

Book xii: History of N.Z., pp. 553–618. Ch. i. Early days. ii. Period of civilisation. iii. Colonisation. iv. Provinces. v. Maori wars.
A "Supplementary Chapter" has article on the Maungatapu murders, pp. 624–7; lament for a chief, pp. 627–8; Maori customs, pp. 628–9; stories, pp. 629–30; fables, pp. 630–1; and proverbs, pp. 631–2.

Blanchard, Emile. La Nouvelle-Zélande et les petites îles australes adjacentes.

I. *Revue des Deux Mondes,* 1ᵉʳ mars 1878, trois. pér., t. xxvi. 34–76.
II. „ „ „ 15 décembre 1879, xxxvi. 766–803.
III. „ „ „ 1ᵉʳ septembre 1881, xlvii. 167–203.
IV. „ „ „ 15 janvier 1882, xlix. 355–394.
V. „ „ „ 1ᵉʳ juin 1884, lxiii. 657–82.
VI. „ „ „ 15 septembre 1884, lxv. 438–54.
VII. „ „ „ 15 octobre 1884, lxv. 908–32.

I. Découverte, pp. 37–46. Premières explorations, pp. 46–70. Première idée de colonisation, p. 62. Nature du pays entrevu, p. 62. Habitans, pp. 63–4.
II. Baleiniers et les chasseurs de phoques, pp. 766–75. Relations de la N.S.W. avec N.Z., pp. 775–83. Missionaires évangéliques, pp. 783–803. (Founded on the *Missionary Register* of 1816 and later years.)
III. Voyages de circumnavigation; récits des capitaines Dumont d'Urville, Laplace, Du Petit-Thouars, Fitzroy, Wilkes, Ross, pp. 177–203.
IV. Colonisation, pp. 355–62. First immigrants and foundation of regular settlements, pp. 362–70. The taking possession by England, pp. 370–5. French settlement at Akaroa, pp. 375–9. Early government, pp. 379–90. Last struggles of native race, pp. 390–4. (Gives an account of De Thierry, Bishop Pompalier, the *Compagnie nantobordelaise*, and the settlement at Akaroa, from the French point of view and from French archives.)
V. Aspect of the country, pp. 658–61. Geology, pp. 661–6. Flora, pp. 667–71. Fauna, pp. 671–82.
VI. Iles Auckland, Macquarie, Campbell, de l'Antipode, Chatham, Norfolk, pp. 438–48. Preuves de l'effondrement d'un continent austral dans l'age moderne de la terre, pp. 448–54.
VII. Premiers habitans. Mélanésiens et Polynésiens. Maoris—traditions et coutumes. Morioris des îles Chatham, pp. 928–9. Etat actuel de la colonie, pp. 929–32.

Blanchard (*ibid.,* Jan. 15, 1892, p. 373) mentions a series of "remarkable articles" on N.Z. in the *Journal des Débats,* Sept. 1839, by L.B.

Buller, Rev. J. Forty Years in New Zealand : | including | a Personal Narrative, | an Account of Maoridom, | and of | the Christianization and Colonization | of the country. | By the | Rev. James Buller. | London : | Hodder and Stoughton, | 27, Paternoster Row. | 1878.
    8°. Pp. viii, 503. Portrait, map, and 16 illus.
      Part i. Personal narrative (1836-76): Hokianga, Kaipara, Wellington, Canterbury, Auckland, Thames. ii. Maoridom: general. iii. Christianization: Marsden, Leigh, Williams, Turner, Pompalier, Bumby, Selwyn, Lawry, Germau mission. iv. Colonization: early history, successive Governors, Kingism, war. Appendix A. Lecture on "New Zealand, the future England of the southern hemisphere." C. Lecture on the Maori war, 1860. D. Epitome of natural history.

Carter, C. R. Round the World | Leisurely. | By | C. R. Carter, | author of | " Victoria, The British El Dorado," " Incidents of Travel," | etc. etc. | Fleet Street, London. | 1878.
    cr. 8°. Title-page, contents, and 120 pp.
      N.Z.: ch. ix., pp. 66-75. General—past and present—the four chief towns.

Elwell, E. Simeon. The Boy Colonists : | or, | Eight Years' Colonial Life in Otago, | New Zealand. | By Rev. E. Simeon Elwell, M.A., | (Worc. Coll., Oxon.) | Burnham, Somerset. | London : | Simpkin, Marshall, & Co. | Oxford : Thos. Shrimpton & Son. | 1878.
    p. 8°. Pp. vi (not numbered), 258. Map.
      Narrative of what occurred to a settler in Otago, 1859-67. "Many of the names are real, and all the facts are related in the order in which they occurred, a greater part of the work being simply an enlargement of a diary."—*Introduction.*

***Filhol,** Henri. [Report on the geology of the Campbell, Auckland, and Stewart Islands.]
    In counection with the French Commission sent to observe the transit of Venus, M. Filhol "fut attaché à la mission do l'île Campbell. . . . Après s'être livré à l'exploration de l'île Campbell, le naturaliste devait visiter les îles Auckland, l'île Stewart, la Nouvelle-Zélande. Il fallait coustater los rapports de ces différentes terres, rechercher si des faits ne témoignent pas de ruptures survenues en des temps reculés. À résoudre des problèmes que suggère la condition actuelle des îles australes, M. H. Filhol a mis infiniment d'intelligence ; il a recueilli un ensemble d'informations neuves."—*Blanchard, Rev. d. D. Mondes,* Mars 1, 1878, p. 36.
      Prof. Huttou mentions a paper by M. Filhol on the Mollusca of Stewart Island (*N.Z. Mollusca,* 1880, p. ii).

Fornander, A. An Account | of | The Polynesian | Race | its Origin and Migrations | and the | *Ancient History* of the Hawaiian People | to the Times of Kamehameha I. | By | Abraham Fornander, | Circuit Judge of the Island of Maui, H.I. | —— | London : | Trübner & Co., Ludgate Hill.
    Three vols. 8°. V. i, 1878; v. ii, 1880; v. iii, 1885. Vol. iii has sub-title : Comparative Vocabulary | of the | Polynesian and Indo-European Languages | —— | With a Preface by | Professor W. D. Alexander, | of Punahou College, Honolulu.
    Vol. i : pp. xvi, 247, with a genealogical table ; ii : pp. vii, 399 ; iii : pp. xii, 292.
      "I believe that I can show that the Polynesian family can be traced directly as having occupied the Asiatic Archipelago, from Sumatra to Timor, Gilolo and the Philippines, previous to the occupation of that archipel by the present Malay family; that traces, though faint and few, lead up through Deccan to the north-west part of India and the shores of the Persian gulf; that, when other traces here fail, yet the language points farther north, to the Aryan stock in its earlier days, long before the Vedic irruption in India; and that for long ages the Polynesian family was the recipient of a Cushite civilisation, and to such an extent as almost entirely to obscure its own consciousness of parentage and kindred to the Aryan stock."—i. 2. The emigration from Sawaii, Samoan group, to N.Z. took place "about fifteen generations previous to 1850, or at the close of the fourteenth or commencement of the fifteenth

Fornander, A.—*continued.*
century A.D."—ii. 7. He denies all ethnological or linguistic connection between the Malay and Polynesian races except such as arose from intercourse between them.

The object of the third volume is to prove that the Polynesian language is "fundamentally a branch of the great Aryan family of languages, and . . . probably the oldest still surviving" (iii. 1). Vol. iii is reviewed in the N.Y. *Nation,* Aug. 26, 1886, and the review is replied to by Fornander in a letter published May 10, 1887. It is reviewed also in the *Saturday Review,* Jan. 9, 1886, lxi. 58–9. His method, the writer says, "sinks to the low level of the etymological school rendered obsolete by the creation of scientific philology."

* **Greffrath,** H. Die Provinz Auckland, Neu-Seeland. *Aus allen Welttheilen,* ix. 238. 1878.

Harris, J. Chantrey. The Southern Guide | to the | Hot-lake District of the North Island | of New Zealand. | By | J. Chantrey Harris. | Under the Auspices of the Union Steam Ship Company | of New Zealand (Limited). | Dedicated to Tourists. | January, 1878. | Dunedin : | Printed at the " Daily Times " Office, Rattray Street.
8°. Pp. viii, 95. Two maps—topographical and coastal.
Descriptive of the district.

In the Matter | of | Dr. Buller's Petition. | Extracts | from the official minutes of evidence taken before | the Public Petitions Committee of the House | of Representatives in the session of 1877. | —— | Wellington : | Printed at the office of James Hughes, Lambton Quay. | 1878.
roy. 8°. Pp. 14.
Alleged an unsatisfied claim of £500 against Provincial Government of Wellington.

Lecoy, A. New Zealand State Forests : | A Mode of Transaction, [*sic*] (*Modus Operandi*) |Combining their Conservation and Improvement | with Financial Advantages. | By A. Lecoy, LL.B., of Paris, | (late of the French Forest Department). | Wellington : | Lyon & Blair, Lambton Quay. | 1878.
roy. 8°. Pp. 24.
Transaction is evidently a mistranslation for *compromise.*

* **Lindsay-Bucknall,** H. A search for fortune : travel and adventure in several parts of the world. London, 1878.
8°.
N.Z. § 14.

* **Merivale,** G. The hot lakes of New Zealand. *Good Words,* xix. 767. 1878.

* **Neuseelands Handel in 1877.** *Preuss. Handelsarchiv,* 1878, no. 51.

* **Neuseelands Schifffahrt und Handel in 1876.** *Preuss. Handelsarchiv,* 1878, no. 35.

Otago Museum : Guide to the Collections of Zoology, Geology, and Mineralogy. Dunedin, 1878.
fcp. 8°.

* **Purnell,** C. W. An Agrarian Law for New Zealand. By Charles W. Purnell. Wellington, 1878.
8°. Pamphlet.

* **Rains,** Fanny L. By Land and Ocean : Journal and Letters of a Young Girl through Australia, New Zealand, China, America, &c. By Fanny L. Rains. London, 1878.
8°.—*Davis.*

Rees, W. L. Sir Gilbert Leigh; | or, | Pages from the History | of | An Eventful Life. | With an Appendix—"The great Pro-consul." | By W. L. Rees. | London : | Sampson Low, Marston, Searle, & Rivington, | —— | 1878.
    p. 8°. Pp. iv, 352.
    The Appendix (pp. 329–52) is a biography and eulogy of Sir George Grey. Another edition published the same year is in two volumes. The appendix is in vol. ii, pp. 231–63.

* **Stewart**, G. Vesey. The Kati-Kati Settlement : sequel and press notices. Omagh, 1878.
    Pamphlet.

Suter, *Bishop* Andrew Burn. Public Works Statement. | Exclusion of Nelson and | Marlborough. | A letter thereon, | to | the Hon. the Premier, | Sir George Grey, K.C.B., | by | the Bishop of Nelson. | 1878. | Nelson : | R. Lucas and Son, Book and General Printers, Bridge-st. | 1878.
    8°. Pp. 8. Nelson, Sept. 5th, 1878.
    On the omission of Nelson and Marlborough from the general scheme of railways accepted by the Legislature.

Thomas, E. C. G. Ryotwarry : | a Solution | of the | Maori Land Question. | By E. C. G. Thomas, A.S., R.A.S., | H.M. Indian C.S. | Price—Sixpence. | Auckland : | William Atkin, | Book and General Printer, High Street. | 1878.
    8°. Pp. 16.
    Proposed application of Ryotwarree tenancy of South India.

Vogel, *Sir* Julius. The colonies generally and New Zealand in particular. *In* Social Notes, edited by S. C. Hall. No. 15, June 15, 1878, pp. 225–8.
    The progress of N.Z. depends on the returns from its land.

Wakefield, E. J. The Taxes | in New Zealand : | Who Pays ? Who Doesn't Pay ? | Who Ought to Pay ? | A Handbook of Taxation Reform, | by | Edward Jerningham Wakefield. | Price : One Shilling. | Christchurch : | Printed at the "Times" office, Gloucester-street. | 1878.
    8°. Pp. 46.
    Part i. Who pays ? who doesn't pay ? pp. 3–18. Part ii. Who ought to pay ? pp. 18–30. Part iii. Taxation reform, and how to get it ?
    Gives a sketch of the history of land-sharking in N.Z., pp. 33–8. Part iii is a summary of proposed reforms in taxation.

Wells, B. The | History of Taranaki | by | B. Wells : | a Standard Work on the History of the | Province | —— | New Zealand : | Edmondson and Avery, "Taranaki News" Office, | New Plymouth. | 1878.
    8°. Preface. Pp. vii, 311.
    Ch. i. [Origin of Maoris.] ii. History of the Ngatiawa tribe. iii. Fall of Pukerangiora and the defence of Ngamotu. iv. European discovery of Taranaki. v. N.Z. Company. vi. Operations of N.Z. Co. vii. Adventures of Dieffenbach in Taranaki (extracted from Dieffenbach's *Travels*). viii. British assumption of sovereignty. ix. Foundation of the settlement. x. Despatch of the pioneer ships. xi. Governor Hobson. xii. Events of 1842. xiii. Events of 1843. xiv. Events of 1844. xv. History of the establishment of various religious denominations in Taranaki: Church of England (pp. 122–7); Roman Catholics (pp. 127–8); Wesleyan Methodists (pp. 128–30); Primitive Methodists (pp. 130–2); Congregationalism (p. 132); Presbyterianism (pp. 132–3); Baptists (p. 134). xvi. Events of 1845–48: Waikanae migration in 1848, pp. 145–6. xvii. Events of 1849. xviii. From 1850 to 1855. xix. Puketapu feud. xx. 1856–58. xxi. 1859. xxii. Taranaki war. xxiii. Truce. xxiv. Renewal of hostilities. xxv. Confiscation of lands and establishment of military settlements. xxvi. Conclusion of war. xxvii. Peace. xxviii. Taranaki pioneers. List of ships which visited the coast of Taranaki in early times, pp. 309–10.

White, J. Plan of the Maori mythology. Napier, 1878.
Chart—a genealogical stemma.
Also published as an appendix to Bastian's *Zur Kenntniss Hawaii's*, 1883.

Wilson, Alexander Johnstone. The | Resources of Modern Countries | Essays towards an Estimate of the Economic | Position of Nations and British | Trade Prospects. | By | Alexander Johnstone Wilson | Reprinted, with Emendations and Additions, from *Fraser's Magazine* | In two Volumes. | Vol. II. | London | Longmans, Green, and Co. | 1878.
8°. Pp. iv (not numbered), 382.
Ch. xii. Australia and New Zealand. N.Z.: pp. 187-98.

1879.

Ballance, J. New Zealand. | The Financial Statement | of | the Hon. J. Ballance, | Colonial Treasurer. | Made in Committee of Ways and Means, Tuesday, 6th August, | 1878. | Wellington : | By authority : George Didsbury, Government Printer. | 1879.
8°. Pp. 67.

[Barr, James.] The | Old Identities : | being Sketches and Reminiscences during | the First Decade | of the | Province of Otago, N.Z. | —By an Old Identity. | Dunedin : | Mills, Dick and Co. | 1879.
cr. 8°. Pp. 395. Illustrated [by James Brown].
Ch. i. Introductory. ii. Personal. iii. Landing. iv, v. Descriptive. vi. Our Chief, and others. vii. The Minister, and others. viii. Tradespeople. ix. Suburban settlers. x, xi. Press in 1848-9. xii. Send back the money. xiii. Sir G. Grey's visit in 1850. xiv. Incidental. xv. Early projects. xvi. Nominee legislation. xvii. Decline of the little enemy. xviii. Tenter-hooks of suspense. xix. Social progress. xx, xxi. Constitution at last. xxii. Dinner to Capt. Cargill. xxiii. Electioneering. xxiv. Up to date (indications of progress). xxv. Opening of first Provincial Council. xxvi. First session. xxvii. Church extension. xxviii. Second session. xxix. Cheap land. xxx. Immigration. xxxi. Otago Maine liquor law league. xxxii. Customs robbery and first Town Board election. xxxiii. First septenary. xxxiv. Discussions of 1856. xxxv. Land sales and leasing ordinance. xxxvi. Banking and steam. xxxvii. Colonist newspaper. xxxviii. Anniversary of 1857. xxxix. Poets of first decade. xl. Loctures. xli. Heave her ahead. Appendix (on the artist, Brown), pp. 393-5.

Barry, W. J. Up and Down ; | or, | Fifty Years' Colonial Experiences | in | Australia, California, New Zealand, India, China, | and the South Pacific ; | being the | Life History of Capt. W. J. Barry. | Written by himself, | 1878. | With Portrait of the Author, | And other Illustrations. | London : | Sampson Low, Marston, Searle, & Rivington, | Crown Buildings, 188 Fleet Street. | 1879.
cr. 8°. Pp. xiii, 307.
Chs. xviii-xxv, pp. 170-294 (with the omission of a few pages), and the appendix, pp. 295-307, relate to N.Z.
Describes life in the interior of Otago in 1863, where the author was storekeeper, farmer, breeder, butcher, and afterwards lecturer.

Blair, W. N. Building Materials | of Otago | and | South New Zealand generally. | By W. N. Blair, M.Inst.C.E. | Papers originally read at the Otago Institute revised and extended. | Dunedin : J. Wilkie & Co., Princes Street. | 1879.
8°. Pp. vii+iv+244. 5 tables.
Introductory, pp. i-iv. Section i. Stones, bricks, concrete, and roofing-slates. ii. Limes, cements, and their aggregates. iii. Timbers. iv. Metals.

Bracken, T. The New Zealand Tourist. | By | Thomas Bracken. | Published by the | Union Steam Ship Company | of New Zealand (Limited). |

Bracken, T.—*continued.*
1879. | Dunedin : | Mackay, Bracken, and Co., Printers, Moray Place. MDCCCLXXIX.
    cr. 8°. Pp. viii, 90. Photograph.
    <small>Generally descriptive of the picturesque parts of both islands.</small>

***Bunbury,** Clement. A visit to the New Zealand Geysers. *Fraser's Magazine,* June, 1879, pp. 761-8. *Popular Science Monthly,* N.Y., 1879.

Centenaire | de la | Mort de Cook | célébré le 14 février 1879 | à l'hôtel de La Société de Géographie | 184, Boulevard Saint-Germain, 184 | Extrait du Bulletin de La Société de Géographie | (Mai 1879) | Paris | Société de Géographie | 184, Boulevard Saint-Germain, 184 | 1879.
    8°. Pp. 140. Map of Cook's voyages.
    <small>Address of Vice-Admiral Baron de la Roncière-Le Noury, Senator, President of the Society, pp. 1-2. Cook, par William Huber, pp. 3-16. Cook et Dalrymple, par le Dr. E. T. Hamy, pp. 17-32. L'Océanie moderne, par C. de Varigny, pp. 33-41. Allocution of the President, pp. 42-3. Catalogue descriptif et méthodique de l'exposition organisée par la Société de Géographie à l'occasion du centenaire de la mort de Cook, par le Dr. E. T. Hamy, sécrétaire de la société, pp. 44-80 (355 articles). Cartographie et bibliographie, par James Jackson, pp. 81-138 (417 numbers—reprinted from the English).</small>
    <small>James Jackson, author of the bibliography of Cook, is "the well-known archiviste-bibliothécaire of the Société de Géographie at Paris."—*Oliver, Madagascar,* ii. 222.</small>

Chambers, William. Judge Bathgate's experiences of New Zealand. *Chambers's Journal,* Oct. and Nov. 1879, pp. 657-60, 737-40; March and June 1880, pp. 161-3, 369-72.
    <small>Derived from conversations with Judge Bathgate and a perusal of his (then unpublished) lectures. Extract from the *Times,* Oct. 21, 1879, describing a movement towards emigration to N.Z. of farmers and landowners in Lincolnshire. Letters from J. Bathgate (June 1880, pp. 368-71) and J. Reid, Elderslie, pp. 371-2). Sir W. Chambers suggested the name Dunedin.</small>

Clayden, Arthur. The | England of the Pacific | or | New Zealand as an English Middle-Class | Emigration-Field. | A Lecture. | By Arthur Clayden, | Together with | A reprint of Letters to the Daily News on the English Agricultural | Labourer in New Zealand ; Notes of a Month's Trip on | Horseback through the North Island of New Zealand, | and of a Forty Days' Trip to Australia ; and a | Few Plain Directions for Intending Emigrants. | Eight Full-Page Illustrations. | Second Edition. | London : | Wyman and Sons, 81, Great Queen Street, | Lincoln's Inn Fields, W.C. | 1879.
    8°. Pp. 65.

Escott, T. H. S. Pillars of the Empire | Sketches of | Living Indian and Colonial Statesmen, | Celebrities and Officials | Edited, with an Introduction, by T. H. S. Escott | London | Chapman and Hall, 193, Piccadilly | 1879.
    p. 8°. Pp. xxxii, 348.
    <small>Sir George Bowen, pp. 1-7; Sir William Jervois (by Major Arthur Griffiths), pp. 149-55; Sir Frederick Aloysius Weld, pp. 333-39 (also by Major Griffiths); Sir Julius Vogel, pp. 322-32.</small>

***Fleming,** P. The financial condition of New Zealand : the bubble bursted. Edinburgh, 1879.
    Pamphlet.

The **Great Medicine Man** | of Dancoyle. | By Policeman X. | Auckland : | Wilsons & Horton, —— | MDCCCLXXIX.
    8°. Pp. 4, double columns.

Grey, James. His Island Home; | and | Away in the Far North. | A Narrative of Travels | in that Part of the Colony north of Auckland. | By James Grey. | Wellington : | Printed at the office of the New Zealand Times Newspaper Company, Limited. | MDCCCLXXIX.

8°. Pp. 54, double columns. Nine photographs of scenes and individuals—Heke, Waka Nene, Patuone, and other Maoris.
Description of Kawau, Bay of Islands district, and Hokianga.

Gudgeon, T. Wayth. Reminiscences | of | the War in New Zealand. | By | Thomas W. Gudgeon, | Lieutenant and Quarter-master Colonial Forces, N.Z. | With twelve portraits. | London : | Sampson Low, Marston, Searle, and Rivington. | Auckland : E. Wayte. | 1879.

cr. 8°. Pp. xiv, 372. Map.
Introduction, pp. v-viii. Preliminary chapter. Ch. i. Landing of troops at Wanganui. ii, iii. Colonial forces under Imperial rule. iv-viii. Origin and progress of Hauhau religion. ix. Capture of the Weraroa pah. x. Relief of Pipiriki. xi, xii, xiii. Opotiki expedition. xv, xvi. East coast expedition. xvii. Murder of Keriti, &c. xviii-xx. Gen. Chute's campaign. xxi-xxiii. McDonnell's campaign. xxiv, xxv. Skirmishes on east coast. xxvi. Outbreak at Napier. xxvii. Titokowaru's outbreak. xxviii. Murders. xxix. Hauhaus' attack on Turu Turu Mokai. xxx, xxxi. Attacks on Te Ngutu. xxxii. Difference between disciplined and undisciplined troops. xxxiii. Reconnoitring; Whitmore commander. xxxiv. Battle of Moturoa. xxxv-xlv. Te Kooti. xlvi-xlviii. Operations against Titokowaru. xlix-lv. Campaign against Uriwera tribe. lvi-lxi. Taupo campaign. lxii. Patatere campaign. lxiii. Operations at Waikare Moana. lxiv.-lxvi. Te Kooti. Conclusion, pp. 307-8. List of killed and wounded, 1869-70, pp. 309-72.

Haast, J. von. Geology | of the | Provinces of Canterbury and | Westland, | New Zealand. | A Report comprising the Results of | Official Explorations. | By Julius von Haast, Ph.D., F.R.S., | Director of the Canterbury Museum, | Professor of Geology in | Canterbury College (New Zealand University), and | late Government Geologist to the Province of Canterbury, | New Zealand. | Christchurch : | Printed at the "Times" office, Gloucester Street and Cathedral Square. | 1879.

8°. Pp. x, 486. Geological maps, coloured and plain. Views from photographs. Both printed at Vienna.
Part i. Historical notes on the progress of the geological survey, pp. 1-171. ii. Physical geography, pp. 172-235. iii. Geology, pp. 236-486.
At pp. 236-9 is given an account of the progress of geological research in Canterbury, with a bibliography.

* The Hau-Haus in New Zealand. *London Quarterly Review*, lii. 427. 1879.

Heaton, John. The Waikato war, 1863-4. Auckland, 1879.
Pp. 100. [With portrait of Rewi.]
"What the author has endeavoured to do is to give an authentic history or detailed account of the operations of both the Imperial and Colonial Forces that were engaged in the Waikato war of 1863 and 1864, obtained from the despatches of General Cameron, the author's own personal observations, and various other authentic sources."—*Preface.*

Heaton, J. Henniker. Australian Dictionary of Dates | and | Men of the Time; | containing the | History of Australasia from 1542 to May, 1879; | by | J. H. Heaton. | Sydney : | George Robertson, 125, Pitt-Street, | and at | Melbourne and Adelaide. | 1879.

roy. 8°. Pp. 232, ii ; 317, 2.
Has biographical notices of J. Ballance, Sir J. Banks, Sir G. Bowen, H. S. Chapman, Capt. Cook, Bishop Cowie, E. J. Eyre, Dr. Featherston, F. D. Fenton, Sir J. Fergusson, Sir W. Fitzherbert, Sir G. Grey, Sir W. Jervois, J. Macandrew, S. Marsden, J. Sheehan, Solander, R. Stout, J. Vogel, F. A. Weld, Col. Whitmore, Bishop Williams.
In pt. ii, pp. 176-79, is a brief chronology of N.Z. history, and (pp. 179-80) of explorations.

Hector, J. Handbook | of | New Zealand. | Sydney International Exhibition, 1879. | By | James Hector, M.D., C.M.G., F.R.S., | Director of the Geological Survey ; | Executive Commissioner for New Zealand. | Published by Direction of the Royal Commissioners for New Zealand. | With Maps and Plates. | Wellington : | Lyon and Blair, Printers, Lambton Quay. | 1879.

8°. Pp. vi (not numbered), 105. Map of N.Z., meteorological map, and 12 statistical diagrams.

Description, history, government, pp. 1-6. Vegetable and animal products, pp. 6-16. Geology, pp. 17-30. Mining and geology, pp. 31-50. Climate, pp. 51-6. Statistics, pp. 57-67. Institutions, pp. 68-86. Forest-trees, pp. 87-95.
Later editions were published in 1880, 1883, 1886.

Hingston, James. The Australian abroad. | Branches from the Main Routes | round the World. | By James Hingston, | ("J. H." of the "*Melbourne Argus*.") | —— | London : | Sampson Low, Marston, Searle, and Rivington, | Crown Buildings, 188, Fleet Street. | 1879.

8°. xii pp., maps, 426 pp. 16 illus. and map relate to N.Z.

Chs. xxix-xliii, pp. 300-426, describe a journey through N.Z., from Hokitika across the island to Christchurch, thence to Dunedin, Wellington, Picton, Nelson, Auckland, the Thames goldfields, and the Lakes. Two chapters (xlii and xliii) describe the Pakeha's progress and the Maori's decline.

Important | Judgments | delivered in the | Compensation Court and Native Land Court. | 1866-1879. | Published : | Under the direction of the Chief Judge, Native Land Court. | 1879.

p. 8°. Pp. v, 147. Maps and pedigrees.

The volume has much historical matter. At pp. 57-81 are sketches of native history by Judge Fenton ; pp. 98-100, by Judge Monro ; pp. 101-8, by Judge Fenton ; pp. 110-23, by Judge Maning.
"By direction of Mr. Fenton I am engaged in collecting information relative to the former history of the native tribes, as far as it can be ascertained from evidence given in the Native Land Courts, with a view to compiling a history of the various tribes since their arrival in New Zealand."—H. Frank Edger to Judge Wilson : see whose pamphlet, p. 81.

*[**Innes**, C. L.] Canterbury sketches, or Life from the early days. By a Pilgrim. Christchurch, 1879.

12°.

Keane, A. H. On the relations of the Indo-Chinese and Indo-Oceanic races and languages. Read Nov. 11, 1879. *Journal of the Anthropological Institute*, ix. 254-89.

The large brown race of Eastern Polynesia (which the author calls the Sawaiori) is Caucasian, coming originally from the Indo-Chinese peninsula, and has absorbed the dark Papuans.

Land and Farming | in | New Zealand. | Information respecting the Mode of | acquiring Land in New Zealand ; with | Particulars as to Farming, Wages, Prices | of Provisions, Etc., in that Colony ; | also the Land Acts of 1877. | With Maps. | Edited by Sir Julius Vogel, K.C.M.G. | London : | Waterlow & Sons Limited, Printers, London Wall ; | and 49, Parliament Street, Westminster. | 1879.

8°. Pp. 189. Two maps.
Notes on N.Z. farming, by Rev. J. Berry, pp. 9-20.

*The Land question in New Zealand and Australia. *Melbourne Review*, 1879, v. 4.

Lecoy, A. The Forest Question | in | New Zealand. | Wellington : | Lyon and Blair. | —— | 1879.

roy. 8°. Pp. 23.

* **Martin,** Josiah. The hot springs and terraces of New Zealand. *Popular Science Review,* xviii. 366. 1879.

* Neuseelands Schifffahrt und Handel in 1877. *Preuss. Handelsarchiv,* 1879, no. 48.

Oliver, G. Homes for the People | in the | Provincial District of Otago. | By George Oliver. | Oamaru : | Printed at North Otago Times Office, Wansbeck Street. | 1879.
    cr. 8°. Pp. 8.
    Suggestions for regulations for land-settlement.

Owen, Richard. Memoirs | on the | Extinct Wingless Birds of New Zealand; | with an appendix | on those of | England, Australia, Newfoundland, Mauritius, and Rodriguez. | By | Richard Owen, C.B., F.R.S. | Foreign Associate of the Institute of France, etc. | —— | London : | John Van Voorst, 1 Paternoster Row. | 1879.
    2 vols. roy. 4°. V. i : pp. x, 465, 48, and woodcuts ; v. ii : 125 plates and map.

      Sir R. Owen states in the preface : The fragment of bone figured in pl. 73 " was brought for sale to the College of Surgeons in 1839 by an individual who stated that he had obtained it in New Zealand from a native, who told him that it was the bone of a great Eagle." Sir R. proceeded to compare it, first with the skeleton of the ox, then with that of the ostrich. Finally, "I arrived at the conviction that the specimen had come from a bird, that it was the shaft of a thigh-bone, and that it must have formed part of the skeleton of a bird as large as, if not larger than, the full-sized male ostrich." He made drawings which, with his descriptions and conclusions, were submitted to the Zoological Society of London, Nov. 12, 1839. There was some hesitation to admit the paper into the Transactions. "On the publication of the volume in 1838 [*sic*], one hundred copies of the paper were struck off; and these I distributed in every quarter of the islands of N.Z. where attention to such evidences was likely to be attracted. . . . The confirmatory response, anxiously expected through . . . 1840, 1841, and 1842, at length arrived," in letters from Rev. W. Cotton and Col. Wakefield, and in the collection of bones transmitted by Rev. W. Williams.

      There are 41 Memoirs, of which four relate to the wingless birds of other countries. The second (on the genus *Dinornis*) reproduces (pp. 73-4) the abstract of the Memoir on the first fragment of bone received, and gives W. Williams's letter to Dr. Buckland (pp. 75-6, *note*). A Memoir (pp. 454-9) adduces from Sir G. Grey, J. White, and Rev. R. Taylor, traditional and other testimonies to the recent disappearance of the moa, and its causes. A "Conclusion" (pp. 460-5) speculates in a Lamarckian vein on the origin of the species by way of degeneration from antecedent winged forms.

      Dr. Mantell sought to claim for Mr. Colenso priority in the discovery of the struthious character of the moa. . The *Quarterly Review,* xc. 404-5, *note,* disposes of the claim. Prof. Owen's first Memoir was despatched to N.Z. in Dec. 1839, and received in 1840. Mr. C.'s paper, dated May 1, 1842, appeared in *Tasmanian Journal,* vol. ii., no. 8, 1844.* The *Athenæum,* no. 850, reports Owen's lecture at the Royal Institution on the wingless birds of N.Z.

      The Quarterly Reviewer, xc. 402, *note,* well remembers seeing the "fragment of the shaft of the femur when it first arrived, and hearing the opinion of the Professor as to the bird to which it must have belonged. He took, in our presence, a piece of paper, and drew the outline of what he conceived to be the complete bone. . . . When a perfect bone arrived, and was laid on the paper, it fitted the outline *exactly.*" The Reviewer was also present when the case of moa-bones sent by W. Williams was opened at the Museum (p. 403).

*. **Pearson,** W. H. In Memoriam Sir John Richardson. Invercargill, 1879.
    8°.

Political | and Other | Ballads, | Compiled from the | "Auckland Free Lance." | Price One Shilling. | Auckland : | Printed and Published by J. D. Wickham, " Free Lance " Office, | Vulcan Lane, Auckland.
    8°. Pp. 22. The " Introduction " is dated April 12, 1879.

---

* No. 7, 1843.

Quatrefages, A. *dc.* The Human Species. | By A. de Quatrefages, | Professor of Anthropology in the Museum of Natural History, Paris. | London : | Kegan Paul & Co., 1, Paternoster Square. | 1879.
  cr. 8°. Pp. x, 498. International Scientific series.
  <small>Polynesian migrations (ch. xvii). Maori colonisation of N.Z., pp. 191-5, 196-7. See earlier works, 1864, 1868.</small>

Report of the Royal Commission appointed by His Excellency to inquire into and report upon the Operations of the University of New Zealand and its Relations to the Secondary Schools of the Colony. Wellington, 1879.
  fcp. f°.

* **Rose,** R. The New Zealand Guide. By R. Rose, fourteen years resident in the colonies. [1879 or 1880.]

* **Russell,** I. C. Sketch of New Zealand. *American Naturalist,* Salem, xiii. 65. 1879.

Simmons, Alfred. Old England | and | New Zealand: | the Government, | Laws, Churches, Public Institutions, and the | Resources of New Zealand, | with an | Historical Sketch of the Maori Race | (the Natives of New Zealand): to which are added Extracts from the Author's | Diary of his Voyage to New Zealand, | in company with 500 Emigrants. | By Alfred Simmons. | London : | Edward Stanford, 55, Charing Cross. | 1879.
  8°. Pp. 143. Map.

Spedding, J. Reviews and Discussions | Literary, | Political, | and Historical, | not Relating to Bacon. | By | James Spedding. | London : | C. Kegan Paul & Co., 1, Paternoster Square. | 1879.
  8°. Pp. vii, 419.
  <small>In article v, pp. 153-86, reprinted from the *Edinburgh Review,* July, 1840, the Wakefield theory of colonization is examined. The next essay, on South Australia in 1841, bears on the same subject.</small>

Stout, R. Address | on | Education : | delivered by the | Hon. Robert Stout, M.H.R., | Attorney-General, | etc., etc., | President of the Otago Educational | Institute, | at the meeting of the Institute held on the | 15th April, 1879. | Lyon and Blair, Printers, Lambton Quay, Wellington. | 1879.
  8°. Pp. 27.
  <small>Progress of education during past year; history of legislation respecting University education in N.Z.; sectarian character of Primary School teaching.</small>

100,000 Tons of Steel Rails | required to be Manufactured | in New Zealand. | Iron and Coal. | Reports on the Mineral Deposits of | the Colony, | addressed to the Hon. the Minister for Public | Works, and published by order of the Government. | With Maps and Plans. | London : | Printed for the Government of New Zealand, by | Wyman & Sons, 81, Great Queen Street, | —— | 1879.
  8°. Pp. 58+1.

Tucker, H. W. Memoir of the Life and Episcopate | of | George Augustus Selwyn, D.D. | Bishop of New Zealand, 1841-1869 ; | Bishop of Lichfield, 1867-1878. | By the | Rev. H. W. Tucker, M.A., | author of " Under his Banner," " Memoir of Bishop Field," etc., etc. | With two Portraits, Lithographs, and Maps. | —— | In two Volumes.— | London : | William Wells Gardner, | 2 Paternoster Buildings. | 1879.
  8°. Vol. i: pp. xii, 399 ; ii : vi, 393.
  <small>Almost a history of church and missionary work in N.Z., 1842-67, derived mainly from the Bishop's letters and journals. Accounts of contemporary events, as the</small>

Tucker, H. W.—*continued*.
Wairau massacre, i. 141–5; Heke's war, i. 166–85; arrival of the Canterbury pilgrims, i. 355–7; the war of 1860–1 (ii. 150–209). Vol. ii, ch. iii, describes the ecclesiastical organisation and the meeting of a Conference to draft a Church Constitution, and gives (ii. 98–108) the Constitution, with Selwyn's address (ii. 108–26).
Reviewed in the *Quarterly*, cxlviii. 33; *Congregationalist*, iii. 677, vii. 304;' *Nation* (by W. H. Bishop), xxix. 44; *Good Words*, xx. 527 (by A. H. Japp); *American Church Review*, xxx. 465.

* **Vogel**, Julius. New Zealand, Australia, and the Pacific Islands. *Princeton Review*, N.S., iii. 435. 1879.

Wakelin, R. Small Farms | and | Small | Farm Settlements. | By | R. Wakelin. | Reprinted from "The Wairarapa Standard." | Greytown: | *Printed at the "Standard" Office, and to be had on order from | any bookseller.* | Price—One Shilling.
8°. Pp. iv, 18. The preface is dated—July 1, 1879.
Chs. v, vi, and vii describe the purchase and occupation of the Wairarapa.

Wallace, Alfred Russel. Stanford's | Compendium of Geography and Travel | Based on Hellwald's 'Die Erde und Ihre Völker' | Australasia | Edited and Extended | by Alfred R. Wallace, F.R.G.S., | Author of 'The Malay Archipelago,' '*Geographical | Distribution of Animals*,' etc. | With | Ethnological Appendix | By A. H. Keane, M.A.I. | Maps and Illustrations | London | Edward Stanford, 55 Charing Cross, S.W. | 1879.
p. 8°. Two maps, and illus.
The part relating to N.Z. is at pp. 545–92. Ch. xxvi gives the physical history of the group. Ch. xxvii is a general survey of the Provinces.

* **Wayte**, G. H. Eighteen months in Australia and New Zealand. 1879.

1880.

Across two Seas. *In the following periodical:*—Sunday. Sunday Reading for Young and Old. Wells, Gardner, Darton and Co., 2 Paternoster Buildings. London, 1880. Printed by Strangeways and Sons, Tower Street, Upper St. Martin's Lane, London.
A story, evidently from actual experience, of settlers' life in the North of Auckland.

* **Armitage**, J. The Wesleyan mission in New Zealand. *Methodist Quarterly*, New York, xl. 338. 1880.

* **Awdry**, F. Life of Bishop Patteson. Illus. 1880.

Bathgate, John. New Zealand | its Resources and Prospects | By | John Bathgate | District Judge, Dunedin | W. & R. Chambers | London and Edinburgh | 1880.
8°. Pp. 121. Map and 22 illus.
Generally descriptive of the country, its industries and institutions.

Berry, J. Farming in north | New Zealand. | By | Rev. J. Berry, | *Wesleyan Minister.* | *With description of proposed Special Arrangements for | assisting the Settlement there of a limited number of | English Farmers.* | London: James Clarke & Co., 13 and 14, Fleet Street. | 1880.
8°. Pp. 62.
Part I. Ch. i. Introduction. ii. Auckland. iii. Climate and natural productions. iv. Does N.Z. farming pay? v. Beginning a farm. vi. Religion and education.—II. (Description of the estates parts of which it is proposed to divide into farms, for sale in England upon deferred payment.) General remarks, pp. 33–6. Eureka estate. pp. 36–40. Stanford estate, pp. 41–43. Bridgewater estate, pp. 44–6.—III. Epitome of information upon N.Z.

Blues and Buffs: a sketch of a contested election. A novel. *Fraser's Magazine*, N.S., xxii. (1880), chs. 30, 31.
   Describes station-life in Canterbury.

* **Bools**, A.   Life and Travels on Sea and Land.   London, 1880.
   8°.   Pp. 47.

Broun, T.   Manual | of the | New Zealand Coleoptera | By | Captain Thomas Broun | Published by Command | Wellington : | Printed at the Office of James Hughes, Lambton Quay. | 1880.
   roy. 8°.   Pp. xxiii, 744.
   Part ii was issued in 1881; pts. iii, iv, in 1886.

* **Brown**, J. K.   A Protective Policy, &c.   Wellington, 1880.
   8°.   Pamphlet.

Brown, R.   The | Countries of the World : | being | a Popular Description of the Various Continents, Islands, Rivers, | Seas, and Peoples of the Globe. | By | Robert Brown, M.A. | Ph.D., F.L.S., F.R.G.S. | *Author of " Peoples of the World,"* etc. etc. | Cassell & Company, Limited : | London, Paris, & New York.
   4°.   6 vols.   Vol. iv, 1880.
   Vol. iv, ch. vii, pp. 87-127, has a general description of N.Z., with sketch-map and 16 large and small illustrations of scenery, towns, and natives.

Buchanan, John.   The | Indigenous Grasses | of | New Zealand. | Illustrated by | John Buchanan, F.L.S., | Draftsman to the Geological Survey Department. | Sixty-four Plates. | Published by Command. | New Zealand. | By Authority : George Didsbury, Government Printer, Wellington. | 1880.
   f°.   Pp. 13 (with title-page and preface) ; 64 plates, with 110 pp. (not numbered) of letter-press.
   The first fasciculus, with 20 plates, appeared in June 1877 ; the second, with 22 plates, in June 1879 ; the third, with 21 plates, in June 1880.—*Prospectus.*
   There are two plates numbered XXIX, two XXXIII, two XXXIV. Plate XXXII appears twice, and there is no XXXI. The Addenda include plates XVII, 2 ; XXVI, 2 ; XXXVI, 2.
   Introduction, pp. 7-10.—Publication of the Colonial Museum.

Buchanan, J.   Manual | of the | Indigenous Grasses | of | New Zealand. | By | John Buchanan, F.L.S. Lond., | Botanist and Draughtsman to the Geological Survey. | Published by Command. | Wellington : | Printed at the office of James Hughes, Lambton Quay. | 1880.
   roy. 8°.   Pp. xv, 174, and plates as in the folio edition.

Buller, James.   New Zealand : | Past and Present. | By the | Rev. James Buller, | *Author of " Forty Years in New Zealand."* | London : | Hodder and Stoughton, | 27, Paternoster Row. | MDCCCLXXX.
   cr. 8°.   Pp. viii, 202.   Map and 8 full-page illus.
   Country—aborigines—missionaries—colony—progress—chief towns and districts —land-laws—emigrant's prospects.

Colenso, William.   A Comprehensive Dictionary of the New Zealand Tongue, including Mythical, Mythological, " Taboo " or Sacred, Genealogical, Proverbial, Poetical, Tropological, Sacerdotal, Incantatory, Natural History, Idiomatical, Abbreviated, Tribal and other Names and Terms of and Allusions to Persons, Things, Acts, and Places in Ancient Times ; also, showing their Affinities with Cognate Polynesian Dialects and Foreign Languages, with Copious Pure Maori Examples.   Part i. Maori-English.

Colenso, William—*continued*.
Part ii. English-Maori.—Appendix to Journals of the House of Representatives of New Zealand, 1880, vol. ii, G.-6.
[Title-page of " Specimen of Mr. Colenso's English-Maori Lexicon." Two more folio pages give—Abbreviations and signs, and part of the letter A.]

Crawford, James Coutts. Recollections | of | Travel in New Zealand | and Australia. | By James Coutts Crawford, F.G.S. | . . . | With Maps and Illustrations. | London : | Trübner and Co., Ludgate Hill. | 1880.
8°. Pp. xvi, 468. 3 maps and 24 illustrations.
First arrival in N.Z. (1839), pp. 21-9. To Queen Charlotte's Sound, pp. 30-4. Across the Straits and back, pp. 35-41. First settlement at Wellington, pp. 42-8. Ride from Wellington to the Manawatu, pp. 52-5. Return to N.Z. in 1846. Bay of Islands, Auckland, and Wellington, pp. 77-81. Walk to the Wairarapa, pp. 82-4. Trip to Taranaki, pp. 85-9. Journey to the Whanganui, pp. 90-4. On the Whanganui river, pp. 95-113. To Lake Taupo and back, pp. 114-51. Topini, pp. 152-65. Return to Whanganui, pp. 166-72. Up the Manawatu river, pp. 173-82. From Upper Hutt to Waikanae, pp. 183-6. From Whanganui to the Waitotara district, pp. 187-90. Journey to explore the main range of Tararua, pp. 191-206. To the northern peninsula of Auckland province, pp. 207-19. Up the Waikato and Waipa, pp. 220-8. Visit to Lake Coleridge, pp. 229-31. Two nights at Motueka, pp. 232-7. Visit to the Hurunui lakes, pp. 238-40. Journey from Christchurch to Dunedin, pp. 241-5. From Dunedin to Lake Wakatipu and Invercargill, pp. 246-50. Invercargill and thence to Dunedin, pp. 251-4. Excursion to Tuapeka, pp. 255-7. Havelock and the Pelorus Sound, pp. 258-63. N.Z. politics, pp. 309-22. Maori language, pp. 323-36. Geology, pp. 337-40. Origin, character, and religion of Maori race, pp. 347-56. N.Z. physically and agriculturally, pp. 357-69.

Description of Mr. Fitzgibbon Louch's Settlement, Bellevue Estate, Province of Auckland, N.Z. Illustrated ; maps and photographs. London : Vacher, 1880.
8°. Pp. 84.—*Davis*.

* **Fritsch**, G. Ueber Julius von Haast, Notes on some Ancient Rock-paintings in New Zealand. *Z. f. Ethnologie*, p. 200. 1880.

* **Grant**, S., *and* **Foster**, J. S. New Zealand : A Report on its Agricultural Conditions and Prospects. With map. London : G. Street & Co. 1880.
Pamphlet. *Davis* gives it under 1881.
The authors were delegates from the tenant-farmers of Lincolnshire.

Halcombe, Arthur F. New Zealand. *Proc. Roy. Col. Inst.*, xi. 320-34. 1880.
Descriptive of provinces in 1880 ; finance ; immigration ; Maoris ; statistics. Discussion (pp. 334-50) : Sir E. Stafford, Broomhall, Beaumont.

Hau-hau. *All the Year Round*, Dec. 4, 1880, pp. 151-7. London.
A description, evidently from some personal knowledge, of the war of 1860.

Hutton, F. W. Manual | of the | New Zealand Mollusca. | A systematic and descriptive | Catalogue | of the | Marine and Land Shells, and of the soft Mollusks and Polyzoa of New Zealand | and the Adjacent Islands. | By | Frederick Wollaston Hutton, F.G.S., C.M.Z.S. | —— | Published by Command. | Wellington : | Printed at the office of James Hughes, Lambton Quay. | 1880.
roy. 8°. Pp. xvi, iv, 224.
Gives a general account of the bibliography of the order (*Intro.*), and refers to M. Jouan's essay on the fauna of N.Z., Mémoires de la Société des Sciences Naturelles de Cherbourg, t. xiv (1869).

* **Hutton**, F. W. Zoological exercises for students in New Zealand. Dunedin, 1880.
sm. 8°.
A manual treating of characteristic types of animals inhabiting N.Z.—*Popular Science Review*, N.S., iv (xix), 261-2.

* **Izett,** F. W. New Zealand as it was in 1870; as it is in 1880. London, 1880.
    8°. Pp. 43.—*Davis.*

* **The Maoris.** *St. James's Magazine*, xlvii. 216. 1880.

Moss, F. J. The Assembly: | What will it do? | By F. J. Moss, M.H.R. | Auckland : | Printed by Wilsons and Horton, "Herald" Office, | —— | MDCCCLXXX.
    8°. Pp. 7, double columns.

Mulvany, T. J. New Zealand | Products and Manufactures. | Suggestions | as to the scope of a proposed inquiry into the best means of | promoting and encouraging | Manufactures and Local Industries | in the Colony. | By | Thomas J. Mulvany, C.E., | —— | Tauranga, 1880.
    8°. Pp. 35, double columns.

* **Oberländer,** R. Die¦ britische Colonie Neuseeland in J. 1879. *Deutsche Rundschau f. Geographie*, ii. 405–461 (1880).

Proceedings | of the | Eighth | General Synod | of the | Church of the Province of New Zealand. | Held at Christchurch April-May, 1880. | Together with | The Constitution, Statutes and Resolutions | of the General Synod, | and | An Appendix containing Reports &c. | Christchurch : | Printed by A. Turner, Gloucester Street, | MDCCCLXXX.
    8°. Pp. x, 58.
    A Report of the Third Session of the Second Synod of the Diocese of Wellington, Sept. 1862, was published in 1862: 8°, pp. 76. It has four Acts (pp. 31–50), and fourteen Resolutions, regulating the Church Constitution.

Purnell, C. W. The Maori and the Moa. *Victorian Review*, i. 570–86. 1880.
    General discussion of ethnology of Maoris (came from Savaii) and date of moa (recent).

* **Rees,** W. L. East Coast Settlement Bill, 1880. Napier, 1880.
    8°. Pamphlet.

* **Scenes from the Life of John Marmon.** Auckland, 1880.
    "Recently, 1880, under the title 'Scenes from the Life of John Marmon'—an erroneous version of the capture of the Wellington, as of many other events, has been published."—*Rusden*, i. 119, *note*.
    "'Cannibal Jack.' Born of convict blood, he was himself a criminal. His 'Reminiscences' were published in 1880 as those of 'John Marmon.'"—*Ibid.*, i. 121, *note.* See also i. 161, *note.*
    A narrative of the massacre in Akaroa harbour, reprinted in *Stories of Banks Peninsula*, pp. 56–61, is professedly in reply to Marmon.

Senior, W. Travel and Trout | in the Antipodes | An Angler's Sketches in Tasmania | and New Zealand | By William Senior | ("Red Spinner") | —— | —— | Melbourne, Sydney, Adelaide, and Brisbane | George Robertson | 1880.
    cr. 8°. Pp. xii, 315.
    Pt. ii, pp. 165–315, describes a tour through N.Z., and fishing in various parts. Ch. xi is on N.Z. fishes, and in ch. viii is a brief account of acclimatisation in Canterbury.

Stewart, G. V. Te Puke, Bay of Plenty: Stewart Special Settlement, No. 3. London: N.Z. Land Corporation. 1880.
    8°. Pp. 56.—*Davis.*

Stout, Robert. Political parties in New Zealand. *Melbourne Review*, Jan. 1880, pp. 56–79. 1880.
    Sketch of political history, 1800–1880; vindication of Grey Ministry.

Tenison-Woods, J. E.   Palæontology of New Zealand | Part IV | Corals and Bryozoa | of the | Neozoic Period in New Zealand | By | the Rev. J. E. Tenison-Woods, F.G.S., F.L.S. ; | —— | Wellington. | By Authority : G. Didsbury, Government Printer. | 1880.
  roy. 8°.   Pp. xvi, 34.

***Toula**, Franz.   Ueber die südlichen Alpen von Neu-Seeland.   *D. Rundschau f. Geographie*, ii. 245 (1880).

Wallace, A. R.   Island Life ; | or, | The Phenomena and Causes of | Insular Faunas and Floras, | including a Revision and Attempted Solution of the | Problem of | Geological Climates. | By | Alfred Russel Wallace, | —— | London : | Macmillan and Co. | 1880.
  8°.   Pp. xvii, 526.   Map showing depth of sea round N.Z.
   Ch. xxi. Anomalous islands : N.Z., pp. 442-56.   xxii. Flora—its affinities and probable origin, pp. 457-76.   The union between Australia and N.Z. in the latter part of the Secondary epoch sufficiently accounts for all the main features of the N.Z. flora.

White, John.   Legendary history of the Maoris (Extracts from a compilation of the).—Appendix to Journals of the House of Representatives of New Zealand, 1880, vol. ii, G.-8.
   i. Memorandum on Maori history.   White, J. (Maori mythology will be expounded as underlying whole of daily life, explaining status of chiefs and rules of war, modes of dressing, cooking and eating food.   Oral traditions of the origin of world and man ; customs, usages, rites and incantations of each stage of existence ; with parallel Polynesian traditions.   History, rites, customs and incantations of each migration.   People found by Maoris in N.Z.—name, treatment, and history.   Parallel between Maori mythology and genealogy of Hawaiiki kings.)   Translations of extracts :—2. History of Tainui migration.   3. Another version.   4. A third.   5. Mauala or Tokomaru migration.   6. Aotea migration.   7. Te Arawa migration.   8. Same.   9. Horouta migration.   10. Another version.   11. Takitumu migration.   12. Paikea migration.   13. Kupe.   14. Nuku-Tawhiti.   15. Ancestors of the Ngatiwhatua.   16. Moriori history.—Maori originals of these extracts.   Genealogical table.

1881.

***Acton**, R.   Our Colonial Empire.   London : Cassell.   1881.
  12°.—*Davis.*

Bateman, William.   The Colonists ; or, The Past and Present Position of New Zealand.   Christchurch, 1880.
  8°.   Papers on farming, grazing, &c.—*Davis.*

Bathgate, Alexander.   Waitaruna : | a Story of New Zealand Life. | By Alexander Bathgate, | Author of " Colonial Experiences." | London : | Sampson Low, Marston, Searle, & Rivington, | —— | 1881.
  cr. 8°.   Pp. vi, 312.
   Pictures of life in Otago, " as it was a short time ago, and to some extent still is "—station-life, work on the diggings, &c.

***Beheim-Schwarzbach**, Br.   Die Maoris auf Neu-Seeland.   Verh. d. Berliner Ges. f. Erdkunde, viii. 146 (1881).

[**Campbell**, *Dr.* J. Logan.]   Poenamo | Sketches of the Early Days | of | New Zealand | Romance and Reality | of | Antipodean Life | in the Infancy of a New Colony. | Williams and Norgate, | 14, Henrietta Street, Covent Garden, London ; | and 20, South Frederick Street, Edinburgh. | 1881.
  p. 8°.   Pp. xii, 359.
   Valuable reminiscences of one of the earliest of Auckland settlers.   Book ii describes settlement in Auckland province in the pre-historic days ; iii, the Maoris ; iv, the foundation of a colony on the Waitemata.

Carpenter, William Lant. On the siliceous and other hot springs in the volcanic district of New Zealand. Proc. Brit. Assoc. 1881, *Report*, ii. 580–2.
    Analyses of Taupo, Hot Lakes, and White Island springs.

Carpenter, W. L. On the hot-lake district and the glacier scenery and fjords of New Zealand. *Ibid.*, ii. 742. 1881.

Cumming, C. F. Gordon. At Home in Fiji | By C. F. Gordon Cumming | author of | 'From the Hebrides to the Himalayas' | In two volumes | —— | With map and illustrations | William Blackwood and Sons | Edinburgh and London | MDCCCLXXXI.
    8°. One illustration—the White Terraces—is of N.Z. scenery.
    Chs. xxiii, xxiv, xxv, relate to N.Z. They describe a visit to Auckland and Sir George Grey at Kawau (xxiii), and to the Hot Lakes (xxiv–xxv).

The early history of Otago.
    Papers with this title appeared in the *Presbyterian* (Dunedin) for September and October, 1881.
    The no. for October contains letters from Rev. Dr. Burns. "Capital we want," he says; "but Scotch capital, and especially Free Church capital, is what we would like best of all" (p. 67).

*****Finsch,** ——. Reise nach Neuseeland. Verh. Berl. Gesellschaft f. Anthropologie, 1881, p. 334.

Hutton, F. W. Catalogues | of the | New Zealand | Diptera, Orthoptera, Hymenoptera ; | with Descriptions of the Species. | By | Frederick Wollaston Hutton, F.G.S., C.M.Z.S., | Professor of Biology at Canterbury College, New Zealand University. | Published by Command. | New Zealand : | By Authority: George Didsbury, Government Printer, Wellington. | 1881.
    roy. 8°. Pp. x, 132. Issued by the Colonial Museum and Geological Survey of N.Z.

Jones-Parry, *Captain* S. H. My Journey | Round the World | via | Ceylon, New Zealand, Australia, | Torres Straits, China, Japan, | and the United States. | By | Captain S. H. Jones-Parry, | Late 102nd Royal Madras Fusileers. | In two Volumes. | —— | London : | Hurst and Blackett, Publishers, | 13, Great Marlborough Street. | 1881.
    2 vols. cr. 8°. Vol. i : pp. x, 312.
    N.Z.: i. 51–117. The Bluff to Wellington, and Wellington Province.

*****Larkworthy,** Falconer. New Zealand revisited. London, 1881.
    Pamphlet.

Massey, Gerald. A | Book of the Beginnings. | Containing an attempt to recover and reconstitute the lost origines | of the myths and mysteries, types and symbols, religion and language, | with Egypt for the mouthpiece and Africa as the birthplace. | By | Gerald Massey. | Volume II. | Egyptian origines in the Hebrew, | Akkado-Assyrian, and Maori. | London : | Williams and Norgate, 14, Henrietta Street. | 1881.
    imp. 8°.
    Section xxi, pp. 523–33: Comparative vocabulary of Maori and Egyptian words: nearly 1,000 Maori words, with as many similar Egyptian words in parallel columns. "This list of words by itself is sufficient to prove the primal identity of the Maori and Egyptian languages" (i. 17).
    Section xxii, pp. 535–98: "African origines of the Maori." Mythology, traditions, "hieroglyphics," and rites and ceremonies prove the Egyptian origin of the Maoris.

Mills, Arthur. New Zealand in 1881. *Contemporary Review*, xl. 438–52. 1881.
    Land question, pp. 439–42. Financial position, p. 443.

The Natural Wonders | of | New Zealand | (the Wonderland of the Pacific) : | its Boiling Lakes, Steam Holes, Mud Volcanoes | Sulphur Baths, Medicinal Springs, and | Burning Mountains. | New Zealand : | Published by G. T. Chapman, Bookseller & Stationer, | Queen Street, Auckland. [1881 ?]
    p. 8°. Pp. 172. Map.
    <small>Guide to the lake-district—description, geology, legend, history.</small>

Nesfield, H. W. A Chequered Career ; | or, | Fifteen Years in Australia | and New Zealand. | London : | Richard Bentley and Son, | —— | 1881.
    p. 8°. Pp. xi, 369.
    <small>Chs. iv-x (pp. 28-123). A station in Hawke's Bay ; the Lakes ; Nelson, West Coast, and Napier ; the Maoris.</small>

* Neu-Seeland als Auswanderungsziel und Exportgebiet. *Export*, iii, no. 31 ff. (1881).

Proceedings of Synod | of the | Presbyterian Church | of | Otago and Southland. | January 1881. | Dunedin : | Printed by Coulls & Culling, Rattray Street, Dunedin. | MDCCCLXXXI.
    8°. Pp. 72 and Table.

Primary Instruction : our State System and its Shortcomings considered, in Two Letters. Christchurch, 1881.
    8°.

Pyke, Vincent, *and* **Thorpe**, Talbot. White hood and blue cap : a Christmas bough with two branches. [And two poems.] Dunedin, 1881.
    8°. Pp. 144.

Quick, W. H. Reasons | for | Not Passing a Bill | intituled | The Church of England in New Zealand Trustees Incorporation Act 1881. | Wellington : | James Hughes, Steam Printer, Engraver, etc., Lambton Quay. | 1881.
    8°. Pp. 8.

Rabbits in New Zealand. By a Run-holder. *Chambers's Journal*, June, 1881, pp. 409–11.

Report | of | Commissioners | appointed by | The County Councils of Vincent, Manio- | toto, and Taieri, in the Provincial | District of Otago, in the | matter of | The Otago Central Railway | Dunedin : | Printed by Mackay, Bracken and Co., Moray Place. | MDCCCLXXXI.

[**Sealy**, H. J.] Are we to Stay here ? | A Paper | on the | New Zealand | Public Works Policy | 1870, | considered specially with reference to the question of | The Settlement | of the Crown Lands, | and the | Incidence of Taxation. | By a Colonist of 22 Years' Standing. | [Timaru, 1881.]
    8°. Pp. 84+2.

Sheep-washing in New Zealand. *Chambers's Journal*, Jan. 1, 1881, pp. 789–92.
    <small>On the north bank of the Waitaki, Nov. 1881.</small>

* Sketches in New Zealand. *Argosy*, xxxi. 484. 1881.

St. Johnston, Alfred. A distant sketching ground. *With six illustrations. Argosy*, Dec. 1881, xxxii. 484.
    <small>Seventy-Mile Bush, Manawatu Gorge, Mount Egmont, Paikakariki Range.</small>

Tea and silk farming in New Zealand. *Chambers's Journal*, March, July, and Aug. 1881, pp. 181–4, 469–72, 538–41.
    <small>Statistic, climatic, and commercial reasons for the encouragement of tea-growing and silk-culture as a combined industry. Suited for the employment of reduced gentlewomen. Leading features of proposed enterprise.</small>

Tinné, T. F. S. Local Industries | of New Zealand : | an enquiry into the means of promoting them, the causes | that hinder their progress, and the measures indis- | pensable for their successful establishment. | By Theodore F. S. Tinné, | Member of the Royal Commission on Local Industries. | —— | Auckland, April, 1881. | Wilsons and Horton.

8°. Pp. 26, double columns.

Whitmee, L. J. The ethnology of the Pacific. Map. *Journal of Trans. Victoria Institute*, xiv. 16–31; discussion, pp. 32–40. 1881.

Proposes the name *Sawaiori* for the natives of Eastern Polynesia and N.Z. Sawaiori race (pp. 22–7) very pure, slightly but rarely mixed with Papuan. May be traced to the Indian archipelago.

Read May 18, 1879.

1882.

***Beheim-Schwarzbach**, Br. Die Maoris auf Neu-seeland. *Westermann's illust. deutsche Monatshefte*, Januar, 1882.

Bell, Sir F. D. The Public Debt of Australasia | A Paper read before | The Royal Colonial Institute | 21st November 1882 | By | Sir Francis Dillon Bell, K.C.M.G. | Agent-General for New Zealand | —— | London | Spottiswoode & Co., Printers, New-Street Square | 1882.

8°. Pp. 40.

Growth of debt; how expended; relation to revenue, taxation, and income; compared with increase in revenue and trade; commercial expansion; growth of agriculture, and of population; railways remunerative; other industries—frozen meat; education.

***Bourke**, Miss E. M. A little history of New Zealand, progressive from discovery to 1880. Sydney, 1882.

18°. An edition seems to have been published in Auckland in 1881.

Buller, Walter L. Manual | of the | Birds of New Zealand | By Walter L. Buller, C.M.G., Sc.D., F.R.S., | Author of " A History of the Birds of New Zealand." | Published by Command. | New Zealand : | By Authority : George Didsbury, Government Printer, Wellington. | 1882.

roy. 8°. Pp. xii, 107. With 37 plates (33 reduced from the drawings by Keulemans in Buller's *History of the Birds of New Zealand*) and many woodcuts.

Preface by Dr. Hector, pp. v-vi (classification and descriptive portion of Hutton's *Catalogue* adopted, but corrections introduced, nomenclature altered, doubtful forms expunged, and newly discovered species added). Introduction, pp. vii-ix. Analytical key to the families, pp. xi-xii.

Cochran, William. Tea and silk farming in New Zealand. Transactions of the Highland and Agricultural Society, 4th series, xiv. 175–249. Edinburgh, 1882.

Auckland province equally suited to produce the teas of China and of Assam. Also a most desirable silk country; account of experiments in sericiculture. Tea and silk farming should go together. Details of proposed enterprise in N.Z.

* Facts relating to New Zealand. By a lady. 1882.

Pp. 71.

To Canterbury.

***Green**, W. S. Eine Reise in die Neuseeländischen Alpen. *Petorm. Mitt.*, 1882, p. 380.

Hay, W. D. Brighter Britain ! | or, | Settler and Maori | in | Northern New Zealand. | By William Delisle Hay, | author of | " Three Hundred Years

Hay, W. D.—*continued.*
Hence," "The Doom of the Great City," etc. | —— | In two Volumes.— | London: | Richard Bentley and Son, | —— | 1882.
p. 8°. Vol. i : pp. viii, 346 ; vol. ii : pp. iv, 320.
<small>Vol. i is mainly on settlers' life in the Kaipara ; v. ii, chs. iii, iv, v, is on :" Maori manners." Ch. vi is on the natural history of the district. An Appendix, ii. 303-14, is list of books on N.Z. Another, ii. 315-21, gives a list of N.Z. journals.</small>

* The immigrant's prospects in New Zealand. London, 1882.
Pamphlet.

Lesson, A. Les Polynésiens | leur Origine, leurs Migrations, leur Langage | Par | Le Dr. Lesson | Ancien Médecin en chef des établissements français de l'Océanie, | Membre de la Société d'Anthropologie | Ouvrage rédigé d'après le Manuscrit de l'Auteur | par Ludovic Martinet | Membre de la Société d'Anthropologie | Paris | Ernest Leroux, Éditeur | —— | 28, Rue Bonaparte, 28 | 1882.
roy. 8°. T. iii : pp. vii, 499 ; carte. T. iv : pp. [iv], 430.
<small>T. iii. Troisième partie. Livre premier. Considérations générales sur la N.Z. Réflexions préliminaires. Ch. i. Géographie et histoire naturelle, pp. 4-52. ii. Maori, pp. 53-109 (gives successive estimates of the population, pp. 55-6).—Livre deuxième. Lieu d'origine des Polynésiens, pp. 110-8. Ch. i. Exposé et réfutation des objections, pp. 119-39. ii. Témoignages favorables, pp. 140-86. iii. Examen linguistique, pp. 187-216. Fables Néo-Zélandaises [Maori and French], pp. 217-23.—Livre troisième. Origine des Néo-Zélandais, pp. 224-341.—Livre quatrième. Ch. i. Recherche de l'Hawahiki. ii. Ile-du-milieu. iii. Peuplement de l'île nord. iv. Provenance des Hawahikiens. T. iv. Quatrième partie. Livre premier. Migrations. Ch. i. Preuves, (ii) Causes, (iii) Date des migrations.—Livre deuxième. Marche des migrations. Ch. i. Dissémination des Maori. ii. Les Maori en Afrique, Amérique, et Asie. [Appendices on the zoology and botany, mythology, legends, and traditions are translated from Taylor's *Te Ika a Maui*.] Index bibliographique [including publications in French], iv. 379-92.
The Polynesians are not of Asiatic origin, nor descended from the Malays, nor emigrants from America. They are the "spontaneous product" of one island, called Hawaiki, which is the Middle Island of N.Z. Thence they spread, at an uncertain date, to the North Island, over the Pacific, and to Africa, America, and Asia. The Maoris are therefore the ancestors of the Polynesians, and Maori the mother-tongue of all the Polynesian dialects.</small>

Michaelis, Hallenstein, *and* **Farquhar.** On the Cultivation of the Wattle or Mimosa in New Zealand. Dunedin, | —— | 1882.
8°. Pp. 6.

* **Mulhall**, Michael G. England's new Sheep-farm. London, 1882.
8°. Pp. 13.

Nicols, Arthur. The Acclimatisation | of the | Salmonidæ at the Antipodes: | its History and Results. | By | Arthur Nicols, F.G.S., F.R.G.S., | —— | —— | London : | Sampson Low, Marston, Searle, & Rivington. | 1882.
cr. 8°. Pp. vii, 238.
<small>The successive shipments of salmon ova for N.Z. are described, pp. 45-89. In the appendix, pp. 207-19, is official correspondence on the subject, with accounts of the hatchings at Wallacetown.</small>

Potts, T. H. Out in the Open: | a Budget of Scraps | of Natural History, | Gathered in New Zealand. | By T. H. Potts, F.L.S. | Christchurch : | Printed by the Lyttelton Times Company, Limited, Gloucester Street. | 1882.
8°. Pp. vii, 301. Photo. of Moriori and illus.
<small>Native gathering at Hikurangi, pp. 9-20. Recent changes in the fauna of N.Z., pp. 221-36. Classified list of N.Z. ferns, pp. 237-60.</small>

Shortland, E. Maori Religion | and | Mythology. | Illustrated by Translations of Traditions, *Karakia*, &c. | to which are added | Notes on *Maori* Tenure of Land. | By | Edward Shortland, M.A., M.R.C.P., | late Native

Shortland, E.—*continued*.
   Secretary, New Zealand, | Author of | " Traditions and Superstitions of the New Zealanders." | London : | Longmans, Green, and Co. | 1882. | ——
      cr. 8°. Pp. xi, 112.
      Ch. i. Primitive religion and mythology. Aryans and Polynesians, pp. 1-9. Ch. ii. Cosmogony and mythology, pp. 10-24. Chs. iii, iv. Religious rites, pp. 25-37, 38-50. Ch. v. The Maori chief of olden time, pp. 51-67. Ch. vi. Claiming and naming land, pp. 68-87. Ch. vii. Land-titles, pp. 88-104. Appendix :—Maori terms of relationship, pp. 106-7 ; vocabulary of words requiring explanation, pp. 107-9. Originals of *karakia* in text, pp. 109-12.
      "The Maori MSS. of which translations are now published were collected by the author many years ago. The persons through whom the MSS. were collected are now, with one exception, no longer living. They were all of them men of good birth, and competent authorities. One who could write sent me, from time to time, in MS. such information as he himself possessed, or he could obtain from the *tohunga*, or wise men of his family. Chapters iii and iv contain selections from information derived from this source. The others not being sufficiently skilled in writing, it was necessary to take down their information from dictation. . . . Chapter ii contains a tradition as to *Maori* Cosmogony more particular in some details than I have ever met with elsewhere."—*Preface.*

Stout, Robert. Moses Wilson Gray. *Melbourne Review*, Jan. 1882, pp. 27-40.
   In N.Z. 1862-75. District Judge of Otago goldfields, 1864-74.

Silkworm-farming in England and New Zealand. Tea and silk farming in New Zealand. *Chambers's Journal*, 1882, pp. 215-6, 660-1. See also *Journal of the Society of Arts*, 1882.

* **Talbot**, Thorpe. New Guide to the Lakes and Hot Springs, and a Month in Hot Water. Auckland, 1882.
      8°.

Thomson, George M. The Ferns and Fern Allies | of | New Zealand | With Instructions for their Collection and Hints on | their Cultivation. | By | George M. Thomson, F.L.S. | Science Teacher in the Dunedin High Schools | With five plates. | George Robertson | Melbourne, Sydney, Adelaide, and Brisbane | —— | MDCCCLXXXII.
      8°. Pp. viii, 132.
      i. Structure of ferns and allied plants. ii. Nomenclature and principles of classification. iii. Enumeration and specific description. iv. Hints on collecting and cultivating. Glossaries.

* **Williams**, W. L. First Lessons in Maori. London, 1882.
      8°. Pp. 97.

1883.

Barker, M. A., *Lady*. Travelling About | over | New and Old Ground. | By | Lady Barker, | Author of " Stories About : —— " " Station Life in New Zealand," &c. | —— | With Maps and Illustrations. | London : | George Routledge & Sons : | —— | 1883.
      cr. 8°. Pp. xii, 353.
      " New Zealand as it was " (a compilation from *Polack*), pp. 45-56. " New Zealand as it is " (from *Dilke* and *Meade*), pp. 57-67, and (from personal observation, of Canterbury, in 1865), pp. 68-76.

Bastian, Adolph. Inselgruppen in Oceanien. | Reisebegebnisse und Studien | von | A. Bastian. | Mit drei Tafeln. | Berlin | Ferd. Dümmlers Verlagsbuchhandlung | Harrwitz und Gossmann | 1883.
      8°. Pp. xxii, Inhalt, 282, and 3 illus.
      N.Z.: pp. 137-220.
      Mythology, pp. 137-58. Priesthood and priestcraft, pp. 158-61. Temples and rites, pp. 161-70. Ranks, pp. 171-7. Migrations, pp. 179-88. Iwi and hapu, pp. 189-90.

Bastian, Adolph—*continued.*
Property in land, p. 100. Tribe and rank as affected by marriage, p. 191. Descent in female line, pp. 190-1. Baptism, dedication, and teaching of children, pp. 191-5. Inheritance, p. 195. Muru, pp. 196-7. Tattooing, p. 197. Weapons, pp. 198-9. Spring and harvest ceremonies, pp. 199-201. Miscellaneous, pp. 201-7. Psychology, pp. 207-8. Mana, pp. 209-10. Death, burial-ceremonies, under-world, pp. 211-7. Cosmogony, pp. 217-20.

Bastian, A. Zur Kenntniss Hawaii's. | Nachträge und Ergänzungen | zu den | Inselgruppen in Oceanien | von | A. Bastian. | Mit 1 Tafel und 2 Beilagen. | Berlin | Ferd. Dümmlers Verlagsbuchhandlung | Harrwitz und Gossmann | 1883.

8°. Pp. xvi, 112+? White's Plan of the Maori Mythology is reprinted.
At pp. 78-104 is an account, partly in German, partly in English, of Maori priestcraft and mythology, derived from John White's lectures on Maori superstitions.

Bradshaw, John. New Zealand | as it is. | By | John Bradshaw, J.P. | for the County of Chester, and the Colony of New Zealand. | London : | Sampson Low, Marston, Searle, and Rivington, | Crown Buildings, 188, Fleet Street. | 1883.

8°. Pp. viii, 392.
Ch. iii. First impressions. iv. Society. v. Station-life. vi. On the farm. vii. Stock and its management. viii. N.Z. Alps. ix. What manner of men we are. x. Financial condition of the colony. xi. Christchurch Exhibition, 1882. xii. Colonial industries. xiii. Public works. xiv. North Island. xv. "How we are governed." xvi. Education. xvii. Religion. xviii. Fragments. Appendix, pp. 363-92 (chiefly statistics).

Bramall, H. The Mineral Resources | of | New Zealand. | By | Henry Bramall, M.Inst.C.E., | Mining Engineer, | *President of the Liverpool Geological Association,* | *President of the Liverpool Engineering Society,* | *Member of the North of England Institute of Mining and* | *Mechanical Engineers.* | An abstract of papers read before | the Liverpool Geological Association. | Re-printed by request from the Transactions of the Association. | Liverpool : | Henry Young, 12, South Castle Street. | 1883.

8°. Sketch-map, title-page, contents, and 60 pp.
Coal, p. 6. Iron, p. 17. Gold, p. 22. Silver, p. 33. Copper, p. 35. Manganese, p. 38. Antimony, p. 40. Chromium, lead, zinc, p. 41. Tin, p. 42. Mercury, p. 43. Arsenic, cobalt, nickel, p. 44. Metallic minerals of minor importance, p. 44. Graphite, p. 45. Petroleum, p. 46. Kauri, p. 47. Sulphur, p. 48. Barytes, p. 49. Non-metallic minerals of minor importance, p. 49. Precious stones, p. 51. Building-stones, limestones, sands and clays, p. 51.

Canterbury Rhymes. | Second Edition : | with Notes and an Appendix. | Edited by W. P. Reeves. | Christchurch : | Printed by the "Lyttelton Times" Company Limited, Gloucester Street. | 1883.

cr. 8°. Pp. viii, 131.
Preface to the second edition, pp. iii, iv. Preface to first edition, p. v.
The Rhymes were written by James Edward FitzGerald, Crosbie Ward, Edward Jerningham Wakefield, Dean Jacobs, Mrs. Raven, Canon Cotterill, Dr. Rouse, William Jukes Steward. They "were written in Canterbury for Canterbury readers, and their best claim to favour on their own soil will be found in . . . the pleasant unpretending record they form of the amusements, quarrels, politics, and progress of Provincial Canterbury." Nine of the original volume are omitted. Of the Appendix "more than half has been taken from the *Canterbury Punch* of 1864-65; this was edited by Mr. Ward, and his hand may be traced in several of the ballads and skits reprinted from it here. The other selections have been mostly chosen from the *Lyttelton Times* and *Canterbury Times.*"—Preface to ed. 2.

* **Colenso,** W. Three Literary Papers | Read before the Hawke's Bay Philosophical Institute, | during the Session of 1882 :— | I. and II. On Nomen-

* **Colenso,** W.—*continued.*
    clature. | III. On "Macaulay's New Zealander." | By W. Colenso, F.L.S., | *Member and Honorary Secretary of the Institute.* | —— | New Zealand : | Printed at the "Daily Telegraph" Office, Tennyson Street, Napier. | 1883.
    roy. 8°. Pp. 41.
    I, II. Errors in use of Maori names (of places, plants, birds, &c.) and words. III. Literary history of the idea.

Coote, Walter. Wanderings, | South and East. | By | Walter Coote, F.R.G.S. | With two Maps and forty-seven Wood Engravings. | Executed under the Direction of Edward Whymper, from | Sketches by the Author, Native Drawings, &c. | New and cheaper Edition. | London : | Sampson Low, Marston, Searle, & Rivington. | —— | 1883.
    p. 8°. Pp. xvi, 369. Two N.Z. illus.
    N.Z.: pp. 31–49. Three months' travelling in both islands, with original sketches.

Domett, A. Ranolf and Amohia : | a Dream of Two Lives. | By | Alfred Domett. | New edition, revised. | —— | London : | Kegan Paul, Trench & Co., 1 Paternoster Square. | 1883.
    2 vols. p. 8°. Vol. i: pp. 307; vol. ii: pp. 339.
    Prelude. Book i. Sailor-student. ii. South-Sea villages. iii. All in a summer night. iv. Latter-day Eden (Canto 5, Fountain-terraces; 6, A geyser yoked). v. Still in Eden. vi. War. vii. Self-sacrifice. At i. 298-9, ii. 334-5, are originals and literal translations of songs of which paraphrases are given in the text.
    Appended to vol. ii is a letter from Mr. Browning, implying identity of Domett with "Waring."

Experiences of a Medical Man in New Zealand; or, Our Hospital at Sopemdown. By Placebo Aspen. Melbourne, 1883.
    8°.

* Facts : or, Experiences in New Zealand. By a Lady. Yalding, 1883.
    8°. Pp. 71.

Fox, *Sir* William. A chapter in the history of New Zealand. The treaty of Waitangi. *Proc. Roy. Col. Inst.*, xiv. 100–11.
    Possession founded on discovery; negotiation of treaty; native estimate of treaty; confiscations; West Coast Commission.
    . Discussion (pp. 112-24): Sir C. Clifford, Bishop of Nelson, C. Pharazyn, F. W. Chesson.

[**Gisborne,** William.] Official Handbook of New Zealand | Edited by | the Agent-General | Parts I and II | With a Map | London | Edward Stanford | 1883 | Price One Shilling.
    8°. Pp. x, 200. Map and tables.
    For part iii see next year.
    Not a revised edition, but an entirely new Handbook.

Green, W. S. The High Alps of New Zealand | or | A Trip to the Glaciers of the Antipodes | with an Ascent of Mount Cook | By | William Spotswood Green, M.A. | Member of the English Alpine Club | London | Macmillan and Co. | 1883.
    cr. 8°. Pp. xvi, 350. One illus. and sketch-map of Tasman glacier.
    Ch. vi. West coast. vii, viii. Canterbury. ix–xvi. Ascent, &c. xvii. Otago, Mount Earnslaw, &c.
    Haast's map of Southern Alps, engraved by the R.G.S., is in *Alpine Journal*, xi, no. 77.

Green, W. S. Fels- u. Gletscherspuren am Mount Cook in Nouseeland. *Peterm. Mitt.*, 1883, p. 53.

Grey, *Sir* G. Auckland Free Public Library. | Address | delivered by | Sir George Grey, K.C.B., | at the Theatre Royal, | Auckland, June 5th, 1883. | Reprinted from the "New Zealand Herald." | Auckland: | Wilsons & Horton, General Printers, Queen and Wyndham Sts. | MDCCCLXXXIII.
    8°. Pp. 29.
    Has a page on "New Zealand's first martyr," and another on "early Maori grammars" (pp. 23-5).

Harven, E. *de*. La | Nouvelle Zélande | Histoire, Géologie, Climat, | Gouvernement, Institutions, Agriculture, etc., etc. | avec cartes et planches | par Emile De Harven | —— | Anvers | Imprimerie et lithographie Veuve de Backer, rue Zirk, 35. | 1883.
    Extrait des Mémoires de la Société royale de Géographie d'Anvers. Ouvrage publié par la Société.
    roy. 8°. Pp. 245, v.
    A compilation mainly from the official handbooks.

Hingston, James. The New Zealand Sounds: a visit to Caswell, George, and Milford Sounds (West Coast). *Victorian Review*, viii. 622-38. Sept. 1883.

Hingston, J. Among the Maoris. *Ibid.*, viii. 689-701. 1883.

* **Land Ho!** A Conversation of 1933 on the Results of the Adoption of the System of nationalizing the Land of New Zealand, 1883. Lyttelton, 1883.
    cr. 8°.

Lendenfeld, R. *von*. Ascent of Hochstetter dome. *Canterbury Times*, April 14, 1883; *Australasian*, May 5, 1883.

[**McIndoe**, James.] Otago. In *Otago Witness*, March 10 to Dec. 8, 1883. Signed I.M.I.
    Part i. Before settlement, March 10, 1883. ii. The selection, March 17. iii. The scheme, March 24. iv. Official, same. v. The first party, March 31. vi. Experiences, April 7. vii. Crown grant (copy of original grant of Otago lands to N.Z. Company), April 14. viii. Climate, *ib.* ix. The ballot (for sections), April 21. x. Occupations, April 28. xi. Officials, May 5. xii. 1848, May 12. xiii. Dissensions, May 19 and 26. xiv. Anniversary, May 26. xiv (*bis*). Various, June 2 and 9. xv. June 9 and 16 (review of the second year). xvi. 1850, June 23. xvi (*bis*). 1850, June 30. xvii. The Bench, July 7. xviii. Settlers' Association, July 21. xix. Institutions, July 28. [xx is apparently omitted.] xxi. Maoridom, Aug. 4. xvi (*sic*). First period, Aug. 18. xvii (*sic*). New era, Aug. 25. xxiii. Delays, Sept. 1, 8, and 15. xxiv. Address of Superintendent, Sept. 22. xxv. General Assembly, Sept. 20. xxvi. Delegations, Oct. 6. xxvii. Second session, Oct. 13, 20. xxviii. General, Nov. 3. xxix. Onward, Nov. 10. xxx. Nov. 17. xxxi. Various, Nov. 24. xxxii, xxxiii. [Dec. 1?] xxxiv. Political, Dec. 8.

New Zealand | Thermal-Springs Districts. | Papers relating to the sale of the | Township of Rotorua, | Established under "The Thermal Springs Districts Act, 1881," | with maps and plans of the district and township: | together with | Information relating to the Hot-Springs Districts, and a Report on | the Mineral Waters. | Second edition. | New Zealand. | By authority: George Didsbury, Government Printer, Wellington. | 1883.
    4°. Pp. 30. Map and three plans, all coloured. 17 lithographs of persons and scenes.
    Announcement and terms of sale, pp. 5-6. Letter from Judge Fenton, p. 7. Description of site of township, pp. 8-11. Remarks on district, by Sir W. Fox, pp. 12-18. Extracts from books by Hochstetter, Gordon Cumming, and Hector, pp. 19-35. Appendix:—Act, pp. 36-8; Proclamations, pp. 38-9.

Official Handbook. Edited by the Agent-General. With Map. London, 1883.
    8°.
    See **Gisborne**, W., *ante*.

Pash, J. Brittain. Report on New Zealand. Read before the Essex Chamber of Agriculture, Chelmsford, May 18, 1883.
 sm. 4°. Pp. 12, double columns.
 Describes the conditions of farming in N.Z.

Peale, A. C. Thermal springs and geysers of New Zealand. Ch. ii of a Report on Thermal Springs by A. C. Peale, M.D., in Twelfth Annual Report of the United States Geological and Geographical Survey for 1878, part ii, pp. 313-20. *In* House Miscellaneous Documents, 1st Session, 47th Congress, 1881-2. Washington, 1883.
 8°. With map and two plates, table of springs, and (p. 435) a bibliography.

Peek, Cuthbert E. On the hot-springs of Iceland and New Zealand, with notes on Maori customs. Proc. Brit. Assoc. 1883, *Report*, ii. 590.
 The Maori customs (only mentioned, in the Abstract) are *mana* and *tapu*.

Quatrefages, A. *de*. Hommes Fossiles | et | Hommes Sauvages : | Etudes d'Anthropologie | Par | A. de Quatrefages | Membre de l'Institut (Académie des Sciences) | Professeur au Muséum d'Histoire Naturelle | Avec 209 gravures intercalées dans le texte et une carte | Paris | Librairie J. B. Baillière et Fils. | 1884.
 8°.
 viii. Migrations polynésiennes, pp. 401-21. ix. Maoris et Morioris, pp. 422-94. See earlier works for statement of views.

* **Quatrefages**, A. *de*. Les Moas et les chasseurs de Moas. *Journal des Savants*, 1883.
 Reviews the controversy on the antiquity of the moa, examines all published data, and concludes that Haast's view cannot be sustained; the largest species, however, were either extinct or dying out when the Maoris arrived.—*Pop. Science Monthly*, xxx. 662.

Rusden, George William. History | of | New Zealand. | By | G. W. Rusden. | In three volumes. | —— | London : | Chapman and Hall, Limited. | Melbourne and Sydney : George Robertson. | 1883.
 8°. Vol. i : pp. vii, 655 ; vol. ii : pp. 606 ; vol. iii : pp. 540. Map and plan.
 Vol. I. Preface, pp. v-viii. Ch. i. The Maoris, pp. 1-63. ii. European discoveries, pp. 64-93. iii. Traffic with Maoris, pp. 94-159. iv. Te Pehi, pp. 160-211. v. Sir George Gipps, pp. 212-91. vi. Spain's court, pp. 292-326. vii. The Wairau, pp. 327-439. viii. The war of 1846, pp. 440-541. ix. Provincial Legislatures, pp. 542-655.
 Vol. II. Ch. x. Colonial office requires information, pp. 1-71. xi. Governor Browne's departure, pp. 72-147. xii. State of the Maoris, pp. 148-266. xiii. Weld Ministry, pp. 267-422. xiv. Native Land Court, pp. 423-46. xv. Sir G. Bowen, pp. 446-519. xvi. Col. Whitmore, pp. 520-606.
 Vol. III. Ch. xvii. Donald McLean and the Maoris, pp. 1-92. xviii. Session of 1874, pp. 93-195. xix. The 'Waka Maori' newspaper. xx. Raid upon Parihaka, pp. 398-465.
 Appendix. Statistics of 1880, iii. 486-7. Papers respecting West Coast Native affairs, iii. 488-504. Index, iii. 505-40.
 "It is nearly half a century since I first saw, in the house of Samuel Marsden, some of his Maori friends. Since that time I have chiefly resided in colonies not far from New Zealand, and have not willingly lost opportunities of becoming acquainted with passing events. In my researches I have been aided by many friends, and many public men."—*Preface*, p. viii. "Compiled with a diligent endeavour to test every statement by reference to the most authentic sources of information."—*Ibid.*, p. vii.
 A passage in vol. ii, pp. 504-5, was the occasion of a law-suit, Bryce *v*. Rusden, tried in the Court of Queen's Bench, 1886. See 1886.
 H. Willoughby gives in the *Australasian*, June 2, 1883, " a personal narrative " of events in the Maori war *à propos* of Rusden's *History*, which he describes as "not a history, but a bitter political pamphlet, extending over 2,000 pages." The article is

Rusden, George William—*continued.*
followed by a letter, signed "J. P. McGregor," vindicating Mr. Bryce from Rusden's charges.
    A debate took place in the Legislative Council, Aug. 1, 1888, on a motion by Hon. J. C. Richmond, who made a self-vindicatory speech: see *Hansard*, pp. 337–40. The speech has been separately published.

Scandrett, W. B. Southland and its Resources. Invercargill, 1883.
    roy. 8°. Pp. 11, double columns.

Shortland, E. How to learn | Maori. | A short Treatise on the Structure and | Idiom of the Language. | By Edward Shortland, M.A., M.R.C.P., | late Native Secretary New Zealand. | Author of "Traditions and Superstitions of the New Zealanders," "Maori | Religion and Mythology," &c. | Auckland : | Upton & Co. | 1883.
    12°. Title-page, preface, and pp. ii, 55.
    Introduction, pp. 1-7. Maori language, pp. 7-10. Syntax, pp. 19-52. Miscellaneous, pp. 52-5.

Smeaton, W. H. O. District High Schools in New Zealand. *Victorian Review*, July 1883.

* **Stewart,** G. Vesey. Guide to the Hot Lakes of Rotorua. London, 1883.
    8°. Pp. 24.

* **Stewart,** G. V. Notes on Special Settlement, No. 4, Bay of Plenty, N.Z. London, 1883.
    8°. Pp. 123.

* **Stewart,** G. V. Reply to the "Truthful" Report by G. E. Barton, made to the Shareholders at the Guildhall Tavern, Gresham-street, London. Tauranga : Edgecumbe. 1883.
    8°. Pp. 10.

Stout, Robert. Governor Gordon and the Maoris. *Melbourne Review*, April, 1883, pp. 164–85.
    Te Whiti movement, 1879–82; Government action and legislation. Recommends that insurgent natives should be tried as ordinary criminals; and this was actually done in 1886.

Stout, R. Politics and Poverty. An address at Dunedin, April 13, 1883.
    8°. Pp. 10, double columns.
    On N.Z. taxation and a proposed National Insurance scheme.

Thomas, Julian. Round about New Zealand. By "The Vagabond." *Australasian*, Melbourne, May 26 to Aug. 18, 1883.
    1. Melbourne to the Bluff. 2. The Bluff to Dunedin. 3. Dunedin to Invercargill. 4. To Lakes Manipouri and Te Anau. 5. On Lake Manipouri. 6 and 7. Camping out on the Lakes. 8. Around Wakatipu. 9. Wakatipu to Cromwell. 10. Lakes Wanaka and Hawea. 11. From the Lakes to the Goldfields. 12. To Christchurch. 13. To the Alps.

Ward, J. P. Wanderings | with the | Maori Prophets, | Te Whiti and Tohu : | (with Illustrations of each Chief) | Being Reminiscences of a Twelve Months' | Companionship with them, from their | Arrival in Christchurch in April, | 1882, until their Return to Pari- | haka in March, 1883. | By John P. Ward. | Price two shillings. | Nelson, N.Z.: | Printed & Published by Bond, Finney, & Co., Waimea-st. | 1883.
    roy. 8°. Pp. 136.

1884.

Blair, W. N. The | Industries of New Zealand. | An Address | delivered to the | New Zealand Manufacturers' Association | at Dunedin, | On the 12th February, 1884, | By | W. N. Blair, M.Inst.C.E. | Price One Shilling. | Dunedin: | Printed at the "Evening Star" Office, Bond Street. | MDCCCLXXXIV.
    8°. Pp. 62; 4 diagrams.

Bracken, Thomas. Lays of the Land of the Maori and Moa. With an Introduction by the Rev. Rutherford Waddell. London, 1884.
    cr. 8°. Pp. 160. Portrait.
    March of Te Rauparaha; Waipounamutu; Orakau; Kaitangata; Canterbury pilgrims; Address at opening of Dunedin Exhibition, 1881; Address at opening of Oamaru theatre, 1883; and other poems, relate to N.Z. subjects or scenes.

Colenso, W. In Memoriam. | An Account of Visits to, and Crossings over, | the | Ruahine Mountain Range, | Hawke's Bay, New Zealand ; | and of the | Natural History of that Region ; | Performed in 1845-1847 : *cum multis aliis*. | In two Papers, read before the Hawke's Bay Philosophical | Institute, 1878 : | with additional and copious notes. | By W. Colenso, F.L.S., Etc., | —— | —— | New Zealand : | Printed at the "Daily Telegraph" Office, Tennyson Street, Napier. | 1884.
    roy. 8°. Pp. vi (not numbered), 72+2.

* Colonist's handbook of New Zealand. S.P.C.K. London, 1884.
    Pamphlet.

Cox, Alfred. Recollections : | Australia, England, Ireland, Scotland, | and New Zealand. | By Alfred Cox. | —— | Christchurch, N.Z. : | Whitcombe and Tombs (Limited). | 1884.
    8°. Pp. vii, 272.
    Chs. x-xxxvi, pp. 66-272, relate to N.Z. Has accounts of many public men— Maning, McLean, Whitaker, Stafford, Fox, Weld, Hall, Sewell, Vogel. Visit to Taupo in 1867, ch. xix. Canterbury newspapers, ch. xxvi. Colonial museums, ch. xxv.

Cumming, C. F. Gordon. Kauri forests of New Zealand. *Lippincott's Magazine*, xxxiii. 366. April, 1884.

Cumming, C. F. G. New Zealand in blooming December. *Century*, xxvii. 919. April, 1884.

* **Fischer**, H. Ueber die Nephrit-Industrie der Maoris in Neuseeland. *Archiv f. Anthropologie*, xv. 403-9 (1884).

Gisborne, William. New Zealand. *In* Encyclopædia Britannica, ed. 9, vol. xvii, pp. 466-71. Edinburgh, 1884.

Gisborne, W. Official Handbook | of | New Zealand | By | William Gisborne, Esq. | [*Edited by the Agent-General*] | Part III | London | Edward Stanford | 1884.
    8°. Pp. 116. Two maps.
    An account of the Provinces.

Graham, W. A. Beetroot | Sugar Manufacture. | —— | Hamilton, Waikato, N.Z. | —— | MDCCCLXXXIV.
    8°. Pp. 21.

Griffin, G. W. New Zealand : | Her Commerce and Resources. | By G. W. Griffin, *United States Consul at Auckland*, | Author of "My Danish Days,"

Griffin, G. W.—*continued.*
"Studies in Literature," " Memoir of C. S. Todd," &c. | —— | Wellington, New Zealand: | Published by George Didsbury, Government Printer. | 1884.
  roy. 8°. Pp. viii, 180. Map.

<small>Financial statistics, pp. 5-21. General statistics, pp. 21-6. Australasian banking, pp. 26-32. Mail routes to Australasia, pp. 32-41. Harbour accommodation, pp. 41-4. Coalfields, pp. 44-57. Goldfields, pp. 57-9. Timber trade, pp. 59-66. Iron and steel trade, pp. 66-72. Watch and clock trade, pp. 72-6. Wine and spirit trade, pp. 76-7. Manganese, pp. 77-80. Wool, pp. 80-8. Woollen manufactures, pp. 81-91. Cattle, pp. 91-8. Frozen and canned meat, pp. 98-103. Canned provisions, pp. 103-6. Fisheries, pp. 106-19. Kauri gum, pp. 119-24. Fungus, pp. 124-8. Flax, pp. 128-32. Rabbit-skins, pp. 132-6. Tanekaha bark, pp. 136-42. Cement, pp. 142-53. Agricultural products, pp. 153-63. Horse-breeding, pp. 163-7. American wooden-ware, pp. 107-70. System of credit, pp. 170-6. Tables of imports and exports by W. N. Blair.

A series of papers furnished to the Department of State, Washington, and printed in the United States Consular Reports. "These papers were written by me at various dates since my appointment as Consul at Auckland, and have had such alterations and additions made to them, in their present form, by Dr. J. Hector . . . and by Mr. W. R. E. Brown, Registrar-General, . . . as were necessary to bring the statistical information up to the latest date."—*Preface.*

Another report on "New Zealand: its history, people, progress, industries, and trade," appeared in the U.S. Consular Reports, no. 36, Dec. 1883, pp. 265-77. Others appeared later.</small>

Harven, E. *de.* La | Nouvelle Zélande | au point de vue économique de la Belgique | par Emile de Harven | *Courtier en Laines* | Conférence donnée à la Société Commerciale, Industrielle | et Maritime d'Anvers | le 28 Janvier 1884 | Prix : 50 centimes. | En Vente | à " l'Office de Publicité " | Rue de la Madeleine, à Bruxelles. || Chez | les principaux librairies du Pays. | Anvers.—Imprimerie Veuve de Backer, Rue Zirk, 35.
  roy. 8°. Pp. 44. The inner title-page omits from *Janvier 1844* to *Anvers,* and adds the date, 1884.

<small>General description; emigration from Belgium; statistics.</small>

Hutton, F. W. Origin of the Fauna and Flora of New Zealand. 1884.
<small>Published; but see Trans. N.Z. Inst.</small>

Jervois, *Sir* William Francis Drummond. The Defence of New Zealand: an Address by His Excellency Sir W. F. D. Jervois, G.C.M.G., C.B., &c. Delivered to the Members of the New Zealand Institute, at the Anniversary Meeting held on the 4th October, 1884. Wellington, 1884.
  f°. Pp. 21, and 19 plates. roy. 8°. Pp. xli; 5 plates.

Kerry-Nicholls, J. H. The King Country; | or, | Explorations in New Zealand. | A Narrative of 600 Miles of Travel through | Maoriland. | By | J. H. Kerry-Nicholls | —With numerous illustrations and a map. | London: | Sampson Low, Marston, Searle, and Rivington, | Crown Buildings, 188, Fleet Street. | 1884.
  8°. Pp. xx, 379.

<small>Introduction, pp. 1-16.—*Frontier of the King country.* Ch. i. The King's camp. ii. The Korero. iii. Ascent of Pirongia.—*Lake country.* Ch. iv. Auckland to Ohinemutu. v. Hot-spring life. vi. Tradition, idolatry, and romance. vii. En route to the terraces. viii. Terraces. ix. Ohinemutu to Wairakei. x. Wairakei.—*Exploration of King country.* Ch. xi. The start. xii. Region of Lake Taupo. xiii. Eastern shore of Lake Taupo. xiv. Tokanu. xv. Rangipo table-land. xvi. Ascent of Tongariro. xvii, xviii, xx. Ascent of Ruapehu. xix. Kaimanawa Mountains. xxi. Kariol. xxii. Forest country. xxiii. Ruakaka. xxiv. Ngatokorua pa. xxv. Hot springs of Tongariro. xxvi. Western Taupo. xxvii. Northern table-land. xxviii. Aukati line.—Appendix: Potatau II. (pp. 345-7). Chiefs (pp. 348-50). List of tribes, with localities (p. 351). Flora (pp. 352-60). Fauna (pp. 360-5). Language (pp. 366-73).

Reviewed in *Academy,* xxvi. 112-3.</small>

Lang, Andrew. Myths of the origin of death. *Princeton Review,* July, 1884, pp. 56–67. New York.
 Examines (pp. 64–6) the Maui-myth, and disputes its solar character.

Lendenfeld, R. *von.* Der Tasman-Gletscher | und seine Umrandung. | Von | Dr. R. v. Lendenfeld | in Christchurch. | Mit einem Lichtdruck, 2 Karten und 10 in den Text gedruckten Skizzen. | (Ergänzungsheft No. 75 zu "Petermann's Mitteilungen.") | Gotha : Justus Perthes. | 1884.
 4°. Pp. iii, 80.
 Introduction, p. 1. The central part of the N.Z. Alps, pp. 2–11. Topography of the glacier and its surroundings, pp. 11–33. Survey of the topography of our province, p. 34. Morphology and dynamics of the ice, pp. 35–50. Geology, flora and fauna, pp. 50–1. Meteorology, pp. 52–64. Tables of altitudes, pp. 64–6. Earlier expeditions to the glacier, p. 67. Our expedition in 1883, pp. 67–79. Bibliography, p. 79. Conclusion, p. 80.

***Lendenfeld,** R. *von.* Eine Expedition nach dem Centralstock der Neuseeländischen Alpen. *Oesterr. Alpenztg.,* vi, no. 146 (1884).

Maoriland | an | Illustrated Handbook | to | New Zealand. | Issued by the | Union Steam Ship Company of New Zealand | (Limited) | George Robertson and Co. (Limited), | Melbourne, Sydney, Adelaide, and Brisbane. | MDCCCLXXXIV.
 cr. 8°. Pp. 355. Illustrations and small maps.
 Nearly all scenes of much interest are described.

***Reinicke,** G. Bemerkungen über Port Lyttelton in Neu-Seeland. *Annal. d. Hydrographie,* 1884, p. 614.

Sala, George Augustus. Land of the Golden Fleece. *Daily Telegraph, New Zealand Herald,* &c., 1884.
 Descriptive narrative of a tour in N.Z.

1885.

A., S. New and Complete Manual | of | Maori Conversation : | containing | Phrases and Dialogues | on | A Variety of Useful and Interesting Topics, | together with | A few General Rules of Grammar ; | and a | Comprehensive Vocabulary : | *By S. A.* | Wellington, N.Z. : | Lyon and Blair, Printers, Lambton Quay | MDCCCLXXXV.
 fcp. 8°. Pp. 197.
 S.A. = Sister Aubert, a Roman Catholic missionary at New Jerusalem, Wanganui River.

Clayden, Arthur. New Zealand in 1884. *Proc. Roy. Col. Inst.,* xvi. 148–66. 1885.
 Industrial position ; social and political position. Discussion (pp. 167–79) : W. Gisborne, Capt. Scott, Douglas McLean, J. B. Thurston.

Cowan, Frank. Fact and Fancy in New Zealand. | The | Terraces of Rotomahana : | a Poem | By Frank Cowan, | —— | To which is prefixed a paper on | Geyser Eruptions and Terrace Formations | By Josiah Martin, F.G.S. | —— | Auckland, N.Z. | H. Brett, Printer, Shortland and Fort Streets. | MDCCCLXXXV.
 p. 8°. Pp. 61.
 J. Martin's paper "contains, among other original observations and discoveries, the first recorded account of the explosive or bomb-like character of the upheavals of water in several of the geysers." Miscellaneous notes to the poem, pp. 43–61.

***Cumming,** C. F. Gordon. The Wonderland of New Zealand. *Overland Monthly,* N.S., v. 1, Jan. 1885.
 U 153

Fenton, Francis Dart. Suggestions for a History | of the | Origin and Migrations | of the | Maori People. | By | Francis Dart Fenton, | Late Chief Judge of the Lands Court of New Zealand. | Auckland, N.Z.: | Printed and Published by H. Brett, "Evening Star" | Office, Shortland and Fort Streets. | 1885.

    8°, Pp. iv, 132.

    Ch. i. Chaldæa. ii. Arabia. iii. Indian Ocean. [Traditions of migration; Maui legend, pp. 67-70.] iv. Islands of Indian and Malay archipelago. v. Pacific Ocean. [Traditions of the voyages to N.Z.; of migration to N.Z.; Hawaiiki, &c.] vi. Concluding observations. Appendices: Legend of Maui (reprinted from Judge Maning's translation), pp. 124-30. Ancient calendar, with translation, pp. 131-2. The Maori spirit-land: a N.Z. poem, is given in translation (F. E. Maning's), pp. 18-20.

    A branch of the Cushite race settled in Arabia under the name Sabaians, who founded colonies in the Indian islands, whence they migrated to the Pacific.

Forbes, Arch. Souvenirs | of | Some Continents | By | Archibald Forbes, LL.D. | London | Macmillan and Co. | 1885.

    cr. 8°. Pp. vi (not numbered), 332.

    At pp. 270-90 is a paper on "Doughtown scrip," describing a drive from Springfield to the West Coast, and a lecture at Hokitika. It appeared in the *English Illustrated Magazine.*

Ginders, Alfred, M.D. The Thermal-Springs, Rotorua, New Zealand: Hints on Cases likely to benefit by Treatment thereat. Wellington. By authority: G. Didsbury. 1885.

    8°. Pp. 10.

Grey, *Sir* G. Polynesian Mythology | [Same as in 1855] Second Edition.— English & Maori. | Auckland: | Printed by H. Brett, Evening Star Office, Shortland Street. | MDCCCLXXXV.

    8°. Pp. xxiii, 255.

    A reprint (by the Government) of the edition of 1855, together with (pp. 199) a reprint of the Maori originals, published in 1854. A new preface by the author, pp. xiii-xx.

Griffiths, G. S. A glacial epoch in the Southern Hemisphere. *Melbourne Review,* Oct. 1855, pp. 403-15.

    Review of F. W. Hutton's theory, pp. 408-14.

The Growth of Colonial England: Australia and New Zealand. *Westminster Review,* xlviii. 412-43. 1885.

    N.Z.: pp. 437-43.

Gudgeon, T. W. The History and Doings | of the | Maoris, | From the Year 1820 to the Signing of the Treaty | of Waitangi in 1840. | By Thomas Wayth Gudgeon, | Author of the Reminiscences of the War in New Zealand. | Auckland: | Printed by H. Brett, "Evening Star" Office, Shortland Street. | MDCCCLXXXV.

    8°. Pp. 225. Pp. 95-225 are covered by White's Lectures: see below.

    Ch. i. Aborigines. ii. Migrations. iii. Traditions. iv. Superstitions. v. Warriors. vi. Witchcraft. vii, viii, ix. War and tapu. x. Former inhabitants of Auckland peninsula. xi. Fragment of early history from an unpublished MS. xii-xx. Tribal wars. xxi. Te Waharoa.

    The narratives are derived from original sources.

    At pp. 95-225 are J. White's lectures on Maori customs and superstitions.

*****Hancock,** Charles. England und die Maori. Berlin: Puttkammer u. Mühlbrecht. 1885.

    8°. A pamphlet. Compare *Ausland,* 1884.

Hutton, F. W. Sketch of the geology of New Zealand. Read before Geological Society, Jan. 29, 1885. Abstract in *Nature,* xxxi. 305.

*Jouan, H. La Nouvelle-Zélande et le Peuplement de la Polynesie. Caen, 1885.

Lewis, T. H. Medical Guide | to the | Mineral Waters of Rotorua | By | T. Hope Lewis, | M.R.C.S., Eng. ; L.S.A., London | (Late Government Resident Medical Officer). | Auckland : | H. Brett, Shortland and Fort Streets. | MDCCCLXXXV.
    cr. 8°. Pp. 60.

Moreton, S. H. A Scramble over the Mountains. By Samuel H. Moreton, *Artist.*
    cr. 8°. Pp. 6, double columns. From the *Weekly Times*, Invercargill, Feb. 7, 1885.

*Mosley, M. Illustrated Guide to Christchurch and Neighbourhood. Christchurch : J. T. Smith. 1885.
    8°. Pp. 229. Sixty-four illus.—*Davis.*

Müller, Max. On the Maui-myth in an article on solar myths, *Nineteenth Century*, xviii. 913–5. 1885.

Murphy, M. Handbook | of | New Zealand Gardening | with a | Chapter on Bee-Keeping | By M. Murphy, F.L.S. | Secretary Canterbury Agricultural and Pastoral Association, and Editor of " New Zealand Country Journal." | Price 2/6 | —— | Christchurch, N.Z. : | Whitcombe & Tombs, Limited. | [1885 ?]
    cr. 8°. Pp. vii, 188. Illus.

Our sister cities : No. 4—Dunedin. *Melbourne Review*, July, 1885, pp. 270–8.

[Raynal, F. E.] Wrecked on a Reef ; | or, | Twenty Months in the | Auckland Isles. | A True Story | of | Shipwreck, Adventure, and Suffering. | With forty Illustrations. | London : | T. Nelson and Sons, Paternoster Row. | Edinburgh ; and New York. | 1885.
    cr. 8°. Pp. xiv, 350.
    Translated from the French, *Les naufragés*, 1873. The appendix contains narratives of the wrecks of the "Invercauld" and the "General Grant" on the same islands.

*Reubank, F. [?] Ein Ausflug nach Neuseeland. *Westermann's illustr. Monatshefte*, Oct. 1884, and Jan. 1885.

Simonin, L. Le monde océanique et les progrès de l'Australie. *Revue des Deux Mondes*, March 15, 1885.
    N.Z. : pp. 435–41.

*A Short Sketch of Some Incidents in the Colonial Life of Mr. Thomas Hancock. Edited by William Coleman. Auckland : Wickham. 1885.
    8°. Pp. 72. Printed for private circulation only.—*Davis.*

Spencer, W. I., *M.R.C.S.* Napier as a Health Resort for Pulmonary Invalids. Napier : R. C. Harding. 1885.
    cr. 8°. Pp. 12.

*Stieda, W. Neu-Seeland in Vergangenheit u. Gegenwart. *Deutsche geogr. Blätter*, viii. 44 (1885).

Stout, R. Address delivered in the Theatre Royal, Auckland, April 14, 1885.
    8°. Pp. 11.
    On political ideals.

Stout, R. Our waifs and strays. *Melbourne Review*, April, 1885, pp. 109–20.
    What N.Z. is doing with her neglected and criminal children.

Stout, R. Public Education in New Zealand. | A Speech | delivered by | The Hon. Robert Stout, | Minister of Education, | in the | House of Representatives, | July 21, 1885. | Wellington. | By Authority: George Didsbury, Government Printer. | 1885.

8°. Pp. 40.

An account of the educational system—University, secondary, primary, technical, Native, reformatory, and deaf-mute.

Strong, H. A. Western sounds of New Zealand. *Good Words,* xxvi. 429. July, 1885.

Tregear, E. The | Aryan Maori. | By | Edward Tregear. | Wellington : | George Didsbury, Government Printer. | 1885.

8°. Pp. iv (not numbered), 107. Plate.

The Maori is an Aryan, who left India and came to N.Z. 4,000 years ago. His language is the most primitive of Aryan dialects, and has embalmed the memory of ancient animals, implements, &c.

* [**Verrall,** John Miles.] The Condition of New Zealand : A Challenge to Sir Julius Vogel, K.C.B., and to the Money-lending Fraternity and Lawyers. By Lieutenant Farmer, Q.C. Christchurch : Whitcombe and Tombs. 1885.

8°. Pp. 23.

Vincent, Ethel Gwendoline. Forty Thousand Miles | over | Land and Water | The Journal of a Tour through the | British Empire and America | By | Mrs. Howard Vincent | With numerous Illustrations | In two Volumes | —— | London : | Sampson Low, Marston, Searle, & Rivington, | —— | 1885.

cr. 8°. Four N.Z. illus.

Vol. i, chs. viii, ix, pp. 150-236, describe a tour through both Islands.

White, J. Maori Customs and Superstitions. *In* Gudgeon's *History and doings of the Maoris,* pp. 95–225. 1885.

1886.

Bonwick, J. The British Colonies | and Their Resources | Including the British Possessions in | America, Australasia, Asia, Africa, and | Europe. | By James Bonwick, F.R.G.S. | —— | London : | Sampson Low, &c. | 1886.

cr. 8°.

Consists of four distinct treatises, separately paged. That on Australasia (pp. 124) contains (spread over the tractate)—the discovery, settlement, climate, population, and description of N.Z., its mineral, forest, pastoral, agricultural, fishery, industrial, and trading resources.

Bonwick, J. Climate and Health | in Australasia, | to which is added | A Chapter on the Land Laws | of the Colony. | New Zealand. | Edited by | James Bonwick, F.R.G.S., | —— | With Map. | London : | Street & Co., 30, Cornhill, E.C. ; | —— | 1886.

cr. 8°. Pp. viii, 78. Maps.

Burrows, *Rev.* R. Extracts from a Diary | kept by the | Rev. R. Burrows | during | Heke's War in the North | In 1845. | Auckland : | Upton and Co. | 1886.

8°. Pp. 58.

Valuable. Disposes of Col. Mundy's legend about Heke's death.

Butler, Annie R. Glimpses of Maori Land | By | Annie R. Butler | —— | London : | The Religious Tract Society | —— | 1886.

cr. 8°. Pp. xii, 260. Illus.

Life in Wellington, Hawke's Bay, and Auckland; chiefly from a religious point of view.

Cox, Alfred. Men of Mark | of | New Zealand | Edited by | Alfred Cox | Christchurch, N.Z. | Whitcombe & Tombs | 1886.
    p. 8°. Pp. iv, 237.
        In the form of a dictionary.

***Cumming**, *Miss* C. F. Gordon. The eruption of Mount Tarawera in 1886. *Leisure Hour*, Oct. 1886.

A Farmer's Views on Land Nationalisation and the Working of the New Zealand Land Act.
    Dated—Palmerston North, April 22, 1886.
    cr. 8°. Pp. 24.

Froude, J. A. Oceana | or | England and her Colonies | By | James Anthony Froude | Moribus antiquis stat res Romana *virisque.—Ennius*. | —— | London | Longmans, Green, and Co. | 1886.
    8°. Pp. xii, 396. With 9 illustrations, 8 of N.Z. scenes.
        Chs. xiv, xv, xvi, xvii, xviii (pp. 238-335), relate to N.Z. Pp. 337-9 report a conversation with a N.Z. colonist. Ch. xiv. Auckland; xv-xvii, the Hot Lakes district. xviii describes Kawau and Sir George Grey, and gives the author's general impression of N.Z. At pp. 257-61 is a report of a conversation with a Mr. F—. The book generally, but particularly the part relating to N.Z., was adversely criticized by E. Wakefield in *Nineteenth Century*, xx. 171, and the N.Z. portion by E. Tregear, *Westminster*, 1887. It is also referred to in *Revue des Deux Mondes*, lxxxiii. 98-9, which has a brief biography of the author and a general review of his works; and in the *Edinburgh*, clxiii (N.Z.: pp. 417-20). It has been more recently examined by J. Bradshaw, *New Zealand of to-day*, 1888.

Geikie, Archibald. The recent volcanic eruption in New Zealand. *Nature*, xxxiv. 320-2; *Contemporary Review*, Oct. 1886, pp. 481-92.

Gisborne, W. New Zealand Rulers | and Statesmen | 1840 to 1885 | By | William Gisborne, | formerly a Member of the House of Representatives, and a Responsible | Minister, in New Zealand. | With numerous Portraits. | London : | Sampson Low, Marston, Searle, & Rivington, | —— | 1886.
    cr. 8°. Pp. viii, 292. Thirty-three portraits.
        A biographical history of the colony from its foundation.

Gordon, H. A. Outline History of the Gold, Coal, and Other Known Mineral Resources of New Zealand. Wellington, 1886.
    8°. Pp. 15.

Grayling, W. I. Taranaki | and its Resources. | *Written by request of the Mayor and Borough Council | of New Plymouth*. | —— | By | W. Irwin Grayling. | 1886. | *New Plymouth*: Printed at the "Taranaki Herald" Office, Devon Street.
    sm. cr. 8°. Pp. 41.

The Great | Volcanic Outbreak | at | Tarawera, New Zealand | 10th June, 1886. | —— | Napier : | Printed by R. Coupland Harding. | 1886.
    cr. 8°. Pp. 48.
        A full narrative of the catastrophe.

Greenwood, T. Free Public Libraries, | Their Organisation, | Uses, | and Management. | By Thomas Greenwood, F.R.G.S., | —— | London : | Simpkin, Marshall & Co. | Stationers' Hall Court, E.C. | 1886.
    p. 8°. Pp. xvi, 463.
    N.Z.: pp. 332-3.

Haast, *Sir* J. The Mineral Resources of New Zealand. *Australian Times and Anglo-New-Zealander*, Aug. 19, 1886, Supplement, pp. 1-3.

Harven, E. *de.* Mission commerciale | en Nouvelle-Zélande. | Rapport général | par | Emile De Harven | Bruxelles | P. Weissenbruch, Imprimeur du Roi | éditeur | 45, Rue du Poinçon, 45 | 1886.

 8°. Pp. xv, 427. Map, with itinéraire du voyage d'exploration commerciale en N.Z. par M. de Harven, Nov. 1884 à Mai 1885. Charts: (1) taux moyen des salaires dans les différents districts de la N.Z., 1884; (2) prix moyens des aliments et du bétail ; (3) statistiques agricoles de l'Australasie, 1873–1883 ; (4) statistiques sommaires, 1853–84 ; (5) immigration et émigration, 1870–1884.

 ii. Personal. iii. General. iv. Natural resources. v. Public works. vi. Financial situation. vii. Maritime. viii. Agriculture. ix. Immigration. x. Industry. xi. Financial establishments. xii. Commerce. xiii. General considerations. Appendix. Cours des valeurs publiques, pp. 418–27; those of banks and finance companies, pp. 222–5.

 M. de Harven was sent out to N.Z. by an association for the opening-up of commercial relations between Belgium and N.Z. A brief biography of him is given in the *New Zealand Herald*, Nov. 15, 1884, Supplement.

***Hayden**, E. The eruption in New Zealand in 1886. *Science*, viii. 68, 135. July, Aug., 1886.

Holgate, C. W. An Account of | the Chief Libraries | of | New Zealand. | With | An Appendix | containing the statutes relating to public libraries in that colony. | By | C. W. Holgate, B.A. | —— | J. Davy and Sons, 137 Long Acre, London. | 1886.

 8°. Pp. 52.

 Has extracts from letters of Sir G. Grey describing his own collection.

Holgate, C. W. The Auckland Free Public Library. In the *Library Chronicle*, July-August, 1886, pp. 115–9.

Hübner, Joseph Alexander, *Baron von.* Through | the | British Empire | By | Baron von Hübner | formerly Austrian Ambassador in Paris and Rome | In two Volumes | —— | With a Map | London | John Murray, Albemarle Street | 1886.

 p. 8°.

 In vol. i, pp. 160–246, is the description of a tour through the colony. Reflections on the Maoris, i. 231–6; and on government and politics, i. 236–47.

 There is a biographical sketch of Hübner in *Men of the Time*.

Keltie, J. Scott. Geographical education.—Report to the Council of the Royal Geographical Society. (*In* Royal Geographical Society's Supplementary Papers, vol. i, pt. 4.) London, 1886.

 roy. 8°.

 "I was present when Professor Kirchhoff [of Halle] was lecturing on New Zealand. He spoke of the Maoris, their origin, relations, implements and weapons ; the discovery of the country, English colonisation, effect of contact of whites with natives, Christianity, language ; the special development of English methods of colonisation ; N.Z. a typical example of the English 'Culture Colony;' climate and exceptional healthiness of N.Z. referred to; compared statistically with Germany; trade, railways, towns " (p. 495).

 The geographical programme of the Collége de France for 1884–85 embraced lectures on N.Z., p. 579.

Kerry-Nicholls, J. H. The origin, physical characteristics, and manners and customs of the Maori race, from data derived during a recent exploration of the King Country, New Zealand. In *Journal of the Anthropological Institute*, vol. xv, pp. 187–209. 1886.

 Introductory, pp. 187–8. Native tradition of the first Maori migration, pp. 188–90. Probable origin of the race, pp. 190–3. Physical characteristics, pp. 193–5; and of half-castes, p. 195. Present condition, pp. 195–7. Religion, pp. 197–202; Hauhauism, pp. 201–2. Domestic arts, pp. 202–5. Manufactures, p. 205. Former healthfulness, p. 206. Medicine and pharmacopœia, pp. 206–7.

* **Leroy-Beaulieu,** Paul. De la Colonisation | chez les | Peuples Modernes | Par | Paul Leroy-Beaulieu | Membre de l'Institut, | Professeur au Collège de France, Directeur de L'*Économiste français*. | —— | Troisième Édition, revue, corrigée et augmentée | Paris: | Librairie Guillaumin et Cie | —— | 1886.
    8°. Pp. xix, 766. (First edition, 1874.)
       N.Z. in 1878: pp. 577-8, &c., describes N.Z. as *cette île*. An account of the Wakefield system is given at pp. 567-75.

* **Leys,** T. W. Volcanic Eruption at Tarawera ; with an Account of the Thermal Springs District. Auckland, 1886.
    4°.

[**McLean,** Patrick Stirling.] History and Policy | of the | Native Land Laws | of New Zealand. | From 1840 to 1886. | Napier, N.Z.: | Printed by Dinwiddie, Walker & Co., Limited, | Tennyson Street. | 1886.
    cr. 8°. Pp. 88.
       Part i. From 1840 to 1856. ii. From 1856 to 1858. iii. From 1858 to 1864. iv. Constitution of the Native Land Court. v. Jurisdiction of the Native Land Court. Investigation of title. vi. Alienation and division of Native lands. vii. Administration of Native lands. viii. Conclusion.
       The " first attempt to bring together the many efforts to settle the vexed questions which are constantly arising upon the administration of Native lands." Careful and impartial.

* Die Maoribevölkerung auf Neu-Seeland, 1886. *Deutsche Rundschau f. Geogr.*, Feb. 1888, p. 229.

The Maoris' fight for life. By a New Zealander. *Chambers's Journal*, Oct. 23, 1886, pp. 673-5.

New Zealand Industrial Exhibition, | 1885. | Prize Essays | on the | Industries of New Zealand. | Published by Authority. | Wellington : | By Authority : George Didsbury, Government Printer. | 1886.
    roy. 8°. Pp. iv, 123.
        Winter, Richard. New Zealand industries: the past, the present, and the future, pp. 3-36.
        Haselden, William Reeve. The present condition and future prospects of the industrial resources of New Zealand, and the best means of fostering their development, pp. 37-104.
        Hart, George Robert. Same title, pp. 105-23.

Northesk, *Lord*. Exhibition of Jade Objects. By the Right Hon. the Earl of Northesk. In *Journal of the Anthropological Institute*, 1886, v. xv, pp. 185-6.
    " Lord Northesk exhibited a very fine collection of jade implements, principally from New Zealand." (May 12, 1885.) " Mr. John Evans made some remarks on the methods by which the jade implements from New Zealand appeared to have been manufactured " (pp. 186-7). Prof. Fischer of Freiburg and Dr. A. B. Meyer of Dresden have treated exhaustively of jade (p. 187).

Old Identity Stories. *Tapanui Courier*, Dec. 1, 1886, Supplement. 2 pp.
    1. History of the past. 2. Tapanui district: its settlement from the earliest times. 3. Notes on the good old days. 4. Tapanui nugget: by Vincent Pyke. 5. Pioneering in Otago.

Petherick, E. A. Catalogue | of the | York Gate Library | formed by | Mr. S. William Silver | An Index to the Literature of Geography | Maritime and Inland Discovery | Commerce and Colonisation | By | Edward Augustus Petherick | F.L.S., F.R.G.S., etc. | Second edition | London | John Murray, Albemarle Street | 1886.
    imp. 8°. Pp. cxxxii+336. Illustrations, facsimiles of maps and titlepages.
       N.Z.: § 79, pp. 271-82, nos. 5401-5606.

Progress of New Zealand. *Science*, viii. 371. Oct. 1886.

Reminiscences | of the | Colonial and Indian Exhibition | Illustrated by Thomas Riley | designer of the Exhibition diploma | Edited by Frank Cundall | —— | London | Published with the sanction of the Royal Commission | by William Clowes and Sons, Limited | 13, Charing Cross, S.W. | 1886.

    4°. Pp. ix, 116.

N.Z.: pp. 65-9. Notes on collections in Maori court by Dr. Buller, pp. 67-9. Engravings of koa, kiwi, and Maori storehouse.

Smith, S. Percy. The | Eruption of Tarawera : | A Report to the Surveyor-General | By | S. Percy Smith, F.R.G.S., | Assistant Surveyor-General, New Zealand. | New Zealand : | By Authority: George Didsbury, Government Printer, Wellington. | 1886.

    roy. 8°. Pp. 84. Plates, maps, and plans.

Description of the Taupo volcanic zone, pp. 6–19; promonitory signs, pp. 19-26; the eruption, pp. 26–35; sympathetic action in neighbouring areas, pp. 35–40; Tarawera and Rotomahana prior to the eruption, pp. 41–5; the great fissure, pp. 45–65; earthquake-cracks, pp. 65–8; conclusion. Appendices, pp. 75–84; ascent of Ruapehu, pp. 78–9; Taupo, pp. 80–4 (both by L. Cussen).

Spencer, W. Baldwin. The parietal eye of Hatteria. *Nature*, xxxiv. 33–5. See also Dallinger, W. H., *Contemporary Review*, July 1886, pp. 147–50.

The lizard known as *Hatteria punctata*, an inhabitant of N.Z., has an (atrophied) invertebrate or molluscoid eye, the occurrence of which suggests that "the tunicates and the vertebrates arose in one stock of enormous antiquity."

Stout, R. Notes | on the | Progress of New Zealand | for Twenty Years, | 1864–1884. | By the | Hon. Robert Stout, | Premier of the Colony. | Wellington : | George Didsbury, Government Printer. | 1886.

    8°. Pp. 39. Twenty-two coloured diagrams.

i. Population, etc. ii. Trade and shipping. iii. Mineral development. iv. Pastoral development. v. Agricultural development. vi. Manufactures. vii. Increase of wealth, advance in credit and general material advancement. viii. Probable future development.

The coloured diagrams show—(1) and (1A) population of N.Z.; (2) ages; (3) birthplaces, (4) religions, and (5) education of the people; (6) and (7) births, deaths, and marriages; (8) and (9) imports and exports; (10) sheep, cattle, and horses; (11) land in cultivation; (12) yield of wheat, oats, and barley; (13) holdings of land under cultivation; (14) and (15) deposits in savings-banks; (16) revenue and expenditure; (17) miles of railway and (18) of telegraph open; (19) shipping, inwards and outwards; (20) deposits in banks; (21) capital invested in industries.

Reprinted in the *Journal of the Statistical Society*, xlix. 539–70. Discussion, pp. 571–80.

* **Tangye**, Richard. Notes of my Fourth Voyage to the Australian Colonies, including Australia, Tasmania, and New Zealand. Birmingham, 1886.

    8°.

"For private circulation. The writer was one of the last visitors at the Hot Springs prior to the eruption of Tarawera."—*Colonial Book Circular*, Sept. 1887.

* **Thomson**, G. M. Acclimatization in New Zealand. *Science*, viii. 426, Nov. 1886.

Tucker, W. H. The English Church | in Other Lands | or | The Spiritual Expansion of England | By the | Rev. W. H. Tucker, M.A. | Prebendary of St. Paul's | Author of . . . 'Memoir of Life and Episcopate of | George Augustus Selwyn, D.D.' etc. | London | Longmans, Green, and Co. | 1886.

    cr. 8°. Pp. xiv, 223. Epochs of Church History series.

General sketch of the history of the Church of England in N.Z., pp. 83–95.

Vaile, S. The | Present Position | and Future Prospects | of the | New Zealand Railways, | with a | Proposed Entirely New Scheme of Levying | Fares and Rates. | Mr. J. P. Maxwell's Report on that Scheme, | and a Reply thereto. | By Samuel Vaile, of Auckland. | Also Extracts from a Paper, | *Read before the Auckland Institute, on the 21st September, 1885,* | on | " The Influence of the Means of Transit | on the | Social Condition of the People," | by Samuel Vaile.
    8°. Pp. 69.

Wakefield, E. Mr. Froude on New Zealand. *Nineteenth Century*, Aug. 1886, pp. 171–82.
    An adverse criticism of Froude's *Oceana*, particularly of the portion relating to New Zealand.

Wallace, J. H. Manual | of | New Zealand History. | By | J. Howard Wallace, | One of the Pioneer Settlers of the Colony | —— | —— | Wellington, New Zealand : | Printed by Edwards & Green, for J. H. Wallace, Jun., Publisher, Grey Street, | —— | 1886.
    8°. Pp. viii, 70.
    A *précis* in 400 paragraphs, some of them very brief. Portions are founded on an announced *Early History of N.Z.* by the author.

*A Wooden Town. By one of its inhabitants. *Cassell's Family Magazine*, Oct. 1886.

1887.

*Der Ausbruch des Tarawera und Rotomahana auf Neu-Seeland. *Deutsche Rundschau für Geogr. und Statistik*, ix Jahrgang, Heft 7, April, 1887, pp. 318–20. Vienna.

Blair, W. N. The | Industries of New Zealand | by | W. N. Blair, M.Inst.C.E. | An Address | delivered to the | Industrial Association of Canterbury, | at Christchurch, N.Z., on | Thursday, February 24, 1887 | Industrial Association of Canterbury Incorporated | F. Jenkins, President of the Association in the Chair. | Christchurch, N.Z. : | Printed by the ' Press' Company, Ltd., Printers and Bookbinders, Cashel Street. | 1887.
    8°. Pp. 96.
    Introductory, pp. 5–6.—What has been done, pp. 7–35. (General sketch; indigenous, pastoral, and agricultural exports; mining; home industries; present position.)—Resources, pp. 36–47. (Preliminary; natural amenities; minerals; vegetable resources; land; general.)—What more can be done, pp. 47–96. (Future industrial development; the great controversy; advantages of manufactures; facilities and difficulties; encouragement to be given.)—Conclusion, p. 96.

Bonwick, J. Romance | of | the Wool Trade. | By | James Bonwick, F.R.G.S., | Fellow of the Royal Colonial Institute, | author of | " Last of the Tasmanians," " Port Phillip Settlement," | etc. | —— | London : | Griffith, Farran, Okeden, and Welsh, | (Successors to Newbery and Harris,) | West Corner of St. Paul's Churchyard, London. | 82, Clarence Street, Sydney, N.S.W. | 1887.
    cr. 8°. Pp. viii, 472.
    Ch. vii is entitled "Sheep and wool in New Zealand," pp. 308–28. It is taken chiefly from Consul Griffin's reports.

Bryce v. Rusden. Privately printed. London, 1887.
    8°. Pp. 638+ii.
    A report of the proceedings in the civil suit, Bryce v. Rusden. The plaintiff was the Hon. John Bryce, formerly Minister for Native Affairs in N.Z.; and the defendant, G. W. Rusden, formerly Clerk of the Parliaments, Victoria, and author of a *History of New Zealand*. The ground of the action (for libel) was especially a passage in

Bryce v. Rusden—*continued.*

Rusden's *History*, ii. 504-5, which charged Lieut. Bryce with cutting down women and young children "gleefully and with ease." The case was heard before the Queen's Bench, March 4 to March 12, 1886.

Carter, C. R. Catalogue of Books | on or relating to | New Zealand; | to which is added | Remarks | on | Book Purchasing and Booksellers | in London. | By C. R. Carter, J.P., | Formerly a Member of the New Zealand House of Representatives and the | Wellington Provincial Council. | Dedicated, by permission, | to | Sir William Fitzherbert, K.C.M.G. | London : | printed by Bowden, Hudson & Co., 23 Red Lion Street. | 1887.

8°. Pp. 42.

365 works are catalogued, by title-pages. In 6 pages of an appendix the compiler gives an account of his hunt for books on N.Z.

Cassell's | Picturesque | Australasia | Edited by | E. E. Morris, M.A. Oxon., | Professor of English, etc., in Melbourne University. | With Original Illustrations. | —— | Cassell & Company, Limited : | London, Paris, New York & Melbourne. | 1887.

4°. Vol. i (1887), ii, iii (1888).

Vol. i. A vanished wonderland, by Prof. T. G. Tucker, pp. 89-100. Dunedin, by R. E. N. Twopeny, pp. 283-95.

Vol. ii. Dunedin to Christchurch, by R. E. N. Twopeny, pp. 140-7. West coast sounds, by J. Mylne, pp. 250-62.

Vol. iii. Christchurch, by R. E. N. Twopeny, pp. 18-29. Wellington to Napier by coach, by W. Waite, pp. 206-11. Lake Wakatipu, pp. 242-53.

Davis, J. D. Contributions | towards a | Bibliography | of | New Zealand. | Collected & annotated by | James Davidson Davis. | —— | Wellington : | Lyon and Blair, Lambton Quay. | 1887.

cr. 8°. Pp. iv, 77.

Catalogues over 600 publications, a few of the earlier ones with biographical and other notes. Many do not relate specially to N.Z. Foreign literature and articles in periodicals are sparsely represented.

Fox, *Sir* W. The | Political Crisis : | by | Sir William Fox. | Marton : | Printed at the office of the Rangitikei Advocate, Broadway. | MDCCCLXXXVII.

8°. Pp. 30. A series of letters reprinted from the *Rangitikei Advocate.*

Letters i and ii show that the Public Works policy is not the cause of the present crisis. iii and iv state the real causes. v, vi, vii, and viii discuss Protection. ix and x are on land-laws. xi adversely criticizes Sir G. Grey's Lands Settlement Bill. xii : educational retrenchment. xiii : administrative retrenchment.

***Geisler,** W. Bilder aus Neu-Seeland. *Deutsche Rundschau für Geogr. und Statistik,* ix Jahr, Hefte 5, 6, Feb. and April 1887, pp. 199-220, 299-307. Vienna.

"His articles treat of the forest scenery and of the Natives of N.Z., with illustrations."—*Colonial Book Circular.*

[**Grey,** William.] Charity and poor law in New Zealand. *Charity Organisation Review,* Aug. 1887, vol. iii, pp. 312-7. London: Longmans, Green, and Co. 1887.

Gudgeon, T. W. The Defenders | of | New Zealand | Being a Short Biography | of Colonists who distinguished themselves in upholding | Her Majesty's Supremacy in these Islands. | By | Thos. Wayth Gudgeon | Author of | "The Reminiscences of the War in New Zealand " | " The Doings of the Maoris from 1820 to the Signing of the Treaty | of Waitangi

Gudgeon, T. W.—*continued.*
in 1840," etc., etc. | Auckland | H. Brett, Printer and Publisher, Shortland Street | MDCCCLXXXVII.
    imp. 8°. Pp. 620, xxxvi. Coloured illustrations, plans, and many portraits.

Introduction, pp. 13–15. Biographical sketches, pp. 19–488. McDonnell's *Maori history*, pp. 491–556, his *Incidents of the war*, pp. 557–87, and his *Tales of the Maori*, pp. 588–620. Addenda:—Alphabetical list of N.Z. medallists, pp. i–xxxiii; officers and men killed, pp. xxxiv–xxxvi.

Hale, Horatio. The giant birds of New Zealand. *Popular Science Monthly* (1887), xxx. 660–3.
    An account of Quatrefages's argument against Haast's view of the antiquity of the moa.

The | Handbook | of | New Zealand Mines | (with Maps and Illustrations). | Part I. | Gold, Silver, Copper, and Antimony Mining, etc. | Part II. | Coal-Deposits and Coal-Mines. | Appendix. | Schools of Mines, Principal Forest-Trees, Building-Materials, | Mineral Waters, Mineral Leases, etc. | —— | Wellington. | By Authority: George Didsbury, Government Printer. | 1887. | Price 5s.
    p. 8°. Pp. xix, v, 392, 55, 82. Three maps, illustrations, and statistical tables. Preface by Hon. W. J. Larnach, pp. v–x.

Part I.—Introduction, pp. xvii–xix. Otago and Southland, pp. 1–94. West Coast (Middle Island), pp. 95–236. Nelson, pp. 237–68. Marlborough, pp. 269–74. Wellington, pp. 275–7. Auckland, pp. 278–343. Economic minerals (republished with slight alterations and additions from Hector's Handbook of New Zealand, 1886), pp. 344–57. Hints to prospectors (by J. A. Miller), pp. 358–68. Improved mining-appliances (by H. A. Gordon), pp. 369–84. Tables of exports, works, and water-races, pp. 385–92.

Part II.—Coal-deposits and coal-mines. Introduction, pp. iii–v. Coal-deposits, pp. 1–9. Coal-mines, pp. 11–54. Auckland and Taranaki, pp. 11–18. Nelson and Marlborough, pp. 19–21. West Coast (Middle Island), pp. 22–9. Canterbury, pp. 30–6. Otago and Southland, pp. 37–54. Statistics, p. 55.

Appendix, pp. 1–56. Schools of mines, pp. 1–22. Principal forest-trees (with slight additions and alterations from Hector's Handbook), pp. 23–36. Building-materials (*ibid.*), pp. 37–43. Mineral waters (*ibid.*), pp. 44–53. Mineral leases, pp. 54–6.

Index, pp. 57–71. Advertisements are paged.
Mr. Patrick Galvin is described as the compiler.

Hoare, E. Brodie. Notes on New Zealand. *National Review*, June, 1887.
    The body of the article is reprinted in the *N.Z. Times*, Aug. 11, 1887.

Hutton, F. W. Report | on the | Tarawera Volcanic District. | By | Professor F. W. Hutton, F.G.S. | Wellington: | By Authority: George Didsbury, Government Printer. | 1887.
    roy. 8°. Pp. 20. 11 plates.

Inglis, J. Our New Zealand | Cousins | by | The Hon. James Inglis | ("*Maori*"), | Minister of Public Instruction in the New South Wales Legislative Assembly; | Author of "Sport and Work on the Nepaul Frontier," | "Our Australian Cousins," etc. etc. | London: | Sampson Low, Marston, Searle, and Rivington | Crown Buildings, 188, Fleet Street. | 1887.
    cr. 8°. Pp. xii+311.

A description, "originally written for the Sydney Press," of a tour through N.Z. in 1885. To describe something of "the startling contrasts and pregnant transformations which have been effected during twenty years of bristling [*sic*] activity and onward progress in a young country like N.Z." is the aim of the author, who had travelled through the Islands twenty years before. Two appendixes reproduce unoriginal matter.

A biographical sketch of the author appeared in the *N.Z. Herald*, Feb. 9, 1889.

Interesting Chapters | from the | Early History of Wanganui ; | and | Wanganui in 1856. | Wanganui, N.Z.: | Printed and Published by A. D. Willis, Caxton Buildings. | 1887.

  8°. Pp. 75. Two illus.

   Partly reprinted from W. Tyrone Power's book. The bulk of the tract is drawn from Dr. Wilson's manuscript diary, May to Aug. 1847, which describes the Native war of that year and the Gilfillan massacre, pp. 20–55. Wanganui in 1856 is by C. Burnett, pp. 61-75.

The Kermadecs. *Chambers's Journal*, May 2, 1887, vol. iv, pp. 214–5 (2½ columns).

  Descriptive of the islands and their successive inhabitants.

* **Kerry-Nicholls**, J. H. The volcanic eruptions in New Zealand in 1886. A paper read before the Society of Arts, London, Jan. 28, 1887.

Lang, A. Myth, Ritual, and | Religion. | By | Andrew Lang. | —— | London : | Longmans, Green, and Co. | 1887.

  cr. 8°. 2 vols.

   Vol. ii, pp. 27–32, discusses Maori metaphysics and myths, which are also discussed in his article on mythology, *Encyc. Brit.*, xvii. 149, translated as *La Mythologie*, Paris, 1886; and in Bastian, *Die heilige Sage der Polynesier*. The Maui-myth is no sun-myth, but a myth of the origin of death (xvii. 149). "In the Maori hymns there are metaphysical ideas and processes which remind one more of Heraclitus than of Hesiod, and perhaps more of Hegel than of either" (ii. 28).

Mackay, J. Our Dealings with | Maori Lands ; | or, | Comments on European Dealings for the Purchase | and Lease of Native Lands, and the | Legislation thereon. | By James Mackay, | Late Civil Commissioner for the Colony of New Zealand, etc., etc., etc. | —— | Auckland : | Kidd and Wildman, Booksellers, Stationers, and Publishers. | MDCCCLXXXVII.

  roy. 8°. Pp. 60; pp. 1–31, 58–60, being in double columns.

   Describes—(1) Maori tenure before arrival of Europeans; (2) dealings of Europeans from arrival till 1840; (3) Government land-purchases, 1840–62; (4) legislation on Native Land Courts and lands, 1862–86; (5) measures to simplify dealings with native lands. At pp. 33–56 are a draft Act, and (pp. 58–60) comments on it.

McDonnell, T. Incidents of the War | Tales | of | Maori Character and Customs, etc., etc., etc., | By | Lieutenant-Colonel McDonnell | of the New Zealand Militia. | Auckland | H. Brett, Printer and publisher, Shortland-street.

  (Bound up with Gudgeon's *Defenders of New Zealand*, of which it forms pp. 557–620.)

McDonnell, T. A | Maori History | being | a Native Account | of the | Pakeha-Maori Wars in New Zealand | By Lieutenant-Colonel McDonnell | of the New Zealand Militia. | Auckland | H. Brett, Printer and publisher, | Shortland Street.

  (Bound up with Gudgeon's *Defenders of New Zealand*, of which it forms pp. 491–556.)

   Introduction, pp. 493–4. "In the following pages I have endeavoured to give a brief Maori account of the early colonization of New Zealand, as also a history of the native wars that have taken place in this colony, which I gathered from a Maori chief, who was an eye-witness of many of the events recorded, and had learned others on good authority. In every instance I have strictly adhered to the facts related, and have allowed my Maori historian to draw his own inferences from them."

Maskell, W. M. An Account | of the | Insects noxious to Agriculture and Plants | in | New Zealand. | The Scale-Insects (Coccididæ). | By W. M. Maskell, F.R.M.S., | Registrar of the University of New Zealand. | Wellington : | By Authority : Geo. Didsbury, Government Printer. | 1887.

  roy. 8°. Pp. iii, 116; 23 plates, most of them coloured, and letter-press opposite ; note appended.

Mivart, St. George. Notes on colonial zoology. *Contemporary Review*, May, 1887, pp. 668–80.
    Hatteria, pp. 673-7.

Pennefather, F. W. On the natives of New Zealand. *Journal of Anthropological Institute*, xvi. 211–6. Read June 29, 1886. Volume published 1887.

Pope, James H. The | State : | the Rudiments of New Zealand | Sociology | For the Use of Beginners | By | James H. Pope, | *Inspector of Native Schools*. | New Zealand : | By Authority : George Didsbury, Government Printer, Wellington. | 1887.
    8°. Pp. viii, 327.
    Part iii, on Government (pp. 218–61), describes the institutions and departments of the N.Z. Government. Part ii, on Political Economy, has constant reference to N.Z. economical problems.

Pyke, V. History | of the | Early Gold Discoveries | in Otago. | By Vincent Pyke, M.H.R., | *Late Warden and Otago Goldfields Secretary*. | Dunedin, N.Z.: | Otago Daily Times and Witness Newspapers Company, Limited. | 1887.
    8°. Pp. vii, 151. Seven illus.
    In twelve chapters, with four additional chapters describing episodes. A narrative of the discovery at Tuapeka in 1861 is given by Gabriel Read at pp. 122-31, appendix B. Impressed by the scarcity of authentic contemporaneous records of the Victorian goldfields, "I made a point of setting down each event as it occurred, after my acceptance of office early in 1862. At the same time I collected every scrap of information obtainable respecting those things which happened before my arrival in the Colony."—*Preface*.

Quatrefages, A. *de*. Les Pygmées. Paris : Germer Baillière et fils. 1887.
    Traces Negritos to N.Z., where they preceded the Maoris.

Sutter, A. Per Mare, per Terras | being | a Visit to New Zealand by Australia, | for the Examination of Certain Lands there | during 1883–84, & America in 1885 | By | Archibald Sutter, C.E. Edin. | Inspector H.M. Land Office ; | Member of the Institution of Civil Engineers, | —— | London | T. Fisher Unwin | 26 Paternoster Square | 1887.
    cr. 8°. Pp. xvi, 281. With maps and illustrations.
    Chs. v-x describe a visit to Auckland province. Valueless.

** 'Taken In.' Being a Sketch of New Zealand Life as seen by ' Hopeful.' London : W. H. Allen & Co. 1887.
    fcp. 8°.

Tregear, E. A flitting ghost. *Westminster*, cxxviii. 404–13.
    A criticism of Froude's *Oceana* in relation to N.Z.

Varigny, C. *de*. L'Oceanie moderne.—III. *Revue des Deux Mondes*, Août 15, 1887.
    A few remarks on N.Z., lxxxii. 924-6.

White, J. The | Ancient History of the Maori, | his | Mythology and Traditions. | Horo-Uta or Taki-Tumu Migration. | By | John White. | Volume I. | Wellington : | By Authority : George Didsbury, Government Printer. | 1887.
    p. 8°. Pp. xiii, 181, 164, three illustrations, and chart of the Maori Mythology, no. 1 (*d*). The Introduction and English translation occupy pp. 1–181. The Maori original is separately paged, pp. 1–164.
    Introduction and notes, pp. 1-6. Ch. i. *Whare-kura:* School of Mythology and History, pp. 8-13. School of Agriculture, pp. 13-15. Astronomical School, pp. 15-16. Ch. ii. *Mythology of creation.* Ch. iii. *Tane and rebellion of spirits.* Ch. iv. *Division of heaven and earth.* Chs. v, vi. *Death of Wahie-roa.* Ch. vii. *Attempt to murder Ta-whaki.* Ch. viii. *Ta-whaki ascends to heaven.* Ch. ix. *Creation of woman.* Ch. x. *God Tane.* Ch. xi. *Creation of man and woman.* Ch. xii. *Deluge.* (Priests and chiefs before the Flood, pp. 165-72. Deluge, pp. 172-81.) Laments, incantations, and

White, J.—*continued.*
prayers are prefixed to chapters and interspersed. Vol. I. was reviewed in the *Saturday Review*, Feb. 18, 1888; and in *Knowledge*, April 2, 1888, pp. 135–6. Prof. Max Müller wrote respecting it to the *Academy*, Jan. 28, 1888.
  Vol. ii. was published in 1887: pp. ix, 194, 177. Illus.—Chs. v, vi, vii, are devoted to the myth of Maui; ch. xi, to the Original Canoes and Migrations.
  Vol. iii, 1887: pp. x, 316, 120. Illus.—Early history. Occupation of South Island and its history. Extermination of the moa.
  Vol. iv, 1888: pp. x, 245, 230. Illus.—Describes the Tai-nui migration. Introduction of the kumara.

***Whitworth,** R. P. Hine-ra; or, The Maori Scout: a romance of the New Zealand war. With glossary. London: G. Routledge and Co. 1887.

1888.

Australasian Colonies. | New Zealand Handbook, | With Map. | Issued by the | Emigrants' Information Office, | 91 Broadway, Westminster, S.W. | —— | London: | Printed for Her Majesty's Stationery Office, | By Eyre and Spottiswoode, | —— | April, 1888.
  8°. Pp. 33. Map.

Australian Poets | 1788-1888 | Being a selection of poems upon all subjects | written in Australia and New Zealand | during the first century of the British Colonization | with brief notes on their Authors and | an introduction by Patchett Martin | Edited by | Douglas B. W. Sladen, B.A. Oxon. | B.A., LL.B. Melbourne, Australia | Author of | "Australian Lyrics," "A Poetry of Exiles," etc. etc. | London: | Griffith, Farran, Okeden and Welsh, | West Corner of St. Paul's Churchyard, | and Sydney, N.S.W. | 1888.
  p. 8°. Pp. xliv, 612.
  Has poems on N.Z. subjects by Mrs. J. G. Wilson, C. Watkins, Alex. Bathgate, T. Bracken, A. Domett, J. L. Kelly, Catherine Richardson, and Eleanor E. Montgomery.

Ballou, M. M. Under | the Southern Cross | or Travels in | ·Australia, Tasmania, New Zealand, Samoa, | and Other Pacific Islands | by | Maturin M. Ballou | —— | Boston | Ticknor and Company | 211 Tremont Street | 1888.
  cr. 8°. Pp. xi, 405.
  Chs. 12, 13, 14, 15, 16, 17, describe a tour through N.Z.—Bluff, Dunedin, Christchurch, Wellington, Auckland, and Hot-Lakes district.

Bradshaw, J. New Zealand | of To-day |·(1884-1887) | by | John Bradshaw | London | Sampson Low, Marston, Searle, and Rivington | *Limited* | St. Dunstan's House | Fetter Lane, | Fleet Street, E.C. | 1888.
  8°. Pp. xii, 402. Two maps of N.Z. and Hot-Lakes district.
  Chs. i, xii. Adverse criticism of *Oceana*. ii. Survey of Colony. iv. Natives. v, vii. Farming. vi. Frozen meat. viii. Solvency. ix. Settlement. x. Hot Lakes. xi. Southern lakes. xii, xiii. Policy. xiii. Railways. xiv. Education. xv. Harbours and industries. xvi. Federation. Statistical appendix, pp. 386-402.

Buller, *Sir* W. L. A History | of the | Birds of New Zealand. | By | Sir Walter Lawry Buller, K.C.M.G., | D.Sc., F.R.S., | F.L.S., F.R.G.S., F.R.C.I., Hon.F.S.Sc. ; | 'Officier de l'Instruction Publique' de la France; | Galileian Medallist of the Faculty of Natural Sciences, Royal University, Florence; | Corresponding Member of the Zoological Society of London, &c. | Second Edition. | Volume I. | London: | Published (for the Subscribers) by | The Author, | 8 Victoria Chambers, Victoria Street, Westminster, S.W. | 1888.
  imp. 4°. Pp. lxxxiv, 250. 24 coloured plates by Keulemans, and many woodcuts.
  The new edition has many alterations and additions. In the Introduction, pp. xlii-lxxxiv, there is a historical sketch of discoveries of moa-bones, and a section on the origin of the N.Z. avifauna.

Colenso, W. Fifty Years Ago | in New Zealand | a Commemoration : a Jubilee Paper : | a Retrospect : | a Plain and True Story. | Read before the Hawke's Bay Philosophical Institute, | October 17th, 1887, | by | William Colenso, | F.R.S., F.L.S., etc., Honorary Member of the Institute. | —— | Napier : | Printed by R. C. Harding, Hastings Street. | 1888.
    8°. Pp. 49. Three sketches from lithographs taken in 1837-8.
    Describes the printing of first book and first New Testament.

Cowie, W. G. Our Last Year | In New Zealand | 1887 | By William Garden Cowie, D.D. | Bishop of Auckland | London | Kegan Paul, Trench and Co., 1, Paternoster Square | 1888.
    cr. 8°. Pp. viii (not numbered), 403.
    Record of a year's church work in Auckland diocese.

[D'Avigdor, H.] Antipodean Notes | Collected on a Nine Months' Tour | Round the World | by | Wanderer. | London | Sampson Low, Marston, Searle, and Rivington | *Limited* | St. Dunstan's House | Fetter Lane, Fleet Street, E.C. | 1888.
    cr. 8°. Pp. viii, 259.
    The Sounds—diggings—Canterbury—farming—frozen meat—hotels and shops—working-man—racing—floods—colonialisms—Nelson—society and books—finance.

Duncan, A. H. The | Wakatipians : | or | Early Days in New Zealand. | By | Alfred H. Duncan, | Author of "Six Months' Kangaroo Hunting ; " "Private Life | of a Ceylon Coffee Planter ; " "Netherton, or | Life in a Scottish Village," &c. | London : Simpkin, Marshall, & Co. | Edinburgh : John Menzies & Co. | Melbourne & Sydney : G. Robertson & Co. | Aberdeen : A. & R. Milne. | Peterhead : W. L. Taylor. | 1888.
    roy. 16°. Pp. viii, 111. Sketch-map of "Wakatip" and illus.
    A "short account of the wild, rough life" of pioneers in Wakatipu Lake district, derived from notes and letters ; "an unwritten page of history."

Featherman, A. Social History | of the | Races of Mankind. | Second division : | Oceano-Melanesians. | By | A. Featherman. | —— | London : | Trübner & Co., Ludgate Hill. | 1888.
    8°. Pp. xxxii, 420.
    Maoris, pp. 160-220. A general account, derived mainly from Taylor.

General Catalogue | of | Grey Collection | Free Public Library. | Auckland | 1888. | Reference Department. | H. Brett, General Printer, Shortland and Fort Streets, Auckland. | MDCCCLXXXVIII.
    roy. 8°. Pp. xxv, 343, 25.
    A large number of publications relating to N.Z.

Gisborne, W. The | Colony of New Zealand | Its History | Vicissitudes and Progress | By | William Gisborne | —— | London | E. A. Petherick & Co., 33, Paternoster Row, E.C. | 1888.
    cr. 8°. Pp. xii, 360. 3 maps.
    Ch. 1. Physical geography, geology, flora and fauna. 2. Maoris. 3. Discovery and colonisation. 4 to 9. History. 10 to 13. Provinces. 14, 15. Miscellaneous. Appendix A : Lists of Governors and Premiers. Other appendices are statistical.
    Reviewed, with Bradshaw's and Payton's books, in the *Athenæum*, Feb. 16, 1889.

***Gunn,** J. The Kermadec Islands. *Scottish Geographical Magazine*, Nov. 1888, pp. 599-604.

Hetley, G. B. The | Native Flowers | of | New Zealand | Illustrated in Colours | in the best style of modern chromo-litho art, from drawings |

Hetley, G. B.—*continued.*
coloured to nature | By | Mrs. Charles Hetley | London : | Sampson Low, Marston, Searle, and Rivington | —— | 1888.
f°. Pp. 8 ; 36 coloured plates, with brief letter-press, index, and 3 supplementary leaves.
<small>A long preface, pp. 1-8, describes the circumstances under which the plants were collected and the plates produced. The book is dedicated to the Queen, and it is briefly noticed in the *Saturday Review*, July, 1888, p. 20.</small>

Hitiri te Paerata. Description | of the | Battle of Orakau, | as given by the Native chief | Hitiri te Paerata, | of the | Ngatiraukawa Tribe, | *At the Parliamentary Buildings, 4th August, 1888.* | Interpreter—Capt. Gilbert Mair. | Wellington. | By authority : G. Didsbury, Government Printer. | 1888.
fcp. 8°. Pp. 14. With genealogical table.

***Kirk,** T. W. The birds of New Zealand. *Ibis,* London, Jan. 1888.

***Knox,** T. W. The Boy Travellers in Australasia. Adventures of Two Youths in a Journey to the Sandwich, Marquesas, Society, Samoan, and Feejee Islands, and through the Colonies of New Zealand, New South Wales, Queensland, Victoria, Tasmania, and South Australia. By Thomas W. Knox. New York : Harper & Brothers. 1888.
sq. 8°. Pp. xvi, 538. Maps and illus.

***Lendenfeld,** R. *von.* Der charakter der Neuseeländischen Alpen. *Globus,* liii. 353–8. Illus. 1888.

*Mission life among the Maories. *Frank Leslie's Sunday Magazine,* Aug. 1888. New York.

***Mortimer,** J. Robert Browning's " Waring." *Manchester Quarterly,* Jan. 1888.

Moser, T. Mahoe Leaves : | being a | Selection of Sketches | of | New Zealand | and its Inhabitants, | and other matters concerning them. | By Thomas Moser. | Second Edition. | Wanganui, N.Z. : H. I. Jones & Son, Victoria Avenue. | 1888.
sm. cr. 8°. Preface (to 1st ed.), 2 pp. ; publishers' note (to 2nd ed.), 2 pp. ; contents ; and 132 pp.
<small>A description of life among Maoris brought into contact with Europeans. "Missionary influence" is the subject of an unflattering first chapter. Pahs, runangas, native courts, sacramental gatherings, witchcraft, and education are the subjects of other chapters. There are burlesque descriptions of individual natives.</small>

Moss, E. G. B. Native lands and their incidents. By E. G. B. Moss, Barrister, Tauruanga [*sic, for* Tauranga]. [1888.]
roy. 8°. Pp. 7, double columns.
<small>i. Native customs. ii. Private purchases. iii. Government purchases and dealings. Suggestions.</small>

*New Zealand : its History, Institutions, and Industries. A Narrative with Statistics. By a Resident. Compiled for the New Zealand Shipping Company. With map. London, 1888.
8°.

The North Island of New Zealand as a field for settlement. By one who has been there. *Field,* July 7, 1888, pp. 38–9. 3 columns.
<small>Describes land and conditions and profits of farming in Auckland province. Denounces Civil Service, land-sharks, mine-brokers, &c.
To a similar effect is a letter in the *Glasgow Herald,* quoted in the *N.Z. Times,* Oct. 11, 1888.</small>

Payton, E. W. Round about New Zealand : | Being | Notes from a Journal of Three Years' | Wanderings in the Antipodes. | By | E. W. Payton. | With Twenty original Illustrations by the Author. | London | —— | 1888.
>large cr. 8°. Pp. xii, 368. Portrait of Rewi, and map.
>>Describes a tour through the colony; with chapters on Labour, Sport, the Natives, and the Social Life.

Payton, E. W. A Set of Fifteen Etchings of New Zealand Scenery. Etched, Printed, and Mounted by E. W. Payton. In portfolio.

Pembroke, George R. C. Herbert, *Earl of.* Roots | A Plea for Tolerance | A new edition | London | Richard Bentley and Son, New Burlington Street | —— | 1888.
>cr. 8°. Pp. vii, 181.
>>See an earlier notice, 1873.

Petrel. In Southern Seas. | A Trip to the Antipodes. | By | 'Petrel.' | With original illustrations drawn | with pen and ink | by 'Twain.' | Edinburgh : R. Grant & Son. | London : Simpkin, Marshall, & Co. | 1888.
>sq. 8° or sm. 4°. Pp. vi, 173. Illus.
>>Ch. 7. Some N.Z. cities. 8. Maoriland. 9. Wonderland (Hot Lakes).

Pompallier, *Bishop.* Early History | of | The Catholic Church | in | Oceania | by the | Rt. Rev. Jean Baptiste François Pompallier | Vicar Apostolic of Western Oceania. | With introduction | by the | Rt. Rev. John Edmund Luck, O.S.B., | Bishop of Auckland | Auckland, N.Z. : | H. Brett, Printer, Star Office, Shortland and Fort Streets. | MDCCCLXXXVIII.
>roy. 8°. Pp. 83, and 1 p. of addenda. Portrait of Bishop Pompallier. Translated from the French by Arthur Herman.
>>Chs. vii-xvi, pp. 35-83, relate to N.Z.
>>Bishop Pompallier arrived at Hokianga in 1838 (misprinted 1858) with a single priest. He learnt English and Maori, and began his mission. The Maoris are described in ch. ix—their manners, customs, and traditions. He was present at the meeting at Waitangi, where he obtained freedom of worship for the Catholics from Governor Hobson. Subsequent chapters refer to the visit of Dumont d'Urville and the arrival of l'Aube, and detail the progress of the misson. At pp. 70-1 he describes a haka, which he pronounced immoral. A last supplementary page gives statistics of the Catholic Church in 1888.

***Preshaw,** G. O. Banking under Difficulties | or | Life on the Goldfields | of | Victoria, New South Wales, and New Zealand | by a Bank Official | Edwards, Dunlop, and Co. | Melbourne, Sydney, and Brisbane | 1888.
>Pamphlet.
>>"Full of anecdotes and experiences of early goldfields days in Westland and Nelson."—*Private letter.*

***Robjohns,** H. T. Bible-work and floods in New Zealand. *Christian World,* London, Sept. 6 and 13, 1888.
>An account of a journey from Nelson to Hokianga.—*Torch,* no. 6, vol. ii.

Rusden, G. W. Aureretanga ; | Groans of the Maoris | Edited by G. W. Rusden, | Fellow of the Royal Asiatic Society. | —— | London. | William Ridgway, 169, Piccadilly. | MDCCCLXXXVIII.
>8°. Pp. v, 178.
>>"The first part of the work compendiously refers to the occupation of New Zealand by Englishmen; to the mission undertaken by the 'Apostle' Marsden; and to the Treaty of Waitangi, 1840. . . . Mr. Rusden then refers to the labours of Bishop Selwyn to avert war and to the war at the Waitara, which he vainly strove to prevent; to the good work done by Sir Donald McLean, and his successful efforts to establish friendly relations with the tribes which adhered to the so-called Maori King ; to the manner in which the lands of the Maoris have been acquired from some of them in the Middle Island and elsewhere ; to the destruction of Te Whiti's peaceful village at

Rusden, G. W.—*continued.*
Parihaka; to the operations of the Native Land Court; to the complaints of the Maoris thereupon, and their desire to retain control of a portion of their lands. Petitions to the Queen for maintenance of the rights guaranteed under the Treaty of Waitangi are also described, with accounts of the deputation of certain Maori chiefs to the Colonial Office in 1882 as well as the more recent deputation of Tawhiao and others to England in 1884, and their reception."—*Colonial Book Circular.*
Aureretanga should be Auwaretanga.

Seffern, W. H. J. The early settlement of New Zealand: a few pages for a New Zealand History. From notes collected during a period of thirty-four years. *European Mail*, June 7, 1888, and following.

* Social life at the capital of New Zealand. *Cassell's Magazine*, March, 1888.

Thomas, A. P. W. Report | on the | Eruption of Tarawera | and | Rotomahana, N.Z. | By | A. P. W. Thomas, M.A., F.L.S., | *Professor of Geology and Biology, University College, Auckland; late Burdett-Coutts | Geological Scholar, University of Oxford.* | New Zealand. | By Authority: George Didsbury, Government Printer, Wellington. | 1888.
roy. 8°. Pp. 74; 2 maps and 19 plates.

Tregear, E. The Maori and the Moa. *Journal of the Anthropological Institute*, xvii. 292-304. 1888.

Whitmore, *Sir* George S. Patriotic Speech | of | Sir G. S. Whitmore, K.C.M.G., | on behalf of | those who defended New Zealand | at a time of national danger.
cr. 8°. Pp. 8.
On Naval and Military Settlers' and Volunteers' Land Bill; in Legislative Council, Aug. 1, 1888.

1889.

Barlow, P. W. Kaipara | or | Experiences of a Settler in | North New Zealand | Written and Illustrated | by | P. W. Barlow | Second Edition. | London | Sampson Low, Marston, Searle, and Rivington | Limited | St. Dunstan's House | Fetter Lane, Fleet Street, E.C. | 1889.
cr. 8°. Pp. xii, 219. Two full-page, and many other, illus.
Auckland—life—auctions—wild pigs—live-stock—balls—forests—fish and shooting—gum-digging—sports—government, and county councils—Maoris—education.

* **Besant**, Walter. Captain Cook. *In* English Men of Action series. Macmillan and Co. *Announced.*

* **Blair**, J. Lays of the Old Identities, and other Pieces suitable for Recitations and Readings. By John Blair, Abbotsford, Otago, New Zealand. Dunedin: R. T. Wheeler. 1889.
Reviewed in *Otago Daily Times*, April 27, 1889.

* **Brown**, J. M. New Zealand. By John Macmillan Brown, Professor of English Literature, Canterbury College, Christchurch. *American Cyclopædia.* New York: Appleton & Co. 1889.

Colenso, W. Ancient Tide Lore. Napier. *In the press.*
About 50 pp.
Relates mainly to Maori tide-lore.

* **Curteis**, G. H. Augustus Selwyn, D.D., late Bishop of New Zealand and of Lichfield. By G. H. Curteis, Canon of Lichfield. London: C. Kegan Paul, Trench and Co. *Announced.*
cr. 8°.

Dale, R. W. Impressions of Australia. III. Education. *Contemporary Review*, Feb. 1889.
    A brief account, not from observation, of the N.Z. educational system is given at pp. 251-4.

* An Early History of New Zealand. Auckland. H. Brett. *Announced*.
    Pp. 700–800. About 200 illus.
    "The early history of the colony up to 1840 is written by Mr. R. A. A. Sherrin. An historical review is contributed by the celebrated Baron de Thierry. Included in the work are historical papers and sketches by the late Rev. R. Taylor and Mr. Colenso. Sir G. Grey has added valuable notes. Judge Wilson, Mr. C. J. Wilson, and others have been laid under contribution."—*N. Z. Times*, May 7, 1889.

Featon, Edward H., *and* S. The | Art Album | of | New Zealand Flora; | being | a Systematic and Popular Description | of the Native Flowering Plants of New Zealand and the | Adjacent Islands. | By Mr. and Mrs. E. H. Featon. | Volume I. | Authors' Edition. | —— | Wellington, N.Z. : | Printed and published at the Office of Messrs. Bock & Cousins, Brandon Street. | Trübner & Co., Ludgate Hill, London, E.C. | 1889.
    roy. 4°. Pp. 180. 39 coloured plates, with letter-press.
    Systematic, Maori, and settlers' names of plants, pp. 177-8.

Hawkins, Robert S. The poor law in New Zealand. *Monthly Review*, Wellington, March, 1889, pp. 129–42.

Hector, *Sir* J. Phormium Tenax | as a | Fibrous Plant. | Edited by | Sir James Hector, K.C.M.G., M.D., F.R.S., &c. | With plates. | Second edition. | —— | New Zealand: | By Authority: George Didsbury, Government Printer, Wellington. | 1889.
    roy. 8°. Pp. xx, 95.
    The plant—its growth, cultivation, fibre, preparation, and properties. Reports to Commissioners. Statistical appendices.

* **Jacobs**, Henry, *Dean of Christchurch*. [History of the Anglican Church in New Zealand.] *In the press*.
    I. The Missionary Period, to 1841. II. The Period of Organization, to 1857. III. From 1857. "The Dean is the author of 424 pages of the work; the material for the remaining 60 pages on the seven Dioceses has been contributed by the respective bishops, or persons appointed by them. The work is the first of a series of colonial Church Histories."—*Typo*, March 30, 1889, p. 29.

* **Jouffroy d'Abbans**, *Comte de, and* **Wakefield**, E. La Nouvelle-Zélande en 1889: après cinquante ans. Paris. *In the press*.

* **Kirk**, T. The | Forest Flora | of | New Zealand. | By | T. Kirk, F.L.S., | Late Chief Conservator of State Forests to the Government of New Zealand. Lecturer on | Natural Science at Wellington College and the School of Agriculture, Lincoln. | Wellington. | By Authority: George Didsbury, Government Printer. | 1889.
    fcp. f°. Pp. xvi, 345. 157 plates.

Picturesque | Atlas | of | Australasia | edited by | Andrew Garran, M.A., LL.D. | The Picturesque Atlas Publishing Co. Limited. | Sydney & Melbourne | 3 vols. 1886–9.
    roy. f° or large 4°.
    Splendidly illustrated, with many N.Z. scenes and accompanying descriptions.
    v. 3 (being published in 1889) relates mainly to N.Z.

* **Wakefield**, E., *and* **Jouffroy d'Abbans**, *Comte*. New Zealand in 1889: after fifty years. *Announced*.

Williams, G. P., *and* **Reeves**, W. P. Colonial | Couplets : | being | Poems in Partnership, | by | George Phipps Williams | and | W. P. Reeves. | Christchurch : | Simpson & Williams. | 1889.
  cr. 8°. Pp. ii, 65.
  <small>The majority of the poems are on N.Z. subjects.</small>

Undated Publications; and Additions.

* Das Aussterben der Maoris auf Neu-Seeland. *Globus*, xxxviii, no. 8.

Barr, J. Poems and songs, descriptive and satirical. By John Barr, Otago. Edinburgh : John Greig & Son. MDCCCLXI.
  12°. Pp. xii, 254.
  <small>Some poems relate to N.Z.</small>

***Berggren**, Suen. Et Besög i de vulkanske Egne paa Ny Zeeland. [The volcanic parts of N.Z.] Dansk. Geogr. Selsk. Tidsr., Bd. 1, pp. 141–4. 2 pls. (views).

***Best**, A. D. Journal of an Excursion into the Interior of the Northern Island of New Zealand.

***Broome**, *Sir* F. Napier. A New Zealand snow-storm. *Cassell's Magazine*, ii.

***Bruck**, Ludwig. Guide to the Health Resorts in Australia, Tasmania, and New Zealand. Edited and compiled by Ludwig Bruck. Centennial Edition.
  cr. 8°.

Buller, W. L. Address | of | Dr. Buller, C.M.G., F.R.S. | (As counsel for the Ngatiapa,) | In the Native Land Court. | Rangatira Block | Printed at the Request of the Ngatiapa Chiefs. | (June–July, 1882.) | Wellington | Lyon & Blair, Printers, Lambton Quay. | 1882.
  roy. 8°. Pp. 32. Two plans.
  <small>Has details relating to Maori history, with legends, songs, and a lament.</small>

[*Lord* George **Campbell's** *Log Letters from " The Challenger,"* 1880, pp. 118–9, and H. N. **Moseley's** *Notes by a Naturalist on the " Challenger,"* 1879, pp. 277–9, have accounts of a short visit to N.Z. At pp. 280–2 of the latter are notes on the Kermadec Islands.]

* Chapman's Traveller's Guide through New Zealand. Auckland, 1872.

Cook, J. [The folio atlas of plates to the Voyages has one relating to N.Z.— "inside of a hippah."]

Crawford, J. Coutts. Geological reports. Council Papers, Wellington Provincial Council, 1861–4.
  sm. f°. Four reports : pp. 19, 30, 47–56, 17.
  <small>A paper by R. Brough Smyth is in third report, pp. 56–9. All relate to Wellington Province.</small>

***Curteis**, *Mrs.* G. Herbert. In Memoriam. A Sketch of the Life of the Right Rev. G. A. Selwyn, late Bishop of Lichfield, &c. Newcastle, 1878.
  Pamphlet.

***Dixon**, George. A Voyage round the World. 1789.
  <small>Given by Featherman as relating to N.Z.</small>

***Droze**, Gustav. Der Krieg in Neuseeland. Mit einer Kriegskarte. Zweite Ausgabe.

Drury, *Capt.* Revised | Sailing Directions, | &c., &c., | for the Northern Part of the Colony of | New Zealand. | By Captain Drury, | H.M.S. "Pandora." | Auckland: | Printed for the New Zealand Government, | By Williamson & Wilson. | 1854.
    12°. Pp. 94.
    <small>Has much descriptive matter.</small>

Fox, *Col.* A. Lane. Note *on the* Use *of the* New-Zealand More. Journal of the Ethnological Society, 1870, pp. 106–9. Illus.

[**Fox,** Sir William. A pamphlet without title-page "for private circulation only," pp. 39. 8°.]
    <small>Correspondence between Mr. Fox, Honorary Political Agent of the Wellington Colonists, and the Colonial Office, pp. 7-9. Minute on the Government of New Zealand, pp. 10-23. Appendix, pp. 24-39.</small>

Farnall, Harry Warner. [Pamphlet without title-page.]
    8°. Pp. 34.
    <small>Correspondence between Mr. Farnall, the Agent-General (Dr. Featherston), Superintendent Gillies, G. Vesey Stewart, and others, relating to free emigration.</small>

Gerland, G. Anthropologie [begun by Waitz].
    Vols. v, vi.

__Greenwood,__ *Major.* Journey to Taupo, from Auckland. By Brigade-Major Greenwood, Thirty-First Regiment. Auckland: Printed by Williamson and Wilson. 1850.
    16°. Pp. 87. Described in the Catalogue of the Grey Library, Capetown.

__Grey,__ *Sir* G. England and the New Zealanders. Auckland, 1847.

Haast, Julius. *On certain* Prehistoric Remains *discovered in* New Zealand, *and on the* Nature *of the* Deposits *in which they* occurred. Journal of the Ethnological Society, 1870, pp. 110–120. Illus.
    <small>An argument for the existence of a pre-Maori race in N.Z.</small>

__Haast,__ J. Report of a geological survey of Mount Pleasant, Canterbury. Lyttelton.

__Handbook__ to the Ferns of New Zealand. Auckland, 1861.

__Hooker,__ *Sir* W. J., *and* **Greville,** R. K. Icones filicum. 1829–31.
    <small>"In 1791, Captain Vancouver arrived in Dusky Bay, . . . having with him as surgeon Mr. Archibald Menzies, a very assiduous collector of Flowerless plants, who procured many species of *Filices, Musci,* and *Hepaticæ,* most of which are described at length and beautifully illustrated in " the above works.—*Hooker, Handbook,* p. 9*.</small>

Illustrated Guide | to the | West Coast | of the | North Island, N.Z. | *Describing the various Towns and adjacent Land* | *available for Settlement, &c.* | By R. W. Pownall. | *Accompanied by ten Drawings on Stone, by W. Potts, from Sketches by R. W. Pownall, A.V.A.* | Wanganui : | A. D. Willis, Printer, Caxton Buildings, Victoria Avenue. | 1885.
    8°. Pp. 83.

__Kerry-Nicholls,__ J. H. Recent exploration of the King country, New Zealand. Proc. Roy. Geog. Soc. (N.S.), vii. 201.

__Knight,__ C., *F.L.S.* Contribution to the Lichenographia of New Zealand.

Knight, C., *and* **Mitten**, —.; **Ralphs**, —. Transactions of the Linnean Society of London, xxiii. 99, 101; Journal of the Linnean Society of London, Bot., iii. 163.

> "As regards Flowerless plants, two valuable papers by Mr. Knight and Mr. Mitten, on some of the Lichens of Auckland (*Transactions*, supra), and by Mr. Ralphs (*Journal*, supra) on the Tree-ferns, are almost the only published contributions made since" 1854 to our knowledge of the Flora of the N. Island.—*Hooker, Handbook*, p. 12*.

* **Knollys**, *Col.* The Victoria Cross in Abyssinia, the Persian war, Bhootan, New Zealand, &c. By Lieut.-Col. Knollys and Major Elliot. London: Dean and Son.
   Illus.

Lindsay, W. Lauder. [See other publications of his, chiefly on the flora of Otago, enumerated in his *Contributions*, 1868.]

[The Missionary Register for 1816, 1817, 1822, 1823, 1826, 1827, and doubtless other years, has reports from N.Z. missionaries.]

* **Mueller**, F. [On the vegetation of Chatham Islands.]
   > "Founded chiefly on Mr. W. Travers's collections."—*Hooker, Handbook*, p. 722.

[The New Zealand Journal, described under 1840, seems to have been published in 1850, 1851, and 1852.]

Ollivant, J. E. Hine Moa, | the | Maori Maiden. | By | Joseph Earle Ollivant, | Author of "A Breeze from the Great Salt Lake," and | Translator of "The Court of Mexico," by Countess Paula Kollonitz. | —— | A. R. Mowbray & Co. | London : | 65, Farringdon Street, E.C. | Oxford : | 116, S. Aldate's Street.
   fcp. 8°. Pp. iv, 187.

> A poem on the legend, pp. 25-116; metrical introduction, pp. 1-24. Appendix, pp. 117-87: Notes on N.Z. animals, vegetable productions, food and fasting in N.Z. (all reprinted from the *Field*), birds, history and mythology, Maori customs, greenstone, canoes, geographical.
> The author passed a few months in N.Z., and in his childhood had seen a Pakeha-Maori (calling himself Pa-he-Rangi) who had been taken prisoner in N.Z., forcibly tattooed, and married to his chief's daughter.

[The Proceedings of the Church Missionary Society for 1819, 1820-1, 1821-2, &c., contain reports from missionaries.]

* Proceedings of the Diocese of New Zealand, 1862-4; of the Synods of the Dioceses of Nelson, Waiapu, and Wellington, 1859-67; are in the catalogue of the Grey Collection, Public Library, Auckland, p. 158.

Province of Canterbury, | New Zealand. | List of Sections | purchased to April 30, 1863. | London : | Edward Stanford, 6 Charing Cross, S.W. | 1863.
   8°. Pp. 115.

* **Pompallier**, *Bishop*. Etat succinct et précis de la Mission Catholique à la Nouvelle-Zélande. Paris, 1859.

* **Pompallier**, *Bishop*. Letter to Matutaera Potatau. Auckland, 1862.

Quoy, —., *et* **Gaimard**, P. Voyage | de Découvertes | de | L'Astrolabe | Exécuté par ordre du Roi, | Pendant les Années 1826-1827-1828-1829, | sous le commandement | de M. J. Dumont D'Urville. | Zoologie | par | MM. Quoy et Gaimard. | —— | Paris | J. Tastu, Éditeur-Imprimeur, | No. 36, Rue de Vaugirard. | 1830.
   5 tomes.

> There is a brief account of the Maoris, i. 19-21, and descriptions of zoological species scattered through the volumes.

Reid, R. C. Rambles | on | the Golden Coast | of | the South Island | of | New Zealand | By | R. C. Reid | London | The Colonial Printing and Publishing Company, Limited | 30 Fleet Street, E.C. | 1886.
    roy. 4°. Pp. 176. 20 illustrations of scenery; 4 (coloured) of ferns. Second edition.
<small>Early explorers and history; descriptions; gold diggings; industries; ferns; and fish.</small>

Report of Proceedings | of the | Otago | Mining Conference | held at Clyde, March, 1874. | Naseby : | Wilson and De Lautour, Commercial and General Printers, Mount Ida | Chronicle Office. | MDCCCLXXIV.
    8°. Pp. 24.

Sherrin, R. A. A. Handbook | of the | Fishes of New Zealand | Prepared, under the instructions of the | Commissioner of Trade and Customs, | by | R. A. A. Sherrin. | Auckland : | Wilsons and Horton, —— | MDCCCLXXXVI.
    p. 8°. Pp. iv (not numbered), 307, iv. Map.
<small>Has accounts of acclimatization, of Macquarie Island seals and sea-elephants, and of the old N.Z. whaling-trade.</small>

The | Sounds, Lakes, & Rivers | of | New Zealand. | *From Photographs and Sketches.* | Published by the Survey Department. | Wellington. | By Authority : George Didsbury, Government Printer. | 1885.
    roy. 4°. 33 plates, with pictorial cover.

*****Walker,** A. West coast of the Middle Island. Proc. Roy. Geog. Soc., ix. 33. 1865.

Warre, *Col.* H. J. New Zealand : its Occupation and Defence against Native Aggression. London, 1863.
    Pamphlet.

Titles of German Periodicals.

Petermann's Mitteilungen (aus Justus Perthes' geographischer Anstalt). Gotha : Perthes.
<small>In the body of the Catalogue the title of this periodical has sometimes been abbreviated *Mith.*, instead of *Mitt.*</small>

Ausland. Stuttgart and München : Cotta.

Globus. Braunschweig : Vieweg.

Zeitschrift für allgemeine Erdkunde. Berlin.

N.F. = Neue Folge (New Series).

Part 2.—Classified Catalogue.

New Zealand generally.

Sparks, Jared. New Zealand. 1823.
Barrow, J. Australasia. 1824.
Craik, G. L. New Zealanders. 1830.
Busby, J. Authentic information. 1832.
Laplace, C. Voyage. 1835.
Nightingale, T. Oceanic sketches. 1835.
New Zealand. 1837.
Wakefield, E. J. British colonization. 1837.
New Zealand. 1838.
House of Lords Committee. 1838.
Rienzi, G. L. Océanie. 1838.
Mann, W. Six years' residence. 1839.
Important information. 1839.
New Zealand. 1839.
Walton, J. Twelve months in N.Z. 1839.
Ward, J. Information. 1839.
Campbell, E. Present state. 1840.
Fourteen years. 1840.
Holman, J. Travels. 1840.
Johnson, J. P. Plain truths. 1840.
New Zealand described. 1840.
    „   „ 1840.
N.Z. Journal. 1840–52.
Reybaud, L. Histoire et colonisation. 1840.
Russell, A. Tour. 1840.
Ward, J. Supplementary information. 1840.
Young, W. C. N.Z. described. 1840.
Bright, J. State and prospects. 1841.
Du Petit-Thouars, A. Voyage. 1841.
Hodgskin, R. Narrative. 1841.
New Zealand in 1841. 1841.
Etonian. New Zealand: a poem. 1842.
Jameson, R. G. New Zealand. 1842.
Present State. 1842.
Russell, M. Polynesia. 1842.
Terry, C. New Zealand. 1842.
Description. 1843.

New Zealand generally—*continued.*

Joplin, R. C. New Zealand : a poem. 1843.
New Zealand. 1844.
Brodie, W. Remarks. 1845.
Brown, W. N.Z. and its aborigines. 1845.
Marjoribanks, A. Travels. 1845.
Martin, S. M. D. New Zealand. 1845.
New Zealand. 1845.
Results of N.Z. inquiry. 1845.
Wakefield, E. J. Adventure. 1845.
Dumont d'Urville. Voyage. 1846.
Ross, J. C. Voyage. 1847.
Byrne, J. C. Twelve years' wanderings. 1848.
New Zealand. 1848.
„   „   under Grey. 1848.
Wakefield, E. J. Handbook. 1848.
Australia and N.Z. 1849.
New Zealand and the Polynesians. 1849.
„   „   its history, &c. 1849.
Power, W. T. Sketches. 1849.
Melville, H. Present state. 1850.
Fox, W. Six colonies. 1851.
Grey, G. Address to N.Z. Society. 1851.
Hursthouse, C. New Zealand. 1851.
New Zealand. 1851.
Mundy, G. C. Our Antipodes. 1852.
Shaw, J. Tramp to the diggings. 1852.
Earp, G. B. New Zealand. 1853.
Martin, R. M. British colonies. 1853.
Reise- und Lebensbilder. 1853.
Swainson, W. Auckland. 1853.
Cholmondeley, T. Ultima Thule. 1854.
Malone, R. E. Three years' cruise. 1854.
Pemberton, R. Happy colony. 1854.
Taylor, R. Te Ika a Maui. 1855, 1870.
Fitton, E. B. New Zealand. 1856.
Swainson, W. New Zealand. 1856.
Baker, A. New Zealand. 1857.
Buller, J. New Zealand. 1857.
Cooper, J. R. N.Z. settlers' guide. 1857.
D'Ewes, J. China, Australia, &c. 1857.
Hursthouse, C. New Zealand. 1857.
New Zealand in 1857.
Puseley, D. Rise and progress of Australia, &c. 1857.
Social progress. 1857.
Boyce, W. B. New Zealand. 1858.
Emigrants' manual. 1858.

New Zealand generally—*continued.*

Neu-Seeland. 1858.
Shaw, J. Gallop to Antipodes. 1858.
Sketches in N.Z. 1858.
Stones, W. New Zealand. 1858.
—— First voyage. 1858.
Fuller, F. Five years' residence. 1859.
Gill, S. G. Rambles. 1859.
Jacobs, A. Les Européens dans l'oceanie. 1859.
New Zealand—progress and resources. 1859.
Thomson, A. S. Story of N.Z. 1859.
Fox, W. War. 1860.
Mittheilungen aus N.S. 1860.
New Zealand. 1860.
    "   " and its affairs. 1860.
Notizen über N.S. 1860.
Hartwig, G. Inseln. 1860.
New Zealand. 1861.
Paul, R. B. New Zealand. 1861.
Reise der Novara. 1861.
Reminiscences of a veteran. 1861.
Schmarda, L. Reise. 1861.
Hodder, E. Memories. 1862.
New Zealand. 1862.
Swainson, W. N.Z. and the war. 1862.
Heywood, B. A. Vacation tour. 1863.
Hochstetter, F. Neu-Seeland. 1863.
Latest from N.Z. 1863.
Life in N.Z. 1863.
N.Z.—past, present, and future. 1863.
Pickering, C. Races of man. 1863.
Scherzer, K. Narrative. 1863.
Silver's guide. 1863.
First week in N.Z. 1864.
Maunoir, —. Nouvelle-Zélande. 1864.
Muter, *Mrs.* Travels. 1864.
N.Z. handbook. 1864.
Sewell, H. N.Z. rebellion. 1864.
Southern Monthly Magazine. 1864.
Carter, S. D. Life in N.Z. 1865.
Second class to N.Z. 1865.
Hoyle, F. W. Journal. 1866.
Hunt, F. Twenty-five years' experience. 1866.
Morison, J. Australia. 1867.
Thomson, *Mrs.* C. Twelve years. 1867.
Life in N.Z. 1868.
Saunders, A. New Zealand. 1868.

New Zealand generally—*continued*.

Taylor, R. Past and present. 1868.
Dilke, C. W. Greater Britain. 1869.
Bates, J. C. New Zealand. 1870.
Braim, T. H. New homes. 1870.
Meade, H. Ride through disturbed districts. 1870.
Money, C. L. Knocking about. 1871.
Baden-Powell, G. S. New homes. 1872.
Barclay, P. Notes. 1872.
Ogilvy, J. P. Facts. 1872.
Christmann, F. Oceanien. 1873.
Harrison, W. G. New Zealand. 1873.
Horne, R. H. Australia and N.Z. 1873.
Kennedy, A. New Zealand. 1873.
B., W. M. Edward Crewe. 1874.
Merewether, H. A. Sea and land. 1874.
Young, F. Past, present, and future. 1874.
All about N.Z. 1875.
Meinicke, C. E. Inseln. 1875.
Official handbook. 1875.
Fox, W. New Zealand. 1876.
Kennedy, D. Colonial travel. 1876.
Spry, W. J. Cruise. 1876.
Broomhall, J. Journey. 1877.
Hamilton, A. Economic progress. 1877.
Montégut, E. Nouvelle-Zélande. 1877.
Notes of a tour. 1877.
Pratt, W. T. Colonial experiences. 1877.
Vogel, *Sir* J. N.Z. and South Sea Islands. 1877.
Carter, C. R. Round the world. 1878.
Lindsay-Bucknall, H. Search for fortune. 1878.
Rains, F. L. By land and ocean. 1878.
Vogel, *Sir* J. Colonies and N.Z. 1878.
Clayden, A. England of the Pacific. 1879.
Hector, J. Handbook. 1879.
Hingston, J. Australian abroad. 1879.
Simmons, A. Old England and N.Z. 1879.
Wallace, A. R. Stanford's compendium. 1879.
Bathgate, J. Resources and prospects. 1880.
Brown, R. Countries of the world. 1880.
Buller, J. Past and present. 1880.
Halcombe, A. F. New Zealand. 1880.
Izett, F. W. N.Z., 1870, 1880. 1880.
Oberländer, R. N.Z. in 1879. 1880.
Senior, W. Travel and trout. 1880.
Jones-Parry, S. H. Journey. 1881.
Larkworthy, F. N.Z. revisited. 1881.

New Zealand generally—*continued*.

Mills, A. N.Z. in 1881. 1881.
Nesfield, H. W. Chequered career. 1881.
Barker, *Lady*. Travelling about. 1883.
Bradshaw, J. N.Z. as it is. 1883.
Cook, W. Wanderings. 1883.
Gisborne, W. Official handbook. 1883, 1884.
Harven, E. Nouvelle Zélande. 1883.
Gisborne, W. New Zealand. 1884.
Sala, G. A. Golden fleece. 1884.
Clayden, A. N.Z. in 1884. 1885.
Vincent, E. W. 40,000 miles. 1885.
Bonwick, J. British colonies. 1886.
Butler, A. R. Glimpses. 1886.
Froude, J. A. Oceana. 1886.
Harven, E. Mission. 1886.
Keltie, J. S. Geographical education. 1886.
Leroy-Beaulieu, P. Colonisation. 1886.
Hübner, *Baron*. British Empire. 1886.
Stout, R. Progress of N.Z. 1886.
Hoare, E. B. Notes. 1887.
Inglis, J. Our N.Z. cousins. 1887.
Sutter, A. Per mare. 1887.
Ballou, M. M. Southern Cross. 1888.
Bradshaw, J. N.Z. of to-day. 1888.
D'Avigdor, H. Antipodean notes. 1888.
Gisborne, W. Colony of N.Z. 1888.
Knox, T. W. Boy travellers. 1888.
Payton, E. W. Journal. 1888.
Petrel. Southern seas. 1888.
Brown, J. M. New Zealand. 1889.

Provinces—

S., W. H. Northern districts. 1844.
Darwin, C. Journal (Auckland). 1845.
Handbook to Otago. 1849.
Hursthouse, C. New Plymouth. 1849.
Shortland, E. Southern districts. 1851.
Rough, D. North of N.Z. 1852.
Adams, C. W. Spring in Canterbury. 1853.
Auckland and neighbourhood. 1853.
Handbook for emigrants—Auckland. 1856.
Paul, R. B. Letters from Canterbury. 1857.
Adam, G. J. Otago. 1858.
Description of Nelson; and Wellington. 1858.
Hodgkinson, S. Canterbury. 1858.
Thomson, J. T. Otago. 1859.

Classified Catalogue

Provinces—*continued.*

Provinz Otago. 1859.
Ridgway, A. F. Auckland. 1860.
Handbook of Otago. 1862.
Marshman, J. Canterbury. 1862, 1864.
Richardson, *Sir* J. Otago. 1862.
Butler, S. Canterbury. 1863.
Hochstetter, F. Nelson. 1863.
Glance at Dunedin. 1864.
Neu-Seeländische Southland. 1864.
New field for agriculture—Southland. 1867.
Pyke, V. Lost at goldfields (Otago). 1867.
Taylor, R. Wanganui. 1867.
Thomson, *Mrs.* C. Twelve years in Canterbury. 1867.
Thomson, J. T. Rambles (Otago). 1867.
Lyttelton, *Lord.* Visit to Canterbury. 1868.
Pyke, V. Otago. 1868.
Barker, *Lady.* Station life (Canterbury). 1870, 1872.
Twenty months in Southland. 1870.
Butler, S. Erewhon. 1873.
Chambers, W. Otago. 1873.
Kennedy, A. New Zealand. 1873.
Pyke, V. Wild Will Enderby (Otago). 1873.
Adam, J. Twenty-five years (Otago). 1874, 1876.
Bathgate, A. Colonial experiences (Otago). 1874.
Kennaway, L. J. Crusts (Canterbury). 1874.
Pyke, V. G. W. Pratt (Otago). 1874.
Official handbook. 1875.
Elwell, E. S. Boy colonists (Otago). 1878.
Greffrath, H. Auckland. 1878.
Wells, B. History of Taranaki. 1878.
Barr, J. Old Identities (Otago). 1879.
Barry, W. J. Up and down (Otago). 1879.
Chambers, W. Judge Bathgate's experiences. 1879.
Innes, C. L. Canterbury sketches. 1879.
Oliver, G. Homes in Otago. 1879.
Blues and Buffs. 1880. (Canterbury.)
Bathgate, A. Waitaruna. 1881.
Campbell, J. L. Poenamo (Auckland). 1881.
Cumming, C. F. G. At home in Fiji (Auckland). 1881.
Early history of Otago. 1881.
Facts relating to Canterbury. 1882.
Hay, W. D. Kaipara. 1882.
Canterbury rhymes. 1883.
McIndoe, J. Otago. 1883.
Scandrett, W. B. Southland. 1883.
Our sister cities—Dunedin. 1885.

Provinces—*continued*.

Grayling, W. I. Taranaki. 1886.
Old Identity stories (Otago). 1886.
Interesting stories about Wanganui. 1887.
Preshaw, G. O. Westland gold life. 1888.
Barlow, P. W. Kaipara. 1889.
See also **New Zealand generally.**

Adjacent islands.

Dumont d'Urville, J. Voyage pittoresque. 1834.
Rienzi, G. L. Océanie. 1838.
Dieffenbach, E. Chatham Islands. 1840.
Dumont d'Urville. Voyage. 1846.
Ross, J. C. Voyage. 1847.
Enderby, C. Auckland Islands. 1849.
Malone, R. E. Three years' cruise. 1854.
Auckland Isles. 1866.
Castaway on Auckland Islands. 1866.
Hunt, F. Twenty-five years' experience. 1866.
Travers, W. Aborigines of Chatham Islands. 1866.
Description of outlying islands. 1868.
Raynal, F. E. Auckland Isles. 1873, 1885.
Blanchard, E. Nouvelle-Zélande. 1878.
Kermadecs. 1887.
Smith, S. Percy. Kermadecs. 1887.
Gunn, J. Kermadecs. 1888.

Discovery and exploration.

Tasman, A. J. Kort verhael. 1674.
———— Journal. 1711, 1744, 1766, 1807, 1813, 1860, 1862.
Valentijn, F. Oud en niew Oost-Indien. 1724.
Brosses, C. Histoire des navigations. 1756.
Callander, J. Terra Australis cognita. 1766.
Dalrymple, A. Historical collection. 1771.
Hawkesworth, J. Cook's voyage. 1773.
Parkinson, S. Journal. 1773.
Forster, G. Voyage. 1777.
Cook, J. Second voyage. 1779.
Crozet. Voyage. 1783.
Ledyard, J. Journal. 1783.
Kippis, A. Life of Cook. 1788.
Vancouver, G. Voyage (Chatham Islands). 1801.
Rochon, A. Voyages. 1802.
Burney, J. Chronological history. 1813.
Blosseville, J. de. Voyage. 1826.
Duperrey. Voyage. 1826.
Sparks, Jared. Life of Ledyard. 1827.

Discovery and exploration—*continued.*
    Craik, G. L. New Zealanders. 1830.
    Polack, J. S. New Zealand. 1838.
    Stokes, J. L. Surveys in Middle Island. 1849, 1851.
    Brunner, T. Explorations in Middle Island. 1851.
    Stokes, J. L. Southern part of Middle Island. 1851.
    Rochfort, J. West coast of Middle Island. 1859, 1862.
    Major, R. F. Early voyages. 1859.
    Haast, J. Exploration of Nelson. 1861.
    Chapman's Magazine. 1862.
    McKerrow, J. Lake districts of Otago. 1864.
    Neueste explorationen. 1864.
    Howitt, W. History of discovery. 1865.
    Chapman's centenary memorial. 1870.
    Clarke, Marcus. Tasman. 1876.
    Blanchard, E. Nouvelle-Zélande. 1878.

Description and physical geography.
    Hawkesworth, J. Cook's voyage. 1773.
    Parkinson, S. Journal. 1773.
    Forster, J. R. Observations. 1778.
    Cook, J. Voyages. 1779, 1784.
    Crozet. Voyage. 1783.
    Nicholas, J. L. Voyage. 1817.
    Cruise, R. A. Journal. 1824.
    Hervey, T. K. Australia. 1825.
    Blosseville, J. Mémoire. 1826.
    Dumont d'Urville, J. Voyage pittoresque. 1834.
    Wakefield, E. J. British colonization. 1837.
    Polack, J. S. New Zealand. 1838.
    Lesson, R. P. Voyage. 1839.
    Description of panorama. 1840.
    New Zealand Journal. 1840–9.
    Swainson, W. Observations on climate. 1840.
    Bidwell, J. C. Rambles. 1841.
    Heaphy, C. Views. 1842.
    Wade, W. R. Journey. 1842.
    Dieffenbach, E. Travels. 1843.
    Churton, —. Letters from Wanganui. 1845.
    Wöhlers, J. F. H. Ostküste. 1846.
    Brees, S. C. Pictorial illustrations. 1847.
    Ross, J. C. Voyage. 1847.
    Guide and description of panorama. 1849.
    Sidney's Emigrant Journal. 1849.
    Cooper, G. S. Journal. 1851.
    Oliver, R. A. Lithographs. 1852.
    Martin, R. M. British colonies. 1853.

Description and physical geography—*continued*.

Rochfort, J. Adventures of a surveyor. 1853.
Richardson, *Sir* J. Summer's excursion. 1854.
Abraham, C. J. Auckland to Taranaki. 1855.
Tancred, *Sir* T. Notes on Canterbury. 1856.
Thomson, J. T. Southern districts of Otago. 1858.
Ausflug nach Mangatawhiri. 1859.
Hamel, B. L. Album. 1859.
Hochstetter's karten. 1860.
Haast, J. Hochstetter's reise. 1860.
———— Southern Alps. 1861.
Hochstetter, F. Skizze. 1862.
———— Auckland. 1862.
———— Rotomahana. 1862.
———— Neu-Seeland. 1863.
Neuseeland in geographischer hinsicht. 1866.
Blair, W. N. Cold lakes. 1867.
Golder, W. N.Z. survey. 1867.
Haast, J. Altitude sections, Canterbury. 1867.
———— Head waters of Rakaia. 1867.
Hochstetter, F. New Zealand. 1867.
M., J. K. Mary Ira. 1867.
Haynes, S. L. Ramble in the bush. 1868.
Bowden, T. A. Manual. 1869.
Haast, J. Topographical map, Southern Alps. 1870.
Whitworth, R. P. Martin's Bay. 1870.
Cooper, H. D. Lake district. 1871.
Domett, A. Ranolph and Amohia. 1872, 1883.
Engler, L. Heisse quellen. 1873.
Roots. 1873, 1878.
St. John, J. H. Rambles. 1873.
Bowen, *Sir* G. *In* Trollope, A. 1873.
Tinné, J. E. Wonderland. 1874.
Mundy, D. L. Rotomahana. 1875.
Barraud, C. D. New Zealand. 1877.
Gully, J. N.Z. scenery. 1877.
Harris, J. C. Hot-lake district. 1878.
Merivale, G. Hot lakes. 1878.
Bracken, T. N.Z. tourist. 1879.
Bunbury, C. N.Z. geysers. 1879.
Grey, J. Island home. 1879.
Martin, J. Hot springs. 1879.
Crawford, J. C. Recollections. 1880.
Toula, F. Südliche Alpen. 1880.
Carpenter, W. L. Hot springs and district. 1881.
Natural wonders of N.Z. 1881.
St. Johnston, A. Distant sketching ground. 1881.

Description and physical geography—*continued*.

Green, W. S. High Alps. 1883.
Hingston, J. N.Z. sounds. 1883.
Lendenfeld, R. Hochstetter dome. 1883.
Peale, A. C. Thermal springs. 1883.
Peek, C. E. Hot springs. 1883.
Thomas, Julian. Round about N.Z. 1883.
Kerry-Nicholls, J. H. King country. 1884.
Lendenfeld, R. Tasman-gletscher. 1884.
Maoriland. 1884.
Reinicke, G. Lyttelton. 1884.
Cowan, F. Rotomahana. 1885.
Cumming, C. F. G. Wonderland. 1885.
Forbes, A. Souvenirs. 1885.
Moreton, S. H. Scramble. 1885.
Mosley, M. Christchurch. 1885.
Strong, H. A. Western sounds. 1885.
Cassell's Picturesque Australasia. 1887.
Payton, E. W. Etchings. 1888.
Picturesque Atlas. 1889.
Drury, *Capt.* Sailing directions. p. 172.
Pownall, R. W. Guide. 1885. p. 173.
Reid, R. C. Rambles. 1886. p. 174.
Sounds, lakes, and rivers. 1885. p. 174.

Geology.

Forster, J. R. Observations. 1778.
Polack, J. S. New Zealand. 1838.
Buch, L. Vulkanische erscheinungen. 1845.
Dieffenbach, E. Geology. 1845.
Ross, J. C. Voyage. 1847.
Chapman, H. S. Earthquakes. 1848.
Dana, J. U.S. Exploring expedition. 1849.
Peppercorne, F. S. Sketches of New Ulster. 1852.
Heaphy, C. Coromandel gold-diggings. 1854.
Crawford, J. C. Port Nicholson district. 1855.
Forbes, T. Geology of N.Z. 1855.
Heaphy, C. Goldbearing district of Coromandel. 1855.
Taylor, R. Te Ika a Maui. 1855, 1870.
Hochstetter, F. Bericht über Auckland. 1859.
————— Auckland. 1859.
————— Nelson. 1859.
————— Auckland coalfields. 1859.
————— Vulkane. 1859.
Goldfelder und fossile knochen. 1860.
Heaphy, C. Volcanic Auckland. 1860.
Expeditionen in den Alpen. 1861.

Y.

Geology—*continued*.

Gold-diggings. 1861.
Haast, J. Exploration of Nelson. 1861.
Chapman's Magazine. 1862.
Goldwäschereien. 1862.
Haast's erforschung der Alpen. 1862.
Lindsay, W. L. Goldfields of Otago. 1862.
——— Goldfields of Auckland. 1862.
New Zealand and goldfields. 1862.
Otago goldfields. 1862.
Gebirge und vulcane. 1863.
Haast, J. Coal measures, Canterbury. 1863.
Haast's forschungen in den Alpen. 1863.
Hector, J. West coast of Otago. 1863, 1864.
Hochstetter, F., *u.* **Petermann,** A. Atlas. 1863, 1864.
——— Neu-Seeland. 1863.
Lindsay, W. L. Illustrations. 1863.
Geschichte der goldlager. 1864.
Haast, J. Mountains and glaciers. Canterbury. 1864.
Hochstetter, F., *and* **Petermann,** A. Geology of N.Z. 1864.
Reise der Novara :—
   Hochstetter, F. Geologie. 1864.
Taylor, R. Age of N.Z. 1864.
Whitcombe's reise. 1864.
Crawford, J. C. Geology of N. Island. 1865.
Hochstetter über die vulkane. 1865.
Neuentdeckten Canterbury-Goldfelder. 1865.
Hector, J. Coal deposits. 1866.
Goldfelder, Canterbury. 1867.
Hochstetter, F. Gletscher. 1867.
——— New Zealand. 1867.
Haast, J. Reise. 1868.
Haast's neueste forschungen in den Alpen. 1868.
New Zealand and goldfields. 1868.
Bowden, T. A. Manual. 1869.
History of Thames goldfield. 1869.
Strelitz. Tagebuch und reise. 1869.
Engler. Gold district, Shortland. 1870.
Goldfelder an der Thames. 1870.
Meinicke. Alpen. 1870.
Haast, J. Hanmer-thermen. 1871.
Nöggerath. Explorationskrater. 1871.
Geology and goldfields, Otago. 1875.
Filhol, H. Adjacent islands. 1878.
Haast, J. Canterbury and Westland. 1879.
Bramall, H. Mineral resources. 1883.
Griffith, G. S. Glacial epoch. 1885.

Geology—*continued*.

Hutton, F. W. Geology of N.Z. 1885.
Gordon, H. A. Mineral resources. 1886.
Haast, J. Mineral resources. 1886.
Handbook of mines. 1887.
Pyke, V. Otago gold discoveries. 1887.
Lendenfeld, R. Alpen. 1888.
Crawford, J. C. Reports. p. 172.
See also Trans. N.Z. Institute.

Eruption of Tarawera.

Cumming, C. F. G. 1886.
Geikie, A. 1886.
Hayden, E. 1886.
Leys, T. W. 1886.
Smith, Percy. 1886.
Hutton, F. W. 1887.
Kerry-Nicholls, J. H. 1887.
Thomas, A. P. W. 1888.

Flora.

Forster, J. R. Observations. 1778.
Richard, A. Flore de la N.Z. 1832.
Wakefield, E. J. British colonization. 1837.
Cunningham, A. Floræ N.Z. precursor. 1838.
Polack, J. S. New Zealand. 1838.
———— Manners and customs. 1840.
Colenso, W. New ferns. 1842.
Wade, W. R. Journey. 1842.
Dieffenbach, E. Travels. 1843.
Suttor, G. Grape vine. 1843.
Colenso, W. Excursion. 1844.
———— Journal. 1844.
———— Ferns. 1845.
Montagne, —. Voyage. 1845.
Raoul, E. Choix de plantes. 1846.
Hooker, J. D. Antarctic voyage. 1847, 1853.
Gray, Asa. Hooker's Flora. 1853.
Taylor, R. Te Ika a Maui. 1855, 1870.
Tancred, T. Notes on Canterbury. 1856.
Stratford, S. P. Natural history. 1857.
Bennett, G. Gatherings. 1860.
Haast, J. Exploration of Nelson. 1861.
Lindsay, W. L. Toot-poison. 1862.
———— Natural history and colonization. 1862.
Hochstetter, F. Neu-Seeland. 1863.
Hooker, J. D. Handbook. 1864.
———— Kermadec Islands. 1864.

Flora—continued.

Reise der Novara:—
  Hochstetter, F. Geologie. 1864.
Travers, W. Canterbury, Nelson, and Marlborough. 1864.
Colenso, W. Botany of N. Island. 1865.
Flora of N.Z. 1865.
Lindsay, W. L. Otago. 1865.
——— Relations of southern to northern. 1865.
Ludlam, A. Cultivation and acclimatization. 1865.
Lindsay, W. L. Lichens. 1866.
Buchanan, J. Kaikoura Mountains. 1867.
Hochstetter, F. New Zealand. 1867.
Lindsay, W. L. Protophytæ. 1867.
——— Contributions. 1868.
——— Conservation of forests. 1868.
——— Obstacles to flax. 1868.
Engler, L. Wälder. 1872.
New Zealand Country Journal. 1877.
Campbell-Walker. State forestry. 1877.
Lecoy, A. State forests. 1878, 1879.
Buchanan, J. Indigenous grasses. 1880.
Wallace, A. R. Island life. 1880.
Potts, T. H. Out in the open. 1882.
Thomson, G. M. Ferns. 1882.
Colenso, W. Ruahine Range. 1884.
Cumming, C. F. G. Kauri forests. 1884.
Hutton, F. W. Origin. 1884.
Murphy, M. N.Z. gardening. 1885.
Hetley, Mrs. Native flowers. 1888.
Featon, E. and S. Art album. 1889.
Kirk, T. Forest flora. 1889.
Hooker, W. Icones filicum. p. 173.
See also Trans. N.Z. Institute.

Fauna.

Forster, J. R. Observations. 1778.
Yate, W. Account. 1835.
Wakefield, E. J. British colonization. 1837.
Owen, R. Memoirs. 1839.
Colenso, W. Fossil bones. 1843.
Dieffenbach, F. Travels. 1843.
Mantell, G. A. Correspondence. 1843.
Voyage of Erebus and Terror. 1844.
Mantell, G. A. Fossil remains. 1848.
——— Notice of Dinornis. 1850.
——— Notice of Notornis. 1850.
Mantell, R. N. Probable age of deposits. 1850.

Fauna—*continued.*

Progress of comparative anatomy. 1852.
Thomson, A. S. Description of two caves. 1854.
Taylor, R. Te Ika a Maui. 1855, 1870.
Tancred, T. Notes on Canterbury. 1856.
Haast, J. Exploration of Nelson. 1861.
Owen, R. Pleiosaurian reptile. 1861.
Sclater, P., *and* **Hochstetter,** F. Genus Apteryx. 1861.
Note on Dinornis. 1862.
Hochstetter, F. Neu-Seeland. 1863.
Reise der Novara :—
   Hochstetter, F. Geologie. 1864.
Buller, W. L. Ornithology. 1865.
Hochstetter, F. New Zealand. 1867.
Potts, T. H. N.Z. birds. 1869.
Wilmer, G. Lowing herd. 1869.
Grey, G. Recent date of Moa. 1870.
Hector, J. Moa remains. 1871.
Hutton, F. W. Catalogue of birds. 1871.
Hector, J. Edible fishes. 1872.
Hutton, F. W. Catalogue of fishes. 1872.
Buller, W. L. History of birds. 1873, 1888.
Hutton, F. W. Land Mollusca. 1873.
———— Marine Mollusca. 1873.
———— Tertiary Mollusca. 1873.
Martens, E. Mollusca. 1873.
Annual Record (Acclimatization). 1874.
Haast, J. Researches. 1874.
Potts, T. H. Recent changes. 1874.
Miers, E. J. Crustacea. 1876.
Wallace, A. R. Geographical distribution. 1876.
Russell, I. C. Giant birds. 1877.
Owen, R. Extinct wingless birds. 1879.
Brown, T. Manual of Coleoptera. 1880.
Hutton, F. W. Mollusca. 1880.
———— Zoological exercises. 1880.
Tenison-Woods, J. E. Corals and Bryozoa. 1880.
Hutton, F. W. Diptera, &c. 1881.
Buller, W. L. Manual of birds. 1882.
Nicols, A. Acclimatization of Salmonidæ. 1882.
Quatrefages, A. Moas. 1883.
Spencer, W. B. Hatteria. 1886.
Hale, H. Giant birds. 1887.
Maskell, W. M. Scale-insects. 1887.
Mivart, St. G. Hatteria. 1887.
Kirk, T. W. Birds. 1888.

Fauna—*continued*.

Sherrin, R. A. A. Fishes. 1886.
See also Trans. N.Z. Institute.

Maoris generally.

Hawkesworth, J. Cook's voyage. 1773.
Parkinson, S. Journal. 1773.
Travels of Hildebrand Bowman. 1778.
Cook, J. Second voyage. 1779.
Crozet. Voyage. 1783.
Labillardiere, J. J. Voyage. 1800, 1802.
Collins, D. English colony in N.S. Wales. 1804.
Savage, J. Account of N.Z. 1807.
Papers of Church Missionary Society. 1816.
Nicholas, J. L. Voyage. 1817.
Cruise, R. A. Journal. 1824, 1825.
Blosseville, J. Mémoire. 1826.
Dillon, P. Voyage. 1829.
Ellis, W. Polynesian researches. 1829.
Craik, G. L. New Zealanders. 1830.
Beechey, F. W. Voyage. 1831.
Character of New Zealanders. 1832.
Earle, A. Narrative. 1832.
Breton, —. Excursions. 1833.
Dumont d'Urville, J. Voyage pittoresque. 1834.
Yate, W. Account. 1835.
Busby, J. Letter. 1837.
Bannister, S. Account. 1838.
Polack, J. S. New Zealand. 1838.
House of Lords Committee. 1838.
Rienzi, G. L. Océanie. 1838.
FitzRoy, R. Narrative. 1839.
Foster, J. Fosteriana. 1839.
Lesson, R. P. Voyage. 1839.
Manners and customs. 1839.
Polack, J. S. Manners and customs. 1840.
Dieffenbach, E. N.Z. and its native population. 1841.
Natives of N.Z. 1842.
Wade, W. R. Journey. 1842.
Dieffenbach, E. Travels. 1843.
Burns, B. Brief narrative. 1844.
Domett, A. Narrative. 1844.
Report select committee. 1844.
New Zealand. 1844.
Brown, W. N.Z. and its aborigines. 1845.
Manners and customs. 1845.
Wilkes, C. Narrative. 1845.

Maoris generally—*continued.*

Angas, G. F. New Zealanders illustrated. 1846.
——— Savage life. 1847.
McKillop, H. F. Reminiscences. 1849.
Polynesians (their decrease). 1850.
Buddle, T. Aborigines. 1851.
New Zealanders. 1851.
Shortland, E. Southern districts. 1851.
Thomson, A. S. Physique. 1853.
——— Native race. 1854.
Maoris. 1855.
Taylor, R. Te Ika a Maui. 1855, 1870.
Shortland, E. Traditions. 1856.
Tancred, T. Notes on Canterbury. 1856.
Maori und N.S. 1858.
Fenton, F. D. Observations. 1859.
Thomson, A. S. Story of N.Z. 1859.
White, J. Lectures. 1861.
Chapman's Magazine. 1862.
Maunsell, R. Fortschritte der Maori. 1862.
Among the Maoris. 1863.
Maning, F. E. Old N.Z. 1863, 1876.
Moser, T. Mahoe leaves. 1863, 1888.
Coleman, J. N. Memoir of R. Davis. 1865.
Lubbock, J. Pre-historic times. 1865.
Maori sketches. 1865.
Shortland, E. Short sketch. 1865.
Sitten- u. Rechtsansichten. 1865.
B., P. C. Two years' experience. 1866.
Industrie der Maoris. 1866.
Colenso, W. Maori races. 1869.
Maori life. 1869.
Scoffern, J. Maoris. 1869.
Wilson, G. H. Ekino. 1869.
Meade, H. Ride through disturbed districts. 1870.
Wood, J. G. Natural history. 1870.
Manning, J. Maoris. 1871.
Figuier, L. Human race. 1872.
K., J. H. Henry Ancrum. 1872.
Maoris of N.Z. 1873.
Johnstone, J. C. Maoria. 1874.
Marryat, E. Amongst the Maoris. 1874.
Spencer, H. Descriptive sociology. 1874.
White, J. Te Rou. 1874.
Wilson, G. H. Ena. 1874.
Brown, R. Races. 1875.
Week at Taupo. 1876.

Maoris generally—*continued*.

Wedderburn, D. Maoris. 1877.
White, J. Legendary history. 1880.
Hay, W. D. Brighter Britain. 1882.
Bastian, A. Inselgruppen. 1883.
Hingston, J. Among the Maoris. 1883.
Kerry-Nicholls, J. H. King country. 1884.
White, J. Maori customs. 1885.
Kerry-Nicholls, J. H. Maori race. 1886.
Maoris' fight for life. 1886.
Pennefather, F. W. Natives. 1887.
Featherman, A. Social history. 1888.

Morioris.

Travers, W. Aborigines of Chatham Islands. 1866.
Quatrefages, A. Moriori et Maori. 1873.
Hunt, W. Twenty-five years. 1866.

Maori ethnology.

Quatrefages, A. Histoire naturelle. 1864.
———— Polynésiens. 1866.
Colenso, W. Maori races. 1869.
Quatrefages, A. Moriori et Maori. 1873.
Whitmee, S. J. Polynesia. 1873.
Ranken, W. *In* N.Z. Magazine. 1876.
Fornander, A. Polynesian race. 1878.
Keane, A. H. Indo-oceanic races. 1879.
Quatrefages, A. Human species. 1879.
Purnell, C. W. Maori and moa. 1880.
Massey, G. Book of the beginnings. 1881.
Whitmee, S. J. Ethnology of Pacific. 1881.
Lesson, A. Polynésiens. 1882.
Quatrefages, A. Hommes fossiles. 1883.
Fenton, F. D. Suggestions. 1885.
Jouan, H. Nouvelle-Zélande. 1885.
Tregear, E. Aryan Maori. 1885.
Quatrefages, A. Pygmées. 1887.
See also **Maoris generally**, *and* Trans. N.Z. Institute.

Maori language.

Savage, J. Account of N.Z. 1807.
Nicholas, J. L. Voyage. 1817.
Kendall, T., *and* **Lee**, S. Grammar and vocabulary. 1820.
Yate, W. Account. 1835.
Lesson, R. P. Voyage. 1839.
Maunsell, R. Grammar. 1842.
Norris, E. Grammar. 1842, 1846.

Maori language—*continued.*

Wade, W. R. Journey. 1842.
Dieffenbach, E. Travels. 1843.
Burns, B. Narrative. 1844.
Williams, W. Dictionary and grammar. 1844.
United States Exploring Expedition. 1846.
Taylor, R. Leaf. 1848.
Pompallier, *Bishop.* Notes grammaticales. 1849.
Shortland, E. Southern districts. 1851.
Williams, W. Dictionary. 1852.
Taylor, R. Te Ika. 1855.
Shortland, E. Traditions. 1856.
Colenso, W. Maori races. 1869.
Taylor, R. Dictionary. 1870.
Williams, W. Dictionary. 1871.
Colenso, W. Dictionary. 1880.
Williams, W. L. First lessons. 1882.
Colenso, W. Literary papers. 1883.
Shortland, E. How to learn Maori. 1883.
A., S. Maori conversation. 1885.

Maori literature.

Savage, J. Account of N.Z. 1807.
Yate, W. Account. 1835.
Marshall, W. B. Personal narrative. 1836.
New Zealand Journal. 1840–52.
Dieffenbach, E. Travels. 1843.
Buddle, T. Aborigines. 1851.
Cooper, G. S. Journal. 1851.
Davis, C. O. B. Maori mementos. 1855.
Taylor, R. Te Ika. 1855, 1870.
Shortland, E. Traditions. 1856.
Grey, G. Proverbs. 1857.
Pompallier, *Bishop.* Prose et poésie. 1859.
White, J. Lectures. 1861.
Chapman's Magazine. 1862.
Hochstetter, F. Neu-Seeland. 1863.
Colenso, W. Maori races. 1869.
Domett, A. Ranolph and Amohia. 1872, 1883.
White, J. Te Rou. 1874.
Musings on *Old New Zealand.* 1877.

Maori religion.

Cruise, R. A. Journal. 1824.
Craik, G. L. New Zealanders. 1830.
Polack, J. S. New Zealand. 1838.
——— Manners and customs. 1840.

Maori religion—*continued*.

Hamlin, J. Mythology. 1842.
Wade, W. R. Journey. 1842.
Grey, G. Polynesian mythology. 1855.
Taylor, R. Te Ika a Maui. 1855, 1870.
Schirren, C. Mauimythos. 1856.
Shortland, E. Traditions. 1856.
Ely, H. Traditions of the Deluge. 1861.
Mythology of Polynesia. 1861.
White, J. Lectures. 1861.
B., P. C. Pai Mariro. 1865.
Lusk, H. Maori Mahommedanism. 1865.
Colenso, W. Fiat Justitia. 1871.
Tylor, E. B. Primitive culture. 1871.
White, J. Plan of mythology. 1878.
Hau-Haus. 1879.
Shortland, E. Maori religion. 1882.
Bastian, A. Kenntniss Hawaii's. 1883.
Lang, A. Maui myth. 1844, 1887.
Müller, Max. Maui myth. 1885.
Fenton, F. D. Suggestions. 1885.
Lang, A. Myth and ritual. 1887.
White, J. Ancient history. 1887.
See also Journals, House of Representatives, 1868, Appendix A.-4, p. 26.

Maori history.

Taylor, R. Te Ika. 1855, 1870.
Schirren, C. Wandersagen. 1856.
Buddle, T. King movement. 1860.
Gorst, J. E. Maori King. 1864.
Maning, F. E. Heke's war. 1864.
Sewell, H. N.Z. rebellion. 1864.
Fox, W. Revolt. 1865.
Gorst, J. E. Conquests. 1865.
Hursthouse, C. Letters. 1865.
Wilson, J. A. Te Waharoa. 1866.
Colenso, W. Maori races. 1869.
Travers, W. T. L. Te Rauparaha. 1872.
Ward, R. Life among Maoris. 1872.
McKay, A. Compendium. 1873.
St. John, J. H. Rambles. 1873.
Davis, C. O. Patuone. 1876.
Important judgments. 1879.
Gudgeon, T. W. History and doings. 1885.
McDonnell, T. Incidents *and* History. 1887.
White, J. Ancient history. 1887.
Hitiri. Battle of Orakau. 1888.

Maori biography.

Mowhee. Quarterly papers of C.M.S. 1816.
—— In Craik's New Zealanders. 1830.
Duaterra. In Nicholas's Voyage. 1817.
Hongi. In Craik's New Zealanders. 1830.
Tupai Cupa. In Craik's New Zealanders. 1830.
Hongi. In Polack's New Zealand. 1838.
Davis, C. O. Kawiti and other warriors. 1855.
Taylor, R. Te Ika. 1855, 1870.
Te Waharoa, by J. A. Wilson. 1866.
Te Rauparaha, by W. T. L. Travers. 1872.
Patuone, by C. O. Davis. 1876.
Te Whiti and Tohu, by J. P. Ward. 1883.

Relations with Europeans.

Turnbull, J. Voyage. 1805.
Dillon, P. Voyage. 1829.
Earle, A. Narrative. 1832.
Marshall, W. B. Personal narrative. 1836.
Coates, D., &c. Christianity. 1837.
Present state of N.Z. 1837.
Reports, Aborigines Protection Society. 1838–87.
Howitt, W. Colonization and Christianity. 1838.
Lang, J. D. N.Z. in 1839. 1839.
Hawtrey, M. Address. 1840.
Holman, J. Travels. 1840.
Coates, D. New Zealanders. 1844.
Domett, A. Wairau massacre. 1844.
Stokes, —. Wairau massacre. 1844.
Martin, S. M. D. New Zealand. 1845.
Results of N.Z. inquiry. 1845.
Wakefield, E. J. Adventure. 1845.
Martin, W. England and the New Zealanders. 1847.
Chamerovzow, L. A. N.Z. question. 1848.
Correspondence, Wesleyan Missionary Committee. 1848.
Question of aborigines. 1848.
Busby, J. Remarks. 1860.
—— Right of a colonist. 1860.
Proceedings of Kohimarama conference. 1860.
Hawtrey, M. Justice to N.Z. 1861.
FitzGerald, J. E. Native policy. 1862.
Ironside, S. N.Z. and aborigines. 1863.
Wakefield, E. J. What will they do? 1863.
Ward, Crosbie. Letter. 1863.
Address of Aborigines Protection Society. 1864.
New Zealand Government and Maori War. 1864.
Protest against confiscation. 1864.

Relations with Europeans—*continued.*

Alexander, Sir J. Notes. 1865.
FitzGerald, J. E. Letters. 1865.
Maoris und der Engländer. 1865.
Busby, J. Colonial empire. 1866.
Williams, T. C. Manawatu purchase. 1868.
────── Letter. 1873.
Rusden, G. W. History. 1883.
Stout, R. Gov. Gordon and Maoris. 1883.
Hancock, C. England u. Maori. 1885.
Rusden, G. W. Aureretanga. 1888.
See also **Missions, History, Land.**

Missions.

Quarterly papers. 1816.
Baseler Magazin. 1817.
Ellis, W. Polynesian researches. 1829.
Craik, G. L. New Zealanders. 1830.
Earle, A. Narrative. 1832.
Yate, W. Account. 1835.
Marshall, W. B. Narrative. 1836.
Coates, D., &c. Christianity. 1837.
Polack, J. S. New Zealand. 1838.
House of Lords Committee. 1838.
Wheeler, D. Letters and journal. 1838.
FitzRoy, R. Narrative. 1839.
Lang, J. D. N.Z. in 1839. 1839.
Journal of a deputation. 1840.
Letter to Lord Chichester. 1840.
Second letter to Lord Chichester. 1840.
Brief reply to Letter to Lord Chichester. 1840.
Missions of C.M.S. 1840.
Polack, J. S. Manners and customs. 1840.
Report, House of Commons Committee. 1840.
Information. 1843.
Domett, A. Narrative. 1844.
Scenes in N.Z. 1845.
Selwyn, G. A. Church and the colonies. 1845, 1846, 1847, 1849.
Marsden's missionary visits. 1846.
Church Missionary Society. 1847.
Hoole, E. Year-book. 1847.
Selwyn, C. J. *and* L. F. Annals. 1847.
Correspondence, Wesleyan Missionary Committee. 1848.
Busby, J. Letter to Lord Chichester. 1850.
Letter to Selwyn. 1850.
Richardson, J. L. C. First Christian martyr. 1851.
Hogg, M. L. Letter. 1853.

Missions—*continued*.

Strachan, A. Life of S. Leigh. 1853, 1855.
Carleton, H. Page from the history of N.Z. 1854.
────── Postscript to Page. 1854.
Christianity in Polynesia and N.Z. 1854.
Church Missionary Intelligencer. 1856.
Marsden, J. B. Memorials of S. Marsden. 1858.
Tucker, *Miss*. Southern Cross. 1858.
Young, R. Southern world. 1858.
New Zealand: a vindication. 1861.
Barrett, A. Life of Bumby. 1864.
Coleman, J. N. Memoir of R. Davis. 1865.
Murder of Volkner. 1865.
Wilson, J. A. Te Waharoa. 1866.
Williams, W. Christianity. 1867.
Christianity among New Zealanders. 1870.
Moister, W. Wesleyan missions. 1871.
Turner, J. G. Pioneer missionary. 1872.
Ward, R. Among Maoris. 1872.
Carleton, H. Life of Williams. 1874.
Yonge, C. M. Life of Patteson. 1874.
Bickford, J. Christian work. 1878.
Buller, J. Forty years. 1878.
Tucker, H. W. Memoir of Selwyn. 1879.
Armitage, J. Wesleyan mission. 1880.
Mission life. 1888.
Pompallier, *Bishop*. Catholic church. 1888.

Church.

Selwyn, G. A. Church and the colonies. 1845, 1846, 1847, 1849.
Selwyn, C. J. *and* L. F. Annals. 1847.
Selwyn, G. A. Charge. 1847, 1850.
Barclay, P. Word of Christ. 1871.
Proceedings of Synods. 1880, and Additions.
　　　　" Presbyterian Synod. 1881.
Quick, W. H. Trustees Incorporation Act. 1881.
Tucker, W. H. English church. 1886.
Cowie, W. G. Last year. 1888.
Pompallier, *Bishop*. Catholic church. 1888.
Jacobs, *Dean*. Anglican church. 1889.

History.

Despard, *Colonel*. Narrative of North campaign. 1846.
FitzRoy, R. Remarks. 1846.
Plain facts relative to war in North. 1847.
McKillop, H. F. Reminiscences. 1849.
War with the Maoris. 1850.

History—*continued.*

Brandes, C. H. Neu-Seeland. 1852.
Mundy, G. C. Our antipodes. 1852.
Collinson, T. B. Military operations. 1853.
Thomson, A. S. Story of N.Z. 1859.
Browne, Harold. Case of the war. 1860.
Hadfield, O. England's little wars. 1860.
Martin, *Sir* W. Taranaki question. 1860.
Neue Aufstand der Maori. 1860.
Taranaki. 1860.
Aylmer, J. E. Difficulty in N.Z. 1861.
Clarke, G. Remarks. 1861.
Gilbert, T. Settlers and soldiers. 1861.
Hadfield, O. Second year. 1861.
———— Sequel. 1861.
Maorikrieg. 1861.
Martin, *Sir* W. Remarks. 1861.
Memorial to Secretary of State. 1861.
New Zealand war of 1860. 1861.
Notes on *Sir* W. Martin's pamphlet. 1861.
Richmond, C. W. Memorandum. 1861.
Taranaki: a tale. 1861.
Flanagan, R. History of N.S. Wales. 1862.
Grayling, W. I. Taranaki war. 1862.
Swainson, W. N.Z. and the war. 1862.
White, W. Sergeant Marjouram. 1862.
Alexander, *Sir* J. Maori war, 1860–61. 1863.
Carey, *Colonel.* Late war. 1863.
Gorst, J. E. Maori King. 1864.
Maning, F. E. Heke's war. 1864.
Origin of N.Z. war. 1864.
Sewell, H. N.Z. rebellion. 1864.
Fox, W. Revolt. 1865.
Gorst, J. E. Conquests. 1865.
Hursthouse, C. Letters. 1865.
Remarks on the credit of N.Z. 1865.
Campaign on West Coast. 1866.
Fox, W. War. 1866.
Taylor, R. Wanganui. 1867.
Williams, W. Christianity. 1867.
Taylor, R. Past and present. 1868.
Wakefield, E. G. Founders of Canterbury. 1868.
Bourne, Fox. Story of our colonies. 1869.
Buller, J. Maori war. 1869.
Hawthorne, J. Dark chapter. 1869.
Hursthouse, C. F. N.Z. wars. 1869.
K., J. H. Henry Ancrum. 1872.

History—*continued*.

Ward, R. Among the Maoris. 1872.
Alexander, *Sir* J. Bush fighting. 1873.
Kennedy, A. New Zealand. 1873.
McKay, A. Compendium. 1873.
Carleton, H. Life of Williams. 1874.
Life and recollections of colonist. 1875.
Facsimiles of Treaty of Waitangi. 1877.
Blair, D. History of Australasia. 1878.
Blanchard, E. Nouvelle-Zélande. 1878.
Buller, J. Forty years. 1878.
Wells, B. History of Taranaki. 1878.
Heaton, J. Waikato war. 1879.
Gudgeon, T. W. Reminiscences. 1879.
Heaton, J. H. Dictionary of dates. 1879.
Tucker, H. W. Memoir of Selwyn. 1879.
Hauhau. 1880.
Scenes from life of Marmon. 1880.
Stout, R. Political parties. 1880.
Bourke, E. M. Little history. 1882.
Fox, *Sir* W. Chapter in history. 1883.
Rusden, G. W. History. 1883.
Stout, R. Governor Gordon and Maoris. 1883.
Cox, A. Recollections. 1884.
Burrows, R. Heke's war. 1886.
Wallace, J. H. Manual. 1886.
Bryce *v.* Rusden. 1887.
Early history. 1889.
See also Appendices to the Journals, House of Representatives.

Biography.

Cook, Captain. By A. Kippis. 1788.
Rutherford, John. *In* Craik's New Zealanders. 1830.
Godley, J. R. By J. E. FitzGerald. 1863.
Bumby, J. H. By A. Barrett. 1864.
Davis, Richard. By J. N. Coleman. 1865.
Turner, Rev. N. By J. G. Turner. 1872.
Williams, H. By H. Carleton. 1874.
Dieffenbach, E. By F. Dieffenbach. 1874.
Patteson, Bishop. By C. M. Yonge. 1874.
Grey, Sir G. By W. L. Rees. *In* Sir G. Leigh. 1878.
Escott, T. H. S. Pillars of the Empire. 1879.
Heaton, J. H. Men of the time. 1879.
Selwyn, Bishop. By H. W. Tucker. 1879.
Gray, M. W. By R. Stout. 1882.
Cox, A. Men of mark. 1886.
Gisborne, W. Rulers and statesmen. 1886.
Gudgeon, T. W. Defenders. 1887.

Emigration.

Alison, A. Speech. 1839, 1840.
Correspondence. 1839.
Matthew, P. Emigration fields. 1839.
Ward, J. Information. 1839.
Emigration speeches. 1840.
R., R. Australia, &c. 1840.
Rudge, J. Address. 1840.
Bright, J. Handbook. 1841.
Carpenter, W. Emigration and colonization. 1841.
Beaven, —. 1842.
Butler, S. Emigrant's Hand-book. 1843.
Randall, —. Address. 1843.
New Zealand Emigrant's Manual. 1851.
Hursthouse, C. Emigration. 1852, 1853.
New Zealand Emigration Circular. 1853.
Esquiros, A. L'Angleterre. 1862, 1863.
Hursthouse, C. Letter. 1866.
———— Remarks. 1871.
Bridges, E. T. Emigration. 1874.
Faithfull, E. Emigration. 1874.
White, J. H. Emigration. 1876.

Colonisation and settlement.

Dalrymple, A. Scheme of a voyage. 1771.
Coates, D. Principles of N.Z. Association. 1837.
Colonization of N.Z. 1837.
Wakefield, E, G. Coates and N.Z. Association. 1837.
Wakefield, E. J. British colonization. 1837.
Beecham, J. Colonization. 1838.
———— Remarks. 1838.
Chapman, H. S. Colonization. 1838.
Hinds, S. Latest documents. 1838.
Colonization of N.Z. 1839.
Instructions from N.Z. Company. 1839.
Lang, J. D. N.Z. in 1839. 1839.
Matthew, P. Emigration fields. 1839.
Molesworth, W. Lord Glenelg and the Ministry. 1839.
Popular account. 1839.
Prospectus of N.Z. Company. 1839.
Bell, F. D. N.Z. 1840.
British colonization. 1840.
Chapman, H. S. N.Z. 1840.
Colonization from Devon and Cornwall. 1840.
Reports of N.Z. Company. 1840–61.
Gipps, G. Speech. 1840.
H., G. N.Z. colonisation. 1840.

Colonisation and settlement—*continued.*

New Zealand Journal. 1840-9.
Report, House of Commons Committee. 1840.
Reybaud, L. Histoire et colonisation. 1840.
Chapman, H. S. Emigration. 1841.
────── N.Z. 1841.
Information relative to New Plymouth. 1841.
Letters from emigrants. 1841.
Birt, J. N. Chatham Islands. 1842.
Index to New Plymouth. 1842.
Fox, W. Colonization and N.Z. 1842.
Heale, T. N.Z. and the N.Z. Company. 1842.
Heaphy, C. Residence. 1842.
Latest information from New Plymouth. 1842.
Letter to J. Somes. 1842.
Mangles, R. D. How to colonize. 1842.
Petre, H. W. Settlements of N.Z. Company. 1842.
Ritter, C. Colonization. 1842.
Ward, —. Nelson. 1842.
Jennings, J. N.Z. colonization. 1843.
Letters from settlers. 1843.
Wood, J. Twelve months in Wellington. 1843.
Bridges, W. N.Z. and Ireland. 1844.
New Zealand. 1844.
Corrected report of debate, House of Commons. 1845.
Correspondence. 1845.
Few plain facts concerning Nelson. 1845.
Martin, S. M. D. New Zealand. 1845.
New Zealand Company. 1845.
Petition of N.Z. Company. 1845.
Results of N.Z. inquiry. 1845.
Wakefield, E. J. Adventure. 1845.
Affairs of N.Z. 1846.
Letter to N.Z. Company. 1846.
On British colonization. 1846.
Letters from N.Z. 1847.
Arrangements, N.Z. Company. 1848.
Otago. 1848.
Otago Journal. 1848.
Plan of Canterbury Association. 1848.
Fox, W. Report on Nelson. 1849.
Wakefield, E. G. Art of colonization. 1849.
Wakefield, F. Colonial survey. 1849.
Canterbury Association. 1849.
    „   Settlement. 1850.
Canterbury Papers. 1851, 1859.
Gouland, H. G. Proposed new colony. 1851.

Colonisation and settlement—*continued*.

Grey, G. Speech on Canterbury Block. 1851.
Wakefield, E. J. Letter to Grey. 1851.
Correspondence *re* Mr. Thomas. 1852.
Canterbury settlement. 1853.
Mutual relations of Canterbury Association, &c. 1853.
Paul, R. B. Account of Canterbury settlement. 1854.
Peel, *Sir* R. Speeches. 1854.
Busby, J. First settlers in N.Z. 1856.
Curr, E. M. Waste lands of Wellington. 1856.
List of land purchasers, Canterbury. 1856.
Waitt, R. Progress of Canterbury. 1856.
Busby, J. Colonies and colonization. 1857.
——— Pre-emptive land claims. 1859.
Canterbury Papers. Second series. 1859.
Fuller, F. Five years' experience. 1859.
Hursthouse, C. Land question. 1859.
Lyttelton, *Lord.* Canterbury colony. 1859.
Hints to colonists. 1859.
Swainson, W. N.Z. and colonization. 1859.
Thomson, A. S. Story of N.Z. 1859.
Busby, J. Illustrations. 1860.
New Zealand Company. 36th report. 1861.
Reminiscences of N.Z. 1861.
Politische eintheilung. 1862.
Deutschen ansiedler in Nelson. 1863.
Godley, J. R. Letters. 1863.
——— Writings and speeches. 1863.
Carleton, H. New Zealand. 1864.
From Auckland to Awamutu. 1864.
How we live at Awamutu. 1864.
Weld, F. A. Hints. 1864.
Hope, *Capt.* Thirty years' policy. 1865.
Middle Island. 1865.
Fox, W. Rangitikei-Manawatu purchase. 1868.
Williams, T. C. Manawatu purchase. 1868.
Wakefield, E. G. Founders of Canterbury. 1868.
Busby, J. Case. 1869.
Stewart, J. B. Kati-Kati settlement. 1877, 1878.
Blanchard, E. Nouvelle-Zélande. 1878.
Spedding, J. Reviews. 1879.
Wakelin, R. Small-farm settlements. 1879.
Across two seas. 1880.
Description of F. Louch's settlement. 1880.
Rees, W. L. East Coast Bill. 1880.
Stewart, G. V. Te Puke. 1880.
New Zealand Thermal Springs district. 1883.

Colonisation and settlement—*continued*.

Stewart, G. V. Notes, and Reply. 1883.
Duncan, A. H. Wakatipians. 1888.
Seffern, W. H. J. Early settlement. 1888.

Land.

Effect of Native Lands Acts. 1873.
Hawke's Bay Native lands. 1873.
Purnell, C. W. Agrarian law. 1874.
────── Land laws. 1876.
Cooper, R. Land purchases. 1877.
Wilson, J. A. Native Land Court. 1877.
Purnell, C. W. Agrarian law. 1878.
Thomas, E. Ryotwarry. 1878.
Land and farming. 1879.
Land question. 1879.
Barry, J. Farming in North N.Z. 1880.
Grant, S. Agricultural conditions. 1880.
Bateman, W. Colonists. 1880. *See* **1881**.
Rabbits in N.Z. 1881.
Land ho! 1883.
Pash, J. B. Report. 1883.
Farmer's views. 1886.
McLean, P. S. Native land laws. 1886.
McKay, J. Dealings with Maori lands. 1887.

Relations with Home Government.

Willis, —. Notes on N.Z. as a dependency. 1840.
Grey, *Earl*. Colonial policy. 1853.
Smith, Goldwin. Empire. 1863.
Mr. Secretary Cardwell. 1866.
Adderley, C. B. Review. 1869.
Sewell, H. Case of N.Z. 1869.
FitzGerald, J. E. Self-reliant policy. 1870.
Hursthouse, C. F. Australasian independence. 1870.
Lang, J. D. Coming event. 1870.
Sir C. Adderley on colonial policy. 1870.
See also **History**.

Government.

Petition for Hobson's recall. 1841.
Chapman, H. S. N.Z. portfolio. 1843.
Martin, S. M. D. New Zealand. 1845.
Domett, A. Petition. 1846.
FitzRoy, R. Remarks. 1846.
Busby, J. Picture of misgovernment. 1853.
Martin, R. M. British colonies. 1853.

Government—*continued.*

Grey, *Sir* G. Memorandum. 1854.
Catechism of the Constitution. 1855.
Mills, A. W. Colonial Constitutions. 1856.
Busby, J. Responsible government. 1857.
—— Federation of colonies. 1858.
Brodie, W. N.Z. and the Constitution Act. 1861.
Russell, J. Singular expedient. 1862.
Wakefield, E. J. What will they do? 1863.
Review of Southland. 1866.
Broadfoot, A. N.Z. banking. 1867.
History of local government. 1868.
Appeal to men of N.Z. 1869.
Broome, F. Crisis in N.Z. 1869.
Weld, F. A. Notes. 1869.
Denison, *Sir* W. Varieties. 1870.
Gillies, T. B. System of government. 1871.
Parliamentary skits. 1871.
Rees, W. L. Coming crisis. 1874.
Fellows, C. Financial policy. 1875.
Grey, *Sir* G. Addresses. 1875.
Macandrew, J. Address. 1875.
Native on Abolition. 1875.
Official handbook. 1875.
Politics. 1875.
Vogel, J. Finances. 1875.
Correspondence, Premier and Superintendent of Otago. 1876.
New Zealand Magazine. 1876.
Bull, W. J. Public works. 1877.
Grey, *Sir* G. Policy of the future. 1877.
Purnell, C. W. N.Z. confederation. 1877.
Treadwell, A. W. Financial statement. 1877.
Wakelin, R. History and politics. 1877.
Vogel, J. Remarks. 1877.
Wilson, A. J. British trade. 1877.
Wakefield, E. J. Taxes. 1878.
Wilson, A. J. Resources. 1878.
Ballance, J. Financial statement. 1879.
Fleming, P. Financial condition. 1879.
Moss, F. J. Assembly. 1880.
Sealy, H. J. Public works policy. 1881.
Bell, *Sir* F. D. Public debt. 1882.
Stout, R. Politics and poverty. 1883.
Fox, *Sir* W. Political crisis. 1887.
Grey, W. Poor law. 1887.
Pope, J. H. State. 1887.
See also Journals, House of Representatives, Appendix.

Industry.

Bell, F. D. Flax-cultivation. 1842.
Enderby, C. British southern whale fishery. 1847.
Hutton, F. W. N.Z. flax. 1870.
Canterbury Flax Association. 1871.
Jackson, J. R. Plants for paper-making. 1875.
Blair, W. N. Building materials of Otago. 1879.
Mulvaney, T. J. Products and manufactures. 1880.
Sheep-washing. 1881.
Tea- and silk-farming. 1881.
Tinné, T. F. Local industries. 1881.
Cochran, W. Tea- and silk-farming. 1882.
Michaëlis. Cultivation of wattle. 1882.
Silkworm-farming. 1882.
Blair, W. N. 1884, 1887.
Fischer, H. Nephrit-industrie. 1884.
Graham, W. A. Beetroot sugar. 1884.
Griffin, G. W. N.Z. resources. 1884.
Harven, E. Nouvelle-Zélande. 1884.
New Zealand prize essays. 1886.
Bonwick, J. Wool trade. 1887.
Hector, J. Phormium tenax. 1889.

Public works.

Crawford, J. C. Remarks. 1861.
Telegraphen-linien. 1866.
Henderson, J. Brogden's proposal for railways. 1873.
Adams, Acton. Nelson railway. 1878.
Suter, *Bishop.* Nelson railway. 1878.
Report on Otago Central Railway. 1881.
Vaile, S. Position and prospects. 1886.
Wakefield, F. Surveying. 1849.
Dawson, R. K. Surveying. 1840.
Thomson, J. T. Survey system of Otago. 1875.
Dobson, E. Public works of Canterbury. 1869.
Jervois, *Sir* W. Defence of N.Z. 1884.

Education.

Bowden, T. A. Memorial. 1868.
Taylor, W. Letters. 1870.
New Zealand Magazine. 1876, 1877.
Report of Royal Commission on University. 1879.
Stout, R. Address. 1879.
Primary instruction. 1881.
Smeaton, W. District high schools. 1883.
Stout, R. Waifs and strays. 1885.
────── Statement. 1885.
Dale, R. W. Impressions. 1889.

Libraries.
Grey, *Sir* G. Address. 1883.
Greenwood, T. Free libraries. 1886.
Holgate, C. W. Chief libraries. 1886.
———— Auckland. 1886.

Health resorts.
Ginders, A. Rotorua. 1885.
Lewis, T. H. Rotorua. 1885.
Spencer, W. I. Napier. 1885.
Bonwick, J. Climate and health. 1886.

Statistics.
Grimstone, S. E. Southern settlements. 1847.
Thomson, A. S. Auckland. 1851.
———— New Munster. 1851.
Palacky, J. Statistik. 1858.
Fenton, F. D. Observations. 1859.
Fyfe, J. H. Census. 1862.
Bevölkerungsstatistik. 1865.
Census of 1867. 1868.
Hamilton, A. Economic progress. 1869.
See also Journals, House of Representatives, Appendix.

Bibliography.
Wakefield, E. J. British colonization. 1837.
New Zealand Journal. 1840–52.
Wakefield, E. J. Handbook. 1848.
Grey, *Sir* G., *and* **Bleek,** W. Catalogue. 1858.
Thomson, A. S. Story of N.Z. 1859.
Hochstetter, F. Neu-Seeland. 1863.
———— Geologie. 1864.
Catalogue, G.A. Library. 1866.
Lindsay, W. L. Contributions to Botany. 1868.
Centenaire de Cook. 1879.
Hay, W. D. Brighter Britain. 1882.
Grey, *Sir* G. Address. 1883.
Petherick, E. A. Silver's library. 1886.
Carter, C. R. Catalogue. 1887.
Davis, J. D. Contributions. 1887.
General Catalogue, Grey Library, Auckland. 1888.

Short Classified List.

General.
Thomson, A. S. Story of New Zealand. 1859.
Taylor, Richard. Te Ika a Maui. Second edition. 1870.
Gisborne, W. Colony of New Zealand. 1888.

Descriptive.
Hector, Sir J. Handbook to New Zealand. Fourth ed. 1886.
Official handbook of New Zealand. [By W. Gisborne.] Edited by the Agent-General. 1883–4.

Geography.
Bowden, T. A. Manual of New Zealand geography. 1869.

Geology.
Geological Survey of New Zealand: reports.

Mineralogy.
Handbook of New Zealand mines. 1887.

Flora.
Hooker, Sir J. D. Handbook of the New Zealand flora. 1864.

Fauna.
Owen, Sir R. Extinct wingless birds of New Zealand. 1879.
Buller, Sir W. L. Manual of the birds of New Zealand. 1882.
———— History of the birds of New Zealand. Second ed. 1888.

Maoris.
Maning, F. E. Old New Zealand. 1876.
White, J. Te Rou. 1874.

Maori Language.
Maunsell, R. Grammar. 1882.
Shortland, E. How to learn Maori. 1883.
Williams, W. Dictionary. Third ed. 1871.

Maori Mythology.
Grey, Sir G. Polynesian mythology. 1885.
White, J. Ancient history of the Maori. *In progress.*

History.
Rusden, G. W. History of New Zealand. 1883.
Gisborne, W. New Zealand rulers and statesmen. 1886.

Church.
Tucker, H. W. Memoir of the life and episcopate of Bishop Selwyn. 1879.

Part 3.—Alphabetical Catalogue.

A.—Authors.

Abraham, C. J. Journal of a walk from Auckland to Taranaki. 1855.
Acton, R. Our colonial empire. 1881.
Adam, G. J. Description of Otago. 1858.
Adam, J. Twenty-five years in the south of New Zealand. 1874, 1876.
Adams, C. W. Spring in Canterbury. 1853.
Adams, W. Acton. Nelson and West Coast Railway. 1878.
Adderley, *Sir* C. Review of Earl Grey's *Colonial policy*. 1869.
Alexander, *Sir* J. E. Bush fighting. 1873.
————— Incidents of the Maori war. 1863.
————— Notes on the Maoris. 1865.
Alison, *Sir* A. Principles of population. 1840.
————— Speech at Glasgow. 1839.
Angas, G. F. New Zealanders illustrated. 1846.
————— Savage life and scenes in Australia and New Zealand. 1847.
Armitage, J. Wesleyan mission in New Zealand. 1880.
Aubert, *Sister*. Manual of Maori conversation. 1885.
Awdry, F. Life of Bishop Patteson. 1860.
Aylmer, I. E. Difficulty in New Zealand. 1861.

B., P. C. Two years' experience of the Maoris. 1866.
————— Pai Marire. 1865.
B., W. M. Narrative of Edward Crewe. 1874.
Baden-Powell, G. S. New homes for the old country. 1872.
Baker, A. New Zealand compared with Great Britain. 1857.
Bannister, S. Changes and present condition of New Zealand. 1838.
Ballance, J. Financial statement. 1879.
Ballou, M. M. Under the Southern Cross. 1888.
Barclay, P. Notes on New Zealand. 1872.
————— Word of Christ in New Zealand. 1871.
Barker, *Lady*. Christmas cake. 1872.
————— Station life in New Zealand. 1870.
————— Travelling about over new and old ground. 1883.
Barlow, P. W. Kaipara. 1889.
Barr, James. Old identities. 1879.
Barr, John. Poems and songs. 1871. P. 172.
Barraud, C. D., *and* **Travers**, W. T. L. N.Z.: graphic and descriptive. 1877.
Barrett, A. Life of the Rev. J. H. Bumby. 1864.
Barrow, J. Australasia. 1824.
Barry, W. J. Up and down. 1879.
Bastian, A. Inselgruppen in Oceanien. 1883.

Authors

Bastian, A. Zur kenntniss Hawaii's. 1883.
Bateman, W. The colonists. 1880.
Bates, J. C. New Zealand. 1870.
Bathgate, Alexander. Colonial experience. 1874.
—— Waitaruna. 1881.
Bathgate, John. New Zealand : its resources and prospects. 1880.
Bayliss, D. Glimpse of shepherd life in New Zealand. 1866.
Beaven, ——. Narrative of a voyage to New Zealand. 1842.
Beecham, J. Colonization. 1838.
—— Remarks on official documents relating to N.Z. 1838.
Beechey, F. W. Voyage to the Pacific and Beering's Strait. 1831.
Beheim-Schwarzbach, Br. Maoris. 1881, 1882.
Bell, *Sir* F. D. New Zealand. 1840.
—— Public debt of Australasia. 1882.
—— *and* **Young**, F. Cultivation of N.Z. flax. 1842.
Bennett, G. Gatherings of a naturalist. 1860.
Berggren, S. Besög i de vulkanske egne paa Ny Zeeland. P. 172.
Berry, J. Farming in north New Zealand. 1880.
Besant, W. Captain Cook. *Announced.*
Best, A. D. Excursion into the interior of the Northern Island. P. 172.
Bickford, J. Christian work in Australia. 1878.
Bidwill, J. C. Rambles in New Zealand. 1841.
Birt, J. N. Colonisation of Chatham Islands. 1842.
Blair, D. History of Australasia. 1878.
Blair, J. Lays of the old identities. 1889.
Blair, W. N. Building materials of Otago. 1879.
—— Cold lakes of New Zealand. 1867.
—— Industries of New Zealand. 1884, 1887.
Blanchard, E. Nouvelle-Zélande. 1878.
Blosseville, J. Mémoire géographique sur Nouvelle-Zélande. 1826.
—— Voyage du capitaine Edwardson. 1826.
Bonwick, J. The British colonies and their resources. 1886.
—— Climate and health in Australasia. 1886.
—— Romance of the wool trade. 1887.
Bools, A. Life and travels on sea and land. 1880.
Bourke, E. M. Little history of New Zealand. 1882.
Bourne, H. R. Fox. Story of our colonies. 1869.
Bowden, T. A. Manual of New Zealand geography. 1869.
—— Memorial upon colonial education. 1868.
Bowen, C. C. Poems. 1861.
Bowen, *Sir* G. F. Inaugural address. 1868.
Boyce, W. B. New Zealand. 1858.
Bracken, T. Lays of the land of the Maori and Moa. 1884.
—— New Zealand tourist. 1879.
Bradshaw, J. New Zealand as it is. 1883.
—— New Zealand of to-day. 1888.
Braim, T. H. New homes. 1870.

Bramall, H. Mineral resources of New Zealand. 1883.
Brandes, C. H. Neu-Seeland in geschichtlichen umrissen. 1852.
Brees, S. C. Pictorial illustrations of New Zealand. 1847.
Breton, *Lieut.* Excursions in New South Wales, &c. 1833.
Bridges, E. T. Emigration to New Zealand. 1874.
Bridges, W. New Zealand and Ireland. 1844.
Bright, J. Handbook for N.Z. emigrants. 1841.
———— State and prospects of N.Z. 1841.
Broadfoot, A. New Zealand, its banking and currency. 1867.
Brodie, W. New Zealand and the Constitution Act. 1861.
———— Past and present state of New Zealand. 1845.
Broome, *Sir* F. N. Crisis in New Zealand. 1869.
———— New Zealand snow-storm. P. 172.
———— Poems from New Zealand. 1868.
Broomhall, J. Journey in New Zealand. 1877.
Brosses, C. *de*. Histoire des navigations. 1756.
Broun, T. Manual of the New Zealand Coleoptera. 1880.
Brown, J. K. Protective policy. 1880.
Brown, J. M. New Zealand. 1889.
Brown, R. Countries of the world. 1880.
———— Races of mankind. 1875.
Brown, W. New Zealand and its aborigines. 1845.
Browne, E. H. Case of the war in New Zealand. 1860.
Bruck, L. Guide to the health resorts in Australia. P. 172.
Brunner, T. Explorations in the Middle Island of New Zealand. 1851.
Buch, L. Vulkanische erscheinungen auf Neu-Seeland. 1845.
Buchanan, J. Botanical notes, Kaikoura Mountains and Mt. Egmont. 1867.
———— Indigenous grasses of New Zealand. 1880.
———— Manual of the indigenous grasses. 1880.
Buddle, T. Aborigines of New Zealand. 1851.
———— Maori King movement. 1860.
Bull, W. J. Public works in New Zealand. 1877.
Buller, J. Forty years in New Zealand. 1878.
———— Maori war. 1869.
———— New Zealand: the future England. 1857.
———— New Zealand: past and present. 1880.
Buller, *Sir* W. L. Address as counsel for the Ngatiapa. 1882.
———— Essay on the ornithology of New Zealand. 1865.
———— History of the birds of New Zealand. 1873, 1888.
———— Manual of the birds of New Zealand. 1882.
Bunbury, Clement. Visit to the New Zealand geysers. 1879.
Burney, J. Chronological history of voyages and discoveries. 1813.
Burns, Barnet. Brief narrative of a New Zealand chief. 1844.
Burrows, R. Diary kept during Heke's war. 1886.
Busby, J. Authentic information relative to New Zealand. 1832.
———— Case of Mr. Busby. 1869.
———— Colonies and colonization. 1857.

Busby, J. Federation of colonies. 1858.
———— First settlers in New Zealand. 1856.
———— Illustrations of responsible government. 1860.
———— Letter to the Colonial Secretary of New South Wales. 1887.
———— Letter to the Earl of Chichester. 1850.
———— Our colonial empire. 1866.
———— Picture of misgovernment and oppression. 1853.
———— Pre-emptive land claims. 1859.
———— Remarks on "The Taranaki Question." 1860.
———— Responsible government. 1857.
———— Right of a British colonist. 1860.
Butler, Annie R. Glimpses of Maori land. 1886.
Butler, S. Emigrant's hand-book. 1843.
Butler, Samuel. Erewhon. 1873.
———— First year in Canterbury settlement. 1863.
Byrne, J. C. Twelve years' wanderings in the British colonies. 1848.

Callander, J. Terra australis cognita. 1766.
Campbell, E. Present state, resources, and prospects. 1840.
Campbell, J. L. Poenamo. 1881.
Campbell-Walker, *Capt*. State forestry. 1877.
Carey, *Col*. Narrative of the late war. 1863.
Carleton, H. Life of Henry Williams. 1874.
———— New Zealand. 1864.
———— Page from the history of New Zealand. 1854.
———— Postscript to *A page from the history of New Zealand*. 1854.
Carpenter, W. Emigration and colonization. 1841.
Carpenter, W. L. Hot-lake district and the glacier scenery and fiords. 1881.
———— Siliceous and other hot springs. 1881.
Carter, C. R. Catalogue of books. 1887.
———— Round the world leisurely. 1878.
Carter, S. D. Life in New Zealand. 1865.
Cawkwell, W. J. Local industry and the Government. 1874.
Chambers, W. Judge Bathgate's experiences. 1880.
———— Word about Otago. 1873.
Chamerovzow, L. A. New Zealand question. 1848.
Chapman, *Mr. Justice*. Colonization of New Zealand. 1838.
———— Earthquakes in New Zealand. 1848.
———— Emigration. 1841.
———— New Zealand. 1840, 1841.
———— *and others*. New Zealand portfolio. 1843.
Cholmondeley, T. Ultima Thule. 1854.
Christmann, Fr., *u*. **Oberländer**, R. Oceanien. 1873.
Churton, —. Letters from Wanganui. 1845.
Clarke, G. Remarks on a pamphlet by J. Busby. 1861.
Clarke, G. M. Resources of New Zealand. 1870.
Clarke, Marcus. Abel Jansen Tasman. 1876.

Alphabetical Catalogue

Clayden, A. England of the Pacific. 1879.
———— New Zealand in 1884. 1885.
Coates, D. New Zealanders and their lands. 1844.
———— Principles, objects, and plan of the N.Z. Association. 1837.
Coates, D., **Beecham,** J., *and* **Ellis,** W. Christianity the means of civilization. 1837.
Cochran, W. Tea- and silk-farming in New Zealand. 1882.
Coleman, J. N. Memoir of the Rev. Richard Davis. 1865.
Colenso, W. Account of some onormous fossil bones. 1843, 1844.
———— Account of visits to the Ruahine Range. 1884.
———— Ancient tide lore. *In the press.*
———— Classification and description of newly-discovered ferns. 1845.
———— Description of some new ferns. 1842.
———— Essay on the botany of the North Island. 1865.
———— Excursion in the Northern Island. 1844.
———— Fiat justitia. 1871.
———— Fifty years ago in New Zealand. 1888.
———— Journal of a naturalist. 1844.
✓ ———— On the Maori races. 1869.
———— Specimen dictionary. 1880.
———— Three literary papers. 1883.
Collins, D. English colony in New South Wales. 1804.
Collinson, T. B. Military operations in New Zealand. 1853.
Cook, J. Voyage towards the South Pole. 1779.
———— Voyage to the Pacific Ocean. 1784.
Cooper, G. S. Expedition from Auckland to Taranaki. 1851.
Cooper, H. T. Lake district. 1871.
Cooper, I. R. New Zealand settlers' guide. 1857.
Cooper, R. Land purchases on the East Coast. 1877.
Coote, Walter. Wanderings, south and east. 1883.
Cowan, F. Fact and fancy in New Zealand. 1885.
Cowie, W. G. Last year in New Zealand. 1888.
Cox, A. Men of mark of New Zealand. 1886.
———— Recollections. 1884.
Craik, G. L. New Zealanders. 1830.
Crawford, J. C. Essay on the geology of the North Island. 1865.
———— Geological reports. P. 172.
———— On the geology of Port Nicholson district. 1855.
———— Recollections of travel in New Zealand. 1880.
———— Remarks upon railways. 1861.
Crozet, —. Nouveau voyage à la mer du Sud. 1783.
Cruise, R. A. Ten months' residence in New Zealand. 1824.
Cumming, C. F. G. At home in Fiji. 1881.
———— Eruption of Mount Tarawera. 1886.
———— Kauri forests of New Zealand. 1884.
———— New Zealand in blooming December. 1884.
———— Wonderland of New Zealand. 1885.

Authors

Cunningham, A. Floræ insularum Novæ Zelandiæ precursor. 1838.
Curr, E. M. Waste lands of Wellington. 1856.
Curteis, G. H. Augustus Selwyn, Bishop of New Zealand. *Announced.*
Curteis, Mrs. G. H. Sketch of the life of Bishop Selwyn. 1878. P. 172.

Dale, R. W. Impressions of Australia. 1889.
Dalrymple, A. Historical collection of voyages. 1770.
——— Scheme of a voyage. 1771.
Dana, J. United States exploring expedition. 1849.
Darwin, C. Journal of researches. 1845.
D'Avigdor, H. Antipodean notes. 1888.
Davis, C. O. Life and times of Patuone. 1876.
——— Maori mementos. 1855.
——— Renowned chief Kawiti. 1855.
Davis, J. D. Bibliography of New Zealand. 1887.
Denison, Sir W. Varieties of vice-regal life. 1870.
Despard, Col. Narrative of the North Campaign. 1846-7.
D'Ewes, J. China, Australia, and the Pacific. 1857.
Dieffenbach, E. Account of the Chatham Islands. 1840.
——— New Zealand and its native population. 1841.
——— On the geology of New Zealand. 1845.
——— Travels in New Zealand. 1843.
Dieffenbach, F. Ernst Dieffenbach, der erforscher Neu-Seelands. 1874.
Dilke, Sir C. W. Greater Britain. 1869.
Dillon, P. Voyage in the South Seas. 1829.
Dixon, G. Voyage round the world. 1789.
Dobson, E. Public works of Canterbury. 1869.
Domett, A. Narrative of the Wairau massacre. 1844.
——— Petition to Parliament. 1846.
——— Ranolf and Amohia. 1872, 1883.
Donlan, —. Letter to absentee landlords. 1844.
Droze, G. Krieg in Neuseeland. p. 172.
Drury, Capt. Revised sailing directions. 1854. P. 172.
Dumont-d'Urville, J. Voyage au Pôle Sud. 1846.
——— Voyage pittoresque autour du monde. 1834.
——— *See also* **Richard** and **Quoy**.
Duncan, A. H. Wakatipians. 1888.
Duperrey, A. Voyage autour du monde. 1826.
Du Petit-Thouars, A. Voyage autour du monde. 1840, 1841.

Earle, A. Narrative of a residence in New Zealand. 1832.
Earp, G. B. New Zealand. 1853.
Eley, H. Traditions of the Deluge. 1861.
Ellis, W. Polynesian researches. 1829.
Elwell, E. S. Boy colonists. 1878.
Enderby, C. Auckland Islands. 1849.
——— Proposal for re-establishing the southern whale fishery. 1847.

Engler, L. Besuch bei den Hoisson Quellen. 1873.
———— Golddistrict Shortland. 1870.
———— Neuseelands wälder. 1872.
Escott, T. H. S. Pillars of the Empire. 1879.
Esquiros, A. Angleterre et la vie anglaise. 1862.
———— English at home. 1863.
Etonian. New Zealand: a poem. 1842.
Evans, C. Strange friendship. 1874.
———— Over the hills and far away. 1874.

Faithfull, Emily. Emigration to New Zealand. 1874.
Featherman, A. Social history of mankind. 1888.
Featon, E. H. *and* S. Art album of New Zealand flora. 1889.
Fellows, C. Financial policy of New Zealand. 1875.
———— Rejoinder on the debts of New Zealand. 1875.
✓**Fenton,** F. D. Native race of New Zealand. 1860.
———— Observations on the aboriginal inhabitants. 1859.
———— Suggestions for a history of the Maori people. 1885.
✓**Figuier,** L. Human race. 1872.
Filhol, H. Report on geology of Campbell, Auckland, and Stewart Islands. 1878.
✓**Finsch,** —. Reise nach Neuseeland. 1881.
Fischer, H. Nephrit-industrie der Maoris. 1884.
Fitton, E. B. New Zealand. 1856.
FitzGerald, J. E. Native policy of New Zealand. 1862.
———— Present state of Maori affairs. 1865.
———— Self-reliant policy in New Zealand. 1870.
Fitz Roy, R. Remarks on New Zealand. 1846.
———— Surveying voyages of Adventure and Beagle. 1839.
Flanaghan, R. History of New South Wales. 1862.
Fleming, P. Financial condition of New Zealand. 1879.
Forbes, Arch. Souvenirs of some continents. 1885.
Forbes, C. Geology of New Zealand. 1855.
✓**Fornander,** A. Account of the Polynesian race. 1878.
Forster, G. Voyage round the world. 1777.
Forster, J. R. Observations during a voyage round the world. 1778.
Foster, J. Fosteriana. 1858. *See* **1839.**
Fox, A. Lane. Use of the New-Zealand mere. 1870.
Fox, *Sir* W. Chapter in the history of New Zealand. 1883.
———— Colonization and New Zealand. 1842.
———— New Zealand. 1876.
———— Political crisis. 1887.
———— Rangitikei-Manawatu purchase. 1868.
———— Revolt in New Zealand. 1865.
———— Settlement of Nelson. 1849.
———— Six colonies of New Zealand. 1851.
———— War in New Zealand. 1866.
Fritsch, G. Haast's notes on rock-paintings. 1880.

Froude, J. A. Oceana. 1886.
Fuller, F. Five years' residence. 1859.
Fyfe, J. H. Census of New Zealand. 1862.

Geikie, A. Recent volcanic eruption in New Zealand. 1886.
✓**Geisler,** W. Bilder aus Neu-Seeland. 1887.
✓**Gerland,** G. Anthropologie der naturvölker. P. 173.
Gibb, *Sir* D. Pata-patoo from New Zealand. 1872.
Gilbert, T. New Zealand settlers and soldiers. 1861.
Gillies, T. B. Our system of government. 1871.
Ginders, A. Thermal-springs, Rotorua. 1885.
Gill, S. G. Rambles in New Zealand. 1859.
Gipps, *Sir* G. New Zealand Land Bill. 1840.
Gisborne, W. Colony of New Zealand. 1888.
——— New Zealand. 1884.
——— New Zealand rulers and statesmen. 1886.
——— Official handbook of New Zealand. 1883, 1884.
Godley, J. R. Letters to C. B. Adderley. 1863.
——— Selection from the writings and speeches. 1863.
Golder, W. New Zealand minstrelsy. 1852.
——— New Zealand survey. 1867.
Gordon, H. A. Gold, coal, and other known mineral resources. 1886.
Gorst, J. E. Conquests in New Zealand. 1865.
——— Maori king. 1864.
Gouland, H. G. Plan of a proposed new colony. 1851.
Graham, W. A. Beetroot sugar manufacture. 1884.
Grant, S., *and* **Foster,** J. S. New Zealand. 1880.
Gray, A. Hooker's Flora of New Zealand. 1853.
Grayling, W. I. Taranaki and its resources. 1886.
——— War in Taranaki. 1862.
Green, W. S. Fels- u. gletscherspuren am Mount Cook. 1883.
——— High Alps of New Zealand. 1883.
——— Reise in die Neuseeländischen Alpen. 1882.
Greenwood, T. Free public libraries. 1886.
Greenwood, *Major*. Journey to Taupo. 1850. P. 173.
Greffrath, H. Provinz Auckland. 1878.
Grey, *Earl*. Colonial policy of Russell's Administration. 1853.
Grey, *Sir* G. Addresses at Auckland. 1875.
——— Address to the New Zealand Society. 1851.
——— Auckland Free Public Library: address. 1883.
——— England and the New Zealanders. 1847.
——— Memorandum on Lord Lyttelton's letter. 1854.
——— Policy of the future. 1877.
——— Polynesian mythology. 1855, 1885.
——— Proverbial and popular sayings. 1857.
——— Recent date of the Moa. 1870.
——— Speech on Canterbury block. 1851.

215

Grey, *Sir G., and* **Bleek,** W. H. I. Grey library, Capetown. 1858.
Grey, J. His island home ; and Away in the far north. 1879.
Grey, W. Charity and poor law in New Zealand. 1887.
Griffin, G. W. New Zealand : her commerce and resources. 1884.
Griffiths, G. S. Glacial epoch in the Southern Hemisphere. 1855.
Grimstone, S. E. Southern settlements of New Zealand. 1847.
Gudgeon, T. W. Defenders of New Zealand. 1887.
———— History and doings of the Maoris. 1885.
———— Reminiscences of the war. 1879.
Gully, J., *and* **Haast,** *Sir* J. New Zealand scenery. 1877.
Gunn, J. Kermadec Islands. 1888.

H., G. New Zealand colonisation. 1840.
Haast, *Sir* J. Coal measures and lignitiferous beds of the Kowai. 1863.
———— Geology of Canterbury and Westland. 1879.
———— Headwaters of the Rakaia. 1866.
———— Hochstetter's reise durch die nördliche Insel. 1860.
———— Mineral resources of New Zealand. 1886.
———— Mountains and glaciers of Canterbury. 1864.
———— Notes on map of Southern Alps. 1870.
———— Physical geography of New Zealand. 1861.
———— Prehistoric remains. 1870.
———— Principal routes across the Southern Alps. 1867.
———— Reise nach den goldfeldern der Westküste. 1868.
———— Researches and excavations. 1874.
———— Southern Alps. 1864.
———— Thermen der Hanmer-Ebene. 1871.
———— Topographical and geological exploration of Nelson. 1861.
Hadfield, O. Ahab's crimes and the Maungatapu murders. 1866.
———— One of England's little wars. 1860.
———— Sequel to " One of England's little wars." 1861.
———— Second year of one of England's little wars. 1861.
Halcombe, A. F. New Zealand. 1880.
Hale, H. Giant birds of New Zealand. 1887.
Hamel, B. L. Album of photographic views. 1859.
Hamilton, A. Economic progress of New Zealand. 1869.
———— Recent economic progress of New Zealand. 1877.
Hamlin, J. Mythology of the New Zealanders. 1842.
Hancock, C. England und die Maori. 1885.
Harris, J. Navigantium atque itinerantium bibliotheca. 1744.
Harris, J. C. Southern guide to the Hot-lake District. 1878.
Harrison, W. G. New Zealand. 1873.
Hartwig, G. Inseln des grossen oceans. 1861.
Harven, E. *de*. Mission commerciale en Nouvelle-Zélande. 1886.
———— Nouvelle Zélande au point de vue économique. 1884.
———— Nouvelle Zélande : histoire, géologie, climat, etc. 1883.
Hawkesworth, J. Voyages in the Southern Hemisphere. 1773.

Hawkins, R. S. Poor law in New Zealand. 1889.
Hawthorne, J. Dark chapter from New Zealand history. 1869.
Hawtrey, Montague. Earnest address to New Zealand colonists. 1840.
——— Justice to New Zealand. 1861.
Hay, W. D. Brighter Britain. 1882.
Hayden, E. Eruption in New Zealand in 1886. 1886.
Haynes, S. L. Ramble in the New Zealand bush. 1868.
Heale, Theophilus. New Zealand and the New Zealand Company. 1842.
Heaphy, C. Coromandel gold diggings. 1854, 1855.
——— Residence in various parts of New Zealand. 1842.
——— Views of the settlements in New Zealand. 1842.
——— Volcanic country of Auckland. 1860.
Heaton, J. H. Australian dictionary of dates. 1879.
Heaton, John. The Waikato war, 1863-4. 1879.
Hector, *Sir* J. Certain early forms of stone instruments. 1876.
——— Coal deposits of New Zealand. 1866.
——— Geological expedition to the west coast of Otago. 1863, 1864.
——— Handbook of New Zealand. 1879.
——— Neue Moa-funde in Neuseeland. 1871.
——— Notes on the edible fishes. 1872.
——— Phormium tenax as a fibrous plant. 1889.
——— Recent Moa remains in New Zealand. 1871.
Henderson, *Capt.* Otago and the Middle Island. 1866.
Henderson, J. John Brogden and Sons' proposal. 1873.
Hervey, T. K. Australia; with other poems. 1825.
Hetley, *Mrs.* Native flowers of New Zealand. 1888.
Heywood, B. A. Vacation tour at the Antipodes. 1863.
Hinds, S. Latest official documents relating to New Zealand. 1838.
Hingston, J. Among the Maoris. 1883.
——— Australian abroad. 1879.
——— New Zealand sounds. 1883.
Hitiri te Paerata. Battle of Orakau. 1888.
Hoare, E. Brodie. Notes on New Zealand. 1887.
Hochstetter, F. Coalfields in the Drury and Hunua district. 1859.
——— Franz-Joseph-gletscher. 1867.
——— Geographische skizze von Neu-Seeland. 1862.
——— Geologie von Neu-Seeland. 1864.
——— Geology of the Province of Auckland. 1859.
——— Geology of the Province of Nelson. 1859.
——— Geolog. untersuchungen in der Provinz Auckland. 1859.
——— Isthmus von Auckland. 1862.
——— Neu-Seeland. 1863.
——— New Zealand. 1867.
——— Provinz Nelson. 1863.
——— Rotomahana oder der warme see. 1862.
——— Vulkane Neu-Seelands. 1859.
——— *and* **Petermann,** A. Geological and topographical atlas. 1664.

Hochstetter, F., *and* **Petermann,** A. Geologisch-topographischer atlas. 1863.
————— Geology of New Zealand. 1864.
Hodder, E. Memories of New Zealand life. 1862.
Hodgkinson, S. Description of the Province of Canterbury. 1858.
Hodgskin, R. Eight months' sojourn in New Zealand. 1841.
Hogg, Lewis M. Letter to the Duke of Newcastle. 1853.
Holgate, C. W. Account of the chief libraries of New Zealand. 1886.
————— Auckland Free Public Library. 1886.
Holman, J. Travels in China, New Zealand, &c., &c. 1840.
Hooker, *Sir* J. D. Botany of the Antarctic voyage. 1847, 1853.
————— Handbook of the New Zealand flora. 1864.
————— List of plants in the Kermadec Islands. 1864.
Hooker, *Sir* W. J., *and* **Greville,** R. K. Icones filicum. 1829-31. P. 173.
Hoole, E. Year-book of missions. 1847.
Hope, *Capt.* Thirty years' policy in New Zealand. 1865.
Horne, R. H. Australia and New Zealand. 1873.
Howitt, W. Colonization and Christianity. 1838.
————— History of discovery in Australia, &c. 1865.
Hoyle, F. W. Fragments of a journal. 1868.
Hübner, *Baron.* Through the British Empire. 1886.
Hunt, F. Twenty-five years' experience in New Zealand. 1866.
Hursthouse, C. Account of the settlement of New Plymouth. 1849.
————— Emigration fields contrasted. 1853.
————— Emigration: where to go, and who should go. 1852.
————— England's New Zealand war. 1865.
————— Letter to the Hon. E. W. Stafford. 1866.
————— Letters on New Zealand subjects. 1865.
————— New Zealand, or Zealandia. 1857.
————— Remarks on New Zealand immigration. 1871.
————— The New Zealand land question. 1859.
Hursthouse, C., *jun.* New Zealand: the emigration field of 1851. 1851.
Hursthouse, C. F. Australasian independence. 1870.
————— Case of New Zealand. 1869.
————— New Zealand wars. 1869.
Hutton, F. W. Catalogue of the birds of New Zealand. 1871.
————— Catalogues of the Diptera, Orthoptera, Hymenoptera. 1881.
————— Catalogue of the Echinodermata of New Zealand. 1872.
————— Catalogue of Fishes. 1872.
————— Catalogue of the Land Mollusca. 1873.
————— Catalogue of the Marine Mollusca. 1873.
————— Catalogue of the Tertiary Mollusca. 1873.
————— Manual of the New Zealand Mollusca. 1880.
————— Manufacture of New Zealand flax. 1870.
————— Origin of the fauna and flora of New Zealand. 1884.
————— Sketch of the geology of New Zealand. 1885.
————— Tarawera volcanic district. 1887.
————— Zoological exercises for students in New Zealand. 1880.
————— *and* **Ulrich,** G. Geology and gold fields of Otago. 1875.

Authors

Inglis, J. Our New Zealand cousins. 1887.
Innes, C. L. Canterbury sketches. 1879.
Ironside, S. New Zealand and its aborigines. 1863.
Izett, F. W. New Zealand in 1870 and 1880. 1880.

Jackson, J. R. New Zealand plants suitable for paper-making. 1875.
Jacobs, Alfred. Tasmanie et la Nouvelle-Zélande. 1859.
Jacobs, Henry. History of the Anglican Church in New Zealand. P. 171.
Jacox, F. Coming man from New Zealand. 1866.
Jameson, R. G. New Zealand and New South Wales. 1842.
Jennings, J. New Zealand colonization. 1843.
Jervois, Sir W. F. D. Defence of New Zealand. 1884.
Johnson, J. Pitts. Plain truths. 1840.
Johnstone, J. C. Maoria. 1874.
Jones-Parry, S. H. Journey round the world. 1881.
Joplin, R. C. New Zealand: a poem. 1843.
Jouan, H. Nouvelle-Zélande et le peuplement de la Polynésie. 1885.
Jouffroy d'Abbans, *Comte de.* La Nouvelle-Zélande en 1889. *In the press.*

K., J. H. Henry Ancrum. 1872.
Kean, C. Adventures in New Zealand. 1846.
Keane, A. H. Relations of Indo-Chinese and Indo-Oceanic races. 1879.
Keltie, J. S. Geographical education. 1886.
Kendall, T., and **Lee,** S. Maori grammar and vocabulary. 1820.
Kennaway, L. J. Crusts. 1874.
Kennedy, A. New Zealand. 1873.
Kennedy, D. Colonial travel. 1876.
Kerry-Nicholls, J. H. King country. 1884.
——— Maori race. 1886.
——— Recent exploration of the King country. P. 173.
——— Volcanic eruptions in New Zealand. 1887.
Kippis, A. Life of Captain James Cook. 1888.
Kirk, T. Forest flora of New Zealand. 1889.
Kirk, T. W. Birds of New Zealand. 1888.
Knight, C. Contribution to the Lichenographia of N.Z. P. 173.
Knollys, *Col.* Victoria Cross in . . . New Zealand, &c. P. 173.
Knox, T. W. Boy travellers in Australasia. 1888.

Labillardière, J. J. Account of a voyage in search of La Perouse. 1802.
——— Rélation du voyage. 1800.
Lang, A. Myth, ritual, and religion. 1887.
——— Myths of the origin of death. 1884.
Lang, J. D. Coming event. 1870.
——— New Zealand in 1839. 1839, 1873.
Laplace, C. P. T. Voyage de la Favorite. 1835.
Larkworthy, F. New Zealand revisited. 1881.
Lecoy, A. Forest question in New Zealand. 1879.

Alphabetical Catalogue

Lecoy, A. New Zealand State forests. 1878.
Ledyard, J. Journal of Captain Cook's last voyage. 1783.
Lendenfeld, R. *von*. Ascent of Hochstetter dome. 1883.
────── Centralstock der Neuseeländischen Alpen. 1884.
────── Charakter der Neuseeländischen Alpen. 1888.
────── Tasman-glotscher und seine umrandung. 1884.
Leroy-Beaulieu, P. Colonisation chez les peuples modernes. 1886.
√**Lesson**, A. Polynésiens: leur origine, leurs migrations, leur langage. 1882.
Lesson, R. P. Voyage autour du monde. 1839.
Lewis, T. H. Medical guide to Rotorua. 1885.
Leys, T. W. Volcanic eruption at Tarawera. 1886.
Lindsay, W. Lauder. Conservation of forests in our colonies. 1868.
────── Contributions to New Zealand botany. 1868.
────── Contributions to the flora of Otago. 1865.
────── Geology of the goldfields of Auckland. 1862.
────── Geology of the goldfields of Otago. 1862.
────── Illustrations of the geology and mineralogy of New Zealand. 1863.
────── Place of natural history in colonisation. 1862.
────── Protophytæ of New Zealand. 1867.
────── Relations of southern to northern flora of New Zealand. 1865.
────── Toot-poison of New Zealand. 1862.
────── Utilization of New Zealand flax. 1867.
Lindsay-Bucknall, H. Search for fortune. 1878.
Lubbock, J. Pre-historic times. 1865.
Ludlam, A. Cultivation and acclimatization of trees. 1865.
Lusk, Hugh. Maori Mahommedanism. 1865.
Lyttelton, *Lord*. New Zealand and the Canterbury Colony. 1859.
────── Visit to the Canterbury Colony. 1868.

M., J. K. The Mary Ira. 1867.
Macandrew, J. Address to the people of Otago. 1875.
McDonnell, T. Incidents of the war. 1887.
────── Maori history. 1887.
Macfarlane, J. S. Craig's troubles. 1871.
McIndoe, J. Otago. 1883.
MacKay, A. Native affairs in the South Island. 1873.
Mackay, J. Dealings with Maori lands. 1887.
McKerrow, J. Lake-districts of Otago and Southland. 1864.
McKillop, H. F. Twelve months' service in New Zealand. 1849.
McLean, P. S. History and policy of the Native land laws. 1886.
Major, R. H. Early voyages to Terra Australis. 1859.
Malone, R. E. Three years' cruise. 1854.
Mangles, R. D. How to colonize. 1842.
Maning, F. E. History of the war in the North. 1864.
────── Old New Zealand. 1863, 1876.
Mann, W. Six years' residence in the Australian provinces. 1839.
Manning, J. Maoris. 1871.

Mantell, G. A. Fossil remains of birds. 1848.
—— Notice of the Notornis. 1850.
—— Notice of the remains of the Dinornis. 1850.
—— *and* **Deane,** J. Correspondence on the Dinornis. 1844.
Mantell, R. N. Extinct colossal birds. 1850.
Marjoribanks, A. Travels in New Zealand. 1845.
Marryat, Emilia. Amongst the Maoris. 1874.
Marsden, J. B. Memoirs of the Rev. Samuel Marsden. 1858.
Marshall, W. B. Two visits to New Zealand. 1836.
Marshman, John. Canterbury. 1862, 1864.
Martens, E. Critical list of the Mollusca. 1873.
Martin, Josiah. Hot springs and terraces. 1879.
Martin, R. Montgomery. British colonies. 1853.
Martin, S. M. D. New Zealand. 1845.
Martin, *Sir* W. England and the New Zealanders. 1847.
—— Remarks on "Notes." 1861.
—— Taranaki question. 1860.
Maskell, W. M. Scale-insects. 1887.
Massey, Gerald. Book of the beginnings. 1881.
Matthew, P. Emigration fields. 1839.
Maunoir, —. Nouvelle-Zélande. 1864.
Maunsell, R. Fortschritte der Maori. 1862.
—— Grammar of the New Zealand language. 1842.
Meade, Herbert. Disturbed districts of New Zealand. 1870.
Meinicke, C. E. Alpen Neu-Seelands. 1870.
✓ —— Inseln des stillen Oceans. 1875.
Melville, H. Present state of Australia. 1850.
Merewether, H. A. By sea and by land. 1874.
Merivale, G. Hot lakes. 1878.
Michaelis, H. Cultivation of the wattle. 1882.
Miers, E. J. Stalk- and sessile-eyed crustacea. 1876.
Mills, Arthur. Colonial constitutions. 1856.
—— New Zealand in 1881. 1881.
Mivart, St. G. Colonial zoology. 1887.
Moister, W. History of Wesleyan missions. 1871.
Molesworth, *Sir* W. Lord Glenelg and the Ministry. 1839.
Money, C. L. Knocking about in New Zealand. 1871.
Montagne, —. Voyage au Pôle sud. 1845.
Montégut, E. Nouvelle-Zélande. 1877.
Moreton, S. H. Scramble over the mountains. 1885.
Morison, J. Australia as it is. 1867.
Mortimer, J. Robert Browning's "Waring." 1888.
Moser, T. Mahoe leaves. 1863, 1888.
Mosley, M. Illustrated guide to Christchurch. 1885.
Moss, E. G. B. Native lands and their incidents. 1888.
Moss, F. J. The Assembly: what will it do? 1880.
Mueller, F. On the vegetation of Chatham Islands. P. 174.

Mulhall, M. G. England's new sheep-farm. 1882.
Müller, Max. Solar myths. 1885.
Mulvany, T. J. New Zealand products and manufactures. 1880.
Mundy, D. L., *and* **Hochstetter**, F. Rotomahana. 1875.
Mundy, G. C. Our antipodes. 1852.
Murphy, M. Handbook of New Zealand gardening. 1885.
Muter, *Mrs.* D. D. Travels of an officer's wife. 1864.

Nesfield, H. W. A chequered career. 1881.
Nicholas, J. L. Voyage to New Zealand. 1817.
Nicols, A. Acclimatisation of the Salmonidæ. 1882.
Nightingale, Thomas. Oceanic sketches. 1835.
Nöggerath, —. Explorationskrater auf Neuseeland. 1871.
Norris, Edwin. Grammar of the New Zealand language. 1842.
———— Neuseeländische grammatik. 1846.
Northesk, *Lord.* Exhibition of jade objects. 1886.

Oberländer, R. Neuseeland in 1879. 1880.
Ogilby, J. P. Facts about New Zealand. 1872.
Oliver, G. Homes for the people in Otago. 1879.
Oliver, R. A. Lithographic drawings. 1852.
Ollivant, J. E. Hine Moa. P. 174.
Owen, *Sir* R. Extinct wingless birds of New Zealand. 1839, 1879.
———— Remains of a pleiosaurian reptile. 1861.

Palacky, J. Statistik von Neu-Seeland. 1858.
Parkinson, Sydney. Journal of a voyage to the South Seas. 1773.
Pash, J. Brittain. Report on New Zealand. 1883.
Paul, R. B. Account of Canterbury Settlement. 1854.
———— Letters from Canterbury. 1857.
———— New Zealand as it was and as it is. 1861.
Payton, E. W. Fifteen etchings of New Zealand scenery. 1888.
———— Round about New Zealand. 1888.
Peale, A. C. Thermal springs and geysers of New Zealand. 1883.
Pearson, W. H. In memoriam Sir John Richardson. 1879.
Peek, Cuthbert E. Hot-springs of Iceland and New Zealand. 1883.
Peel, *Sir* R. Speeches. 1853.
Pemberton, R. Happy colony. 1854.
Pembroke, *Earl of.* Roots. 1888.
Pennefather, F. W. Natives of New Zealand. 1887.
Peppercorne, F. S. Geological sketches of New Ulster. 1852.
Petherick, E. A. Catalogue of the York Gate Library. 1886.
Petre, *Lord.* Settlements of the New Zealand Company. 1842.
Petrel. In southern seas. 1888.
Pickering, C. Races of man. 1863.
Polack, J. S. Manners and customs of the New Zealanders. 1840.
———— New Zealand. 1838.
Pompallier, *Bishop.* History of the Catholic Church in Oceania. 1888.

Pompallier, *Bishop.* Letter to Matutaera Potatau. 1862.
——— État de la Mission catholique à la Nouvelle-Zélande. 1859.
——— Notes grammaticales sur la langue Maorie. 1849.
——— Prose et poésie chretienne en Néo-Zélandais. 1859.
Pope, J. H. The State. 1887.
Potts, T. H. Breeding habits of New Zealand birds. 1869.
——— Out in the open. 1882.
——— Recent changes in the fauna of New Zealand. 1874.
Power, W. Tyrone. Sketches in New Zealand. 1849.
Pratt, W. T. Colonial experiences. 1877.
Preshaw, G. O. Banking under difficulties. 1888.
Purnell, C. W. Agrarian law for New Zealand. 1874.
——— Maori and the Moa. 1880.
——— New Zealand confederation. 1877.
——— Our land laws. 1876.
Puseley, D. Rise and progress of Australia. 1857.
Pyke, Vincent. Adventures of George Washington Pratt. 1874.
——— History of the early gold discoveries in Otago. 1887.
——— Lost at the goldfields. 1867.
——— Province of Otago. 1868.
——— Story of Wild Will Enderby. 1873.
——— *and* **Thorpe,** Talbot. White hood and blue cap. 1881.

Quatrefages, A. Hommes fossiles et hommes sauvages. 1884.
——— Human species. 1879.
——— Moas et les chasseurs de Moas. 1883.
——— Polynésiens et leurs migrations. 1864, 1866.
——— Pygmées. 1887.
——— Races Moriori et Maori. 1873.
Quoy, —, *et* **Gaimard,** P. Découvertes de l'Astrolabe. 1830.
Quick, W. H. Church of England Trustees Incorporation Act. 1881.

R., R. Australia, Van Diemen's Land, and New Zealand. 1840.
Rains, Fanny L. By land and ocean. 1878.
Randall, —. Address on New Zealand emigration. 1843.
Raoul, E., *and* **Decaisne,** —. Plantes de la Nouvelle-Zélande. 1846.
Raynal, F. E. Naufragés. 1878.
——— Wrecked on a reef. 1885.
Rees, W. L. Coming crisis. 1874.
——— East Coast Settlement Bill. 1880.
——— Sir Gilbert Leigh. 1878.
Reid, R. C. Rambles on the golden coast of the South Island. 1886.
Reinicke, G. Bemerkungen über Port Lyttelton. 1884.
Reubank, F. Ausflug nach Neuseeland. 1884.
Reybaud, L. Histoire et colonisation de la Nouvelle-Zélande. 1840.
Richard, A. Découvertes de l'Astrolabe. 1832.
Richardson, *Sir* J. L. C. First Christian martyr in New Zealand. 1851.
——— Sketch of Otago. 1862.

Richardson, *Sir* J. L. C. Summer's excursion in New Zealand. 1854.
Richmond, C. W. Memorandum in reply to a pamphlet. 1861.
Ridgway, A. F. Voices from Auckland. 1860.
✓**Rienzi**, G. L. Océanic. 1838.
Ritter, C. Colonization von Neu-Seeland. 1842.
——— Colonization of New Zealand. 1842.
Robjohns, H. T. Bible-work and floods in New Zealand. 1888.
Rochfort, J. Adventures of a surveyor in New Zealand. 1853.
——— Expeditions to the west coast of the Middle Island. 1862.
Rochon, A. Voyages aux Indes orientales. 1802.
Rose, R. New Zealand guide. 1879.
Ross, *Sir* J. C. Voyage of discovery and research. 1847.
Rough, D. North of New Zealand. 1852.
Rudge, J. Address to the New Zealand emigrants. 1840.
Rusden, G. W. Aurerctanga. 1888.
——— History of New Zealand. 1883.
Russell, A. Tour through the Australian colonies. 1840.
Russell, I. C. Giant birds of New Zealand. 1877.
——— Sketch of New Zealand. 1879.
Russell, John. Account of a singular expedient. 1862.
Russell, M. Polynesia. 1842.

S., W. H. Survey of the northern districts of New Zealand. 1844.
Sadler, W. E. Roving diggers to become colonial settlers. 1869.
Sala, G. A. Land of the Golden Fleece. 1884.
Saunders, A. New Zealand, its climate and soil. 1868.
Savage, John. Account of New Zealand. 1807.
Scandrett, W. B. Southland and its resources. 1883.
Scherzer, K. Narrative of the circumnavigation of the globe. 1863.
Scheube, H. Unter den schafbaronen Neuseelands. 1875.
Schirren, C. Wandersagen der Neuseeländer. 1856.
Schmarda, L. Reise um die Erde, 1853-57. 1861.
Sclater, P. L. Birds of the genus Apteryx in New Zealand. 1861.
Scoffern, J. The Maories. 1869.
Sealy, H. J. Are we to stay here? 1881.
Seffern, W. H. J. Early settlement of New Zealand. 1888.
· **Selwyn**, *Bishop*. Charge to the clergy of New Zealand. 1850.
——— Church in the colonies. 1845, 1846, 1847, 1849.
Selwyn, C. J. *and* L. F. Annals of the diocese of New Zealand. 1847.
· **Senior**, W. Travel and trout in the Antipodes. 1880.
Sewell, Henry. Case of New Zealand. 1869.
——— New Zealand rebellion. 1864.
Shaw, J. Gallop to the Antipodes. 1858.
——— Tramp to the diggings. 1852.
Sherrin, R. A. A. Handbook of the fishes of New Zealand. 1886.
Shortland, E. How to learn Maori. 1883.
——— Maori religion and mythology. 1882.

✓ **Shortland,** E. Sketch of the Maori races. 1865.
─────── Southern districts of New Zealand. 1851.
─────── Traditions and superstitions of the New Zealanders. 1856.
Simmons, A. Old England and New Zealand. 1879.
Simonin, L. Monde océanique et les progrès de l'Australie. 1885.
Smeaton, W. H. O. District high schools in New Zealand. 1883.
Smith, Goldwin. The Empire. 1863.
Smith, S. Percy. Eruption of Tarawera. 1886.
─────── Kermadec Islands: their capabilities and extent. 1887.
Sparks, Jared. Life and travels of John Ledyard. 1828.
─────── New Zealand. 1823.
Spedding, J. Reviews and discussions. 1879.
Spencer, H., *and* **Duncan,** D. Descriptive sociology. 1874.
Spencer, W. B. Parietal eye of Hatteria. 1886.
Spencer, W. I. Napier as a health resort. 1885.
Spry, W. J. J. Cruise of the Challenger. 1876.
St. John, J. H. H. Pakeha rambles through Maori lands. 1873.
St. Johnston, Alfred. Distant sketching ground. 1881.
Stewart, G. V. Guide to the Hot Lakes. 1883.
─────── Kati-Kati settlement. 1877, 1878.
─────── Notes on special settlement. 1883.
─────── Reply to the report by G. E. Barton. 1883.
─────── Te Puke, Bay of Plenty. 1880.
Stieda, W. Neu-Seeland in vergangenheit u. gegenwart. 1885.
Stokes, J. L. Letter on the Wairau massacre. 1844.
─────── Surveys in the Middle Island. 1849, 1851.
Stones, W. My first voyage. 1858.
─────── New Zealand and its resources. 1858.
Stout, *Sir* R. Address at Auckland. 1885.
─────── Address on education. 1879.
─────── Governor Gordon and the Maoris. 1883.
─────── Moses Wilson Gray. 1882.
─────── Notes on the progress of New Zealand, 1864-84. 1886.
─────── Our waifs and strays. 1885.
─────── Political parties in New Zealand. 1880.
─────── Politics and poverty. 1883.
─────── Public education in New Zealand. 1885.
Strachan, A. Life of Rev. Samuel Leigh. 1853, 1855.
Stratford, S. P. Natural history of New Zealand. 1857.
Strelitz, —. Reise nach Neuseeland. 1869.
─────── Tagebuch eines goldgräbers in Neuseeland. 1889.
Strong, H. A. Western sounds of New Zealand. 1885.
Suter, *Bishop.* Public Works Statement. 1878.
Sutter, A. Per mare, per terras. 1887.
Swainson, William. Auckland. 1853.
─────── New Zealand. 1856.
─────── New Zealand and its colonization. 1859.

Swainson, William. New Zealand and the war. 1862.
———— Observations on the climate of New Zealand. 1840.

Talbot, Thorpe. Guide to the Lakes and Hot Springs. 1882.
Tancred, *Sir* T. Notes on the natural history of Canterbury. 1856.
Tangye, Richard. Fourth voyage to the Australian colonies. 1886.
Tasman, A. J. Journal van de reis naer het onbekende Zuidland. 1860.
———— Kort verhael uyt het journael. 1674.
Taylor, R. Age of New Zealand. 1864.
———— Leaf from the natural history of New Zealand. 1848.
———— Maori and English dictionary. 1870.
———— Past and present of New Zealand. 1868.
———— Te Ika a Maui. 1855, 1870.
———— Wanganui, its past, present, and future. 1867.
Taylor, W. Education of the people. 1870.
Tenison-Woods, J. E. Palæontology of New Zealand. 1880.
Terry, C. New Zealand, its advantages and prospects. 1842.
Thomas, A. P. W. Eruption of Tarawera and Rotomahana. 1888.
Thomas, E. C. G. Ryotwarry. 1878.
Thomas, Julian. Round about New Zealand. 1883.
Thomson, A. S. Description of two caves in the North Island. 1854.
———— Native race of New Zealand. 1854.
———— Physique of the inhabitants of New Zealand. 1853.
———— Statistical account of Auckland, 1848. 1851.
———— Statistics of New Munster to 1848. 1851.
———— Story of New Zealand. 1859.
Thomson, *Mrs.* C. Twelve years in Canterbury. 1867.
Thomson, G. M. Acclimatization in New Zealand. 1886.
———— Ferns and fern allies of New Zealand. 1882.
Thomson, J. T. Rambles with a philosopher. 1867.
———— Sketch of the Province of Otago. 1858.
———— Survey of the southern districts of Otago. 1858.
———— Survey system of Otago. 1875.
Tinné, J. E. Wonderland of the Antipodes. 1874.
Tinné, T. F. S. Local industries of New Zealand. 1881.
Tomlinson, H. Diary of voyage to New Zealand. 1875.
———— Farm labourer's report on New Zealand. 1876.
Toula, F. Südliche Alpen von Neu-Seeland. 1880.
Travers, W. T. L. Destruction of the aborigines of Chatham Island. 1865.
———— Flora of Canterbury, Nelson, and Marlborough. 1864.
———— Life and times of Te Rauparaha. 1872.
Treadwell, J. W. New Zealand, June 30, 1877. 1877.
Tregear, E. Aryan Maori. 1885.
———— Flitting ghost. 1887.
———— Maori and the Moa. 1888.
Trollope, Anthony. Australia and New Zealand. 1873.
Tucker, H. W. English Church in other lands. 1886.

Authors

Tucker, H. W. Life and episcopate of Bishop Selwyn. 1879.
Tucker, *Miss.* Southern Cross and southern crown. 1858.
Turnbull, J. Voyage round the world, 1800–1804. 1805.
Turner, J. G. Pioneer missionary. 1872.
Tylor, E. B. Primitive culture. 1871.

Vaile, S. Present position and future prospects of N.Z. railways. 1885.
Valentijn, F. Oud en niew Oost-Indien. 1724–6.
Vancouver, G. Voyage of discovery to the North Pacific. 1801.
Varigny, C. *de.* Océanie moderne. 1887.
Verrall, J. M. Condition of New Zealand. 1885.
Vincent, E. G. Forty thousand miles over land and water. 1885.
Vogel, *Sir* Julius. Colonies generally and New Zealand in particular. 1878.
——— Finances of New Zealand. 1875.
——— New Zealand, Australia, and the Pacific islands. 1879.
——— New Zealand and the South Sea islands. 1877.
——— Remarks on the resources of New Zealand. 1877.

Wade, W. R. Journey in the Northern Island. 1842.
Waitt, R. Progress of Canterbury. 1856.
Wakefield, E. Mr. Froude on New Zealand. 1886.
——— *and* **Jouffroy,** *Comte.* New Zealand in 1889. *Announced.*
Wakefield, E. G. Founders of Canterbury. 1868.
——— Mr. Dandeson Coates and the New Zealand Association. 1837.
——— View of the art of colonization. 1849.
Wakefield, E. J. Adventure in New Zealand. 1845.
——— Handbook for New Zealand. 1848.
——— Letter to Sir George Grey. 1851.
——— Taxes in New Zealand. 1878.
——— What will they do in the General Assembly? 1863.
——— *and* **Ward,** J. British colonization of New Zealand. 1837.
Wakefield, Felix. Colonial surveying. 1849.
Wakelin, Richard. History and politics. 1877.
——— Small farms and small farm settlements. 1879.
Walker, A. West coast of the Middle Island. 1865.
Wallace, A. R. Australasia. 1879.
——— Geographical distribution of animals. 1876.
——— Island life. 1880.
Wallace, J. H. Manual of New Zealand history. 1886.
Walton, J. Twelve months in New Zealand. 1839.
Ward, Crosbie. Letter to Lord Lyttelton. 1863.
Ward, John. Information relative to New Zealand. 1839.
——— Supplementary information relative to New Zealand. 1840.
Ward, J. P. Wanderings with the Maori prophets. 1883.
Ward, R. Life among the Maories. 1872.
Ward, —. Nelson, the latest settlement of the New Zealand Company. 1842.
Warre, H. J. New Zealand: its defence against Native aggression. 1863.

Wayte, G. H. Eighteen months in Australia and New Zealand. 1879.
✓ **Wedderburn**, *Sir* D. Maoris and Kanakas. 1877.
Weld, F. A. Hints to intending sheep-farmers. 1864.
————— Notes on New Zealand affairs. 1869.
Wells, B. History of Taranaki. 1878.
Wheeler, D. Letters and journal. 1838.
White, J. Ancient history of the Maori. 1887.
————— Legendary history of the Maoris. 1880.
————— Maori customs and superstitions. 1856, 1861, 1885.
————— Plan of the Maori mythology. 1878.
————— Te Rou; or, The Maori at home. 1874.
White, J. H. Emigration to New Zealand. 1876.
White, W. Memorials of Sergeant William Marjouram. 1862.
✓ **Whitmee**, S. J. Ethnology of the Pacific. 1881.
✓ ————— Mr. Wallace on the ethnology of Polynesia. 1873.
Whitmore, *Sir* G. S. Patriotic speech. 1888.
Whitworth, R. P. Hine-ra; or, The Maori scout. 1887.
————— Martin's Bay settlement. 1870.
Wilkes, C. United States Exploring Expedition. 1845.
Williams, G. P., *and* **Reeves**, W. P. Colonial couplets. 1889.
Williams, T. C. Letter to W. E. Gladstone. 1873.
————— Manawatu purchase completed. 1868.
Williams, W. Christianity among the New Zealanders. 1867.
————— Dictionary of the New Zealand language. 1844, 1852, 1871.
Williams, W. L. First lessons in Maori. 1882.
Willis, —. Notes on the acquisition of New Zealand. 1840.
Wilmer, G. Lowing herd; and Zealandia. 1869.
Wilson, A. J. British trade. 1877.
————— Resources of modern countries. 1878.
Wilson, G. H. Ena; or, The ancient Maori. 1874.
————— Ekino; and other poems. 1869.
Wilson, J. A. Native Land Court. 1877.
————— Story of Te Waharoa. 1866.
Wilson, *Mrs.* R. New Zealand; and other poems. 1851.
Wohlers, J. Ostküste der neuseeländischen insel Poenamu. 1846.
Wood, J. Twelve months in Wellington. 1843.
✓ **Wood**, J. G. Natural history of man. 1870.

Yate, W. Account of New Zealand. 1835.
Yonge, Charlotte M. Life of John Coleridge Patteson. 1874.
Young, Frederick. New Zealand—past, present, and future. 1874.
Young, W. C. New Zealand described. 1840.
Young, R. Southern world. 1858.

Part 3.—Alphabetical Catalogue.

B.—Titles of anonymous and pseudonymous publications.

Aborigines Protection Society: reports. 1838, 1840.
Account of several late voyages and discoveries. 1711.
Across two seas. 1880.
Address of the Aborigines Protection Society. 1864.
Adventures of British seamen in the Southern Ocean. 1827.
Affairs of New Zealand. 1846.
All about New Zealand. 1875.
Among the Maoris. 1863.
Annual Record of science and industry for 1873. 1874.
Antipodean notes. [By H. D'Avigdor.] 1888.
Appeal to the men of New Zealand. 1869.
Arrangements for the adjustment of questions relating to land. 1848.
Arthur Thomson's Geschichte der unterverfassung. 1860.
Auckland and its neighbourhood. 1853.
Auckland Isles. 1866.
Ausbruch des Tarawera. 1887.
Ausflug an den Waikato. 1859.
Aussterben der Maoris.
Australasian colonies. New Zealand Handbook. 1888.
Australia as it is. [By J. Morison.] 1867.
Australia, Van Dieman's Land, and New Zealand. 1849.
Australian poets, 1788–1888. 1888.

Bemerkungen über einige häfen. 1876.
Beschreibung einiger häfen der Nordinsel. 1874.
Bevölkerungsstatistik Neu-Seelands. 1865.
Bishop of Australia's visit to New Zealand. 1838.
Blick auf Neuseeland. 1877.
Blues and Buffs. 1880.
Brief reply to a letter, &c. 1840.
British colonization of New Zealand. 1840.
Bryce v. Rusden. 1887.

Campaign on the West Coast. 1866.
Canterbury Association for emigration to New Zealand. 1850.
Canterbury Flax Association. 1871.
Canterbury in 1864. [By J. Marshman.] 1864.
Canterbury Papers. 1851, 1859.
Canterbury rhymes. 1883.
Canterbury Settlement. 1850, 1853.
Canterbury sketches. [By W. L. Innes.] 1879.
Case of Messrs. Lundon and Whitaker. 1871.
Cassell's Picturesque Australasia. 1887.

Alphabetical Catalogue

Cast away on the Auckland Islands. 1866.
Catalogue of books relating to New Zealand. 1866.
Catechism of the Constitution. 1855.
Census von Neu-Seeland, 1867. 1869.
Centenaire de la mort de Cook. 1879.
Chapman's Centenary memorial of Captain Cook. 1870.
Chapman's New Zealand Monthly Magazine.
Chapman's Traveller's guide. 1872.
Character of the New Zealanders. 1832.
Christianity among the New Zealanders. 1867, 1870.
Christianity in Melanesia and New Zealand. 1854.
Church Missionary Intelligencer. 1856.
Church Missionary Society. New Zealand land question. 1847.
Coates on the New Zealanders. 1844.
Colonial policy in the government of coloured races. 1866.
Colonist's handbook of New Zealand. 1884.
Colonization of New Zealand. [By H. S. Chapman.] 1838.
Colonization of New Zealand. 1824, 1837, 1838.
Colonization of New Zealand from Devon and Cornwall. 1840.
Cookery book from New Zealand. 1848.
Corrected report of debate in House of Commons. 1845.
Correspondence between Colonial Office and N.Z. Company. 1839.
Correspondence between Premier and Superintendent of Otago. 187 .
Correspondence between Secretary of State and N.Z. Company. 1845.
Correspondence between Wesleyan Committee and Earl Grey. 1848.
Correspondence re Mr. Thomas and the Canterbury Association. 1852.
Cruise —— New Zealand. 1825.
Cruise's residence in New Zealand. 1824.

Dark chapter from N.Z. history. [By J. Hawthorne.] 1869.
Description of Fitzgibbon Louch's settlement. 1880.
Description of the Province of Nelson; and of Wellington. 1858.
Description of New Zealand. 1843.
Description of the outlying islands. 1868.
Description of a view of the Bay of Islands, New Zealand. 1840.
Deutschen ansiedler in Nelson und ihre schicksale. 1863.
Dieffenbach's travels in New Zealand. 1842.
Dr. Hochstetter's Karten von Neu-Seeland. 1860.

Early history of New Zealand. *Announced.*
Early history of Otago. 1881.
Earle's residence in New Zealand. 1832.
Edw. Shortland über Neu-Seeland. 1857.
Effect of the Native Lands Acts. 1873.
Emigrants' manual to New Zealand. 1858.
Emigration to New Zealand. 1840.
Erste eisenbahn auf Neu-Seeland. 1864.
Expeditionen in den Alpen-regionen. 1861.
Experiences of a medical man in New Zealand. 1883.

Fac-similes of the Declaration of Independence. 1877.
Facts: or, Experiences in New Zealand. 1883.

Titles

Facts relating to New Zealand. 1882.
Farmer's views on land nationalisation. 1886.
Ferdinand von Hochstetter über den bau der vulkane. 1865.
Few plain facts concerning Nelson. 1848. *See* **1845**.
First ten years' quarterly papers of Church Missionary Society. 1826.
First week in New Zealand. 1864.
Flora of New Zealand. 1865.
Fourteen years in New Zealand. 1840.
From Auckland to Awamutu. 1864.
Full history of the Maungatapu murders. 1866.

Gebirge u. vulkane auf Neuseeland. 1863.
General catalogue of Grey Collection, Auckland. 1888.
Geschichte der entdeckung der goldlager in Neu-Seeland. 1864.
Glance at Dunedin. 1864.
Gold-diggings of New Zealand. 1861.
Goldfelder an der Thames in Neu-Seeland. 1870.
Goldfelder an der Westküste, Canterbury. 1867.
Goldfelder und fossile knochen in Neu-Seeland. 1860.
Goldwäschereien auf Neu-Seeland. 1862.
Great medicine man of Dancoyle. 1879.
Great volcanic outbreak at Tarawera. 1886.
Growth of colonial England. 1885.
Guide and description of the panorama of New Zealand. 1849.

Haast's erforschung der Alpen. 1862, 1868.
Handbook for emigrants to New Zealand. 1856.
Handbook of New Zealand mines. 1887.
Handbook of Otago and Southland. 1862.
Handbook to the ferns of New Zealand. 1861.
Handbook to the suburban and rural districts of Otago. 1849.
Hau-hau. 1880.
Hau-haus in New Zealand. 1879.
Hawke's Bay Native Lands Alienation Commission. 1873.
Hints to colonists. By "Uncle John." 1859.
History of local government in New Zealand. 1868.
History and description of Thames goldfields. 1869.
How we live at Awamutu. 1864.

Ika-na-Mawi. Sagen und gewohnheiten der Neuseeländer. 1856.
Illustrated guide to the west coast of the North Island. 1885.
Illustrated narrative of the Maungatapu murders. 1866.
Illustrations to 'Adventure in New Zealand.' 1845.
Immigrant's prospects in New Zealand. 1882.
Important information about New Zealand. 1839.
Important judgments in the Native Land Court. 1879.
Index reference to New Plymouth. 1842.
Industrie der Maoris auf der allgemeinen austellung in Auckland. 1866.
Information for the missionary deputation to Lord Stanley. 1843.
Information relative to New Plymouth. 1841.
Instructions from the New Zealand Land Company. 1839.
Interesting chapters from the early history of Wanganui. 1887.
In the matter of Dr. Buller's petition. 1878.

Jahresbericht des Norddeutschen Bundesconsuls zu Wellington. 1870.
J. Haast's forschungen in den Alpen Neu-Seelands. 1863.
Journal of a deputation of the London Missionary Society. 1840.

Kermadecs. 1887.

Laing's [sic] Letters on New Zealand. 1839.
Land and farming in New Zealand. 1879.
Land ho! 1883.
Land question in New Zealand and Australia. 1879.
Last of the Moas. 1864.
Latest from New Zealand. 1863.
Latest information from New Plymouth. 1842.
Letter to the Bishop of New Zealand. 1850.
Letter to J. Somes, Esq., about the capital of New Zealand. 1842.
Letter to the directors of the New Zealand Company. 1846.
Letter to the Earl of Chichester. 1840.
Letters from emigrants. 1843.
Letters from settlers and labouring emigrants. 1843.
Letters from New Zealand. 1847–48.
Life and recollections of a New Zealand colonist. 1875.
Life in New Zealand. 1863.
List of original land-purchasers. 1856.

Mahoe leaves. [By T. Moser.] 1863, 1888.
Manners and customs in New Zealand. 1839, 1845.
Maoribevölkerung auf Neu-Seeland, 1886. 1888.
Maorikrieg auf Neu-Seeland. 1861.
Maoriland. 1884.
Maori life. 1869.
Maori sketches. 1865.
Die Maori und Neu-Seeland. 1858.
Maoris. 1855, 1873, 1880.
Maoris' fight for life. 1886.
Maoris und der Engländer auf Neuseeland. 1865.
Marsden's missionary visits to New Zealand. 1846.
Memorial to the Secretary of State for the Colonies. 1861.
Middle Island. 1865.
Mission life among the Maoris. 1888.
Missions of the Church Missionary Society. 1840.
Mittheilungen aus Neu-Seeland. 1860.
Moa bird or Dinornis. 1877.
Mr. Robert Graham's remarks on a pamphlet. 1871.
Mr. Secretary Cardwell and the right of petition. 1866.
Murder of the Rev. C. S. Volkner. 1865.
Musings on Manning's [sic] 'Old New Zealand.' 1877.
Mutual relations between the Canterbury Association, &c. 1853.
Mythology of New Zealand. 1860.
Mythology of Polynesia. 1861.

Native on Abolition. 1875.
Natives of New Zealand. 1842.
Natural wonders of New Zealand. 1881.

Titles

Neue aufstand der Maori. 1860.
Neuentdeckte Canterbury-goldfelder. 1865.
Neue volkszählungen in Neu-Seeland. 1848.
Neueste explorationen in Neu-Seeland. 1864.
Neu-Seeland als auswanderungsziel und exportgebiet. 1881.
Neu-Seeland, ein günstiges auswanderung-gebiet. 1858.
Neuseeland in geographischer hinsicht. 1866.
Neuseelands schifffahrt und handel in 1876, 1877.   1878, 1879, 1887.
Neu-Seelandische Provinz Southland. 1864.
New field for agricultural and pastoral pursuits. 1867.
New Zealand.   1838, 1839, 1844, 1857, 1860, 1861.
New Zealand and its affairs, past and present. 1860.
New Zealand and its claims. 1845.
New Zealand and its goldfields.   1862, 1868.
New Zealand and the Polynesians. 1849.
New Zealand and Van Diemen's Land. 1839.
New Zealand Company: its claims to compensation considered.
New Zealand Company. Reports.   1840, 1842, 1861.
New Zealand Country Journal. 1877.
New Zealand described. 1840.
New Zealand Emigrants' Manual. 1853.
New Zealand Emigration Circular. 1853.
New Zealanders.   [By G. L. Craik.]   1830.
New Zealanders. 1851.
New Zealand Government and the Maori war. 1864.
New Zealand Handbook. 1864.
New Zealand in 1841. 1842.
New Zealand in 1857. 1857.
New Zealand Industrial Exhibition, 1885 : Prize essays. 1886.
New Zealand Institute. 1870.
New Zealand : its history and present state. 1849.
New Zealand : its history, institutions, and industries. 1888.
New Zealand : its progress and resources. 1859.
New Zealand Journal. 1841.
New Zealand Magazine.   1876, 1877.
New Zealand—past, present, and future. 1863.
New Zealand proverbs and legends. 1876.
New Zealand station. 1871.
New Zealand thermal-springs districts.   Township of Rotorua. 1883.
New Zealand under Governor Grey. 1848.
New Zealand zauberflöte. 1850.
New Zealand. A vindication of the missionaries. 1861.
New Zealand war of 1860. 1861.
Nicholas's Voyage to New Zealand. 1817.
North Island of New Zealand as a field for settlement. 1888.
Note on the coexistence of Man with the Dinornis. 1862.
Notes of a tour through various parts of New Zealand. 1877.
Notes on Sir W. Martin's pamphlet, The Taranaki Question. 1861.
Notizen über Australien und Neu-Seeland. 1860.

Official Handbook of New Zealand. 1883.
Old Identities.   [By James Barr.]   1879.

Old Identity stories. 1886.
On the British colonization of New Zealand. 1846.
Origin of the New Zealand war. 1864.
Otago. 1847, 1848.
Otago. [By J. McIndoe.] 1883.
Otago: its goldfields and resources. 1862.
Otago Journal. 1848.
Otago Museum: Guide to the collections. 1878.
Our sister cities: Dunedin. 1885.

Paläontologie von Neu-Seeland. 1864.
Parliamentary skits and sketches, by Silver Pen. 1871.
Petition for the recall of Governor Hobson. 1841.
Petition of the New Zealand Company. 1845.
Petre's account of New Zealand. 1841.
Piako. 1876.
Plan of the Association for founding the Settlement of Canterbury. 1848.
Picturesque atlas of Australasia. 1886–9.
Plain facts relative to the war in the north of New Zealand. 1847.
Poenamo. [By J. Logan Campbell.] 1881.
Polack on New Zealand in 1831–37. 1838.
Political and other ballads. 1879.
Politische eintheilung und bevölkerung im Neu-Seeland im 1861. 1862.
Politics: a contribution to the question of the day. 1875.
Polynesian legends and fairy stories. 1876.
Polynesian mythology. 1855.
Polynesians: and New Zealand. 1850.
Popular account of New Zealand as a field for British colonization. 1839.
Present state of New Zealand. 1837, 1842.
Primary instruction: our State system and its shortcomings. 1881.
Proceedings of the Eighth General Synod. 1880.
Proceedings of the Kohimarama Conference. 1860.
Proceedings of Synod of the Presbyterian Church of Otago. 1881.
Progress of comparative anatomy. 1852.
Progress of New Zealand. 1886.
Prospectus of New Zealand Land Company. 1839.
Protest against the confiscation of Native lands in New Zealand. 1864.
Protestantische missionen auf Neu-Seeland. 1847.
Province of Canterbury. List of sections purchased. 1868.
Province of Otago. [By V. Pyke.] 1868.
Provinz Otago in Neu-Seeland. 1859.

Question and rights of the aborigines. 1849.

Rabbits in New Zealand. By a Run-holder. 1881.
Rambles with a philosopher. [By J. T. Thomson.] 1867.
Reise der österreichischen fregatte Novara. 1861, 1864.
Reise- und lebensbilder aus Neu-Holland und Neu-Seeland. 1853.
Remarks on the credit of New Zealand. 1865.
Reminiscences of the Colonial and Indian Exhibition. 1886.
Reminiscences of New Zealand. 1861.
- Reminiscences of a veteran. 1861.
Report of Commissioners, Otago Central Railway. 1881.

Titles

Report of proceedings of the Otago Mining Conference. 1874.
Report of the Royal Commission on the University of New Zealand. 1879.
Report from the Select Committee on New Zealand. 1840, 1844.
Report from the Select Committee of the House of Lords. 1838.
Results of the New Zealand inquiry. 1845.
Review of the position of Southland. 1866.
Ritter on the colonization of New Zealand. 1842.
Roots. [By Lord Pembroke.] 1873, 1888.

Savage's account of New Zealand. 1807.
Savings-bank in the school. 1875.
Scenes from the life of John Marmon. 1880.
Scenes in New Zealand. 1845.
Second-class to New Zealand and back. 1865.
Second letter to the Earl of Chichester. 1840.
Sheep-washing in New Zealand. 1881.
Short sketch of incidents in the life of Thomas Hancock. 1885.
Sidney's Emigrant Journal. 1849.
Silkworm-farming in England and New Zealand. 1882.
Silver's Guide to Australasia. 1863.
Sir Charles Adderley on colonial policy. 1870.
Sketch of Otago. [Sir J. Richardson.] 1862.
Sketches in New Zealand. 1858, 1881.
Social life at the capital of New Zealand. 1888.
Social progress at the Antipodes. 1857.
Sounds, lakes, and rivers of New Zealand. 1885.
Southern Monthly Magazine. 1864.
Steam to Australia and New Zealand. 1850.
Supplement to the Review of the position of Southland. 1866.
Sydney Herald. 1836-7.

'Taken in :' being a sketch of New Zealand. 1887.
Taranaki : a tale of the war. 1861.
Tea- and silk-farming in New Zealand. 1881.
Telegraphen-linien in Neu-Seeland. 1866.
Terra australis cognita. [By John Callander.] 1766.
Thirty years' policy in New Zealand. [By Capt. Hope.] 1865.
Thomson's Story of New Zealand. 1860.
100,000 Tons of steel rails. 1879.
Traditions and superstitions of the New Zealanders. 1855.
Transactions and proceedings of the New Zealand Institute. 1869.
Travels of Hildebrand Bowman, Esquire. 1778.
Tristan d'Acunha's New Zealand [sic]. 1841.
Trosième voyage de Cook. 1782.
Twenty months in Southland, 1867-69. 1870.

United States Exploring Expedition. 1846.

Voyage of H.M.S. Erebus and Terror. 1844.

War with the Maoris. 1850.
Week among the Maoris of Lake Taupo. 1876.
Whitcombe's reise durch die südlichen Alpen. 1864.
Wissenschaftliche forschungen in Neu-Seeland. 1871.
Wooden town. 1886.

Corrections.

Page 11. *Over* **Burney,** J., *place* **1813.**
" 22. *Delete* **Bannister,** S. Condition, &c.
" 31. *Delete* **Heale,** T., first entry.
" 39. *For* **Majoribanks** *read* **Marjoribanks.**
" 48, line 6. *For* Neu *read* Neue.
" 77. *For* **Schmarda,** L., *read* **Schwarda,** T.; *and for* 1853–67 *read* 1853–57.
" 116, line 14. *Transpose* Ernst *and* Ferdinand.
" 128. *Delete* **Purnell,** C. W. Agrarian law.
" 140. *For* **Whitmee,** L. J., *read* S. J.
" 160. *For* **Tucker,** W. H., *read* H. W.

BY AUTHORITY: GEORGE DIDSBURY, GOVERNMENT PRINTER, WELLINGTON, N.Z.

www.ingramcontent.com/pod-product-compliance
Lightning Source LLC
Chambersburg PA
CBHW020809230426
43666CB00007B/923